READING EPHESIANS & COLOSSIANS

Smyth & Helwys Publishing, Inc.
6316 Peake Road
Macon, Georgia 31210-3960
1-800-747-3016
© 2020 by David I. Starling
All rights reserved.

Unless otherwise noted, quotations from Scripture are in the author's translation. Titles of journals, books of the Bible, and ancient works are abbreviated according to the *SBL Handbook of Style*, 2nd edition.

Library of Congress Cataloging-in-Publication Data

Names: Starling, David Ian, author.
Title: Reading Ephesians and Colossians : a literary and theological
  commentary / by David I. Starling.
Description: Macon, GA : Smyth & Helwys, 2020. | Series: Reading the New
  Testament, second series | Includes bibliographical references.
Identifiers: LCCN 2020042452 (print) | LCCN 2020042453 (ebook) | ISBN
  9781641732772 (paperback) | ISBN 9781641732789 (ebook)
Subjects: LCSH: Bible. Ephesians--Commentaries. | Bible.
  Colossians--Commentaries.
Classification: LCC BS2695.53 .S73 2020 (print) | LCC BS2695.53 (ebook) |
  DDC 227/.507--dc23
LC record available at https://lccn.loc.gov/2020042452
LC ebook record available at https://lccn.loc.gov/2020042453

Disclaimer of Liability: With respect to statements of opinion or fact available in this work of nonfiction, Smyth & Helwys Publishing Inc. nor any of its employees, makes any warranty, express or implied, or assumes any legal liability or responsibility for the accuracy or completeness of any information disclosed, or represents that its use would not infringe privately-owned rights.

Reading Ephesians & Colossians

A Literary and Theological Commentary

David I. Starling

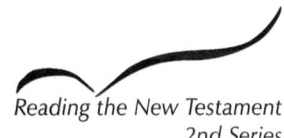

Reading the New Testament
2nd Series

Also by David I. Starling

UnCorinthian Leadership: Thematic Reflections on 1 Corinthians

Not My People: Gentiles as Exiles in Pauline Hermeneutics

Hermeneutics as Apprenticeship: How the Bible Shapes our Interpretive Habits and Practices

Dedication

To Nicole, whose companionship and
encouragement are a daily delight;

and

to Peter O'Brien, whose commentaries are nowhere quoted
in this volume but whose influence is pervasively present

Contents

ACKNOWLEDGMENTS ix
EDITOR'S FOREWORD xi

EPHESIANS
Introduction to Ephesians 1
  Authorship and Destination 1
  Relationship to Colossians 7
  Situation and Date 10
  Purpose 11
  Structure 13
  Theological Emphases and Contemporary Significance 14

One new humanity (Eph 1:1–3:21) 17
  To the saints (1:1-2) 17
  Blessed be the God . . . who has blessed us in Christ (1:3-14) 20
    Remembering you in my prayers (1:15-23) 32
      And you . . . he made alive (2:1-10) 41
      You . . . have been brought near (2:11-22) 50
      The grace of God that was given to me for you (3:1-13) 61
      I bow my knees to the Father (3:14-19) 72
  To him be glory (3:20-21) 79

To walk worthily (Eph 4:1–6:20) 81
  I urge you therefore (4:1) 81
  One body (4:2-16) 83
  No longer . . . as the Gentiles (4:17-24) 98
    As beloved children (4:25–5:2) 106
    As children of light (5:3-14) 116

  Not as unwise . . . but as wise (5:15-21) 128
  Submitting to one another in reverence toward
   Christ (5:21–6:9) 136
  Be strong in the Lord (6:10-20) 156
  Tychicus . . . peace . . . and grace (6:21-24) 167

COLOSSIANS
Introduction to Colossians 173
  Authorship 173
  Destination 175
  Situation and Date 176
  Purpose 179
  Relationship to Philemon and Ephesians 180
  Structure 181
  Theological Emphases and Contemporary Significance 182

The gospel which you heard (Col 1:1–2:5) 185
  To the saints (1:1-2) 185
  We always thank God . . . when we pray for you (1:3-8) 188
  Asking that you may be filled with the knowledge of his will
   (1:9-14) 194
  . . . for in him all the fullness was pleased to dwell (1:15-20) 206
  And you . . . he has now reconciled (1:21-23) 217
  Now I am rejoicing in my sufferings for your sake (1:24–2:5) 221

So walk in him (Col 2:6–4:18) 231
  Just as you received Christ Jesus as Lord (2:6-7) 231
  See to it that no one takes you captive (2:8-23) 233
  Therefore, if you have been raised with Christ . . . (3:1-17) 252
  Wives . . . Husbands . . . Children . . . Fathers . . . Slaves . . .
   Masters (3:18–4:1) 267
  Redeeming the time (4:2-6) 274
  Final commendations and greetings (4:7-18) 277

WORKS CITED 285

Acknowledgments

Over the course of writing this commentary I have incurred numerous debts of gratitude to people whose friendship, help, and support have made its completion possible.

I must begin by expressing my thanks to Prof. Todd Still, who invited me to contribute a commentary to this series and offered warm encouragement and wise advice along the way. Leslie Andres and the rest of the team at Smyth & Helwys also gave expert assistance and direction through the process of revising the manuscript and preparing it for publication.

Closer to home, I am grateful to God for the team in which I serve at Morling College. I owe a particular debt to my biblical studies colleagues, Tim MacBride, Andrew Sloane, and Anthony Petterson, not only for the time they gave to reading and giving feedback on this and other writing projects, but also (and much more so) for the daily blessing of their friendship and partnership in ministry. The college as a whole, along with the Australian College of Theology and the University of Divinity, has given generous and ongoing support to my work in research and writing, including the semester of study leave that I was granted in 2017 and the opportunities within and beyond that semester to travel to scholarly conferences and participate in the wider conversations of colleagues around the world whose research interests intersect with mine.

Among those colleagues, special mention should go to Greg Beale, Michael Bird, Jeannine Brown, Alan Cadwallader, Simon Gathercole, Tim Gombis, Kyle Harper, Peter Head, Teresa Morgan, Steve Runge, Mark Seifrid, Frank Thielman, Paul Trebilco, Kevin Vanhoozer, Larry Welborn, Joel White, Jarvis Williams, and Tom Wright, all of whom gave generously of their time to offer ideas and insights in conversations and email exchanges that arose out of the issues discussed in this commentary.

The bulk of my study leave semester in 2017 was spent as a visiting researcher in the Ancient History department at Macquarie University, which provided me with a welcoming and stimulating scholarly home for the duration of my time there. Two particular highlights of that visit were the frequent conversations with Chris Forbes about the Greco-Roman world in which Paul ministered and the weekly seminars that Ros Kearsley conducted on the inscriptions of Roman Asia.

Two last words of thanks remain to be added. Peter O'Brien was a wise and gracious mentor to me, during both my original undergraduate studies in theology and the years in which he served as associate supervisor for my PhD research. I am privileged to have learned from him and to have followed in his steps as a commentator on these two books. Finally (but by no means least!), I am thankful for my wife, Nicole, who is my strongest earthly support, my closest partner in ministry, and my most cherished companion. Her love and encouragement continue to be a daily delight and blessing.

Editor's Foreword

Like its predecessor (Reading the New Testament) and its companion series (Reading the Old Testament), Reading the New Testament: Second Series seeks to help readers—whether students or scholars, ministers or laypeople—gain a greater understanding of and appreciation for biblical texts in their original contexts. To this good end, commentaries in this series attend not only to lexical, historical, and critical concerns but are also attuned to and interested in, as the subtitle of each volume signals, literary matters and theological meaning.

Whereas some commentaries are committed to the necessary and salutary task of commenting on every jot and tittle (see Matthew 5:18), works in this series seek to trace the thought and observe the craft of biblical authors in a less atomistic manner. While attending to various trees, they are also intent on not missing the forest. Relatedly, while technically undergirded and academically informed, the commentaries within this series are intended for and are meant to be accessible and valuable to a broad readership. The seventeen volumes that will make up Reading the New Testament: Second Series, then, are written *by* scholars but are not exclusively, or even primarily, *for* scholars.

Contributors to this commentary series are accomplished academics, experienced teachers, capable communicators, and professing Christians who are committed to explicating Scripture thoughtfully, clearly, and sympathetically. To the extent that this series results in people reading the twenty-seven New Testament documents with greater skill, care, insight, devotion, and joy, the contributors and editor of Reading the New Testament: Second Series will be grateful and gratified.

—Todd D. Still
Baylor University
George W. Truett Theological Seminary
Waco, Texas

Introduction to Ephesians

Authorship and Destination

Ephesians announces itself in its opening verse as a letter from "Paul, an apostle of Christ Jesus," to "the saints who are [in Ephesus] and faithful in Christ Jesus." On both scores—the authorship of the letter and its address to believers in Ephesus—the content and style of what follows raise questions that have been the topic of vigorous debate among commentators since the late eighteenth century (cf. the survey and analysis of views on the authorship of Ephesians in Hoehner 2002, 6–20).

Scholarly doubts over the authorship of Ephesians are typically based on a combination of several of the letter's features, none of which is sufficient on its own to rule out Paul as the author but the sum of which, taken together, is deemed by many to tip the scales in favor of pseudonymity. Ernest Best, for example, sees problems for the assumption of Pauline authorship of Ephesians in the letter's literary style, rhetorical form, and theological emphases (Best 1998, 27–35). To these could be added the letter's striking lack of specific reference to the recipients and their circumstances and the arm's-length nature of the way in which the writer's relationship with them is described (e.g. 1:15; 3:2)—features that would seem odd in a letter addressed by Paul to believers living in a city in which (according to Acts 19:10) he lived and ministered for more than two years.

The stakes in the discussion are raised by the features of the letter (e.g., the description in 4:21 of Tychicus's role as letter-bearer), which, if the letter is not authentically Pauline, are difficult to reconcile with the claim made by some commentators that it was a transparently pseudonymous text that would have been immediately recognized as such by the original readers. The frequently made claim that transparent, nondeceptive pseudepigraphy of this sort was a well-established first century practice within and beyond the church is open to serious question (Ehrman 2014, 93–145).

Within such discussions and deliberations, not all theories have an equal claim. While the question of the letter's *destination* is complicated by the absence of the words *en Ephesō* ("in Ephesus") from the earliest surviving manuscripts, on the matter of its *authorship* the onus of proof rests on those who dispute its Pauline origins, not those who defend them. Given the assertion of Pauline authorship that is made in the opening verse of Ephesians (and also, explicitly, in 3:1), uniformly present throughout the manuscript tradition, and accepted without controversy within the letter's patristic reception history, the letter should be regarded as Pauline until proven otherwise by a better explanatory hypothesis.

The features of Ephesians that have given rise to the modern scholarly debate over its authorship are not trivial or easily swept aside. As commentators frequently point out (e.g., Best 1998, 27; Thielman 2010, 5–7), the differences of vocabulary and style between Ephesians and the other letters of the Pauline corpus are sufficiently striking to have been commented on by interpreters writing long before the rise of the historical-critical method. Erasmus, for example, declared that "the style differs so much from the other epistles of Paul that it could seem to be the work of another person, did not the heart and soul of the Pauline mind assert clearly his claim to this letter" (CWE 43:300n12, cited in Thielman 2010, 7).

The vocabulary of the letter includes expressions that are used in Ephesians but never in the undisputed Pauline letters (e.g., "in the heavenly places" [*en tois epouraniois*]; 1:3, 20; 2:6; 3:10; 6:12), and words that can be also found in the undisputed Paulines but are used in Ephesians with a different sense or in a different context (e.g., "spiritual" [*pneumatikos*] in 6:12 to refer to evil powers and "holy" [*hagios*] in 3:5 as an adjective applied to the apostles and prophets). The syntax of the letter is equally distinctive, standing out for its long, meandering sentences (e.g., 1:3-14; 1:15-22; 3:1-7) and its extended sequences of genitive nouns and pronouns (e.g., 1:18, "the riches of his glorious inheritance in the saints" [*ho ploutos tēs doxēs tēs klēronomias autou*]; and 1:19, "the working of the might of his strength" [*tēn energeian tou kratous tēs ischyos autou*]).

The rhetoric of the letter, too, employs a noticeably different strategy from the argumentative rhetoric that is common in the undisputed Pauline letters. Rhetorical questions are almost entirely absent (4:9 is the solitary exception), in keeping with a general preference for reminder and exhortation over diatribe and polemic, and inferential or explanatory particles such as *gar* ("for") and *oun* ("then"; "therefore") are thin on the ground. Apart from the broad and generically worded warning in 5:6, the letter makes no explicit mention of opponents or rival teachers within the church.

The distinctive theological emphases that Best highlights as features that distinguish Ephesians from the undisputed Pauline letters include the universal scope of its ecclesiology (e.g., 1:22-23; 2:19-21; 3:10), its lack of any reference to the co-crucifixion of believers with Christ, the exalted role it gives to the apostles and prophets in the economy of revelation (e.g., 2:20; 3:5), its use of "reconciliation" language to refer to horizontal reconciliation between believers (e.g., 2:16), its depiction of the whole cosmos as being "filled" through Christ's redeeming work (e.g., 1:23; 4:10), its emphasis on the already realized elements of believers' salvation (e.g., 2:6), and the focus of its ethical instruction, particularly the household code of 5:21–6:9, on the internal relationships of the Christian household.

In addition to the issues that Best lists, two other features of Ephesians that are frequently noted by interpreters as problematic for the assumption of Pauline authorship are the absence from Ephesians of the "justification" language (along with "righteousness" used in a forensic sense) that is so prominent in earlier letters such as Galatians and Romans (Talbert 2007, 10), and the strikingly different way in which the situation of Gentiles within the church is depicted. While the Jew/Gentile issues that are a major theme in Galatians and Romans are no less prominent in Ephesians (esp. 2:11-22; 3:1-14), the full inclusion of uncircumcised Gentiles within the church appears in Ephesians to be an accomplished reality to be remembered and celebrated rather than a contested claim for which an argument must be mounted (Talbert 2007, 11).

A third, closely related issue is the way in which the Old Testament is used within the letter. Andrew Lincoln, for example, draws a sharp contrast between the role Scripture plays in Ephesians and the way it functions in the arguments that Paul mounts in Galatians 3–4 and Romans 4, 9–11, and 15, where it serves as a uniquely authoritative resource that Paul can mine for proofs that the justification of the Gentiles was "promised beforehand" by God. In Ephesians, Lincoln argues, Scripture is merely "one source among a number of authoritative traditions which [the writer] employs," interpreted in a framework that already presupposes the eschatologically revealed mystery of Gentile inclusion (3:5) and deployed in the service of the writer's aim to shape the readers' conduct and reinforce their sense of identity (Lincoln 1990, xciii; cf. Lincoln 1982, 44–50).

The cumulative weight of these various observations, taken together, is considerable, but it is hardly enough to overturn the *prima facie* claim of the letter to have been written (or dictated or commissioned) by Paul. The stylistic distinctives of Ephesians can be explained, at least in part, by its homiletic genre and epideictic rhetorical species (Witherington 2007, 2–3,

7–10, 219–23), by its frequent recourse to the use of traditional and liturgical material as a strategy for reinforcing the social identity of the readers (Campbell 2014, 334–36), and by the hypothesis that Paul or his amanuensis adapted its style to the Asiatic conventions that would have been familiar to the letter's intended audience (Witherington 2007, 4–6, 223).

Nor are the theological emphases of Ephesians so different from those of the undisputed Pauline letters as to render it inexplicable as a development of Paul's own thought or a recontextualization of his ideas to address the situation of the letter's intended readers. The ecclesiology of Ephesians, for example, is not as far removed from that of the undisputed Pauline epistles as it is sometimes painted. While the letter certainly encourages its readers to view themselves as members of a single, cosmic *ekklēsia*, "built on the foundation of the apostles and prophets" (2:20), the concrete exhortations that follow in chapters 4–6 still assume a primary sphere of application within the local, visible community of believers (e.g., 4:1-16, 25-32); nor, conversely, is the idea of a trans-local "church," comprising all who belong to Christ, a notion that is absent from the undisputed letters (cf. Gal 1:13; 1 Cor 10:32; 15:9; Phil 3:6). The familiar Pauline metaphors of the church as body (1 Cor 12:12-31; Rom 12:4-5) and building (1 Cor 3:9-17) have undeniably been adapted in the way that they are used in Ephesians. Whereas the "head" of the body in 1 Corinthians 12 is merely a high-status member of the congregation, the head in Ephesians is Christ (1:22-23; 4:15); and the respective roles of Paul and Christ in 1 Corinthians 3 as foundation-layer and foundation for the building that is the church have been recast in Ephesians 2, where the "foundation" of the church is the apostles and prophets, and Christ is the "cornerstone" (2:20). But to appeal to this as proof that Ephesians could not have been written by Paul is seriously to underestimate the freedom and fluidity with which Paul employs his metaphors. Even within 1 Corinthians itself, the metaphor of the temple and dwelling place of the Spirit can be applied, within the space of a few chapters, to both the church (3:16-17) and the individual believer (6:19), without any evidence that Paul was concerned this might create an impression of inconsistency or contradiction. Within Ephesians, there are obvious contextual reasons for the adaptation of the body metaphor, including the way it enters the discourse as a development of the prior metaphor of Christ as head (1:22). The adaptation of the building metaphor, too, can readily be explained as a consequence of the way its function differs from that of the building metaphor in 1 Corinthians 3, where the agency and accountability of Paul and his fellow builders are the chief issues under discussion.

The illusion of an unbridgeable gulf between the thought world of Ephesians and that of the undisputed Pauline epistles is created, at least in part, by the scholarly habit of treating Galatians and Romans as the quintessence of authentic Paulinism and treating the arguments he mounts in those letters in favor of the justification of Gentiles, apart from the works of the law, as the defining center of his theology (cf. the criticisms of that tendency in Campbell 2014, 331–32; Anderson 2016, 384–91). The preference of Ephesians for the language of "salvation" and "wrath" over the more overtly forensic categories of "justification" and "condemnation," for example, is entirely consistent with the soteriological language of 1 Thessalonians, and the focus of Ephesians on teaching Gentiles to live in accordance with their newly conferred status as the holy people of God corresponds closely to the purposes of 1 Thessalonians and 1 Corinthians (and, for that matter, much of Gal 5–6 and Rom 12–15). Charles Talbert's observation that "[w]hile Romans and Galatians, genuine Pauline letters, are focused on the problem of the Gentiles, Colossians and Ephesians are concerned with the problems of Gentile Christians" (Talbert 2007, 11) could just as easily have been framed to make the opposite point: "First Thessalonians and 1 Corinthians, genuine Pauline letters, are focused on the problem of Gentile Christians, and a similar concern can be seen in Colossians and Ephesians." Similarly, Lincoln's sharp dichotomy between the way Scripture is used in Ephesians and the way it functions in the authentically Pauline letters relies on a reductionistic account of the latter. When due allowance is made for the rich variety of ways that Paul can draw on Old Testament traditions in support of his rhetorical and pastoral purposes, the hermeneutic at work in Ephesians can be seen to fit comfortably within the landscape of Pauline hermeneutics (cf. the more detailed discussion in Starling 2011, 201–208).

Where the theological categories and emphases of Ephesians differ from those of the undisputed Pauline epistles, those differences can, in most instances, be explained as contextualizations or developments of Paul's thought, rather than as a fundamental departure from it. Thus, for example, the heavy stress that Ephesians places on the already realized dimensions of the readers' salvation and the power of God that has accomplished them makes perfect sense as an application of Paul's gospel to the social situation of the readers and their interaction with the powers (both cultural/political and supernatural) that dominated their world (Arnold 2010, 43, 48), without in any way implying that the future horizons of salvation and judgment have been forgotten (see comments below on 1:13-14; 21; 2:5-7; 5:6). Similarly, the disappearance of narrowly focused polemics against "works of the law" as a basis for justification (cf. Gal 2:16; 3:2, 5, 10; Rom 3:20, 28), in favor of the more sweeping declarations of Ephesians 2:8-9 that the readers' salvation is "not of yourselves" (*ouk ex hymōn*) and "not because of works" (*ouk ex ergōn*), can be plausibly and elegantly explained in terms of the trajectory of Paul's developing thought (cf. Marshall 1996; Anderson 2016, 227–64).

The question of the letter's destination arises in part from its lack of personal greetings and specific, concrete references to the circumstances and concerns of the recipients. It is made more pressing by the secondhand way in which the author's relationship with the recipients is depicted (e.g., 1:15; 3:2) and the hypothetical terms in which their conversion and catechesis are depicted in 4:21—both of which would seem odd if the letter was addressed by Paul to a church to whom he was as deeply connected as the church in Ephesus. The discussion is complicated still further by the absence of the phrase *en Ephesō* ("in Ephesus") from the oldest surviving manuscripts of the letter and by the fact that the letter to the Colossians (which includes in 4:7-8 a commendation of Tychicus as letter-bearer that is strikingly similar to the commendation of Tychicus in Eph 6:21-22) makes reference to "the letter from Laodicea" (Col 4:16) and the prayers that Paul prays "for you, and for those in Laodicea, and for those who have not seen my face in the flesh" (Col 2:1).

Various solutions have been proposed to the text-critical puzzle posed by the opening verse of Ephesians. Although the external evidence for the shorter reading (*tois hagiois tois ousin kai pistois en Christō Iēsou* ["to the saints who are also faithful in Christ Jesus"]) includes the three oldest surviving manuscripts of Ephesians ($\mathfrak{P}^{46}$, ℵ*, B*), the extreme grammatical oddity of the syntax counts against the theory that this was the original reading (Anderson 2016, 201–202; Thielman 2010, 12–15). The theory that the original text included a blank space into which the names of various towns and cities could be inserted by the copyists (Lightfoot 1893, 392–93; Witherington 2007, 217–19) is ingenious, but in the absence of any surviving ancient manuscripts in which that practice is followed, or any surviving copies of Ephesians in which the name of another town or city has been inserted into the greeting, it must be regarded as entirely speculative. Equally speculative is the proposal that the place name was originally omitted, without a blank space, and left to be supplied by the letter-bearer as the letter was read (Anderson 2016, 206–207).

Despite the unconvincing nature of these theories, the absence of *en Ephesō* from the earliest manuscripts of Ephesians still requires some explanation. The best and simplest way of accounting for its absence is the theory that Ephesians was originally composed as a kind of circular homily, addressed to Ephesus with the expectation that further copies would be made and distributed to the churches of the surrounding region (including the church in Laodicea), and that early in the history of the text's transmission copies were made in which those words were deleted to facilitate that intended function of the letter (cf. the removal of "in Rome" from Rom 1:7 in Codex G) (Thielman 2010, 16; Arnold 2010, 28; Metzger 1994, 505). On this reading of the evidence, the "letter from Laodicea" that Paul refers to in Col 4:16 could still, in all likelihood, have been the circular homily that we call Ephesians, without implying that it was composed exclusively or primarily for the Laodiceans; Paul describes it to the Colossians as "from Laodicea" rather than "from Ephesus" simply because Laodicea would have been the closest town to Colossae to which Ephesians was delivered by Tychicus.

If Paul, as he dictated the letter, already had in mind a wider audience than merely the believers in Ephesus, then the lack of specific reference to individuals and circumstances in Ephesus becomes a good deal less surprising than it would be if the letter were composed exclusively for the Ephesians. The same can be said of the remote and hypothetical way in which he describes his relationship with his intended readers (1:15; 3:2). And if, as I will argue below, the most likely date of composition for Ephesians is in the early 60s, during Paul's first Roman imprisonment, then even in Ephesus a large proportion of his intended readers would have been people who had come to faith during the interval that had elapsed between his departure from the city in the mid-50s and his writing of the letter, approximately half a dozen years later.

In this commentary, therefore, I will be reading Ephesians as an authentically Pauline composition, written as a circular homily intended for believers in Ephesus and the towns and villages of the surrounding region. Given that hypothesis, and the paucity of information provided within the letter itself regarding the immediate situation of the churches Paul is addressing, I will not be presupposing any detailed reconstruction of the particular circumstances of the original readers, or of events within the churches to which they belonged. Rather, I will be focusing (as the letter does) on their status as Gentile believers in Christ, their situation as relatively recent converts to the faith, and their relationship to the powers (both visible and invisible) that dominated the politico-religious context in which they lived (cf. Arnold 2010, 29–41).

Relationship to Colossians

The conclusion for which I have argued above regarding the authorship and destination of Ephesians anticipates the discussion in this section about the letter's relationship to Colossians. On even a cursory reading of the two letters, it is difficult not to notice the verbal and conceptual similarities between them; particularly striking examples can be seen in the instructions of the household code regarding the way slaves should relate to their masters (6:5-6, cf. Col 3:22), the exhortations about wisdom, speech, and song in 5:15-20 (cf. Col 3:16-17; 4:5), and the commendation of Tychicus in 6:21 (cf. Col 4:7, though in this case the extent of the verbal similarity is somewhat less if, as I argue below in the comments on Col 4:8, the most likely original wording of that verse is the variant reading attested in $\mathfrak{P}^{46}$, C, and D^1).

Striking as the similarities between Ephesians and Colossians are, the evidence of the two letters is not of the sort that can be neatly explained by a theory of slavish literary dependence of one on the other (see especially Best 1997b). Fragments of one letter turn up in the other, but not always at corresponding points in the structure of the letter; verses that express similar ideas (e.g., Eph 6:18 and Col 4:2; Eph 6:4 and Col 3:21; Eph 3:5 and Col 1:26) do not always do so in the same vocabulary, and the changes of wording are difficult to explain if one letter was composed with the other open in front of its imitator (cf. Best 1998, 22). If different authors wrote the two letters, then (with the possible exception of 6:21) the author of the latter letter made creative and eclectic use of words and ideas from the former one, rather than leaning heavily and dependently on it.

The simpler explanation is that the two letters have a common author, who composed them at (almost) the same time, with a similar pool of thoughts and phrases occupying his mind. If that author was Paul, and the words about Tychicus are to be taken at face value, then the close similarities of wording have an obvious explanation in the fact that the arrangements for the delivery of the two letters were almost identical, as were the expectations Paul had in each case for the role of Tychicus as letter-bearer.

The points at which the two letters diverge from one another (at times using similar vocabulary and imagery to express slightly different ideas) are not so widely disparate as to require the conclusion that they were the work of different authors (contra Mitton 1951, 82–97; Dibelius 1913, 113–14). While the word *mystērion* ("mystery"), for example, can be used to refer to a slightly wider range of hidden-but-now-revealed truths in Ephesians (1:9; 3:3-6; 5:32) than in Colossians (where, in 1:26-27; 2:2; 4:3, it refers consistently to Christ), the scope of the realities that the word refers to in Ephesians is no wider than in the undisputed Pauline letters, and (as argued below in the comments on 3:4) they are all interrelated within Paul's mind as part of "the mystery of Christ." Even in Colossians the phenomenon of Gentile inclusion (which is the focus of the "mystery" to which Paul refers in Eph 3:3-6) is also in view in 1:26-27. Nor is the fact that the mystery is said in Col 1:26 to have been revealed by God "to his saints" inconsistent with the claim in Eph 3:5 that it has been made known "to his holy apostles and prophets," since the latter group is clearly depicted in Ephesians 3 as a conduit of revelation to all of God's people (cf. 3:8-9; 1:9-10).

If Paul composed both letters, under the same circumstances and at almost the same time, then the question of which letter was composed first is of considerably less importance than it would be if one were the Pauline template from which a pseudo-Pauline imitator composed the other. While it is difficult to make a definitive pronouncement, the most likely scenario is one in which the immediate spur to write was provided by the circumstances that occasioned Colossians and Philemon (including the news that Paul had received from Epaphras about the circumstances of the Colossian church). On this scenario, the writing of Ephesians was Paul's opportunistic response to the fact that Tychicus would already be traveling through Ephesus (and the towns of the Lycus valley) on his way to Colossae, and could deliver another, more general letter *en route*. Under those circumstances, Colossians was probably the letter that was written first, and Ephesians was a reworking of some of its themes for the broader audience of "those in Laodicea, and . . . those who have not seen my face in the flesh" (Col 2:1), who were also on Paul's mind during his imprisonment (cf. the "you also" [*kai hymeis*] in 6:21 and the discussion in the comments on that verse, below). That being said, if "the letter from Laodicea" that Paul refers to in Col 4:16 is Ephesians, then the intention to write that letter was already formed in his mind as he dictated Colossians, even if the composition and dictation of its details was still to take place.

A sequence of this sort is consistent with some of the more observable differences between the two letters. It is more likely, for example, that Paul would have added into Ephesians the explicit OT references that are nowhere present in Colossians than that he would have carefully removed them all in the process of redacting Ephesians for the believers in Colossae. Similarly, it is easier to envisage Paul expanding on the brief word to husbands in Col 3:19 to produce the much longer and more theologically developed exhortations in Eph 5:25-32 than to envisage him, having already composed the household code of Ephesians, pruning it back to the cursory instructions contained in the Colossian code. On the other hand, the places where Ephesians is brief and Colossians expansive can generally be explained as expressions of the particular pastoral concerns that motivate the letter to Colossae, which would have been less immediately relevant to the intended readers of Ephesians. The sweeping Christological assertions of Col 1:15-23, for example, have undoubtedly played an enduring role in the history of Christian dogmatics, but within the original context of the letter their more immediate function is to prepare the way for the polemics and exhortation of 2:6-23; it is not difficult to imagine Paul viewing that paragraph as having been composed specifically for the situation he was addressing in Colossae and filling the equivalent spot in Ephesians with the brief reflections of 1:19b-23 on Christ's resurrection, ascension, and headship over the powers.

Reconstructions of this sort are unavoidably speculative and should not be asked to bear too much weight. Within this commentary, where words and phrases in Ephesians have a close parallel in Colossians, I will interpret them primarily in light of their immediate context in Ephesians, taking note of the way they are used in Colossians as one factor that may shed light on their meaning in Ephesians, without ruling out the possibility that they may be doing slightly different work in one letter from the function that they perform in the other.

Situation and Date

If, as I have argued above, Ephesians is best understood as a letter composed by Paul under the same circumstances as those in which he composed the letters to Philemon and the Colossians, then the question of the letter's situation and date must be answered in conjunction with the quest for the situation and date of the other two letters.

Among the few details that the three letters provide about the circumstances in which Paul is writing, the most prominent and frequently mentioned is the fact that he is "in chains" (Eph 6:20; Col 4:13, 18; Phlm 10, 13) as a "prisoner" (Eph 3:1; 4:1; Col 4:10; Phlm 1, 9, 23). The only two cities that are named within the New Testament as places where Paul was held as a prisoner (apart from his brief internments in Philippi and Jerusalem) are Caesarea (Acts 23:23–26:32) and Rome (Acts 28:11-31; cf. Phil 1:13), though in 2 Corinthians, written prior to the imprisonments in Caesarea and Rome, Paul makes reference to multiple earlier imprisonments in unspecified locations (2 Cor 6:5; 11:23). It is tempting, given the relative proximity of Colossae to Ephesus, to speculate that the imprisonment in which Onesimus had become a "son" to Paul was not his later imprisonment in Rome (or Caesarea) but an earlier, Ephesian imprisonment left unrecorded in Acts. But the main problem this reconstruction attempts to solve (i.e., that of the long journey Onesimus would have needed to make from Colossae to Rome) is more apparent than real, given the close connections of trade and transport between Rome and Ephesus. It is by no means beyond the realms of possibility that Onesimus, in his quest to appeal to Paul as an *amicus domini*, could have made his way to the capital and found Paul there, or that Paul could have harbored hopes of making his way from Rome to Colossae after his anticipated release from prison (Phlm 22). It is, however, somewhat more difficult to explain why an imprisonment long enough to include the forging of the bonds between Paul and Onesimus that are described in Philemon 10-13 could have been left unmentioned by Luke in the relatively long and detailed narrative of Paul's time in Ephesus that he offers in Acts 19. The hypothesis of an early date (ca. AD 55, or even, as Campbell proposes, AD 50; Campbell 2014, 337) for Paul's prison letters is also a little more difficult to square with the fact that he is able to describe himself to Philemon as an "old man" (Phlm 9) at the time of the letter's composition.

The theory of an Ephesian provenance for all three letters would additionally create problems for the traditional assumption that Ephesians was written *to* Ephesus and would require an explanation for how the words *en Ephesō* ("in Ephesus") found their way into the opening verse of the letter in so many of the surviving manuscripts. These problems would not necessarily be fatal for the theory; it is possible, for example, that Paul, even if his imprisonment were in Ephesus, may still have included the believers of that city among the addressees of a letter composed during his imprisonment. But they do count, at least to some degree, against the theory of an Ephesian provenance for the prison letters if Ephesians is included as one of them.

For these and other reasons, the majority of interpreters who regard Ephesians as an authentically Pauline letter opt for Rome as the most likely location of its composition and date the letter as originating from the same imprisonment as the one referred to in Acts 28, which lasted from approximately AD 60 to AD 62. Sometime during AD 60, according to Tacitus (*Ann.* 14.27), the city of Laodicea suffered a major earthquake, but because of the uncertainty regarding the extent of the damage it inflicted on Laodicea (and also, according to Eusebius, Colossae), the question of whether the writing of Ephesians, Colossians, and Philemon pre- or post-dated that event should not be decisive for the dating of the letters. For the purposes of this commentary, I will assume a Roman provenance for Ephesians and a date of composition somewhere between AD 60 and 62, reading the letter as relatively late within the trajectory of Paul's developing thought (Anderson 2016, 226–378) and relating its contents to the social and religious context of Roman Asia in the early 60s.

Purpose

There is little within Ephesians to suggest that the letter was occasioned by news that Paul had received from the churches to which he is writing in the letter. The exhortations of the letter's second half do not offer any indication that Paul is responding to particular instances of disunity, immorality, or other problems that have been reported to him (cf. the methodological issues discussed in Gupta 2012). Even the appeal to the readers in 3:13 not to be "discouraged" by Paul's sufferings is not in itself a sufficient basis to conclude that he had received news that they were disheartened by his imprisonment (though the likelihood that this was the case would probably have been a plausible assumption for Paul to make). Nor (contra Moritz 1996b) is there any clear indication within the letter that it is framed as a contribution to an ongoing theological controversy within the churches that Paul is writing to.

The prayer reports of 1:16b-19 and 3:14-19 are probably the clearest indication we have in the first half of the letter of what Paul's hopes were for his readers and (by implication) what he was aiming to accomplish in writing to them. Lincoln may perhaps be a little overconfident in his attempt to mirror-read these verses as evidence that the writer is reacting to a perceived problem suffered by his readers, judging them to be "lacking in appreciation for or awareness of" the themes that are the focus of these prayers (Lincoln 1990, lxxviii). He is, however, on stronger ground when he highlights the ways these prayers (together with the content of chs. 1–3 more broadly) suggest a desire on the writer's part to deepen and confirm the readers' sense of identity as Gentile Christians and members of the church, to fortify their resolve in the face of an intimidating array of hostile powers (Lincoln 1990, lxxviii–lxxix).

The fact that the letter goes on, in its second half, to encourage the readers to live a life in keeping with the identity established in chapters 1–3 is not enough to support the conclusion drawn by Lincoln (and developed by his student Roy Jeal) that the letter shifts in its purpose and rhetorical species from an epideictic first half to a deliberative second half (cf. Lincoln 1990, xlii; Jeal 2000, 43). Rather, as Witherington suggests, the exhortations of the letter's second half serve primarily as reminders to readers who have already (in behavior as well as in doctrine) "learned Christ" (4:20):

> Throughout this discourse the audience is being asked to learn or remember (e.g., 1:13-14; 2:11-22; 4:17ff; 5:8), not to change their conduct. The peroratio in Ephesians 6 makes it perfectly clear that the audience is being asked to stand firm and equip themselves with armor that they already have ready to hand, not change direction. (Witherington 2007, 222)

Structure

The structure of Ephesians reflects the letter's twofold purpose: to reinforce the readers' sense of identity and to encourage them to shape their conduct and relationships in accordance with it.

The first three chapters have as their core a series of three narratives that function to remind the readers of the story that has transformed their situation and given them their new identity. The first two of these focus directly on the transformation they themselves have experienced: once they were dead, but now they have been made alive together with Christ (2:1-10); once they were far off, separated from God and his people, but now they have been brought near (2:11-22). The immediate focus of the third narrative is on Paul, whose imprisonment (v. 1) and sufferings (v. 13) serve as its frame. But the explanation Paul provides for his sufferings becomes in turn an account of how "the mystery of Christ, which in other times was not made known" has "now" come to be "proclaim[ed] to the Gentiles" (vv. 5, 8); the story of the suffering apostle turns out, in the end, to be a third story about the transformed situation of the readers, who have now come to be "fellow heirs, fellow members of the body, and sharers in the promise in Christ Jesus" (v. 6).

Wrapped around these three narratives are reports of Paul's prayers for the readers (1:15-23; 3:14-19), and encasing these, in turn, are the doxologies that open (after the brief greeting in 1:1-2) and close the first section of the letter (1:3-14; 3:20-21). The structure of the letter's first half is, thus, a concentric one (cf. Sellin 2008, 52):

A. Doxology (1:3-14)
   B. Prayer report (1:15-23)
      C. Salvation-historical narratives (2:1–3:13)
   B'. Prayer report (3:14-19)
A'. Doxology (3:20-21)

The effect is to surround Paul's words to the Ephesians about the things that God has done for their salvation with words that implicitly invite them to join with Paul in offering up to God prayers and praises. The Ephesians are to understand themselves not only as a redeemed community but as a worshiping community who live in daily dependence on God and exist to give him glory.

The second half of the letter (chs. 4–6) builds on the first, urging the readers to "walk worthily" (4:1) of the calling and identity that Paul has reminded them of in chapters 1–3. The opening exhortations of 4:1-3 focus on the internal dynamics of relationships within the body of Christ, an emphasis that continues to the end of verse 16. The longer series of exhortations in 4:17–6:9, however, combines a continuing emphasis on that theme with a series of reminders about the ways the lives of believers must differ from those of their pagan neighbors (4:17), and from their own conduct before they "learned Christ" (4:20) and were taught to "put on the new humanity" (4:22).

Three aspects of their new identity are brought into focus in the subsequent paragraphs, as a basis for Paul's exhortations: their new status as "beloved children" who are to live in imitation of their Father (4:25–5:2); their consequent calling, as "children of light," to display the fruit of the light in their conduct and character (5:3-14); and their privileged situation, "not as unwise . . . but as wise," which should be expressed in the way they relate to their surrounding culture and to one another (5:15–6:9).

Embedded within this third subsection, and making up the bulk of it, is the "household code" of 5:21–6:9. Verse 21 ("submitting to one another in reverence toward Christ") thus serves as a bridge between the call to live wisely in 5:15-21 and the specific injunctions that follow in 5:22–6:9. These injunctions are grouped as three sets of reciprocal pairs, addressed to wives (5:22-24) and husbands (5:25-33), children (6:1-3) and fathers (6:4), slaves (6:5-8) and masters (6:9).

The body of the letter concludes in 6:10-20 with a call to the readers to "be strong," clothing themselves with the armor of God (vv. 11-17) and devoting themselves to prayer (vv. 18-20). These two closely interconnected paragraphs comprise the *peroratio* of the homily that makes up the bulk of the letter; as such, they function as both the climax of the series of exhortations introduced in 4:1 and as a recapitulation of key themes and motifs from chapters 1–3 (e.g., the reminders in 1:20-23; 2:1-6; 3:10 of the readers' participation in Christ's victory over the powers, and the prayer in 3:14-19 for God's strengthening work in their hearts). Finally, in 6:21-24, Paul closes the letter by commending Tychicus as the letter carrier (vv. 21-22) and offering a prayer wish for the readers (vv. 23-24).

Theological Emphases and Contemporary Significance

Like the structure of the letter, its theological themes are consistent with its purpose. The depictions of the character and action of God in the letter's first half emphasize his grace, mercy, and love (e.g., 1:2, 3, 6, 7; 2:4, 5, 7, 8; 3:2, 7-8, 17, 19), the glory that is his and is to be given to him (e.g., 1:6, 12, 14, 17; 3:16, 21), his power, might, and strength (e.g., 1:19-20; 3:7, 20), and the way he works things out in accordance with his wisdom, purpose, and will, for his own good pleasure (e.g., 1:4, 5, 9-10, 11; 3:9, 11).

The power of God and the wealth that he pours out in his generosity are both described by Paul as "surpassing" (*hyperballon*) in their magnitude (1:19; 2:7), language that invites comparison with the powers, both visible and invisible, that dominate the readers' world and the splendor and generosity of the patrons whose gifts were celebrated in the honorific inscriptions that pervaded the public spaces of the cities of Roman Asia. But the God who raised Christ from the dead is not just one power among others; in the resurrection of Christ, he has demonstrated once and for all his transcendent sovereignty over the powers and has seated his Son "high above all rule and authority and power and dominion, and every name that is named" (1:21). For readers who felt themselves hemmed in on every side by the various and mutually reinforcing power structures of the social world that they inhabited, the realities that Paul reminds them of are not abstract theology but essential elements of a worldview and liturgical practice that made it possible for them to live the kind of culturally resistant lifestyle that they are called to in the second half of the letter.

The relationship between the doctrine of the letter's first half and the ethics of its second half goes beyond the frequently articulated dynamic in which grace (chs. 1–3) is met with gratitude (chs. 4–6). The life the readers are urged to live in the exhortations of the letter's second half is not merely a generically good life, motivated by grace but directed by the norms and expectations of a moral code that is self-evident to all; it is, rather, to be lived out as a kind of performance or manifestation of the particular and distinctively Christian truth that is "in Jesus" (4:21) (Gombis 2010, 15). As a community of men and women who have "learned Christ" (4:20), they are to clothe themselves with a new identity (4:22-24) and live as "imitators of God" (5:1) (cf. the discussion in Starling 2019).

Their calling as the new community thus calls for both a peaceable, harmonious unity (4:1-16; cf. 2:14-22) and a holy distinctiveness that stand out like light from darkness against the backdrop of their previous way of life and the lives of their pagan neighbors (4:17–6:9; cf. 2:1-3, 10). Their social existence is to be a public, embodied display of the richly variegated, "intricately complex" (*polypoikilos*) wisdom of God (3:10), demonstrated in both the diversity of the church's composition, knitted together with one another in love (2:14–18; 4:7–16), and the varied, complementary ways in which they embody the gospel in their differing roles and situations (5:21–6:9).

For us as twenty-first century readers, in a time torn apart by the tensions between a soulless globalization and the mutually antagonistic tribalisms that react against it (cf. Chua 2018; Goodhart 2017; Haidt 2012), the social vision that Paul commends in Ephesians stands out as both enticingly attractive and dauntingly difficult. It is all too easy for the church to conform itself to the norms of a consumer capitalist society, marketing spirituality to an experience-hungry culture, or to allow itself to be co-opted into the belligerence and self-righteousness of one side or the other in the culture wars of our time. It is much harder, and infinitely more beautiful, to live out the way of life that Paul urges the readers of Ephesians to pursue, performing an identity that is grounded not in soil, skin, nostalgia, or utopianism but in the person of Christ, and asserted not in anger and coercion but in gentleness and love. Like our predecessors in every generation of the church's history, we need the soaring visions that Paul paints in Ephesians of God's grace and glory, power and purpose, as they converge in the story of Christ, so that we can play our part within that story, anticipating the day when not just the church but all things will be summed up in him.

One new humanity

Ephesians 1:1–3:21

To the saints (1:1-2)

(1) Paul, an apostle of Christ Jesus through the will of God; to the saints who are [in Ephesus] and faithful in Christ Jesus. (2) Grace to you and peace from God our Father and the Lord Jesus Christ.

1:1. In keeping with ancient Greco-Roman and Jewish letter-writing custom, Ephesians commences with a prescript that identifies the sender ("Paul, an apostle of Christ Jesus through the will of God") and the recipients ("to the saints who are [in Ephesus] and faithful in Christ Jesus"), then adds a greeting ("Grace to you and peace from God our Father and the Lord Jesus Christ"). As is the case in Paul's other letters, though less so here in Ephesians than in most other Pauline letter prescripts, these standard elements are modified and expanded to highlight the things he wishes to emphasize about himself, his readers, and his purposes in writing.

In v. 1a, Paul identifies himself as "an apostle of Christ Jesus through the will of God," foreshadowing the references later in the letter to the "apostles and prophets" given by Christ to the church (cf. 2:20; 3:5; 4:11), and his own unique role as "as servant [of the gospel] according to the gift of the grace of God" (3:7). Although explicit references within Paul's prescripts to his calling as an apostle are sometimes a reflection of the fact that his apostleship is being challenged in the churches he is writing to (cf. Gal 1:1; 1 Cor 1:1; 2 Cor 1:1), there is no indication within Ephesians that this is the case among the people he is writing to in this instance. Rather, as is the case in Rom 1:1 and Col 1:1, the explicit reference to his apostleship here and elsewhere in the letter appears to reflect his consciousness of the fact that many of the people he is writing to will not be his converts and will not (in most cases) have experienced his ministry firsthand (cf. 1:15; 3:2; Thielman 2010, 32).

There are two main reasons that this is likely to have been the case, despite the fact that Paul—according to the account in Acts 19—had spent more than two years in Ephesus, teaching first in the synagogue (19:8) and then subsequently in the lecture hall of Tyrannus (19:9). In the first place, if we grant the hypothesis that Ephesians was written during Paul's Roman imprisonment, at some point in the two years that he spent there under house arrest (Acts 28:30; cf. the argument in the introduction in favor of a Roman origin for Ephesians and a date in the early 60s), then many of the Christians in Ephesus would have become believers during the years that had elapsed between his departure from Ephesus (ca. AD 55) and the writing of the letter (AD 60–62). And in the second place, given the role of Ephesus as the mother city of the Roman province of Asia and the way in which, according to Luke, the gospel had radiated out from there even during the time when Paul had been present in the city (cf. Acts 19:10), Paul would have been conscious as he wrote that he was addressing not only the churches that met within Ephesus itself but also the churches that had been established across the preceding decade in the nearby villages and towns to the east, south, and north of the city.

The probable function of Ephesians as a circular homily, addressed not to a single community in Ephesus but to a network of house churches within and beyond the city, is the most likely explanation for the omission of "in Ephesus" within the oldest surviving manuscripts of the letter—probably not because those words were missing from the original but because, early in the history of the text's transmission, copies were made in which those words had been deleted to facilitate the letter's use, in keeping with Paul's intentions, in churches outside of Ephesus.

Paul addresses his readers in v. 1b as "the saints who are [in Ephesus] and faithful in Christ Jesus." The absence of an article in front of "faithful" suggests that Paul has in mind a single group of recipients who are addressed as both "saints" and "faithful" (Larkin 2009, 2; Wallace 1996, 282) rather than, as some argue (Kümmel 1975, 355; Robinson 1963, 50–53; Witherington 2007, 225–26), two separate groups, identified respectively as "the saints" (i.e., Jewish believers) and "the faithful" (i.e., Gentile believers). Describing the readers as "saints" emphasizes the activity of God in consecrating them as his people (cf. 1:13); describing them as "faithful" emphasizes the trust and fidelity with which they have responded to the message of the gospel (cf. 1:13, 15, 19; 2:8; 6:21).

The primary function of the phrase "in Christ Jesus" that ends the verse is probably not to specify Christ Jesus as the object of their trust (cf. 1:15: "your faith in the Lord Jesus") but (given the parallel with the unambiguously locative "in Ephesus" and the slightly stronger implications of fidelity that the adjective *pistos* has, compared to the noun *pistis* and the verb *pisteuō*) to depict Christ Jesus as the metaphorical "sphere" in which their trust and allegiance have been exercised (cf. 6:21). Paul's use of the expression here in v. 1 thus anticipates the way in which the phrase functions in vv. 3-14 to refer to the readers' relational location "in Christ" as the sphere within which they have experienced the blessings of God and now live as his people.

By expanding his description of the letter's recipients in this way, Paul begins the work that he will continue across the first three chapters of the letter, reinforcing his readers' awareness of their identity as a community defined by the gracious purposes of God in Christ and the exhortations to them in the letter's second half to live a life in keeping with that identity.

1:2. The prescript concludes in v. 2 with a greeting that wishes the readers "grace . . . and peace from God our Father and the Lord Jesus Christ." The same greeting (with minor variations) is found in all the canonical Pauline letters. It combines the customary Greek "greetings!" (*chairein*), transformed into a prayer wish for "grace" (*charis*), with the traditional Hebrew/Aramaic *šālôm/šĕlām*, translated into a wish for "peace" (*eirēnē*) (Lieu 1985). The "grace" for which the greeting prays can refer (here in Ephesians and elsewhere in Paul's letters) both to the divine disposition of favor and kindness from which all of God's blessings proceed (cf. 1:6) and to the outpoured gifts that flow from that generous disposition (cf. 1:7). The "peace" that is joined to it refers principally to the harmony and well-being that God's salvation creates, both "vertically," between God and his people, and "horizontally," within the human relationships of the reconciled community (cf. 2:17; 4:3; 6:15, 23). Here, too, the gift is inseparable from the giver, since it is Christ himself, according to Paul in 2:14, who "is" our peace.

Both the grace and the peace that Paul wishes for his readers are spoken of as proceeding "from God our Father and the Lord Jesus Christ." Here as elsewhere in Paul's letter greetings, this form of words does not imply that "God our Father" and "the Lord Jesus Christ" are to be thought of as two separate sources of blessing; rather, as the following verses go on to make clear (cf. 1:3-14), the picture he wishes to convey is one in which the agency of God and that of Christ are exercised in an inseparable unity, such that the blessings believers receive from the Father are both accomplished and experienced in the Son—and, for that matter, the Spirit (cf. vv. 13-14). Nor is the relationship between the Father and the Son represented as a merely instrumental one; in speaking "the Lord Jesus Christ" (1:2, 3), Paul is implying that the risen Jesus participates in the very identity of YHWH himself as "Lord" (*kyrios*), anticipating what he goes on to say in 1:21 about the way in which Christ has been "seat[ed] . . . high above all rule and authority and power and dominion, and every name that is named."

Blessed be the God ... who has blessed us in Christ (1:3-14)

(3) Blessed be the God and Father of our Lord Jesus Christ, who has blessed us in Christ with every spiritual blessing in the heavenly places, (4) in so far as he chose us in him before the foundation of the world, in order that we should be holy and unblemished before him in love, (5) because he predestined us for adoption to him through Jesus Christ, according to the good pleasure of his will, (6) for the praise of the glory of his grace, with which he has graced us in the Beloved, (7) in whom we have redemption through his blood, the forgiveness of trespasses, according to the riches of his grace, (8) which he lavished upon us with all wisdom and understanding, (9) by making known to us the mystery of his will, according to his good pleasure, which he purposed in him (10) as a plan for the fullness of the times, to sum up all things in Christ—the things in the heavens and the things on the earth, in him— (11) in whom we have also been made inheritors, having been predestined according to the purpose of the one who works all things according to the council of his will, (12) in order that we, who first hoped in Christ, might be for the praise of his glory; (13) in whom you also, having heard the word of truth, the gospel of your salvation (in whom having also believed) you were sealed with the Holy Spirit of promise (14) who is a guarantee of our inheritance until the redeeming of the possession, for the praise of his glory.

1:3. In almost all of Paul's letters (cf. Rom 1:8-10; 1 Cor 1:4-9; Phil 1:3-11; Col 1:3-11; 1 Thess 1:2–2:13; 2 Thess 1:3-12; 2 Tim 1:3; Phlm 6-7), his initial greeting is followed immediately by a report of the prayers of thanksgiving and intercession that he prays for the readers. Here, however, the prayer report is deferred to vv. 15-23 and preceded by an outpouring of praise to God for the blessings that God has extended to his people.

Paul's praises to God take the form of a *berakah*—a liturgical form derived from the OT and from the prayers of Jewish synagogue worship, which ascribes blessing to God on the basis of his saving deeds. The *berakah* of 1:3-14 combines with the benediction in 3:20-21 to encase the first half the letter within an *inclusio* of praise. The liturgical character that it gives to the letter breaks with normal epistolary conventions—one of numerous ways in which the letter exhibits features more like those of an early Christian homily than those of a letter addressed to a particular community and occasioned by the community members' immediate circumstances (Witherington 2007, 215–26; Lincoln 1990, xxxix–xl). In a letter that is aimed at strengthening and deepening the Ephesians' sense of identity, Paul begins not with them but with God. His readers are to understand themselves as objects of God's choosing, adopted members of his family, beneficiaries of his salvation, and participants in his story. And by beginning with a *blessing* of God, in which the readers are implicitly invited to join, Paul reminds them of the first and most basic implication of this way of constructing their identity: they are a worshiping people who exist not only because of God but also (as Paul reminds them repeatedly within the opening paragraphs) "for the praise of his glory" (cf. vv. 6, 12, 14).

The structure of the *berakah* is intricate and expansive. It hangs together as a single, long sentence of 202 words, cascading down the page via a series of subordinating syntactical connections. The most prominent among them are the active-voice aorist participles, *proorisas* ("because he predestined . . . ," v. 5) and *gnōrisas* ("by making known known . . . ," v. 9), referring to the planning and revealing action of God, and the relative clauses that commence in v. 7 ("in whom we have redemption . . ."), v. 11 ("in whom we have also been made inheritors"), and v. 13 ("in whom you also . . . were sealed"). All three of these relative clauses contain principal verbs in the first- or second-person plural, and they point to Christ as the one in whom "we" or "you" have experienced the actions to which they refer. Despite its sprawling clause structure, the unit is held together by the recurring structural device of the reminders in vv. 6, 12, and 14 that all of these things have taken place "for the praise of the glory of his grace" (v. 6) or, more simply, "for the praise of his glory" (vv. 12, 14). These have the effect of recalling the words of blessing with which the *berakah* commenced and reinforcing its liturgical character as an expression of praise offered up to God.

The opening words of the *berakah*, in v. 3, pick up on the language of the greeting in the previous verse and speak of the God to whom its praises are directed as "the God and Father of our Lord Jesus Christ" (cf. 1:17; Col 1:3; 2 Cor 1:3). He is further identified in v. 3b as the one "who has blessed us in Christ with every spiritual blessing in the heavenly places." This double reference to Christ is a reminder of the central place that he occupies for Paul, both in the naming and knowing of God and in the enacting and experiencing of God's saving plans and purposes in the world (Hurtado 2003, 139).

It is difficult to decide whether Paul's "in Christ" language (both here in v. 3 and throughout the *berakah*, with minor variations, in vv. 4, 6, 7, 9, 10, 11, 12, 13) is intended to be read in an instrumental sense (i.e., Christ as the one by/through whom the choosing and saving and revealing work of God has taken place) or a locative sense (i.e., Christ as the metaphorical "place" in which the various blessings of God are located and experienced). The fact that Paul can draw upon the alternative expression, "through Jesus Christ" (v. 5; cf. v. 7), when he wishes to speak unambiguously of the role played by Christ in the former, instrumental sense (together with the way in which "in

Christ" language is used in connection with the first-person plural, active-voice verb in v. 7: "in whom we have redemption") suggests that the latter, locative idea may be the one at the front of Paul's mind here and elsewhere in vv. 3-14 when he employs the "in Christ" formula (contra Campbell 2012, 82–84).

The blessings that believers receive in Christ are "spiritual," not because they have no bearing on the everyday, bodily experience of life in the world but because they are granted through the work of the Spirit (cf. vv. 13-14). This work has taken place "in the heavenly places"), i.e., in the invisible, spiritual realm in which both the work of the Spirit of God and the work of his unseen, supernatural enemies (also "spiritual") can be spoken of as occurring (6:12; cf. 2:2).

1:4. Having pronounced a blessing on God in v. 3 and identified him as the source of "every spiritual blessing" that the readers have received in Christ, Paul goes on in vv. 4-14 to string together a list of the blessings included within that gift. The immediate function of the list within the syntax of vv. 3-14 is to provide the reasons God is to be blessed; the *kathōs* at the start of v. 4 functions not as a comparison between *eulogēsas* and *exelexato* ("who blessed us . . . just as he chose us") but as a signal of a causal relationship between *exelexato* (and all that follows) and *eulogētos*, i.e., "Blessed be God . . . in so far as he chose us . . ." (Larkin 2009, 7; Best 1998, 119).

If the phrase "in Christ" (along with its various equivalents) is, as I have argued above, to be read in a primarily locative sense throughout vv. 3-14, then Paul's depiction of believers as having been chosen "in him" is not so much about the participation of Christ in the divine act of choosing (contra Arnold 2010, 80) as it is about Christ as the metaphorical "place" in which God's electing mercy is located. The metaphor is probably best unpacked in terms of the representative headship of Christ as the chosen Messiah and Servant (cf. Pss 78:67-70; 89:3, 19; 105:6, 26; Isa 41:8-9; 42:1; 44:1-2; 45:4) and the participation of his people in him. A similar idea is implied in 1 Cor 1:18-31, where the pattern of God's electing wisdom is depicted by Paul as centered on the person of Christ crucified, which in turn implies God's choice of "the foolish . . . the weak . . . the low-born and the despised . . . the things that are not" (and, among them, the Corinthian believers).

This corporate, christocentric understanding of election by no means rules out the election of individual believers; the picture Paul paints in 1 Corinthians is one in which believers can still be reminded that "because of him (*ex autou*) you are in Christ Jesus" (1:30), and that "God placed the members, each one of them, in the body, just as he willed" (12:18). It does, however, have the effect of tying any notion of individual election tightly to the collective identity that believers share with one another as a single people, participating together in Christ (cf. 1 Cor 12:12-27; Eph 2:14-22).

This electing wisdom of God, according to Paul, can be traced back to "before the foundation of the world," language that implies both a high view of God's sovereignty (cf. vv. 5, 11) and the gracious, unmerited nature of his choice (cf. vv. 6-8; Rom 9:11; 2 Tim 1:9) (Thielman 2010, 48–49). Although (implicitly) "unconditioned" (i.e., not contingent on prior merit) the choice of God as Paul depicts it in v. 4 was not "unconditional" (i.e., with no expectations or obligations imposed on its recipients) (Barclay 2015, 562–63): those who were chosen by God in Christ were chosen with a purpose in mind, "that we should be holy and unblemished before him in love."

"Holy" and "unblemished" are both words that, in line with their OT background, might be read as suggesting the possibility of a cultic metaphor in which the chosen people are depicted as a sacrificial animal offered up to God—a possibility that, some argue, implies that it is not the conduct of believers in view here but simply their consecrated situation before God (Caragounis 1977, 123; Best 1998). Paul's use of similar terms elsewhere, however (e.g., Col 1:22, where "holy" and "unblemished" are placed in parallel with "above reproach" [*anenklētous*], and Phil 2:15, where "unblemished" is paralleled with "blameless" [*amemptoi*] and "innocent" [*akeraioi*]), suggests that what he has in mind is not merely the status of believers as a consecrated people but the "holy" and "unblemished" nature of the life they are intended to live.

This reading is supported by the prepositional phrase "in love," which concludes the verse. It is syntactically possible that the phrase could, as some argue (Best 1998, 123; Larkin 2009, 7), belong with what follows ("because he predestined us in love . . ."), and it is true that the love of God is an important idea within Ephesians (cf. 2:4, 6:23, and the references to the love of Christ in 3:19 and 5:2). The phrase "in love," however, is used in almost all instances in contexts that have to do with the conduct and dispositions of believers (4:2, 15, 16; 5:2; the exception is 3:19). In light of that pattern of usage, a stronger case can probably be made for reading "in love" in connection with what precedes it rather than what follows. Read in this way, it is a reminder of the central role that love plays in determining the content of the "holy and unblemished" life to which believers are called (cf. 1:15).

1:5-6. The choice of God's people and his purpose that they be "holy and unblemished before him" are, as Paul goes on to say in v. 5, grounded in his decision to adopt them as his children. Although the aorist particle, *proorisas*, is syntactically subordinate to the preceding verb, *exelexato* ("he chose"), it would be a mistake to read their relationship as a chronological one ("First he predestined, then he chose . . .") (cf. Wallace 1996, 625, correctly). A more likely explanation is that the participle's relationship to the main verb is a causal one ("because he predestined . . . he chose . . ."), with the filial relationship that God purposed to have with his adopted children supplying the reason for his election of a people and his desire that they imitate him in living a life of love (cf. 5:2).

Behind the language of adoption stands the double background of Greco-Roman legal custom and the adoption of Israel as "firstborn son" of YHWH in the OT (Exod 4:22-23; cf. Hos 11:1). Despite the absence of the word *huiothesia* ("adoption") from the LXX, the surrounding context here in Eph 1:3-14, with the story of election, redemption, and revelation it tells, suggests that here, as elsewhere in Paul (Scott 1992, 267), it is the OT background of the image that is of primary importance. What Paul's readers are to understand themselves as having been predestined for in the purposes of God is a relationship that is both analogous to and (as vv. 11-14 will make clear) continuous with the relationship of Israel to YHWH, as it has now been fulfilled in Jesus the Messiah.

The readers' adoption into this relationship has taken place, according to vv. 5b-6 "through Jesus Christ, according to the good pleasure of his will, for the praise of the glory of his grace, with which he has graced us in the Beloved." Three aspects of their adoption are highlighted: first, the mediating role of Jesus the Messiah, through whose actions believers have been adopted and into whose own sonship their adoption has brought them (cf. 2 Sam 7:14; Isa 43:6; 2 Cor 6:18); second, its grounding in the "good pleasure" of God's will, reiterating the references to the divine will already implied in vv. 4-5a by the language of election and predestination, but adding the connotations of pleasure and freedom implied by the term *eudokia* (cf. Pss 51:18 [LXX 50:20]; 69:13 [LXX 68:14]; Sir 15:15; 33:13); and third, its purpose, which is "the praise of the glory of his grace." This last phrase recurs, with slight variations, as a threefold refrain in vv. 6, 12, and 14. In each case, the purposive nature of the construction (*eis epainon* . . .), together with the way it is linked to the language of God's "good pleasure" (v. 5), "will" (vv. 5, 11), "counsel" (v. 11), and "purpose" (v. 11), suggests that the praises of God are not only the outcome of God's saving actions but their *intended* outcome.

The particular focus of those praises, here in v. 6, is "the glory *of his grace.*" This is the first explicit occurrence of the word since the greeting in v. 2, though the concept has been implied in the intervening verses by the references to God's abundant blessings (v. 3) and the prevenient nature of his election (v. 3). Having introduced the word, Paul immediately repeats it, describing God's generosity as "his grace, with which he has graced us."

While this rhetorical amplification has the effect of placing the emphasis here in v. 6 on God's grace, the word "glory" should not be allowed to fade out of view altogether, or be shunted as far into the background as an adjectival translation ("his glorious grace") might imply. "Praise" (*epainos*) and "glory" (*doxa*) are closely related concepts, especially when they are viewed against the honor-shame horizons of the first century cultural context, and the interest of Paul in the manifest, public glory of God and the honor accorded to his generous actions is confirmed by the shortened form of the refrain in vv. 12 and 14 (not "for the praise of his grace" but "for the praise of his glory").

The grace that believers have received, and for which God is to be praised, is a grace that was extended to its recipients "in the Beloved" (v. 6). In keeping with the line of thought behind the earlier references to the blessings of God granted and experienced "in Christ"/"in him" (vv. 3, 4), Paul first appropriates to Christ language that is used in the OT for the collective status of the people of Israel as the beloved (*ēgapēmenos*) of God (cf. Isa 5:1, 7; LXX Isa 44:2; cf. Bar 3:36), then extends that status back out again to the people who are included in him.

In almost all of the OT texts that speak of Israel as the "beloved" of YHWH, the context is one that highlights the nation's failure to live up to that status; the "love song" that YHWH sings for his beloved is a song about bloodshed where there should have been justice, and an outcry where there should have been righteousness (Isa 5:1-7). Readers of Ephesians whose ears are closely attuned to resonances such as these may already hear them evoked by the language of v. 6, which speaks of Christ as the one who has picked up the discarded mantle of Israel, and the "grace" that has been "graced" to those who are in him.

1:7-8. For those who do not pick up that faint, whispered echo of Israel's story, as it is evoked in v. 6, there is a louder one in v. 7, where the form that the grace of God takes, as it is extended to his people, is specified as "redemption through his blood, the forgiveness of trespasses." The language of "redemption" (*apolytrōsis*) with its echo of the cognate verb, *lytroō* (the favorite word employed in Deuteronomy to describe the liberation of the Hebrew slaves from Egypt; e.g., Deut 7:8; 9:26; 13:5; 15:15; 21:8; 24:18; also Exod 6:6; 15:13), is the first explicit indication in Ephesians that the grace of God, as it is offered within the history of a fallen world, is given to a people who are captive, helpless, and in need of rescue. More than that: the fact that it is accomplished "through his blood" and consists, in part at least, in "the forgiveness of trespasses" makes it clear that the plight from which believers are rescued includes not only subjection to hostile powers but also culpability for the wrongs that they themselves have done (cf. 2:1-3).

Although the language of "redemption," read against the background of OT usage (e.g., Exod 6:6), does not necessarily imply the payment of a ransom price, a redemption that is accomplished "through . . . blood" and consists in "forgiveness" does suggest that possibility. Some among Paul's readers may have been able to discern in his language echoes of texts such as 4 Macc 17:21-22, in which the deaths of the Maccabean martyrs are depicted as "having become like a ransom (*hōsper antipsychon*) for the sin of our nation," such that "through the blood of those devout ones (*dia tou haimatos tōn eusebōn ekeinōn*) . . . divine Providence delivered Israel that previously had been mistreated" (cf. Williams 2015). Others, for whom the memory of this particular story may not have been evoked, would still have been aware of the broader background of Greco-Roman language and custom, in which the verb "redeem" (*apolytroō*) implied the liberation of a slave through the payment of a price (cf. Let. Aris. 12, 33; LXX Exod 21:8 for Jewish uses of the word in this sense). Interpreted against backgrounds such as these, Paul's language would probably have suggested to his readers the idea of Christ's death as a *lytron* (cf. Mark 10:45) or *antilytron* (cf. 1 Tim 2:6) offered as payment for the freedom of others (without necessitating any further extension of the metaphor, e.g., by specifying the person to whom the ransom was paid).

The likelihood of this is increased still further by the language of vv. 7b-8a, which speak of the redemption and forgiveness the readers have experienced not as a deliverance accomplished through divine power but as a gift granted "according to the riches of his grace, which he lavished upon us." Although Paul can place heavy emphasis elsewhere in the letter (e.g., 1:19-23; 3:7, 16-18, 20-21; 6:10-20) on the power that God has exerted in delivering his people, the focus here is not on power but on wealth, and on wealth generously disbursed for the salvation and enrichment of others.

Included within the riches that God's grace has bestowed, and bound up with the redemption and forgiveness spoken of in the previous verse, is the gift of "all wisdom and understanding" (v. 8b). Some commentators (e.g., Arnold 2010, 86; Larkin 2009, 10) tie this phrase to the following verse (". . . by making known to us in all wisdom and understanding the mystery of his will"), pointing out the obvious connections between "wisdom and understanding" and the knowledge of God's will. Despite the importance of those connections, however, there is no need to break the pattern that prevails throughout the rest of vv. 3-14, in which the prepositional phrases consistently modify what precedes rather than what follows (Thielman 2010, 62; Hoehner 2002, 213). Nor does it make best sense to read "in all wisdom and understanding" as a reference to the wisdom exercised by God (either in lavishing his grace or in making known the mystery of his will). Given the way in which closely similar language is used in Colossians to refer unambiguously to the wisdom and understanding granted by God to believers (Col 1:9), or hidden for them as "treasures" in Christ (Col 2:3), it makes best sense to read Paul's language in v. 8b as referring to the human wisdom and understanding granted by God to his redeemed people as part of their deliverance from the "darkened . . . understanding" (4:18) that was characteristic of their former existence.

1:9-10. At the heart of this wisdom is the knowledge of God's will, to which Paul goes on to refer in v. 9 (cf. Col 1:9; 2:2-3). Here (as with *proorisas*, "because he predestined," in v. 5) the relationship between the aorist participle (in this case, *gnōrisas*, "by making known") and the verb it modifies (*eperisseusen*, "lavished") is not chronological ("first he made known, then he lavished . . ."). Rather, it offers an elaboration on the means by which God lavished his grace (including the gifts of "wisdom and understanding" referred to in v. 8b) on the readers. The "knowledge of [God's] will" to which this verse is referring is not a series of piecemeal revelations concerning the will of God for this matter and that within their lives. What Paul is speaking of here is the singular revelation of the "mystery" that he goes on to unfold in vv. 9b-10 and returns to repeatedly across the rest of the letter (3:3-4, 9; 6:19).

As is the case elsewhere in the NT, and in the LXX and Second Temple Jewish texts (e.g., Dan 2:18-19, 27-30, 47), the word *mystērion* does not imply something inherently cryptic or paradoxical but simply a piece of knowledge that was once hidden but has now been made known by God. Like the *mystērion* made known in the dream of Daniel 2 (cf. Dan 2:45), the content of the Ephesian *mystērion* is eschatological, concerning the plans of God "for the fullness of the times" (v. 10a; cf. Gal 4:4; Mark 1:15; 2 Bar 40:3). Strictly speaking, what Paul is writing about in vv. 9b-10 is not the content of the mystery but the purposes of God that informed his decision to make the mystery known (cf. 3:4-6). Nevertheless, given the close relationship in vv. 3-14 between the language of "good pleasure" (vv. 5, 9), "purpose" (vv. 9, 11), and "will" (vv. 5, 9, 11), it would seem strange if the "good pleasure" and "purpose" unfolded in vv. 9b-10 did not coincide, or at least overlap, with the "will" that constitutes the content of the mystery in v. 9a (cf. Thielman 2010, 65).

The plan of God for the fullness of the times is one that he "purposed in Christ" (v. 9). The verb *proetheto* can also carry the meaning of "set forth" or "published," and that sense would not be out of place here in the context of an account of how a "mystery" has been "made known"; the cognate noun *prothesis* is, however, used with the unambiguous sense of "purpose" in 1:11 and 3:11, which tips the scales in favor of a translating the verb as "purposed" here in 1:9. As is the case throughout vv. 3-14, the expression "in Christ" probably refers not to the participation of Christ in the framing of God's plans (contra Arnold 2010, 87) but to the way in which those plans are centered on and contained in him, as Paul goes on to say in v. 10b.

The immediate relevance of those plans for Paul's Gentile readers consists in their own inclusion in the Jewish messiah Jesus; that, according to Paul in 3:4-6, is the once-hidden "mystery" that has now been revealed, and it becomes the focus of the final section of the *berakah* in 1:11-14. But before that, here in v. 10, Paul locates that particular mystery (no small thing in itself!) within the larger purpose of God to "sum up all things in Christ."

The word *anakephalaiōsasthai*, which Paul uses to speak of that "sum[ming] up," is a technical term drawn from the vocabulary of ancient and literary theory (e.g., Quintilian, *Inst.* 6.1.1; Dionysius of Halicarnassus, *Ant. rom.* 1.90.2; cf. Rom 13:9). It implies a metaphor in which Christ functions as the summary and climax of the story of the universe, the unifying narrative to which all the other disparate parts and people are in some way related (cf. Aristonicus, *De signis Odysseae* 23.310–43, describing the way in which Odysseus's short speech to Penelope after their reunion functions as the *anakephalaiōsis* of the whole long and winding tale that has been told across the preceding twenty-three books). Although the story of Christ has already been played out on earth (cf. 4:9-10) and the mystery made known to the church (cf. 1:9; 3:4-9), there is still a future dimension to the metaphor (cf. Caragounis 1977, 144); what the church has received in the message of the gospel is an advance notice of the fact that it is this story that will one day turn out to have been the one in which God has drawn together the threads of all things.

Paul's statement of what is included in the "all things" that are summed up in Christ is explicitly and emphatically comprehensive: "the things in the heavens and the things on the earth" (v. 10). This does not imply that each and every thing and person in the universe will become a willing participant in the worship of Christ; the future horizon of Ephesians still includes a day when "the wrath of God" will come upon "the sons of disobedience" (5:5-6). Nevertheless, like the similar language used in Colossians 1:15-20, it does imply a vast, broad vision of God's restoring purposes, the scope of which extends far beyond the salvation of individual believers and the gathering together of a church. One day, as Paul puts it in 4:10, the Christ who now fills the church will fill all things (cf. 1:23).

1:11-12. Up until this point in the *berakah*, the first-person plural pronouns that Paul has employed have been transparently and uncomplicatedly inclusive in their reference; there is no reason to imagine that the scope of the "we" who have received the various blessings catalogued within vv. 3-10 is any narrower than that of the "we" implied by the references to "our Father" and "our Lord Jesus Christ" in vv. 2-3, or that it excludes the members of the "you" who are greeted in v. 2. In vv. 11-14, however, the picture becomes somewhat more complicated. The "we" implied in v. 11 as the subject of *eklērōthēmen* ("we have been made inheritors") can still be read without restriction, in line with the first-person plurals of vv. 3-10. But the referent of the "we" (*hēmas*) in v. 12 is specified more narrowly as "we, who first hoped in Christ," preparing the way for a distinction in v. 13 between the members of that group and "you also," who heard the message of the gospel, believed, and were sealed with the Holy Spirit.

It is possible, as some argue (e.g., Lincoln 1990, 36–37; Thielman 2010, 75–76), that the *pro-* prefix on the verb *proēlpikotas* ("hoped," or "first hoped") does not carry its normal sense of "ahead of time" or "beforehand" but functions merely to reinforce the temporal content already present in the idea of the verb *elpizō* ("hope") in its simple form. (Instances of *proelpizō* being used in this sense, to mean simply "anticipate" or "intensely hope," can be found, for example, in Athenaeus, *Deip.* 9.20 and Themistius, *Or.* 5.65a.) On this reading, the *kai hymeis* ("you also") in v. 13 becomes "even you," so that its effect is not to distinguish between two different groups (the "we" of v. 12 and the "you" of v. 13) but merely to "[narrow] the focus from all Christians to the readers of this letter in particular" (Arnold 2010, 91). This is a somewhat forced way to read the syntax of the verse, however, especially when the "we" of v. 12 has been specified in the way that it has.

A more likely way to understand the "we"/"you" distinction in these verses is to read it as the first instance of the Jew/Gentile distinction that will become the focus of so much attention in the subsequent chapters of the letter (cf. especially 2:1-3, 11-22; 3:1-13; 4:17). On this reading, the "we" of v. 12 refers not to all Christians but to the Jewish Christians who "first" put their hope in Jesus the Messiah, and v. 13 signals not merely a narrowing of focus on the readers but an epoch-making turning point in the history of salvation, anticipating the narratives of Gentile salvation and inclusion that the readers are reminded of in 2:1–3:13 (MacDonald 2000, 203–204; Witherington 2007, 237; Abbott 1897, 21–22).

This interpretation of the intended reference of the "we" in v. 12 may also shed some light on the peculiar form taken by the description of God's purpose in v. 12 ("in order that we, who first hoped in Christ, might be for the praise of his glory"). Here, unlike the parallel expressions in vv. 6 and 14, the phrase *eis epainon tēs doxēs autou* ("for the praise of his glory") functions not to modify a verb of action (cf. "he predestined us," v. 5, and the verbal noun, "the redeeming . . . ," v. 14) but to provide the predicate of *einai*, "to be." The "we" of v. 12 were made inheritors in order that they "might *be*" for the praise of God's glory; what is in view here is not merely the reason for a particular event but the purpose of their very existence. As Barth points out (Barth 1974, 113–15), the closest analogies to this sort of language can be found in OT texts that use similar language to speak about the purpose of Israel's existence (e.g., Isa 62:7; Deut 26:19; Jer 13:11), and in the etymological interpretation of the name "Judah" that is given in Gen 29:35 (cf. the Hebrew verb *yādḏāh*, "to praise") and appropriated by Paul in Rom 2:29.

The action of God that constituted them as a people for his praise is the one that was described in v. 11 by the verb *klēroō*. The first-person passive form of the verb (*eklērōthēmen*), which Paul uses here, could be translated either as "we have been made inheritors" or "we have been made an inheritance." Although it is true that the OT can speak of Israel as the inheritance of YHWH (an idea to which Paul alludes in v. 18), the closer connection of this verse is with what Paul says in v. 14, where he assumes the existence of an "inheritance" belonging to believers, of which the Holy Spirit is "a guarantee . . . until the redeeming of the possession." It is probably better, therefore, to translate the verb in v. 11 as "we have been made inheritors" and take it as a reference to the promise that has been given by God to his adopted children.

Here in v. 11, as earlier in vv. 4-5, Paul goes out of his way to emphasize the deep roots of God's saving action within his sovereign plans and purposes: "we have . . . been made inheritors, having been predestined according to the purpose of the one who works all things according to the counsel of his will." The context of this assertion is not a philosophical discussion of divine providence; Paul's focus is not on the sovereignty of God *per se*, but on the way in which God's sovereign purposes have been carried out in the salvation and adoption of his people. Nevertheless, Paul is happy to frame his depiction of that particular, saving exercise of God's sovereignty within a larger, explicitly comprehensive assertion about God as the one who "works all things according to the counsel of his will" (v. 11), reinforcing his readers' confidence in the stability and certainty of the divine purposes within which they have been included.

1:13-14. While the "we" of v. 12 is (as I have argued above) specified as the "we" who "first hoped in Christ" and distinguished from the (implicitly Gentile) "you" of v. 13, there is no compelling reason to take the "we" of v. 11 as similarly restricted. The inclusion of the "you" of v. 13 in the adoptive purposes of God referred to in v. 11 is signaled by the repeated "in whom" at the start of that verse. Gentiles who were once outsiders and strangers to God heard the message of the gospel, believed in Christ, and were sealed with the Spirit.

Paul's description in v. 13 of the Spirit as "the Holy Spirit of promise" is a reminder of the OT texts (e.g., Isa 32:15; 44:3; Ezek 36:26-27; 37:14; 39:29; Joel 2:28-29) that promise a future outpouring of the Spirit upon the restored people of Israel. By pouring out that same Spirit on Gentiles who heard and believed the gospel, God has "sealed" them as his own, certifying them as heirs of the covenants of promise from which they were once excluded (cf. 2:12; 3:6; Gal 3:1–4:7; 2 Cor 1:20-22) (Starling 2011, 203–204). The outcome of this double work, in both the "us" of v. 12 and the "you" of v. 13, is to create a single people of God, possessors of the one Spirit who is not only the seal of the Gentiles' inclusion in Christ but also the guarantee, for Jew and Gentile alike, of their common inheritance, "until the redeeming of the possession, for the praise of his glory."

As we have already hinted at several points in the paragraphs above, the list of blessings that Paul supplies in the *berakah* of 1:3-14 is not only a catalogue but a story; the blessings for which God is praised are strung together in a loosely narrative sequence, commencing with the readers' election before the foundation of the world (v. 4) and tracing its outworking through their adoption as children of God (v. 5), their redemption (v. 7), their receipt of the revelation of God's will (v. 9), and (in prospect) their eventual entrance into the inheritance which is theirs as the people of God (v. 11-14) (cf. Starling 2014b, 142–43, from which the material in the following paragraphs is adapted).

The language used to describe these blessings and the sequence in which they are arranged are reminiscent of the exodus narrations of the OT. Thus, for example, the grounding of the salvation story in the readers' prior election in Christ echoes the way the exodus narrations within the early chapters of Deuteronomy are grounded in God's election of Israel, which is in turn based on his prior love for the patriarchs (e.g., Deut 4:37-38; Deut 7:7-8). Similarly, as discussed above, the adoption language of v. 5 echoes the strong connection within the OT between the exodus and the special position of Israel as the "son" of YHWH; the language of "redemption" echoes the favorite word employed in Deuteronomy to describe the liberation of the Hebrew slaves from Egypt; the assertion that God has "made known (*gnōrisas*) to us the mystery of his will" echoes the sequence of the OT exodus narrations, in which the exodus event was immediately followed by the great act of revelation at Sinai, in which God made known (LXX: *egnōrisa*) his law to Israel at

Sinai (e.g., Ezek 20:11; Neh 9:14); finally, here in Ephesians, as in the OT exodus narrations, the climax of the story is the "inheritance" into which the redeemed people are brought as the destination of their journey (Exod 15:17; Deut 32:9).

If the shape and content of the *berakah* implies that at one level the readers' salvation in Christ is a typological echo of the exodus salvation of Israel, it also offers a number of hints that the readers should view their salvation as the fulfilment of the second exodus and new covenant promises of the prophets. Like the promised new covenant of the second exodus (and unlike the scriptural narrations of the original exodus), the deliverance that they have experienced is described as being, at its heart, not merely a defeat of hostile powers but a "forgiveness of . . . trespasses" (cf. Jer 31:34; 33:8; Ezek 16:63). Additional hints are added in v. 13, with the references to "the gospel of your salvation" (cf. LXX Isa 52:7) and the "the Holy Spirit of promise" (cf. Isa 32:15; 44:3; Ezek 36:26-27; 37:14; 39:29; Joel 2:28-29), both of which carry the implication that the prophetic promises of the postexilic restoration of Israel have somehow been proclaimed to and fulfilled among the Gentiles.

In both form and content, then, the opening benediction of Eph 1:3-14 is replete with echoes of the exodus traditions of the OT and the new exodus promises of the prophets. Paul wants his readers to know that they have a salvation history of their own, analogous to and emerging from within the salvation history of Israel's scriptures, and made theirs through their inclusion in Christ. It is that story, as it is encapsulated here and reiterated in the reminders of 2:1-10, 2:11-22, and 3:1-13, that will function to ground their sense of identity, direct their hearts toward the praise of God, and provide the rationale and motivation for the way in which he encourages them to live in chapters 4–6.

Remembering you in my prayers (1:15-23)

(15) For this reason, I in particular having heard of your faith in the Lord Jesus and your love for all the saints (16) do not stop giving thanks for you, remembering you in my prayers: (17) that the God of our Lord Jesus Christ, the Father of glory, may give to you the Spirit of wisdom and revelation in the knowledge of him (18) so that, the eyes of your heart having been enlightened, you may know what is the hope that derives from his calling, what are the riches of the glory of his inheritance in the saints, (19) and what is the surpassing greatness of his power for us who believe, according to the working of the might of his strength, (20) which he exerted in Christ by raising him from the dead and seating [him] at his right hand in the heavenly places,

(21) high above all rule and authority and power and dominion, and every name that is named, not only in this age but also in the coming one. (22) And he subjected all things under his feet, and gave him as head over all things to the church, (23) which is his body, the fulness of the one who is filling all things in every way.

1:15. After the *berakah* that Paul inserts in 1:3-14, he turns in vv. 15-23 to the prayer report with which he typically follows the initial greeting in his letters (cf. Rom 1:8-10; 1 Cor 1:4-9; Phil 1:3-11; Col 1:3-11; 1 Thess 1:2–2:13; 2 Thess 1:3-12; 2 Tim 1:3; Phlm 6-7). Like the *berakah* of vv. 3-14, the prayer report is a single, long sentence, replete with accumulations and redundancies. Although it begins with thanksgiving (vv. 15-16), the bulk of its content is petition, the chief focus of which is a prayer for Spirit-enabled knowledge and understanding (vv. 17-19). The list of realities that Paul prays his readers will be enabled to understand includes both echoes of the content of the *berakah* (e.g., v. 17, cf. 1:8-9; v. 18, cf. 1:12, 14) and anticipations of the salvation-historical reminders in 2:1–3:13 (e.g., vv. 20-22, cf. 2:5-6; v. 23, cf. 2:16; 3:6). Even within the prayer report itself, as Paul elaborates in vv. 19b-23 on the power of God that he prays his readers will know, the line between prayer report and reminder becomes somewhat blurry. Rhetorically, then, the prayer becomes both an indication of what Paul sees as his readers' greatest need (Lincoln 1990, lxxviii, 53–54; Witherington 2007, 239) and a part of his strategy for addressing it.

The prayer report begins (v. 15) with a connecting phrase (*dia touto*; "for this reason…"), which probably refers backward to the closing verses of the *berakah* rather than forward to the participial construction that follows. The particular connection between the contents of the *berakah* and the fact that *Paul* prays for the readers (v. 15: *kagō*; "I in particular") lies in the fact that they—or at least the majority of them—are Gentiles (the "you also" of vv. 13-14), and fall within the sphere of Paul's special responsibility (3:1-2, 8; cf. the similar connection that Paul draws in Rom 1:5-6, 9-15) (Thielman 2010, 93).

The participial clause that completes v. 15 ("having heard of your faith in the Lord Jesus and your love for all the saints") supplies the timeframe in which Paul's prayers and thanksgivings have been offered, part of the reason he prays and gives thanks for them, and the implied content of his thanksgiving. Given the way in which the *en Christō* phrases of vv. 3-14 have functioned, a good argument can be made for interpreting the phrase "in the Lord Jesus" here as referring not to the object of their faith but to the sphere in which it is exercised (Lincoln 1990, 54–55; Thielman 2010, 94).

In favor of the alternative interpretation, however, is the parallelism between "in the Lord Jesus" and "for all the saints," which would seem to support a reading in which the former refers to the object of their faith and the latter to the objects of their love. Further support for this reading can be found in the thanksgiving-report of Philemon 5, which includes a reference to Philemon's faith that is described unambiguously as "the faith which you have toward [*pros*] the Lord Jesus"; as Thielman concedes, "it would be very difficult to make a convincing case that something in the historical context of Philemon drove Paul to emphasize the object of his readers' faith whereas something in the context of Col. 1:4 or Eph. 1:15 led him to emphasize the sphere of their faith" (Thielman 2010, 94–95). On balance, then, the latter alternative (i.e., a reference to "the Lord Jesus" as the object of their faith) is probably to be preferred (cf. Morgan 2015, 311; Campbell 2012, 171).

Along with the readers' faith, Paul thanks God for their love, which has been shown to "all the saints." Given the way in which the readers themselves (all of whom, one can only assume, are included within the "you" of this verse) have been described in v. 1 as "saints," the same word used here in v. 15 almost certainly refers not to a Jewish-Christian subset of the church (contra Caird 1976, 43) but to all believers everywhere.

As discussed above (see introduction and comments on v. 1), the fact that Paul has only "heard" of their faith and love is presumably due to the passage of time between his two years in Ephesus and the writing of this letter, and the likely function of the letter as a kind of circular homily addressing communities of believers beyond the confines of Ephesus itself, in the towns and villages of the surrounding region. The principal and most recent avenue through which Paul has heard of their (continuing) faith and love is probably the report that he has received from Epaphras, whose journey from Colossae to Rome would have taken him through Ephesus (cf. Col 1:8, assuming that the description in Phlm 23 of his status as a "fellow prisoner" is either metaphorical or referring to his voluntary sharing in Paul's imprisonment upon his arrival). (The terms on which Tychicus, the letter carrier, is introduced and commended to the readers in Eph 6:21 and Col 4:7 make it unlikely that he had already been the one who had brought their news to Paul; contra Arnold 2010, 102).

1:16. Having made reference to the reports that he has received of the Ephesians' faith and love, Paul goes on to tell his readers that "I do not stop giving thanks for you, remembering you in my prayers." Although the report that follows is composed mainly of the petitions that he prays for them, it is his prayers of thanksgiving that he mentions first, implicitly underlining both his conviction that their faith and love are the product of God's work in them and the confidence that informs his prayers for the continuing of that work (cf. Phil 1:6).

1:17. The content of his prayers is spelled out in vv. 17-19: "that the God of our Lord Jesus Christ, the Father of glory, may give to you the Spirit of wisdom and revelation in the knowledge of him, so that you, having been enlightened with respect to the eyes of your hearts, may know what is the hope that derives from his calling, what are the riches of his glorious inheritance in the saints, and what is the surpassing greatness of his power for us who believe."

Paul's prayers are addressed to "the God of our Lord Jesus Christ, the Father of glory." The elaborate over-specification (Paul could have simply written "God") is in keeping with the tendency toward amplification and redundancy that is a characteristic of the letter's rhetorical style (Witherington 2007, 4–10). It also functions to recall the way in which God has already been described in 1:3 and the threefold references to God's glory in 1:6, 12, 14, strengthening the connections between the prayer report and the *berakah* and implicitly reminding the readers that the God to whom Paul prays is the one whose praises have been the focus of the previous paragraph. The description in this context of God as "the God of our Lord Jesus Christ" (cf. 1:3) is consistent with the way in which Paul speaks of believers as having been adopted "through Jesus Christ" (1:5) and having access to the Father "through him" (2:18); their prayers are joined with Christ's prayers, and they pray as participants in his sonship.

What Paul asks the Father to do for his readers is to "give [them] the Spirit of wisdom and revelation in the knowledge of him." Some commentators (e.g., Abbott 1897, 28) balk at the idea that Paul could be asking that God give the Spirit to readers to whom the Spirit has already been given (cf. 1:13), proposing instead that the expression should be translated as "a spirit of wisdom and revelation" (cf. 2 Tim 1:7; Rom 8:15). This is unlikely to have been Paul's meaning, however, given the OT and Second Temple Jewish background to the expression "the Spirit of wisdom" (e.g., Isa 11:2; Exod 31:3; cf. 1 En. 49:3. Deut 34:9 and Wis 7:7 are disputable, but should probably be translated in the same way) and the difficulty of deriving any coherent meaning from the expression "a spirit of revelation," if it is taken as a reference to the human spirit (Fee 1994, 676). Paul's prayer is not that they might be given the Spirit for the first time but that God might continue to pour the Spirit out on them more and more, to grant them the wisdom and understanding that they require (cf. his prayer in 3:17 "that Christ may dwell in your hearts through faith," which can hardly be read as implying that Christ does not already dwell there). Although the range of possible kinds of "wisdom" and "revelation" that could be granted by the Spirit is wide (cf. Exod 31:3; Dan 2:22-23), Paul's prayer is focused on the particular wisdom that contributes to and resides within the sphere of the knowledge of God (v. 17b: *en epignōsei autou*), and consists chiefly in a deepened awareness and understanding of the realities to which he goes on to refer in vv. 18b-19.

1:18. The grammar of v. 18 is somewhat difficult, and capable of multiple interpretations. The four main options are (i) that Paul is praying that God would give the Ephesians "enlightened eyes" (reading *pephōtismenous . . . ophthalmous* as a second direct object of *dōē*, "may give," in v. 17) (e.g., Abbott 1897, 28; Best 1998, 164); (ii) that Paul is describing the Ephesians as men and women who have already been enlightened at their conversion (reading *pephōtismenous*, "enlightened," as modifying *hymin*, "you," in v. 17, and *tous ophthalmous* as an accusative of respect) (e.g., Lincoln 1990, 47); (iii) that *pephōtismenous . . . ophthalmous* is an accusative absolute construction, describing the outcome of the gift of the Spirit of wisdom and revelation for which Paul prays (Porter 1992, 92); or (iv) that *pephōtismenous* is modifying the *hymas*, "you," of v. 18b and has been fronted by Paul, ahead of the *eis to eidenai* that follows, to emphasize the circumstances in which (and the means by which) he prays that the readers will know the realities to which he goes on to refer in vv. 18b-19 (Larkin 2009, 21).

Proponents of option (i) have difficulty explaining the lack of an article before *pephōtismenous* and the lack of a *kai* connecting this phrase with the preceding one. Proponents of option (ii) have difficulty explaining the lack of grammatical concord between the accusative *pephōtismenous* and the dative *hymin*, and proponents of option (iii) have trouble explaining why Paul has used the rare accusative absolute construction rather than the much more common genitive absolute. In both cases, they tend to resort to the hypothesis that the accusative case of *pephōtismenous* is the result of attraction to the accusative *hymas* that follows; a hypothesis of this sort starts to blur the distinction between those two options and option (iv), which is probably the one to be preferred.

The metaphor of "the eyes of your heart," which Paul employs in v. 18, draws on imagery that was common in both Greco-Roman and Second Temple Jewish usage (see Best 1998, 165 for examples), as does the language of "enlightened . . . eyes" or the "enlightened heart" (cf. Ps 19:8; 1 QS 2.3; 4.2, and the somewhat different use of the metaphor in Ezra 9:8 and Bar 1:12). The "heart," in keeping with Paul's use of the same word elsewhere in Ephesians, should not be viewed either as an exclusively cognitive faculty or as an entirely non-cognitive organ of emotion. Paul's assumption here, as elsewhere, is that the affections, the will, and the intellect are all interrelated and mutually informing faculties; stubbornness of heart can give rise to "ignorance" and a "darkened . . . understanding" (4:18), and (conversely) the presence of Christ in the hearts of a people who are grounded in his love can empower them to "comprehend" and "know" that love (3:17-19). Enlightened eyes not only perceive the existence of what they look upon but also have a sense of its "glory" and "greatness" (vv. 18b-19; cf. 2 Cor 4:6) that motivates them to choose and delight in it. It is that kind of enlightenment—simultaneously cognitive, affective, and volitional—that Paul is praying for here.

The knowledge Paul prays that God will grant his readers is summed up in vv. 18b-19 as a list of three realities: "what is the hope that derives from his calling, what are the riches of his glorious inheritance in the saints, and what is the surpassing greatness of his power for us who believe."

The first ("the hope that derives from his calling") is probably—given the parallelism between the three constructions—a reference to the future realities that are the object of Christian hope (*spes quae speratur*) rather than to the disposition of hopefulness that looks forward to these things (*spes qua speratur*); the same sense is probably also carried by the similar language in 4:4. This hope "derives from his calling" because it has its source in the purposes of God, within which and for which the readers have been called (cf. 4:1, 4).

The second reality that Paul prays his readers will know is "the riches of the glory of [God's] inheritance in the saints" (v. 18b). Although inheritance language has been used earlier in this chapter (vv. 11, 14) to refer to the inheritance that believers have been granted by God, it is used here to refer to the complementary reality of the "inheritance" that God possesses in his people (cf. Deut 32:9; 1 Sam 10:1; 26:19, etc). Paul wants his readers to know how precious and valued they are to God, as are all the saints among whom they have come to belong.

1:19-20. Finally, thirdly, Paul prays that God will enable his readers to know "the surpassing greatness of his power for us who believe" (v. 19a). Within a context in which believers could all too easily feel overwhelmed and intimidated by the vast array of powers, political and religious, visible and invisible, with whose claims their faith has brought them into actual or potential conflict (see especially Rowe 2009, 41–51), Paul wants them to know the "surpassing" (*hyperballon*) greatness of God's power in Christ. Paul's language here is explicitly and emphatically comparative, recalling the language of the magical papyri and the Ephesian honorific inscriptions (e.g., the invocation in PGM XII.284, addressed to the "Greatest God, who surpasses every power [*Thee megiste, hos hyperballeis tēn pasan dynamin*]") (Betz 1986, 163–64, who also cites PGM IV.649 and IvE 11a.15-19; cf. Arnold 1997, 73) and anticipating what is said in v. 21 about the way in which the resurrection and ascension of Christ have placed him "high above all rule and authority and power and dominion, and every name that is named."

Paul not only wants his readers to know the magnitude of God's power; he also wants them to know that it is directed toward their benefit. In the words of the prayer report, it is power "for us who believe." In contrast to the capriciousness of the powers that the prayers and incantations of the magical papyri sought to harness and control, the power of God, Paul reassures his readers, is consistently and reliably "for us."

The magnitude and kind of the power Paul has in mind is best understood, he goes on to tell his readers, "according to the working of the might of his strength, which he exerted in Christ by raising him from the dead . . ." (vv. 19b-20). Here, as elsewhere in Ephesians, synonymous or near-synonymous terms (in this case, "power . . . working . . . might . . . strength") are accumulated together into a kind of crescendo of emphasis. If there is a distinction worth drawing between the terms Paul uses, it is the distinction between "power" (*dynamis*), as a term for the potential that a person or thing possesses, and "working" (*energeia*), as a term for the outworking of that potential in actuality (cf. Aristotle, *Metaphysics* 1045b–48b; Eph 3:7, 20). The measure and standard of what God is able to do can be seen in what he has already done in raising Christ from the dead.

What Paul wants his readers to remember about the resurrection is not only the magnitude of the power that can be seen in it but also the way that power "surpass[es]" that of all other powers (including those under which Christ was crucified; cf. Col 2:15; 1 Cor 2:8) and is exercised "for us who believe" (v. 19a). Thus, having made reference to the resurrection in v. 20a, he goes on in vv. 20b-23 to remind his readers that God exerted his power not only by raising Christ from the dead but also by "seating [him] at his right hand in the heavenly places, high above all rule and authority and power and dominion," and that he "subjected all things under his feet" and "gave him as head over all things to the church."

Paul's description in v. 20b of the risen and ascended Christ as "seat[ed] at [God's] right hand in the heavenly places" is an allusion to Ps 110:1, where the anointed king of Israel is represented as having been summoned to the place of honor at the right hand of YHWH. Here in Eph 1:20b, the exaltation of Christ is depicted as an event that has taken place "in the heavenly places" (cf. 1:3; 2:6; 3:10, 6:12)—that is, in the unseen realm in which the activity of spiritual powers (including God's own Spirit as well as the spiritual beings that oppose him) takes place.

1:21. The effect of Christ's resurrection and ascension is to place him "high above all rule and authority and power and dominion, and every name that is named, not only in this age but also in the coming one" (v. 21). The list that Paul constructs clearly includes the "spiritual forces of evil in the heavenly places" to whom he refers later in the letter (6:12), but the elaborate inclusiveness of the list suggests that he has in mind not only the invisible powers of this sort but also the all-too-visible social and political powers (as co-opted and corrupted by the invisible powers of evil) within whose hegemony his readers conducted their daily lives (Gombis 2010, 35–58; Thielman 2010, 20–23, 108). The likely effect that Paul intended this reminder to have for his readers would have been not only to liberate them from the widespread dependence on magical practice that was endemic within their cultural context (cf. Acts 19:17-20, and the long list of magical names invoked syncretistically in PGM XII.285–301) but also to embolden them in the face of the demands and threats made by the powers that exercised sway within the political and economic system under which they lived (cf. Acts 19:23-41).

1:22. The depiction of the anointed king in Ps 110:1 as seated at YHWH's right hand goes on to anticipate a day when all of his enemies will be made into a "footstool" for his feet. That part of the verse is not alluded to directly here in Ephesians 1, but Paul does allude in v. 22 to the similar image in Ps 8:6, depicting Christ's supremacy over all things in a form of words (*panta hypetaxen hypo tous podas autou*) that closely resembles the wording of extant Greek versions of the psalm (cf. LXX Ps 8:7: *panta hypetaxas hypokatō tōn podōn autou*). In the psalm, the subjection of all things beneath the feet of humanity is celebrated as something already established by God within the ordering of creation (though see also the eschatological and Christological reading of that verse in Heb 2:8-9); here in Eph 1:22, somewhat similarly, it is depicted as having been accomplished already in the resurrection and ascension of Christ. It would be a mistake, however, to conclude that the eschatological vision of v. 22 is an entirely realized one. In light of the distinction in v. 21 between "this age" and "the coming one" (and to the extent that the echo in v. 20 of Ps 110:1 generates an allusion to the second half of that verse, the future horizon implied by YHWH's invitation to his anointed to "sit . . . until I make your enemies a footstool for your feet"), it makes best sense to read Paul's image in v. 22 as implying a kind of inaugurated eschatology. Christ has already been installed as king *de jure*, but the *de facto* subjection of all things to him is still in the process of being accomplished (cf. the way in which Paul appropriates and interprets Pss 110:1, 8:6 in 1 Cor 15:20-28).

1:23. A reading along these lines also helps in making sense of the way Paul's prayer report closes, in v. 23. Here, Paul completes his depiction of the way God has exerted his power in Christ by reminding his readers that God "gave [Christ] as head over all things to the church, which is his body, the fullness of the one who is filling all things in every way." The depiction of Christ as having been "g[iven]" by God to the church anticipates the language of Eph 4:11, where the same word is used for Christ's gift of apostles, prophets, evangelists, and pastor-teachers. In the latter instance, the list of Christ's gifts to the church is preceded in the immediately previous verse by a statement about the purpose of Christ, through descending in the incarnation and ascending above the heavens, to "fill all things" (4:10). The similarity of language and ideas between 4:10 and 1:23 suggests that the language Paul uses in the latter instance (*to plērōma tou ta panta en pasin plēroumenou*) should be interpreted not in a passive sense ("the fullness of the one who is continuously and completely filled") (contra Thielman 2010, 114–16) but in an active or middle-voice sense ("the fullness of the one who is filling [for himself] all things in every way") (Larkin 2009, 26; Lincoln 1990, 76–77; Barth 1974, 200–10).

Although the image in v. 23 of Christ "filling all things in every way," read against the background of Stoic panentheism, could be taken in a timeless sense as referring to the way in which Christ, like the *logos* in Stoic metaphysics, pervades the universe, the more immediately relevant background is the one provided by the OT echoes and allusions in vv. 20, 22 and the eschatological framework implied in v. 21. In a manner that is analogous to (and a fulfillment of) the way YHWH's glory fills the temple (e.g., LXX Isa 6:1; 2 Chr 7:1) and will one day fill the earth (e.g., Hab 2:14; Ps 72:19), Christ now fills the church with his presence and glory, and that glory will one day fill all things. On that reading, the present-tense form of the participle (*plēroumenou*) is, as Arnold correctly argues, to be understood in a progressive sense, "indicating that Christ's activity in filling the world through the church is a dynamic process that is ongoing" (Arnold 2010, 119).

The image in v. 23a of the church as "[Christ's] body" echoes the similar imagery in 1 Corinthians 12 and Romans 12, but with the important difference that here the *ekklēsia* Paul has in mind—principally, at least—is not the local assembly of believers but the whole, universal body of all who belong to Christ. A further difference from Paul's earlier descriptions of the church as the body of Christ is the way the image is preceded here by the reference in v. 22b to Christ as "head" (note the contrast with 1 Cor 12:21, where the head is simply a particularly high-status member of the body).

The latter metaphor speaks not only of Christ's relationship to the church (to whom he is "g[iven]" as head) but also of his relationship to the whole creation, as "head over [*hyper*] all things" (v. 22). The immediate implication of that image, reading v. 22b against the horizon of vv. 21-22a, is the subjugation of the powers and dominions of the created world to Christ's lordship; its larger, eschatological implication (read against the horizon of v. 23b) is the creation's eventual restoration and the filling of all things with his glory and rule. Any dichotomy that might be implied in v. 22 between Christ's headship as "headship over" and Christ's headship as "headship for" is thus relativized and transcended in v. 23 by the image of Christ as the one who "fills" both the church and (ultimately) all things.

And you . . . he made alive (2:1-10)

(1) And you, when you were dead in your trespasses and sins, (2) in which you once walked, according to the age of this world, according to the ruler of the realm of the air, according to the spirit that is now at work among the sons of disobedience, (3) among whom we too all once conducted our lives, in the passions of our flesh, doing the desires of the flesh and of the thoughts; and we were by nature children of wrath, like the rest . . . (4) . . . but God, being rich in mercy, because of the great love with which he loved us, (5) even when we were dead in trespasses, made us alive with Christ—by grace you have been saved— (6) and raised us up with him, and seated us with him in the heavenly places, (7) in order that in the coming ages he might show the surpassing riches of his grace in kindness toward us in Christ Jesus; (8) for it is by grace you have been saved, through faith, and this is not of yourselves; [it is] the gift of God, (9) not because of works, so that no one may boast, (10) for we are his handiwork, created in Christ Jesus for good works, which God prepared in advance, so that we might walk in them.

2:1-2. Ephesians 2:1-10 is the first of three narrative-shaped salvation-historical reminders (2:1-10; 2:11-22; 3:1-13) that make up the core of Ephesians 1–3. In each of them, Paul addresses his mainly Gentile readership and reminds them of the story of their salvation and inclusion among the people of God. The narratives contribute to Paul's identity-forming purposes by reminding the readers of the story that has made them who they are and that (as he goes on to exhort them in chs. 4–6) is to shape their conduct and relationships in the present.

The opening narrative, in 2:1-10, is in essence a story of salvation through resurrection—a reminder to the readers that they were once dead through trespasses and sins but have now been made alive together with Christ, becoming participants in the triumph of his resurrection. It unfolds from the reminder of the resurrection and enthronement of Christ that concludes the prayer report of 1:15-23, taking the key verbs of 1:20-23 (*egeiras, kathisas*) and converting them into *syn-* compounds that speak of the way in which believers have been "raised with" (*synēgeiren*) and "seated with" (*synekathisen*) Christ in the heavenly places (v. 6; cf. 1:20).

The *kai hymas* ("And you . . .") at the start of v. 1 thus functions as a kind of hinge between what precedes and follows, linking what is said about Christ in 1:20-23 (1:20: *egeiras auton ek nekrōn*; "by raising him from the dead") with what is said about "you" in 2:1 (*kai hymas ontas nekrous*; "and you, when you were dead") and about "us" in 2:3, 5 (*kai hēmeis pantes . . . kai ontas hēmas nekrous*; "we too all . . . even when we were dead").

While the language of "Jews" and "Gentiles" is absent, the references in vv. 1-5 to "you" and "us" show that the discussion of 1:11-14 has not been forgotten (cf. Barth 1974, 216; contra Thielman 2010, 125; Arnold 2010, 132) and play an important role in preparing the way for the more explicit discussion of the overcoming of the estrangement of the Gentiles from Israel and from God in vv. 11-22 (cf. Wright 2009, 145). The inclusive "we" of 2:4-10 emerges out of what has been said in the previous verses about the Gentile "you" (vv. 1-2) and the Jewish "we" (v. 3), and the equivalence of plight that both groups experienced prior to their salvation in Christ.

The narrative begins in vv. 1-2 with a description of the situation from which the readers ("you [Gentiles]") have been delivered. Their pre-conversion plight is depicted as one of death in "trespasses and sins" (v. 1)—the trespasses and sins that were once the characteristic lifestyle of the readers ("in which you once walked").

The world (v. 2) whose ways they followed is not merely "*the* world" but "*this* world"—more literally, "the age of this world" (*ton aiōna tou kosmou toutou*)—defined in opposition to the age of the world to come and ruled by hostile powers opposed to God and his people (cf. 6:12). Although the primary sense of *aiōn* ("world") here in 2:2, in line with its meaning in 1:21 and 2:7, is a temporal one, the parallel between this phrase and the following ones ("the ruler of the realm of the air, the spirit that is now at work among the sons of disobedience") hints at the possibility of a personification, in which the present age is represented as an enslaving power like "sin" and "death" in Romans 5–8 (Thielman 2010, 123, 128–29).

The two parallel phrases that make up the remainder of v. 2 ("according to the ruler of the realm of the air, the spirit that is now at work among the sons of disobedience") should probably best be read as standing in apposition to one another, with the genitive case of *tou pneumatos* ("the spirit") the result of attraction to the genitives that precede it (Larkin 2009, 28). Both expressions ("the ruler" and "the spirit") make best sense read as referring in parallel to the same personal, supernatural being (cf. "the devil," 4:27; 6:11), who exerts sway over the invisible, airy realm in which unseen spiritual powers do their work (cf. Plutarch, *Mor.* 274b; Diogenes Laertius, *Vit. phil.* 8.32; Philo, *Giants* 1.6, 8).

The expression Paul uses to refer to the people who live under his influence ("the sons of disobedience") is an obvious Hebraism, which occurs again in 5:6 as a description of unconverted Gentiles, describing the same people referred to as *ta ethnē* in 4:17, and it is reasonable to suppose that the expression has the same Gentile connotations here in 2:2. Before their conversion, Paul reminds his readers, the ways they walked in were alien to the life of the coming age, shaped by the influence of hostile spiritual powers as it was mediated through the influence of pagan customs and mores.

2:3. Having painted the direst possible picture of the pre-conversion life of the Gentiles, Paul goes on in v. 3 to say the same things emphatically about himself and his fellow Jews ("among whom we too all . . ."). The "among whom" language of v. 3 carries an implied spatial metaphor, reminiscent of the situation of Israel in exile. Within the context of the language and imagery that surrounds it in vv. 1-3, it is possible to hear within the phrase an allusion to the description of the house of Israel in Ezekiel 36, living "among the nations" (LXX: *en tois ethnesin*, six times within the five verses of Ezek 36:19-23), under God's wrath and profaning his name by both their conduct and its punishment (cf. Starling 2014b, 145). A further parallel with Ezekiel 36 can be found in the language and imagery of death that pervade that chapter, spilling over into the vision of the valley of dry bones in the chapter that follows (cf. Martin 1989, 190; Suh 2007, 715–33).

The language with which Paul describes the pre-conversion existence of himself and his fellow Jews in v. 3 is comprehensive in its scope. It embraces not only their outwardly visible conduct ("conducted our lives") but also the invisible dispositions and desires from which it sprang ("in the passions of our flesh, carrying out the desires of the flesh and of the thoughts"), concluding with the summary statement that "we were by nature children of wrath, like the rest." The same language that Paul uses elsewhere to speak of the distinction "by nature" between Gentile and Jew (cf. Gal 2:15; Rom 2:27; 11:21, 24) functions here to speak of their common predicament: "we [Jews]" were, "like the rest [i.e., the Gentiles]," by nature children of wrath. The latter expression almost certainly refers not to the human wrathfulness that characterized their own attitudes (cf. 4:26, 31) but to the divine wrath that is, as Paul reminds his readers again in 5:6, the destiny of the sons of disobedience.

In speaking of humanity outside of Christ as "children of wrath," Paul is not necessarily implying that God's wrath is already bent toward them; it is, rather, in line with OT expressions such as "a son of stripes" (Deut 25:2) and "son[s] of death" (e.g., 1 Sam 26:16; 2 Sam 7:5; cf. "son of wrath," *Apoc. Mos.* 3), a depiction of them as deserving of wrath (cf. LXX Deut 25:2), liable to it, and in danger of it (Abbott 1897, 45). Nor does the fact that men and women are in that situation "by nature" imply a doctrine of imputed guilt or a one-dimensionally genetic etiology of human sinfulness. The multiple references to conduct and character in vv. 1-3, together with the explicit statement in 5:6 that it is "because of these things" that "the wrath of God comes," make it clear that the wrath Paul has in mind is not something that human beings inherit in the womb, irrespective of their own personal blameworthiness. And the mode of life described in vv. 1-3 as incurring that blameworthiness is depicted as the consequence of interrelated and mutually inextricable causes, including not only the implicitly fallen, inherited "nature" referred to in v. 3 but also the influence of custom and culture ("the age of this world"), the oppressive, supernatural power exerted by "the ruler of the realm of the air . . . the spirit that is now at work among the sons of disobedience," and the decisions of the individual person, made as outworkings of "the desires . . . of the thoughts."

2:4-6. Having painted a picture in vv. 1-3 of the common plight in which "you" and "we" once languished, Paul turns in vv. 4-7 (leaving the sentence commenced in v. 1 unfinished) to speak of the saving activity of God: "but God, being rich in mercy, because of the great love with which he loved us, even when we were dead in trespasses, made us alive with Christ—by grace you have been saved—and raised us up with him, and seated us with him in the heavenly places, in order that in the coming ages he might display the surpassing riches of his grace in kindness toward us in Christ Jesus."

The depiction of God in v. 4 as "rich in mercy" echoes both the language of 1:7 ("the riches of his grace"; cf. 2:7) and the frequently occurring OT descriptions of YHWH as "abounding in steadfast love" (LXX *polyeleos*; e.g., Exod 34:6; Ps 145:8 [LXX 144:8]), pointing to the abundance of God's mercy as the cause of the actions narrated in vv. 5-6.

Side by side with the description of God in v. 4a as "rich in mercy," and roughly equivalent to it, is a reference to "the great love with which he loved us" (v. 4b), the cognate accusative construction (*tēn . . . agapēn . . . hēn ēgapēsen*) joining with the qualifier, "great," to place further emphasis on the love of God. These two causal constructions, both of which locate the reasons for God's saving actions in his merciful and loving character, are followed by a brief reminder in v. 5a ("even when we were dead in trespasses") of the plight of the people whom he saved, as he had already sketched it in vv. 1-3. Although there is a logical relationship between v. 4b and v. 5a ("the great love with which he loved us, even when we were dead in trespasses"), the grammatical function of the *hymas* ("us") in v. 5a as the object of the verb *synezōopoiēsen* ("made us alive together with") in the second half of the verse suggests that the primary connection of v. 5a is with what follows: "God . . . even when we were dead in trespasses, made us alive with Christ." Verse 5a is, therefore, to be understood resumptively, picking up the language of v. 1 (and broadening its scope from the "you" of v. 1 to the inclusive "we" of v. 5) to forge a link between the contents of the unfinished sentence commenced in vv. 1-3 and the principal verbs in vv. 5b-6.

Finally, in v. 5b, the first of these three verbs arrives. The action of God matches and reverses the plight of the readers, so that people who were "dead in trespasses" are "made . . . alive with Christ." The verb Paul uses (*synezōopoiēsen*) can be found nowhere else in the extant Greek literature from before Paul, and it may well have been one that he himself coined to link the salvation of believers with God's prior action in raising Christ from the dead. It is followed in v. 6 by two similar verbs, *synēgeiren* ("raised us up with him") and *synekathisen* ("seated us with him"), each of which derives from the verbs used in 1:20 to speak of the resurrection and enthronement of Christ.

In between, in v. 5b, Paul breaks the sequence of the three verbs with an interjected, parenthetical reminder that "by grace you have been saved," anticipating the longer excursus of vv. 8-10. Here, as in those verses, the language of salvation functions against the backdrop of the plight described in vv. 1-3 to imply a comprehensive deliverance from both the enslaving powers under which the readers were held captive (v. 2) and the divine wrath to which they were liable (v. 3).

All three of the *syn-* verbs in vv. 5-6 are used here in an aorist form and narrative sequence that imply they should be taken as referring to events that have already occurred (cf. Col 3:1). Similarly, the periphrastic perfect form of *este sesōsmenoi* ("you have been saved") implies a focus on the present state that results from an action already experienced (Larkin 2009, 31; Fanning 1990, 319). These facts, taken together, are appealed to by some as evidence that the text could not have been written by Paul, given the way he speaks in the undisputed letters about being "saved" as a future event (e.g., 1 Thess 2:16; 1 Cor 3:15; Rom 5:9-10) and pours sarcastic criticism on the idea that believers in Corinth have "already . . . become kings" (*ēdē . . . ebasileusate*; 1 Cor 4:8). While the difference of emphasis is striking, the two ways of speaking are not as unreconcilable as they are sometimes painted to be. Already in the undisputed letters, Paul is capable of describing believers in the present tense as "being saved" (e.g., 1 Cor 1:18; 15:2), depicting the present age as "the day of salvation" (2 Cor 6:2), and on one occasion (in Rom 8:24) using the aorist tense to say that believers "were saved" (though in a context that emphasizes the fact that they were saved "in hope"). The idea of a present existence that involves participation in the resurrection of Christ is implied, too, in the image of the believer as being "alive to God in Christ Jesus" (Rom 6:11) and summoned in the present to "walk in newness of life" (Rom 6:4). And here in Ephesians 2, the striking claims about the present situation of believers as already "saved" and the accomplished actions of God who has already "raised" and "seated" them with Christ are still qualified by an element of eschatological reserve: it is "in the heavenly places" that they have been seated with Christ, a situation that is, by implication, not yet manifest in their physical circumstances or their social standing, and it is only "in the coming ages" (Eph 2:7) that the way they have been enriched by the grace of God will be publicly exhibited for all to see (cf. Col 3:3-4).

By emphasizing what God has already done for believers, Paul is able to highlight two key realities that are of importance for his pastoral purposes in the letter. In the first place, he is able to focus his readers' attention on the power that God has already exerted in raising Christ from the dead and liberating them from their previous lives of enslavement to pagan gods and hostile spiritual forces, thereby encouraging them to resist any temptation to be intimidated or overawed by the powers (visible and invisible) that still dominate the lives of their neighbors and the city that they live in. And in the second place, hand in hand with that, his emphasis on what God has already done enables him to draw a sharp clear line between their past and their present, preparing the way for his exhortations in the second half of the letter, in which he urges them to live out the new identity that they have been given in Christ (cf. 4:1, 17-23).

2:7. Paul's account of the saving acts of God on behalf of his people concludes in v. 7 with a statement of their purpose: "in order that in the coming ages he might display the surpassing riches of his grace in kindness toward us in Christ Jesus." The description of the riches of God's grace as "surpassing" (*hyperballon*), like the reference to his "surpassing power" in 1:19, may imply an intentional comparison—in this case, between the wealth and generosity of the pagan benefactors, whose patronage was celebrated in the innumerable honorific inscriptions of a Greco-Roman city like Ephesus, and the infinitely surpassing wealth of God, exhibited in his kindness toward the helpless and undeserving (cf. Harrison 2003, 231). By locating the "display" of this kindness in "the coming age," Paul implies not only the everlasting remembrance of God's kindnesses but the present hiddenness of their full effect in the life and situation of their recipients (cf. Col 3:3-4). The effect of v. 7, therefore, is not only to disclose the purpose of the already completed divine actions referred to in vv. 5-6 but also to point toward a final, future chapter in which the story will be completed (cf. the similar—and similarly indirect—eschatological climaxes of 1:10 and 1:14).

2:8-9. In the final paragraph of this section (vv. 8-10), having completed the "once . . . but God" story of vv. 1-7, Paul takes a step back from the narrative sequence of the preceding paragraphs to offer a commentary on the story's meaning and implications: "For it is by grace you have been saved, through faith; and this is not of yourselves—it is the gift of God, not because of works, so that no one may boast. For we are his handiwork, created in Christ Jesus for good works, which God prepared in advance, so that we might walk in them."

The "for" (*gar*) that links v. 8 with its preceding context is primarily explanatory in function: the saving actions of vv. 5-6 can rightly be described as a display of God's kindness (v. 7) because, as vv. 8-10 explain, they were motivated by divine grace and not accomplished or merited by the works of their recipients. This point is made in vv. 8-9 with the greatest possible emphasis, beginning with the way the phrase "by grace" (or better, perhaps, "by this grace," reading the definite article of *tē . . . chariti* as a reference back to the previously mentioned grace of vv. 5-7) is brought forward to the front of its clause, highlighting its importance within the sentence. Additional emphasis on the gracious nature of God's saving activity is added by the point/counterpoint elaborations in vv. 8b-9 ("and this is not of yourselves— it is the gift of God, not because of works") (cf. Runge 2010, 283–84).

The gracious nature of salvation, as Paul portrays it here, does not imply the passivity of those who receive it: salvation, accomplished by God and unmerited by any human deserving, is still to be received "through faith" (v. 8; cf. 1:1, 13, 15, 19). But the instrumentality of faith as the means through which faith is received is not something that Paul sees as in any way detracting from the fact that salvation is God's work and not our own. Most recent commentators are dismissive of the tendency among older interpreters (Barth 1974, 1.225; Hodge 1954 [1856], 118–19; Caird 1976, 53; cf. Augustine *Persev.* 2) to read the "this" (*touto*) in v. 8b as referring back directly to the "faith" in v. 8a, insisting that a reading of this sort runs counter to the grammar of the sentence by taking the neuter pronoun *touto* as referring back to the feminine *pistis* as its antecedent. It is worth pointing out, however, in defense of the older interpretation, that it is by no means unknown in Ancient Greek for *touto* to be used with a feminine or masculine antecedent (e.g., Herodotus, *Hist.* 3.82; 4.23; Plato, *Resp.* 9.583e; LXX Gen

2:22-23; Isa 6:6-7; Phil 1:29), and a reading of this sort did not seem problematic to the Greek fathers (e.g., Chrysostom, *Hom. Eph.* 4 [*PG* 62.33–34]; Theodoret, *Comm. Pauli Epist.* [*PG* 82.521–22]) (cf. Olliffe 2017). Whichever reading of the grammar is followed, the gist of what Paul is saying is much the same: "this" (whether the faith by which believers are saved or the whole experience of salvation, as it has been described in v. 8a) "is not of yourselves—it is the gift of God, not because of works, so that no one may boast."

The grace/works dichotomy that these verses construct has a long pre-history within Paul's letters (cf. Anderson 2016, 226–81). In its earliest surviving form, in his letter to the Galatians, Paul's defense of the grace of God is focused sharply on the particular issues raised by the advocates of Gentile circumcision. His axiomatic conviction that the grace of God must not be nullified is deployed against the idea that righteousness could be obtained *dia nomou* ("through the law"; 2:21), and the "works" in view as a false basis for justification are consistently characterized as *erga nomou* ("works *of the law*"; cf. 2:16; 3:2, 5; italics added). In his letter to Rome written several years later, Paul's references to "works of the law" persist, as do his arguments regarding the place of the law of Moses within the history of salvation, but they sit alongside more general formulations regarding "works" (e.g., Rom 4:2, 6; 9:12, 32; 11:6) and "the one who works" (Rom 4:4), grounding the particular point about the works prescribed by the law of Moses in a larger, more general claim about works of any kind. Here in Eph 2:8–10, it is the broad form of the dichotomy that we find, and the focus is squarely on the nature of salvation as a gracious and unconditioned gift (though the issues regarding circumcision, the law, and the boundary between Jews and Gentiles have by no means been forgotten; cf. 2:11-22).

The function of the reminder, emphatic as it is, within the larger rhetorical context of the chapter suggests that its primary purpose is not to fire a shot in a theological battle such as the one between Paul and the agitators in Galatia. Important as such battles had been in shaping the terms in which Paul articulated and applied his gospel in his subsequent correspondence, his letter to the Ephesians does not contain any direct evidence of a polemical context of that sort. The reminder seems to be intended as a preventative measure, staving off the ever-present danger of a self-congratulatory response to the privileges granted in salvation ("so that no one may boast," v. 9; cf. Deut 9:4-5), and a spur to the kind of praise and gratitude that Paul has already modeled in the previous chapter.

2:10. The section concludes in v. 10 with an explanatory expansion on the claims of vv. 8-9: "for we are his handiwork, created in Christ Jesus for good works, which God prepared in advance, so that we might walk in them." The depiction of the readers as "[God's] handiwork" functions as a warrant for the reminder in the previous verse that their salvation is "not because of works, so that no one may boast." Given the nature of salvation, as it has been depicted in vv. 1-7, as a resurrection from the dead, Paul's readers are encouraged to think not only of their salvation but of their very selves as the work of God's hands.

The word *poiēma* ("handiwork") can be used in a general sense to refer to the works (of any kind) that a person has made or the deeds that they have performed; it can also frequently be used in a narrower, more specialized sense to refer to artistic and literary productions that function to communicate a theme or to express the creativity of their maker (e.g., Philo, *Moses* 1.3; Dionysius of Halicarnassus, *Ant. rom.* 1.41). The only other occurrence of the word in the NT is in Rom 1:20, where Paul uses it to refer to the things that God has created as a visible expression of his power and divine nature. In both contexts, the broader, more general sense of *poiēma* is sufficient for Paul's meaning, but the more specialized sense is not out of the question, particularly (in the case of Eph 2:10) given the care and design implied by the way Paul goes on to say that God "prepared in advance" (*proētoimasen*) the good works to be performed by believers. In either case, however, the emphasis implied by the syntax, in which *autou* ("his") is brought forward to the front of the clause, is not on the fact that "we are his *handiwork*" but on the fact that "we are *his* handiwork" (and not our own).

Because of this (and not despite it!), the verse concludes with a glance in the direction of the "good works" that God has prepared for his people to perform. The relationship of v. 10b to vv. 8-9 is not constructed by Paul as one of qualification or counterbalance: Paul's message is not that salvation is by grace but must subsequently be repaid with good works. Verse 10b, rather, continues and elaborates on the line of thought in vv. 8-9, representing the gracious salvation of God as a creative work that includes the "prepar[ing]" of good works for believers to walk in, reversing the state of affairs under which they once lived, when they "walked . . . in . . . trespasses and sins" (2:2), under the power of alien and enslaving forces.

At this point, therefore, there is a sense in which we are already on the threshold of the exhortations that Paul gives to his readers in chapters 4–6, commencing with his encouragement to them in 4:1 to "walk worthily of the calling to which you have been called" (cf. 4:17; 5:2, 8, 15). Before we take that next step, however, Paul has two more salvation stories for us to hear (2:11-22 and 3:1-13), further reinforcing his readers' grasp of their identity and of the story they have been caught up in, followed by a second prayer report in 3:14-19 (balancing the earlier prayer report in 1:15-23) and a doxology in 3:20-21 (balancing the *berakah* in 1:3-14).

You . . . have been brought near (2:11-22)

(11) Therefore remember that once you who are Gentiles in the flesh, those who are called "uncircumcision" by what is called "circumcision" (done in the flesh by hands), (12) that you were at that time without Christ, alienated from the political community of Israel and strangers to the covenants of promise, not having hope, and Godless in the world, (13) but now in Christ Jesus, you who once were far off have become near, by the blood of Christ. (14) For he is our peace, who has made the two one, and has destroyed the wall of partition, the hostility, in his flesh (15) by abolishing the law of commandments in the form of ordinances, in order that he might make the two into one new person in him, making peace (16) and might reconcile both in one body to God, through the cross, having put to death the hostility in himself. (17) And he came and preached peace to you who were far off and peace to those who were near, (18) for through him we both have access in one Spirit to the Father. (19) So then, you are no longer strangers and aliens, but you are fellow citizens with the saints and members of the household of God, (20) having been built on the foundation of the apostles and prophets, Christ Jesus himself being the cornerstone, (21) in whom the whole building, being joined together, grows into a holy temple in the Lord; (22) in whom you too are being built together into the dwelling place of God in the Spirit.

2:11. If the movement in 2:1-10 is from death to life, the movement in 2:11-22 is from separation to inclusion, narrating the salvation of the letter's Gentile readers as a recapitulation of Israel's return from exile, in language and imagery borrowed from the exilic prophets. The centrepiece of the section is v. 17, which provides the link between the language of "far off" and "near" introduced in v. 13 (summarizing vv. 11–13) and the language of "peace" introduced in vv. 14–16 (cf. Starling 2014b, 146–48).

The principal theme of the section, like that of the preceding one, is soteriological, but the language and categories in which it tells the story of the readers' salvation are more explicitly social and ecclesiological than those employed in 2:1-10. It should be read, therefore, neither as a simple reiteration of the themes of 2:1-10 nor (contra Schnackenburg 1991, 102) as the beginning of a completely new, ecclesiologically focused section of the letter that leaves behind the soteriological themes of 2:1-10 to address Jew-Gentile tensions within the churches that Paul is writing to. Rather, it extends and builds upon the previous section, further deepening the readers' sense of their collective identity by reminding them of the story of God's saving works, with the accent on the way in which their salvation has brought them "near" to God and joined them with their Jewish fellow believers in a new, reconciled community. Like the previous section, too, it continues to prepare the way for the exhortations of chapters 4–6, especially the encouragements toward unity and mutual love that those chapters contain.

The predicament described in the opening verses (2:11-12) includes both the alienation of Gentiles from Jews and (climactically, in v. 12) the alienation of Gentiles from God: "Therefore, remember that once you who are Gentiles in the flesh—those who are called 'uncircumcision' by what is called 'circumcision' (done in the flesh by hands)—that you were at that time without Christ, alienated from the political community of Israel and strangers to the covenants of promise, not having hope, and Godless in the world."

The *dio* ("Therefore, . . .") with which v. 11 commences is inferential, performing the task (as it does in 3:13 and 4:25) of linking the teaching in the immediately preceding context to the exhortation that follows (Larkin 2009, 36). In this case, however, the exhortation (the first and only imperative in chs. 1–3) is simply to "remember" the story that Paul goes on to tell and, in particular, the reminder of the readers' previous situation outside of Christ, contained within the two *hoti* ("that . . .") clauses of vv. 11-12, which are both directly governed by the command to remember.

Verse 11 continues with a description of the Gentile identity of the readers, constructed in Jewish categories and viewed from a pre-Christ perspective that Paul goes out of his way to distance himself from. They are Gentiles "in the flesh" (i.e., in their uncircumcision; cf. Gen 17:11-12; Rom 2:28), "called" uncircumcision by what is "called" circumcision, the latter being merely the visible, physical circumcision that is "done in the flesh by hands" (cf. Col 2:11-12; Rom 2:28-29; Phil 3:3). Given the fact that his readers' flesh continues (one can only assume) to be as uncircumcised as it ever was, it is probably best (contra Larkin 2009, 36; Best 1998, 234) to read *ta ethnē* ("Gentiles") in v. 11 attributively, as a description of his readers that continues to be the case, rather than as the predicate of an implied *ēte* ("you were"). Paul, in other words, is not reminding his readers that they used to be Gentiles but reminding his Gentile readers that they used to be alienated from Christ, from Israel, and from God.

2:12. The readers' former predicament is presented in v. 12 as one of multiple and interrelated deprivations and estrangements: "without Christ, alienated from the political community of Israel and strangers to the covenants of promise, not having hope, and Godless in the world." The first of these, "without Christ," recalls the repeated references in 1:3-14 and 2:4-10 to the blessings and salvation that are located "in Christ" (Thielman 2010, 154) and anticipates the reversal of fortunes that Paul is about to describe in v. 13 as having taken place "now, in Christ Jesus." The second and third items of the list are joined as a pair: "alienated from the political community of Israel and strangers to the covenants of promise." The former describes the socio-political alienation of Gentiles from the community of the people of God; the latter describes one consequence of that—the exclusion of the readers from having any stake in promises that were embedded within covenants to which they were not a party. The fourth and fifth items, too, belong together as a pair: "not having hope, and Godless in the world." In saying that they were "without hope," Paul is not necessarily implying that they lacked any subjective sense of hopefulness; his focus, rather, is on the objective hope that they lacked, as people who were excluded from the promises of God and destined for the "wrath" of his final judgment (cf. 1:18; 2:2; 5:6).

The final, climactic item in the list depicts the readers before their conversion as *atheoi en tō kosmō* ("Godless in the world"). At one level, this description is far from the truth; as first century Greco-Roman pagans, they would presumably have had many gods, and would have used the same word *atheoi* to describe Jews and others who denied the existence of those gods or refused to participate in the traditional ceremonies that honored them (cf. Josephus, *Ag. Ap.* 2.148). From Paul's perspective, however, as people who did not believe in the one true God, they were the true *atheoi*, "alienated from the life of God because of . . . ignorance" (4:18).

2:13. Having reminded his readers in vv. 11-12 of their predicament "without Christ," Paul turns in v. 13 to narrate the fact that "now, in Christ Jesus, you who once were far off have become near, by the blood of Christ." The "now" (*nyni*) with which Paul commences the verse combines with the *pote* in v. 11 to complete a *pote . . . nyn* ("once . . . now") contrast between their former situation (summarized here in v. 13 as a predicament of having been "far off") and their present existence in Christ as people who have been "brought near."

The language Paul uses here anticipates the allusion that he makes in v. 17 to Isa 57:19 and echoes the language used elsewhere in the OT to speak of Israel as the people "near" to YHWH (cf. Ps 148:14). Lincoln also points out a series of texts (Deut 28:49; 29:22; 1 Kgs 8:41; Isa 5:26; Jer 5:15) as examples of the way in which "the Gentile nations can be described as 'far off'" (Lincoln 1990, 138), but the examples he cites—with the partial exception of 1 Kgs 8:41—use the term to speak of geographical remoteness or cultural strangeness rather than Gentile identity and exclusion *per se*, and are less relevant to Paul's line of thought here in Ephesians. (Even in the case of

1 Kgs 8:41, the surrounding context includes a distinction between enemy nations that are "far off" and "near" [v. 46], reinforcing the sense that it is the distant origins of the foreigner in v. 41, not merely his Gentile status, that are in view.)

The means through which the readers have been brought near, as Paul reminds them at the end of v. 13, is "the blood of Christ"—language that recalls what Paul has already said in 1:7 about "redemption through his blood" and is further unpacked in what he goes on to say in vv. 14-16: "For he is our peace, who has made the two one, and has destroyed the wall of partition, the hostility, in his flesh, by abolishing the law of commandments in the form of ordinances, in order that he might make the two into one new person in him and might reconcile both in one body to God, through the cross, having put to death the hostility in himself."

2:14. The *autos gar* ("For he . . .") that commences v. 14 suggests that the function of vv. 14-16 is to elaborate on and explain what was said in v. 13, with a particular focus on that verse's assertions that it was "in Christ Jesus . . . by the blood of Christ" that the readers have been brought near to God. "He" (i.e., Christ) is, therefore, brought into focus as the subject of the sentence, and indeed of every verb in the paragraph. What is claimed about Christ in v. 14a goes beyond the idea that Christ is merely the instrument through whom peace is granted, or even that he is the agent or source of peace; he "is" our peace in the sense that the peace he accomplishes and grants is accomplished "in his flesh" and experienced in union with him, within the "one new person" that he creates in himself. In keeping with the reconciliation that Paul is speaking about, the Gentile "you" of vv. 11-13 is now absorbed into the inclusive "we" of v. 14, referring to the members of the new community of Jews and Gentiles created by Christ's death.

The syntax of the remainder of vv. 14-15 is notoriously difficult, as reflected in the variety of English translations of these verses. The key points of difficulty relate to the two expressions, *tēn echthran* ("the hostility") and *en tē sarki autou* ("in his flesh"), at the end of v. 14, and the question of whether they should be related grammatically to what precedes them in v. 14 or what follows them in v. 15. In the case of *tēn echthran*, a decision must be made as to whether it is functioning in apposition to *to mesotoichon tou phragmou* ("the wall of partition") or *ton nomon* ("the law"). Both options have their difficulties. The former requires us to overcome the hurdle of the participle *lysas* ("has destroyed") between the two apposited noun phrases; the latter requires us to leap over the prepositional phrase, *en tē sarki autou* ("in his flesh"). On balance, the arguments for the former are stronger, partly because the sense of "the enmity" can be equated slightly more readily with "the wall of partition" than with "the law." In the case of the immediately following phrase, *en tē sarki autou*, the decision is between a connection with *lysas . . . tēn echthran* ("has destroyed . . . the hostility") and a connection with *ton nomon . . . katargēsas* ("by abolishing the law"). Once again, the former option is the more likely, since it preserves the parallelism with the roughly equivalent expression, *apokteinas tēn echthran en autō* ("having put to death the hostility in himself") at the end of v. 16 (cf. Larkin 2009, 40; Thielman 2010, 167–68).

If we follow this reading of the syntax, then v. 14b strings together two interrelated descriptions of Christ: "who has made the two one," and "[who] has destroyed the wall of partition, the hostility, in his flesh." The (neuter plural) "two" that he has made into "one" could either be two peoples (*genē*) or the two regions (*chōria*) on either side of the now-destroyed wall, but either way the surrounding context makes it clear that what is in view is the reconciling of Jew and Gentile in the one body of the church (cf. v. 15).

The expression "the wall of partition" (*to mesotoichon tou phragmou*) brings together two rare and roughly synonymous terms to refer to the metaphorical division between Jew and Gentile that Christ has torn down to make peace. The former term, *to mesotoichon*, resembles the language that Josephus uses (*ton meson toichon*) to speak of the wall between the holy of holies and the rest of the temple (*Ant.* 8.71), and the word itself can be found in several surviving third century BC inscriptions from Didyma in Asia, referring to a wall in a pagan temple (I. Didyma 25a.13; 26b.21; 27a.88; cited in Arnold 2010, 160); these examples, together with the "access" and "temple" imagery of vv. 18-22, suggest that Paul has in mind—and would have expected his readers to have in mind—the wall in the Jerusalem temple that separated the court of the Gentiles from the inner courts into which only Jews could enter (cf. Josephus, *Ant.* 15.417; *J.W.* 5.193-95; Arnold 2010, 159–60; contra Thielman 2010, 165; Best 1998, 253–54). The image of "partition" (*phragmos*) may also carry connotations of the way Jewish writers could speak of God as having "fenced" (*periephraxen*) Israel off from the nations by means of the law of Moses (cf. Let. Aris. 139), an association that is strengthened by what Paul goes on to say in v. 15.

It would be a mistake, however, to take the image of "the wall of partition" in v. 14 as referring directly and univocally to either the law or the wall within Herod's temple; what Paul has in mind, according to the further specification of the metaphor in v. 14b, is not the law *per se*, or the wall in the temple, but the frontier of hostility (*tēn echthran*) that coincides with the line between Gentile and Jew that was inscribed by the law and the cultic exclusions institutionalized in the temple. This, Paul says, Christ has destroyed "in his flesh"—the latter expression referring to Christ's physical death on the cross (cf. Col 1:22: "in his body of flesh, through death").

2:15. The way in which Christ has accomplished this, according to what Paul goes on to say in v. 15, is "by abolishing the law of commandments in the form of ordinances." Various unconvincing attempts have been made to qualify the starkness of that assertion—e.g., by proposing that it is the ceremonial and not the moral law that is set aside (e.g., Kaiser 1996, 397), that the law in its divisiveness and not in its commanding force is what is abolished (e.g., Barth 1974, 287–91), or that the thing done away with by Christ's death is not law but "legalism" (e.g., Schlier 1957, 125–26). Certainly, as Paul's appeal in 6:2-3 to the commandment to honor fathers and mothers makes clear, what he has in mind here by speaking about Christ "abolishing" (*katargēsas*) the law is not the end of its capacity to function as Scripture and shape Christian conduct. The simplest resolution to the hermeneutical tensions that are created when 2:15 is read alongside 6:2-3 is to follow the line of thought that Paul himself suggests by his elaborately specified reference in v. 15a to "the law of commandments in the form of ordinances"; the abolition he speaks of is probably best understood in terms of the bringing to an end of the Mosaic covenant and the associated power of the law to function as a legal code, "in the form of ordinances" (*en dogmasin*), for those under its authority (cf. Rom 3:31; 7:6, and the comments in Thielman 2010, 169–70).

The purpose clause in vv. 15b-16 should probably be read as modifying both *to mesotoichon tou phragmou lysas, tēn echthran* ("has destroyed the wall of partition, the hostility") in v. 14 and *ton nomon . . . katargēsas* ("by abolishing the law . . .") in v. 15a. The purpose Paul goes on to speak of is a double one that includes not only the "horizontal" reconciliation of Jew and Gentile ("in order that he might make the two into one new person in him, making peace") but also the "vertical" reconciliation of both to God ("and might reconcile both in one body to God, through the cross, having put to death the hostility in himself"). The former purpose relates more directly to the destruction of the wall of hostility spoken of in v. 14; the latter relates to the fact that this was accomplished by means of the abolition of the law as a commanding, covenantal authority over Israel. The logic here is not, strictly, that the vertical reconciliation effects the horizontal or that the horizontal effects the vertical, but that the cross effects both, by implication, through the "abolition" of the law, whose broken ordinances would otherwise have spelled wrath and condemnation for Jew and Gentile alike (cf. Col 2:14; Eph 2:1-3; Thielman 1994, 226; Starling 2012c, 197).

The way in which Paul articulates the former purpose ("in order that he might make the two into one new person in him, making peace") draws on the language Paul has already used in 2:10 to speak of believers as having been "created (*ktisthentes*) in Christ Jesus." Here, however, it is Christ rather than God that Paul speaks of as the creator, and the object of his creative work is not individual believers but the "one new person" (*heis kainos anthrōpos*) that is his body, the church (cf. 1:22-23). This new person is created "in him" (*en autō*), the personal pronoun functioning reflexively (Larkin 2009, 41) to express the incorporative union of the church with Christ.

2:16. The "peace" that is spoken of in v. 15 as the result of Christ's work is a horizontal peace between Jew and Gentile within the church. It is, however, inseparably linked in Paul's thought with the vertical peace that Christ's work accomplishes between a once-alienated humanity and God. The interconnectedness between these two realities is reflected in the way Paul expresses the latter of the two purposes that he describes in vv. 15b-16: "and might reconcile both in one body to God, through the cross, having put to death the hostility in himself." The reconciliation in view here is between humanity (Jews and Gentiles alike) and God, but the fact that it is "both" that are reconciled, "in one body," makes it clear for Paul's readers that there can be no reconciliation with God that does not also simultaneously involve reconciliation between former enemies within the church.

This reconciliation is accomplished "through the cross," a violent death that, paradoxically, has the effect of "put[ting] to death" the hostility that Christ intended to overcome. Although the earlier reference to "hostility" in v. 14 was exclusively to the hostility between Jew and Gentile, the scope of the word's reference here in v. 16 broadens, in line with the reconciliation of which the verse is speaking, to include the hostility between God and an alienated humanity (cf. Thielman 2010, 172). It is difficult to say whether the *en autō* that concludes the verse should be translated as "in it" (referring back to the cross) or "in himself" (functioning reflexively, like the *en autō* in the previous verse, and referring to Christ); the latter is, on balance, to be preferred as preserving consistency between the referents of the various forms of *autos* within vv. 14-16 (cf. Lincoln 1990, 146).

2:17. The transition to the third movement of the section, in vv. 17-18, is made by means of syntax that suggests the continuation of a narrative sequence (*kai elthōn euēngelisato*) rather than a summary, explanation, or argument in support of what has been said in the preceding verses: the peace that has been "made" on the cross (v. 15) is now "proclaimed" by Christ, through his agents the apostles (cf. Sandnes 1991, 226; Arnold 2010, 166).

In order to narrate this event of the coming of the gospel to Jew and Gentile, Paul employs a composite Scripture citation made up of words drawn from Isa 57:19 and Isa 52:7 (cf. Starling 2011, 170–72): "And he came and preached peace to you who were far off and peace to those who were near." The scriptural words in which the event is narrated make explicit the connection between the key terms of vv. 11-13 (*makran, engys*) and vv. 14-16 (*eirēnē*), implicitly identifying the whole sequence of vv. 11-16 as in some way promised or typologically foreshadowed in Scripture.

Paul's use of Scripture in v. 17 raises an obvious question about the way in which the original reference of the two terms, *makran* and *engys*, appears to have been altered in his reuse of the words. Whereas in the context of Isaiah 57 the "far" and "near" function as references to the Jews of the diaspora and those living in the land, respectively, the same terms are used in Ephesians 2 to refer to Gentiles (identified explicitly as *hymin tois makran*, "you who were far off") and Jews. The implicit warrant for this reappropriation of the scriptural end-of-exile promise of Isa 57:19 can be found in the earlier reminder that Paul gives to his readers in 2:1-3 of the solidarity of Jew and Gentile in the spiritual death that was the continuation or the antitype of Israel's exile. Gentiles can find themselves addressed in a promise originally given to exiled Israelites because the predicament of exile that the promises addressed corresponded so precisely with their own predicament as Gentiles, spiritually dead and far off from God (Starling 2011, 193).

2:18. The peace described in v. 17 as having been proclaimed by Christ to the "far" and the "near" is explained in v. 18 in terms of the "access" (*prosagōgē*) that both groups have to the Father through him. Although the word Paul employs here could be used in political contexts to refer to an audience with a king or other official person (e.g., Xenophon, *Cyr.* 7.5.45), the references here to God as "Father," together with the cultic language of v. 13 and the temple imagery in vv. 21-22, combine to suggest that the primary background Paul had in mind was the use of the cognate verb, *prosagō*, in the LXX for the bringing of offerings, prayers, and people into the presence of God (e.g., Lev 1:2-3; 7:35; Tob 12:12; cf. Thielman 2010, 174; Lincoln 1990, 149). This access, Paul once again stresses (cf. "both . . . one" in v. 16), is granted to "both" Jew and Gentile, in the "one" Spirit, the latter expression probably functioning primarily in a locative sense to speak of the Spirit as the one "in" whom the members of the church stand together as they enter the presence of God (cf. v. 22; Fee 1994, 682).

Here, and throughout this whole section, the particular aspect of the church's unity that is in view is the unity of Jew and Gentile, which has a uniquely important place within the unfolding of God's purposes (cf. Rom

15:7-13); nevertheless, the language with which Paul celebrates that unity carries the potential for wider application to innumerable other points of division and hostility that have been overcome by the work of Christ and the gift of the Spirit (cf. 4:1-6; Gal 3:28; Col 3:11-15; 1 Cor 12:12-13).

2:19. The final paragraph of this section (vv. 19-22) picks up the thread of the *pote . . . nyn* contrast introduced in vv. 11-13 and reiterates it, with slight variation in language (*ouketi este . . . alla este*) and with stress not on the "once . . ." but on the "now . . ." half of the contrast: "So then, you are no longer strangers and aliens, but you are fellow citizens with the saints and members of the household of God, having been built on the foundation of the apostles and prophets, Christ Jesus himself being the cornerstone, in whom the whole dwelling, being joined together, grows into a holy temple in the Lord, in whom you too are being built together into the dwelling place of God in the Spirit."

As was the case in vv. 11-13, "horizontal" and "vertical" dimensions are tied tightly together all the way to the final verse, and the descriptions of the readers' new status in Christ seem to be arranged so as to ascend through increasing degrees of proximity and intimacy ("fellow citizens . . . members of the household of God") toward a climax in vv. 21-22 ("a holy temple . . . the dwelling place of God").

The terms Paul uses in v. 19 to describe what the readers are no longer—*xenoi* ("aliens") and *paroikoi* ("strangers")—draw on both the categories of the LXX (e.g., Ruth 2:10; 2 Sam 15:19; Exod 12:45) and Greco-Roman socio-political language used to describe the outsiders (transient and resident aliens, respectively) whose place within the city was contrasted with that of its citizens (*politai*) (cf. Thielman 2010, 178; Elliott 1981, 25–27).

This status has now been exchanged for that of "fellow citizens (*sympolitai*) with the saints and members of the household (*oikeioi*) of God." The former expression reverses the outsider status implied by the socio-political categories of "aliens" and "strangers" in v. 19a, as well as the description of the readers in v. 12 as having formerly been "alienated from the political community (*politeia*) of Israel." Although the alienation described in v. 12 was from "Israel," the status that is described in v. 19 as having replaced it—that of "fellow citizens with the saints"—is probably best understood as referring not to a new relationship with Israel but to membership within the community of the church, in line with the Gentile-inclusive references to "the saints" elsewhere in the letter (cf. Lincoln 1990, 151; Thielman 2010, 179; contra Barth 1974, 269; Schüssler Fiorenza 2017, 26–28). The latter expression ("members of the household of God"), given its proximity to the political categories (*xenoi, paroikoi,* and *sympolitai*) that precede it, carries connotations of the common Greco-Roman metaphor in which the citizen was pictured as a "householder" of the city (e.g., Plato, *Leg.* 8.842e; Demosthenes, *1 Philip.* 27). Its primary sense, however, in line with the image in v. 18 of "access . . . to the Father" (and the earlier adoption imagery in 1:5), is probably domestic rather than political (cf. Gal 6:10; 1 Tim 5:8; Best 1998, 278–79; Lincoln 1990, 152). The image carries implications of both relationship with God as father (reversing the former "Godlessness" of v. 12) and membership within the church as a community of brothers and sisters.

2:20. The image of the church as a household in v. 19 gives way in v. 20 to the image of the church as a house and of believers as "having been built on the foundation of the apostles and prophets, Christ Jesus himself being the cornerstone." Like the previous metaphor, it implies permanence and belonging; the compound verb *epoikodomeō*, in its aorist passive participle form, depicts believers as having been not only built into the structure of the church but also "built on" the solid foundation that the structure rests upon.

Unlike the similar metaphor that Paul uses in 1 Cor 3:10-15, where the focus is on the judgment of (human) builders, the implied builder here is God, and the apostles and prophets are not builders but part of the building's foundation. Christ, who functioned within the metaphor in 1 Cor 3:11 as the church's foundation, is pictured here as its *akrogōniaios*. The precise meaning of this term is notoriously difficult to determine, with arguments being mounted for either the keystone that crowns and completes the structure (Jeremias 1963, 792; Lincoln 1990, 155–56) or the cornerstone that holds the foundation together (Arnold 2010, 170–71; Thielman 2010, 180). In favor of the former interpretation, Jeremias cites the use of the word in T. Sol. 22:7, where it refers unambiguously to a stone placed "at the head of the corner" (*eis kephalēn gōnias*) when the temple was completed. In favor of the latter, however, is the use of the word in LXX Isa 28:16, where the *akrogōniaios* is laid in Zion "for its foundations" (*eis ta themelia autēs*), and the fact that Paul's metaphor, as he goes on to develop it in v. 21, requires Christ to be already present within the structure as it is being built. Paul's syntax, too, with its emphatic reference to "Christ Jesus himself," suggests that he feels the need to set apart Christ's role within the building from that of the apostles and prophets—a need that would not be as pressing if they were not located together within the foundations.

The "apostles and prophets" to whom Paul is referring in v. 20 are almost certainly to be understood as the apostles and prophets of the NT church, rather than a combination of OT prophets and NT apostles. In favor of this interpretation is the order in which they are listed (with "apostles" preceding "prophets") and the parallel references in 3:5 and 4:11. The foundational nature of the apostles' role in testifying the to the gospel and establishing churches is not difficult to see (cf. 1 Cor 3:10; 15:1-11). It is a little less obvious how the same can be said of the prophets, given the ongoing, week-by-week nature of their ministry within the church as Paul depicts it in passages such as 1 Cor 14 and 1 Thess 5:19-20. What Paul probably has in mind, given the way in which "prophets" are joined with "apostles" in 3:5 as those to whom the inclusion of Gentiles within the church "has now been revealed . . . by the Spirit," is the pivotal role that the prophets played in the early church's turn toward the Gentiles and its decision to welcome them as members (e.g., Acts 13:1-3; 15:22, 32; cf. Thielman 2010, 180; Best 1998, 283).

2:21. In the final two verses of the passage, the building metaphor introduced in v. 20 is further specified as a temple in which God himself makes his home: "in [him] the whole building, being joined together, grows into a holy temple in the Lord, in whom you too are being built together into the dwelling place of God in the Spirit." The jumping-off point for these final verses is the image in v. 20 of Christ as the "cornerstone" of the building into which believers are being incorporated. Now, developing that idea, Paul speaks of the building as being "joined together" (*synarmologoumenē*) in him, using a compound verb coined from a specialist architectural term, *harmologeō*, meaning "fit together" (cf. P.Ryl. 233.6, cited in Thielman 2010, 183–84), to which Paul has added the prefix *syn-* ("together"). What is joined together is "the whole building" (translating a phrase that would normally mean "every building" but is clearly referring here to a single metaphorical structure; cf. the similar expressions in Matt 3:15; LXX Lev 9:5; 16:33).

The building not only is "joined together" but "grows" (*auxei*). Although the word Paul uses here refers in its most literal sense to the organic growth of a body or a plant (e.g., Col 2:19; cf. the related verb, *auxanō*, in 1 Cor 3:6), metaphorical possibilities of this sort are left undeveloped here, and Paul maintains his focus on the architectural image of a church that "grows into a holy temple in the Lord." The latter expression ("in the Lord") carries the same locative sense as the "in Christ" language of chapter 1 and speaks of the Lord Jesus as the metaphorical sphere in which the community of his people exists as a temple. The image is a dynamic one: although believers have already been "built" into the church, the church is still in the process of "grow[ing]" into a temple (cf. the similar idea in 1 Cor 3:10-15, preceding the declaration of v. 16 that "you are God's temple").

2:22. Verse 22 reiterates the image of v. 21, but with a more explicit focus on Paul's Gentile readers, concluding the chapter with a reminder that "in [him] you too (*kai hymeis*) are being built together into the dwelling place of God in the Spirit." The verb, *synoikodomeisthe* ("are being built together"), is the last of the series of *syn-* compounds that has extended across the chapter (cf. vv. 5, 6, 19, 21), the first three of which (*synezōopoiēsen*, *synēgeiren*, and *synekathisen* in vv. 5-6) describe the way believers were joined with Christ in his resurrection and enthronement, and the last three of which (*sympolitai*, *synarmologoumenē*, and *synoikodomeisthe* in vv. 19-22) describe the way the believers (Jew and Gentile alike) are joined together with each other as members of the church.

The description of the metaphorical temple constituted by the church as the "dwelling place (*katoikētērion*) of God" trades on the overlap between the concepts of "house" and "temple" (cf. 2 Sam 7:13; Exod 15:17; LXX Ps 75:3), melding the two ideas of believers as *oikeioi theou* ("members of the household of God," v. 19) and the church as a *naos hagios* ("holy temple," v. 21) into a single, somewhat mixed metaphor. The dual emphases of the verse, on the inclusion of the Gentiles and the function of the church as a place in which God dwells *en pneumati* ("in the Spirit"), complete the reversal of the readers' plight as it was described in vv. 11-12. In both cases, despite the explicitly social and ecclesiological categories that Paul employs throughout vv. 11-22, the climax of the description is theocentric and soteriological in its orientation: Gentiles who were once "Godless in the world" (v. 12) are now members of a community that is "the dwelling place of God" (v. 22).

The grace of God that was given to me for you (3:1-13)

(1) For this reason I, Paul, the prisoner of Christ [Jesus] for the sake of you Gentiles— (2) if indeed you have heard about the responsibility of administering the grace of God that was given to me for you, (3) that the mystery was made known to me by revelation, just as I earlier wrote to you in brief, (4) concerning which, by reading, you can know my insight into the mystery of Christ, (5) which in other times was not made known to the sons of human beings as it has now been revealed to his holy apostles and prophets by the Spirit: (6) that the Gentiles are fellow heirs, fellow members of the body, and sharers in the promise in Christ Jesus, through the gospel, (7) of which I became a servant, according to the gift of the grace of God which was given to me according to the working of his power. (8) To me, the very least of all the saints, this grace was given: to proclaim to the Gentiles the good news of the immeasurable riches of Christ, (9) and to enlighten all with regard to what is the plan of the mystery that was hidden from ages past in God, who created all things, (10) in order that now, through the church, the intricately complex wisdom of God might be made known to the rulers and authorities in the heavenly places, (11) according to the purpose from the ages, which

> he carried out in Christ Jesus our Lord, (12) in whom we have boldness and access with confidence through faith in him. (13) Therefore I ask you not to be discouraged because of my sufferings for you, which are your glory.

3:1. In 3:1 Paul commences the sentence that he eventually resumes in verse 14, but he has scarcely begun before he breaks it off unfinished and commences a digression (3:2-13) that ends by becoming a third salvation narrative alongside the previous two. The focus of this third narrative is not directly on the readers but on Paul, whose imprisonment (v. 1) is the circumstance that occasions the digression and whose sufferings (v. 13) are the theme of its conclusion. Both the imprisonment and the sufferings, however, are described as being "for you" (*hyper hymōn*), and the story of how Paul came to be "the prisoner of Christ for the sake of you Gentiles" turns out to be the story of how "the mystery of Christ, which in other times was not made known" came to be "proclaim[ed] to the Gentiles" (vv. 5, 8). Behind the story of Paul's apostleship and imprisonment is a story about the transformed situation of the readers, which has the same "once . . . now" structure as the previous two narratives (cf. the contrast in v. 5 between "in other times" and "now").

The fact that a reference to his imprisonment occasions the digression and a reference to his sufferings concludes it suggests that his purpose in recounting it to his readers is to guard against the danger that they might become "discouraged" by the news of those events (v. 13). The bold, triumphant tone of the previous two narratives, in which Paul has depicted his readers as already "raised up" and "seated" with Christ (2:6) and the end-of-exile prophecies of Isaiah 57 as already accomplished (2:17), may well have jarred with the circumstances of Paul himself as a prisoner of Rome, confined and suffering under the very powers that Christ had—according to Paul—conquered in his resurrection and ascension. Rather than attempt to minimize the resultant cognitive dissonance by skirting around the issue of his sufferings, Paul reframes them as part of the same story of "the working of [God's] power" (v. 7) that he had already narrated in 1:20–2:22, and therefore as something that his readers can understand not as a cause for shame and discouragement but as their "glory" (v. 13).

The section begins in v. 1 with a transitional phrase, *touto charin* ("for this reason"), which points back to the material in the immediately preceding context (especially 2:11-22) as the reason for the prayer that he is about to pray. In the remainder of the verse, Paul begins to paint a picture of himself as he prays: "I, Paul, the prisoner of Christ for the sake of you Gentiles . . . ." (The longer reading of the verse, in which Paul describes himself as a prisoner of "Christ Jesus," is probably best explained as the result of scribal assimilation to Phlm 1, 9.) One obvious rhetorical effect of the picture is to heighten the pathos of the prayer report that follows and reinforce the ethos of Paul as its writer (cf. the brief reminders of Paul's sufferings in Eph 4:1; Gal 6:17; Phlm 9; Col 4:18). A further possible connection between his imprisonment and his prayer may lie in the fact that it is his imprisonment that keeps him from seeing his readers face to face, with the consequence that praying and letter-writing are the main forms in which his concern for them can be expressed (cf. Col 2:1, 5; 4:12; Rom 1:9-13).

The self-descriptions of v. 1 are not merely reminders of the fact of Paul's imprisonment; they also function, in two important ways, to anticipate the reframing of that imprisonment that follows in vv. 2-13. In the first place, here in v. 1, Paul portrays himself not as "the prisoner of Caesar" but as "the prisoner of Christ"; the genitive case of "Christ" functions primarily in a possessive sense to point to Christ as the one to whom Paul belongs, but with the possible additional implication that it is because of Christ that Paul has become a prisoner (cf. Phlm 13; 2 Cor 2:14; Barth 1974, 360–62; Abbott 1897, 77). And in the second place, Paul describes his imprisonment as being "for the sake of you Gentiles," language that represents his imprisonment not as a pointless catastrophe but as part of a larger, purposeful pattern of life and ministry that is directed toward the readers' benefit, modeled on the sacrificial sufferings of Christ (cf. Col 1:24; Thielman 2010, 191–92).

3:2. Having described himself in this manner, Paul breaks the flow of ideas mid-sentence to offer a reminder in vv. 2-13 of how it was that he came to be "the prisoner of Christ for the sake of you Gentiles." The focus of the explanation that follows is more on the latter part of the phrase ("for the sake of you Gentiles") than on the former ("the prisoner of Christ"), though Paul's concluding remarks in v. 13 make it clear that his sufferings and imprisonment have not been forgotten. Paul wants his readers to understand his imprisonment as the outworking of his commission to proclaim Christ, and to understand that commission as both a gift of God's grace to him and a part of the larger story of God's plan to make Christ known among the Gentiles.

The digression begins in v. 2 with a phrase (*ei ge*, "if indeed") that, as Paul employs it in his letters, typically combines an element of hypothetical doubt with a rhetorical underlining of his awareness that the validity of what he has just said depends on the truth or falsehood of what follows (cf. 4:21; Gal 3:4; 2 Cor 5:3; Col 1:23; Abbott 1897, iv–v; Moule 1959, 164). What hinges on the question raised by the "if . . ." clause in this instance is, therefore, probably not (contra Arnold 2010, 185–86) the exhortation in 3:13 but simply the validity (from the readers' vantage point) of Paul's self-description in the previous verse as "the prisoner of Christ for the sake of you Gentiles." The fact that this verse leaves open, at least in theory, the question of whether the readers have heard of Paul's commission as apostle to the Gentiles is not a strong argument against the authenticity of the letter; as argued in the introduction, there would have been a considerable change in the membership of the Ephesian churches during the years between Paul's time in the city and the writing of Ephesians, and the letter may also have been intended to be read by believers in satellite churches that had sprung up in the surrounding region.

Paul describes his commission as "the *oikonomia* of the grace of God that was given to me for you." The word *oikonomia* is one that he has already used in 1:10 to refer to the "plan" of God for administering the times. Here in 3:2, however, it carries a different (though not unrelated) meaning, in line with the way it is used in Col 1:25 to refer not to the plan of God but to the responsibility that has been "given" to Paul as part of that plan. Strictly speaking, what is said to have been given to Paul here in Eph 3:2 is not the *oikonomia* but "the grace of God," but the close conceptual and verbal parallels between the two verses suggest that the *oikonomia* Paul has in mind is the responsibility generated by the receiving of that grace. The "grace," in turn, given to Paul for the sake of the Gentiles, should be understood not in a directly soteriological sense (as it is, for example, in 1:6-7; 2:5, 7-8) but as a reference to the particular privilege and responsibility conferred on Paul by the call of Christ (cf. 3:8; Rom 1:5; 15:15; 1 Cor 9:17).

3:3-5. The content and origin of that responsibility are further unfolded in v. 3: ". . . that the mystery was made known to me by revelation, just as I earlier wrote to you in brief." The *hoti* ("that") at the start of the verse is omitted in a number of important early manuscripts, but it is more likely that the omission resulted from a copyist's attempt to shorten Paul's long sentences than that the word was added by a copyist in order to combine two short sentences into one long one (Best 1998, 299). What was made known to Paul was "the mystery"—the content of which Paul goes on to define in 3:6: "that the Gentiles are fellow heirs, fellow members of the body, and sharers in the promise in Christ Jesus, through the gospel." Here in v. 3, however, Paul's focus is not yet on the mystery's content but on the fact that it was made known to him "by revelation." Elsewhere, when Paul uses language of this sort in connection with his call as an apostle to the Gentiles, he makes it clear that the revelatory event to which he is referring is his encounter with the risen Jesus on the road to Damascus (cf. Gal 1:16). If, as seems likely, that is the case here too, then the inclusion of Gentiles with Jews as "fellow heirs, fellow members of the body, and sharers in the promise in Christ Jesus" (v. 6) is bound up in Paul's mind with the identity of Jesus as Messiah, in a single, multidimensional mystery that can be described, as in v. 4, as "the mystery of Christ" (reading the genitive "of Christ" as a genitive of reference, i.e., "the mystery that concerns Christ" cf. Col 1:27; 2:2; 4:3; cf. Larkin 2009, 50–51).

What we are to think of, then, is probably not a series of discrete, unmediated, supernatural revelations, one of which was about the inclusion of uncircumcised Gentiles within the people of the Messiah. Rather, as Paul goes on to imply in v. 3b, we are to envisage a comprehensive rereading of the scriptural story of salvation in light of the Messianic identity of the crucified and risen Jesus, so that the Scriptures themselves become the medium through which a mystery is made known that their original readers had never glimpsed (cf. the similar picture in Rom 16:25-26 of "the mystery that was kept quiet for long ages but . . . has now been made known . . . through the prophetic writings").

The way the mystery was revealed to Paul can thus be described as being "just as I earlier wrote to you in brief"—probably, given the close similarities in wording and ideas between 3:6 and 2:11-22, a reference to the immediately preceding paragraph rather than to an earlier letter that Paul had written (Lincoln 1990, 175; Best 1998, 302). "By reading" (i.e., by reading the retrospectively reinterpreted story of salvation told in 2:11-22), Paul tells the Ephesians in v. 4, "you can know my insight into the mystery of Christ." Paul's "insight" (*synesis*), in other words, is not an inscrutable private revelation that his readers will simply need to take on trust from him. It can be known and understood by means of a perusal of the story told in 2:11-22 about how the death of Christ and his subsequent proclamation of peace in the gospel have made Gentiles heirs of the promises to which they had previously been strangers (2:12, 14-18; 3:6; cf. Starling 2011, 184–85). Nor was this reconfigured understanding of the story of salvation given exclusively to Paul; it was, rather, made known by Christ, through the Spirit (*en pneumati*), to all of "his holy apostles and prophets" (a group that presumably coincides with the "apostles and prophets" of 2:20 and 4:11).

3:6. The description in v. 6 of the mystery's content strings together another series of three *syn-* compounds—*synklēronoma* ("fellow heirs"), *syssōma* ("fellow members of the body"), and *symmetocha tēs epangelias* ("sharers in the promise")—recalling the earlier strings of *syn-* compounds in 2:5-6 and 2:19-22. All three terms, too, contain verbal reminiscences of the stories told in 1:11-14 and 2:11-22 (*synklēronoma*, cf. 1:14; *syssōma*, cf. 2:16; *symmetocha tēs epangelias*, cf. 1:13; 2:12). All three of these things have come to be true of the Gentile readers of the letter "in Christ Jesus, through the gospel," a double-barreled formulation that recalls the language and ideas of the berakah in 1:3-14.

3:7. Paul's mention in v. 6 of the gospel as the means through which the Gentiles have become sharers in Christ and members of his people leads him back in v. 7 to his own role in the story. The gospel by which the Gentiles came to be included in Christ is the gospel "of which I became a servant, according to the gift of the grace of God which was given to me according to the working of his power." His self-description as a "servant" is characteristic (cf. 1 Cor 3:5; 2 Cor 3:6; 6:4; 11:23; Phil 1:1); here, as in Col 1:23, he describes himself as a servant "[of] the gospel," in line with the way he describes the focal point of his service in passages such as 1 Cor 1:17; 4:1; 9:15-23 and Rom 1:1; 15:16. According to the account of his ministry that Paul offers to his readers in Rom 15:14-21, his work as "a minister of Christ Jesus to the Gentiles" (Rom 15:16) is to be understood as a completion or extension of Christ's own work as "a servant to the circumcised" (Rom 15:8), with the consequence that Christ's work through Paul constitutes a fulfillment of the mission of the Isaianic servant (Rom 15:21; cf. Isa 52:15). This dimension of Paul's self-understanding may help explain why the two places where Paul describes himself as a "servant of the gospel," here and in Col 1:23, are both closely connected in his thinking with the sufferings that he endures in fulfillment of his calling (cf. White 2016), and how it is that Paul sees his sufferings as "fill[ing] up" those of Christ (Col 1:24).

Because it is this commissioning, as Paul has already implied in 3:1, that has led to his imprisonment, and his imprisonment that has occasioned the digression in 3:2-13, he goes out of his way in v. 7b to characterize his commissioning as an event that took place "according to the gift of the grace of God, which was given to me according to the working of his power." The double emphasis on grace ("gift . . . grace . . . given") and power ("working . . . power") links Paul's description of his own vocation as a servant of the gospel with the way he has described the saving activity of God in the preceding chapters (cf. 1:6-8, 19-23; 2:3-10) and prepares the way for his exhortation in 3:13. Paul wants his readers to think of his labors and sufferings as a servant of the gospel not as meritorious works that place God in his debt but as part of a privileged vocation that was granted to him by the grace of God (cf. Phil 1:29-30); equally, he wants them to think of his imprisonment under Rome not as a failure of God's plans but as part of the intended outworking of God's power (cf. Phil 1:12-20). The juxtaposition of "grace" and "power" in v. 7 is reminiscent of the words of the risen Jesus that Paul recounts to the Corinthian church in 2 Cor 12:9 ("My grace is sufficient for you, for power is made perfect in weakness"). The fact that Paul's use of those terms in v. 7 is framed by references to his imprisonment (v. 1) and sufferings (v. 13) suggests that the theology of weakness that he articulates in 2 Corinthians has not given way to a triumphalist, over-realized eschatology here in Ephesians.

3:8. The emphasis of v. 7 on the grace of God continues in v. 8, which highlights the unmerited, incongruous nature of God's choice of Paul to serve as a preacher of the gospel to the Gentiles: "To me, the very least of all the saints, this grace was given: to proclaim to the Gentiles the good news of the unsearchable riches of Christ." The syntax of the verse brings Paul, as the recipient of God's grace, into focus at the beginning of the sentence and describes him with deliberate over-specification as "the very least of all the saints." Further emphasis is conveyed by the use of the word *elachisteros* ("the very least"), which is something of a grammatical oddity—the comparative form of an adjective that is already superlative in meaning—and functions to underline Paul's unworthiness for the task that was entrusted to him. (The rarity of the expression should not be overstated, however; cf. Thielman 2010, 211).

Paul's self-description here has similarities to the language and ideas of 1 Cor 15:9 and 1 Tim 1:15, where, in both cases, the reason given for the damning assessment of Paul's life before he was called to be an apostle is his activity as a persecutor of the church. Here, however, that is left unstated, and the focus is not so much on the particular form in which his pre-conversion sinfulness was manifested (though that would, in itself, have contributed to the unlikeliness of his commissioning as a preacher of Christ to the Gentiles; cf. Gal 1:23; Acts 9:21) as it is on the graciousness of God in calling Paul into his service.

The emphasis of v. 8 on the grace of God can be seen not only in the calling of the undeserving Paul to be a preacher of the gospel but also in the content of the gospel that he was given to preach: "the good news of the unsearchable riches of Christ." The expression "the riches of Christ" could be read as either an epexegetical genitive, depicting Christ as the one in whom the riches consist, or a possessive genitive, depicting Christ as the one to whom the riches belong (and by whom they are given). Despite the fact that the earlier instances within the letter of the expression "the riches of . . ." are epexegetical genitives (cf. 1:7; 1:18; 2:7), the fact that we are speaking here of a person, Christ (who is himself "rich"; cf. 2 Cor 8:9), tips the scales in favor of the latter option (Larkin 2009, 53; contra Lincoln 1990, 183–84; Best 1998, 318). Just as the "riches of . . . grace" referred to in 1:7 and 2:7 (see also 2:4) are riches that belong to and are bestowed by God, so the "riches" proclaimed by Paul, according to 3:8, are riches that belong to and are given by Christ. They are, like the ways of God more broadly (as Paul describes them in Rom 11:33), "unsearchable" (*anexichniaston*); that is to say, they are beyond tracing out, incapable of being adequately explained or comprehended by any human logic or enquiry (cf. Pr Man 6; LXX Job 5:9; 9:10).

The earlier references in 1:7 and 2:4, 7 to the "riches" of God's grace and mercy make it clear that the riches in view here in 3:8 consist in, or have been poured out in the form of, Christ's abundant generosity (cf. 2 Cor 8:2, 9, and the discussion in Barclay 2013). They are depicted here by Paul not merely as background to the gospel or an entailment of it but as integral to its content. Paul's gospel cannot be reduced to the mere idea of "grace" as a formula or an abstract principle—it is "the riches *of Christ*" that he proclaims; but, equally, the form of words that he uses here leaves no room for a way of proclaiming Christ that is not, at its very heart, a declaration and manifestation of the grace of God (cf. Gal 2:21).

3:9. Verse 9 adds to v. 8b a further description of the content of the commission entrusted to Paul as a gift of God's grace: "to enlighten all with regard to what is the plan of the mystery that was hidden from the ages in God, who created all things." This description overlaps with but is not identical to the previous one. The word "all" in v. 9 is broader than "the Gentiles" in v. 8b, implying that Paul understands the scope of his mission as including Jews as well as Gentiles, believers as well as unbelievers (cf. Col 1:28; Rom 1:14-16; 1 Cor 9:19-23; 10:32-33). And the description Paul offers in v. 9 of the content of the message with which he has been entrusted implies not only the initial proclamation of the gospel to unbelievers but also the unfolding and explaining of the gospel's entailments for believers, so that they may be "enlightened" (cf. 1:18) in their understanding of the plans and purposes of God (Arnold 2010, 195; Best 1998, 319).

The description Paul gives of those plans and purposes ("the plan of the mystery that was hidden from the ages in God, who created all things") reiterates language and ideas from earlier in the letter (esp. 1:4, 9-10; 3:4-5). The expression "from the ages" is best understood in a temporal sense (i.e., "from ages past"), in line with his use of the same term elsewhere in the letter (esp. 1:21; 2:7) and the similar statement in Col 1:26, rather than as a reference to the spiritual forces that the term can sometimes be used to refer to in the language of second century Gnosticism (cf. Irenaeus, *Haer.* 1.1.1; 1.30.2). The "mystery" to which Paul refers is presumably the same as the one he has just spoken of in v. 6 (i.e., the full inclusion of the Gentiles, alongside the Jews, within the church), as a subset and prototype of the larger, all-inclusive plan of God for the summing up of all things in Christ (cf. 1:9-10). The description of God as the one who "created all things" reinforces the echo of what Paul has already said about the cosmic scope of the plans of God in 1:9-10, 22-23, and offers a further reminder of the wisdom and sovereignty of God (cf. 1:4, 11; 2:10), which events such as Paul's imprisonment may have thrown into doubt. In speaking of the plan of the mystery as having been hidden "in" God, Paul implies a spatial metaphor similar to the ones he employs in 1 Cor 2:10 and Rom 11:33, portraying the mind and wisdom of God as a vast reservoir or expanse, unsearchable to human enquiry.

3:10. Verse 10 gives the purpose of the activities that Paul has been commissioned to undertake (and, by implication, the purpose of God in entrusting that commission to Paul): "in order that now, through the church, the intricately complex wisdom of God might be made known to the rulers and authorities in the heavenly places." The "now" in which that purpose is to be fulfilled functions primarily to distinguish the time period in view from the ages past, in which the plans of God remained hidden (v. 9), but also implies a distinction between the present and the "coming ages" (1:21; 2:7), in which what is imperfectly and provisionally displayed in the church will be perfectly and universally visible in the restored and reordered cosmos.

In saying that God's purpose is for the wisdom of God to be "made known" (*gnōristhē*) through the church, Paul uses a verb that he employs elsewhere in the letter (cf. 1:9; 3:5; 6:19, 21; possibly also 3:3) to refer to the verbal communication of a message. But the same verb can also be used (e.g., Rom 9:22-23; LXX Ps 97:2; 105:8) to refer to the communicative actions that do not necessarily involve the speaking or writing of words. In this instance, the fact that the audience to whom the wisdom of God is to be made known is "the rulers and authorities in the heavenly places" suggests that what Paul has in mind is not the church's verbal proclamation of the gospel but the way it enacts and displays the wisdom of God in its conduct, its composition, and its very existence:

> In her total being, that is, as founded and ruled by the Messiah; as composed of Jews and Gentiles formerly dead in sins and divided in hostility; as a people daring to live on the basis of forgiveness; as a community boldly looking to God's face and speaking to him; as a suffering and struggling, poor and yet enriched nation—this way the church is God's display, picture window, legal "proof" (2:7), lighthouse (5:8). (Barth 1974, 364)

The wisdom the church is to make known is an "intricately complex" (*polypoikilos*) wisdom. The term Paul uses implies both beauty and variety (cf. the "multi-colored" veil in Euripides, *Iph. taur.* 1150, and the "ingeniously wrought" garland of flowers in Eubulus, *Fragmenta* 105.2), suggesting that the way the church displays that wisdom includes both the diversity of its membership and the harmony with which they live out their common life together in their various, mutually complementary roles and situations (cf. 4:1-16; 5:21–6:9).

The primary audience to whom this wisdom is to be made known is "the rulers and authorities in the heavenly places"—i.e., the invisible, spiritual powers that co-opt and corrupt the visible powers of the social and political world and do battle against God and his people (cf. 1:21; 2:2; 6:1). The invisible nature of the watching audience does not take away from the visible nature of the church's witness to the wisdom of God. Nor are the invisible rulers and authorities the only ones by whom the church's display of God's wisdom will be seen; the church that has been called out of darkness to light is itself to shine as a light within its social environment, as a testimony to the truth of the gospel. That thought is a latent implication of what Paul says here in 3:10 about the function of the church as a display of God's wisdom, which he goes on to develop later in the letter (cf. 5:8-14). In the present context, however, the focus is not on the evangelistic effect the church's witness has for the men and women who are exposed to it but on the way it demonstrates to the principalities and powers the paradoxical wisdom of God, which they have neither understood nor overcome (cf. 1 Cor 2:6-9). The relevance of that notion to the immediate context in 3:1-13 lies in the references to Paul's sufferings and imprisonment in 3:1, 13, and his concern that the readers may become "discouraged" by these circumstances (v. 13), interpreting them as a sign that the plans of God were failing in the face of the powers of this age.

3:11. The role that Paul describes for the church in v. 10 is, as he goes on to say in v. 11, "according to the purpose [of God] from the ages, which he carried out (*epoiēsen*) in Christ Jesus our Lord." Once again, as in v. 9, his readers are reminded of the sovereignty of God and the age-old origins of his purposes. Commentators differ over whether the word *epoiēsen* should be translated as "carried out" or "formed." Abbott, for example, argues in favor of the latter option, insisting that "the natural meaning of *poiein pr[othesin]* . . . is to form a purpose" (Abbott 1897, 90), but he offers little proof for his assertion, brushing aside the evidence of roughly equivalent expressions such as *poiountes ta thelēmata* ("carrying out the desires," 2:3) and paying no attention at all to more closely parallel expressions from further afield (e.g., *tēn tēs patridos prothesin . . . poiein*, "to accomplish . . . the design of his own government," in Polybius, *Hist.* 18.36.7). The evidence of those parallels, together with the emphasis on fulfillment in the surrounding context (esp. 3:10, 12), suggests that Paul is speaking here of plans that were "carried out" by God in Christ, so as to bring about the state of affairs that he goes on to describe in v. 12 (cf. Arnold 2010, 198).

3:12. That state of affairs, according to v. 12, is one in which "in [Christ] we have boldness and access with confidence through faith in him." Paul can use the word *parrēsia* ("boldness") elsewhere to note the frankness with which he can speak to his fellow believers (e.g., Phlm 8; 2 Cor 7:4) or the boldness with which the gospel is to be proclaimed in the world (e.g., Eph 6:19-20; 1 Thess 2:2; Phil 1:20). In this context, however, the fact that the word is combined in a composite expression, sharing a single article, with the reference to "access with confidence" that follows (cf. Larkin 2009, 56), suggests that he is referring primarily to the right of entry into the presence of God that believers exercise when they pray (cf. LXX Job 22:26; Heb 4:16; 10:19; 1 John 5:14).

Believers possess and exercise that right of entry *dia tēs pisteōs autou*— an expression that could be translated as either "through his faithfulness" (e.g., Wallace 1996, 115–16; Barth 1974, 347) or "through faith in him" (e.g., Arnold 2010, 199; Larkin 2009, 57). The absence of any reference elsewhere in the letter to the "faithfulness" of Christ and the use of closely similar expressions in 2:8 and 3:17, referring unambiguously to the faith of believers, combine to suggest that the latter translation should be followed. The fact that this involves a slight element of redundancy ("with confidence . . . through faith") is hardly a fatal objection, given the pervasive presence of redundancy as a feature of Paul's rhetoric throughout the letter (cf. Thielman 2010, 219).

3:13. Finally, in v. 13, Paul brings his digression to a close with a concluding exhortation to the readers: "Therefore, I ask you not to be discouraged because of my sufferings for you, which are your glory." The *dio* ("therefore") at the start of the verse signals the fact that the exhortation is intended to draw out the implications of what Paul has just said in 3:2-12 and apply them to the readers. Paul's sufferings, because they are endured as part of his vocation as a preacher of the gospel to the Gentiles, are to be viewed not as failures on the part of Christ to protect his apostle or (merely) as ominous portents of the similar misfortunes that the believers in Ephesus may endure. They are to be understood as sufferings "for you," an expression that echoes the language of 3:1 ("the prisoner of Christ for the sake of you Gentiles") and functions as a compressed version of the more expansive formulation in Col 1:24: "Now I rejoice in my sufferings (*pathēmata*) for you (*hyper hymōn*), and fill up in my flesh what is lacking in Christ's afflictions (*thlipseis*) for the sake of his body, that is, the church." Paul's sufferings as a "servant . . . of the gospel" (3:7; cf. Col 1:23), like those of Christ himself, were integral to his vocation and directed toward to the well-being and salvation of others—in Paul's case, the Gentile believers whom he continued to serve, even in his imprisonment, by example, by letter-writing, and by prayer. His sufferings should therefore, he concludes, be regarded by the believers in Ephesus not as a matter of shame or consternation but as their "glory," interpreted through the paradoxical lens of the Isaianic servant songs and the theology of power in weakness and glory in suffering that Paul drew from them.

Paul's concern that his readers might become "discouraged" by his sufferings probably includes an element of solicitude for their emotional well-being (cf. Phil 2:17-18, 25-29), but his use of the same verb, *enkakein*, elsewhere in his letters (cf. 2 Cor 4:1, 16; Gal 6:9; 2 Thess 3:13) suggests that his focus is not only on their inward emotional state but also on their perseverance in the outward, visible practices in which it is made manifest; his desire is not merely that they will not be saddened but that they will not be saddened so as to lose motivation and give up. Paul's encouragement here in v. 13 thus prepares the way for both the prayer for strengthening that follows in vv. 14-19 and the exhortations of chapters 4–6.

I bow my knees to the Father (3:14-19)

(14) For this reason I bow my knees to the Father, (15) from whom every family in heaven and on earth is named, (16) [praying] that he may grant you, according to the riches of his glory, to be strengthened with power through his Spirit, in the inner person, (17) so that Christ may dwell in your hearts through faith, in order that you, being rooted and grounded in love, (18) might be strengthened to grasp, together with all the saints, what is the breadth and length and height and depth (19) and to know the love of Christ, which surpasses knowledge, so that you might be filled up to all the fulness of God.

3:14. In verses 14-19 Paul picks up the thread that he had left dangling in 3:1 and supplies the prayer report that completes the unfinished sentence commenced in that verse. The prayer report that follows, like the earlier one in 1:15-23, makes frequent use of both the language of "strength" and "power" (3:16, 18; cf. 1:19, 21) and the language of "knowledge," "wisdom," and "understanding" (3:18-19; cf. 1:17, 18). Like the earlier prayer report, too, it concludes with a twofold reference to "filling" and "fullness" (3:19; cf. 1:23).

The two prayer reports are clearly related but not identical in content. The themes of hope and inheritance that are touched on briefly in the first prayer report (1:18) are not explicitly present in the second. And the second prayer report, for its part, includes a focus on the love of Christ (3:17-19), which is not an explicit element of the first. Even where their themes overlap, the relationship between them is configured somewhat differently. While the first prays that the readers would "know . . . [God's] power" (1:18-19), the second prays that they would "be strengthened . . . to know" (3:18-19); and while the first describes the church as "[Christ's] body, the fullness of the one who is filling all things in every way" (1:23), the second prays that the readers would "be filled up to all the fullness of God" (3:19).

At one level, therefore, it is true to say that the second prayer focuses on realities that the first prayer has asked God to make the readers aware of, praying that those realities will be present and effective in the readers' lives (cf. Arnold 2010, 204). At the same time, somewhat paradoxically, it must also be said that the "strengthen[ing]" for which the second prayer asks is, in part at least, strengthening "to know" the love of Christ, and that it is through this knowledge that Paul envisages the readers being "filled up" toward the measure of God's fullness. This reciprocal relationship between knowledge and empowerment is crucial to both the epistemology and the pastoral strategy of Ephesians. Knowledge and understanding, according to Paul, are spiritual matters as well as cognitive ones. Understanding comes through spiritual empowerment, and spiritual empowerment comes through understanding. And both, in turn, are required if the readers are to be in a position to live out the exhortations of chapters 4–6.

The phrase *toutou charin*, which commences v. 14, recalls the earlier use of the same phrase at the start of the unfinished sentence in 3:1, signaling that Paul is now resuming the train of thought that he had left off at the end of that verse. It makes sense, therefore, to look for the "reason" Paul is referring to here, in part at least, in the paragraph that immediately precedes the original *toutou charin*. Because, as Paul has reminded the readers in 2:11-22, his readers, together with Paul, have access to God in prayer (2:18), and because, as Gentiles who have been reconciled to God in Christ, they are now being built into a community that is "the dwelling place of God in the Spirit" (2:11, 16, 22), Paul, as apostle to the Gentiles (cf. 3:1-2), turns to God in prayer for them, asking that "Christ may dwell in your hearts through faith" (3:17).

Building on these already implied connections with 2:11-22 established by the original *toutou charin* in 3:1, the reiteration of the phrase here in 3:14 suggests the possibility of a further source of reasons for Paul's prayer within the content of the digression in 3:2-13. In addition to the motifs of Gentile inclusion and access to God in prayer, already present in 2:11-22 and reiterated in 3:6-8, 12, the digression contributes to the reasons for Paul's prayer via the concluding appeal to the readers in v. 13 not to be "discouraged" by Paul's sufferings; accordingly, the prayer that follows asks that they will be "strengthened" in their "inner being" (v. 16; cf. 2 Cor 4:16) so that this will not be the case.

Paul's description of his posture in prayer ("I bow my knees to the Father," v. 14) represents him as praying with deliberate earnestness and humility. Prayer with bowed knees was by no means the universal custom in either Jewish or Greco-Roman tradition; Jews, for example, frequently stood when they prayed (e.g., 1 Sam 1:26; 1 Kgs 8:22; Matt 6:5; Mark 11:25; Luke 18:11, 13; cf. Arnold 2010, 208), and sometimes prostrated themselves completely before God (e.g. Gen 17:3; Matt 26:39). But kneeling in prayer was by no means unknown; drawing on the social custom of kneeling when requesting a favor from a powerful superior, Jews would on occasion bend their knees before God, frequently in contexts of particular urgency, seriousness, or contrition (e.g., Ezra 9:5; Luke 22:41; Acts 7:60; cf. the metaphorical use of the motif in Pr Man 11).

The prayer that Paul prays is directed to "the Father, from whom every family in heaven and on earth is named" (vv. 14b-15). The directing of prayer to the Father is standard practice for Paul (cf. 1:17, and the proto-Trinitarian image of "access . . . through [Christ] . . . in one Spirit to the Father," in 2:18; 2 Cor 12:8 is worth noting as a possible exception). Although there is undoubtedly an element of privilege and intimacy implied by the depiction of God as Father and Paul's access to him in prayer, Paul's bowed knees are a reminder that there is nothing casual or taken for granted about this access.

3:15. That note is reinforced in v. 15 by the description of God as the one "from whom every family in heaven and on earth is named." The meaning of Paul's language here is a matter of long-standing debate. One line of interpretation, stretching back as far as the translators of the early Latin and Syriac versions, understands *patria* not as "family" but as "fatherhood" (Latin: *paternitas*), but there is no convincing precedent for reading the Greek word *patria* as carrying an abstract meaning of that sort. Another common interpretation (e.g., Caird 1976, 69) reads *pasa patria* not as "every family" but as "[his] whole family," referring to the church as the household of God (cf. 2:19) and alluding to the imperial propaganda that spoke of Augustus (and various other emperors after him, including Caligula, Claudius, and Nero) as *pater patriae* to the people of Rome. The grammatical awkwardness involved in reading the expression in that way is not a fatal objection, given the precedent in 2:21 (cf. Matt 3:15; LXX Lev 9:5; 16:33), but it is difficult nonetheless to make sense of what Paul has in mind by the portion of that one family that is "in heaven," if that interpretation is followed. The more likely interpretation, therefore, as most recent commentators agree (e.g., Best 1998, 338–39; Lincoln 1990, 202–203), is that Paul is speaking of "every family" and that the heavenly families he has in mind are the various groupings and categories of angelic beings (cf. 1 En. 69.3). In saying that they are "named . . . from" God the Father, Paul is not representing them as members of a family that bears his name; he is, rather, speaking of the sovereignty of God as the creator who assigned the names of all created things (cf. Ps 147:4; Isa 40:26).

3:16. The remainder of the paragraph, in vv. 16-19, provides the content of Paul's prayer: "that he may grant you, according to the riches of his glory, to be strengthened with power through his Spirit, in the inner person, so that Christ may dwell in your hearts through faith, in order that you, being rooted and grounded in love, might be strengthened to grasp, together with all the saints, what is the breadth and length and height and depth, and to know the love of Christ, which surpasses knowledge, so that you might be filled up to all the fullness of God."

The standard or measure of the giving that Paul prays for from God is "the riches of his glory" (v. 16)—language that recalls Paul's earlier references to the riches of God's mercy (2:4) and grace (2:7) and "the unsearchable riches of Christ" (3:8). Here, the abundant wealth of God is pictured as being poured out in generous giving to his people. The currency in which God's riches are described as consisting is "glory" (*doxa*)—a word that can carry various meanings and connotations, including visible splendor and public renown. Here, however, as is occasionally the case elsewhere in Paul's letters (e.g., Col 1:11; Rom 6:4), it is treated by Paul as roughly equivalent to "might" or "power."

The gift Paul prays that God may grant to his readers is that they will be "strengthened with power through his Spirit, in the inner person." The strengthening for which he prays is, in part at least, a preventative against the discouragement that he has earlier (in 3:13) envisaged as a danger for them. It is a strengthening, accordingly, that takes place "in the inner person"—language that resembles Paul's picture of himself and his fellow missionaries in 2 Cor 4:16: "Therefore, we do not lose heart; although our outer person is wasting away, our inner person is being renewed day by day."

3:17-18. The means through which he prays that this strengthening will occur is the work of the Spirit (cf. the earlier prayer in 1:17), and its effect is "that Christ may dwell in your hearts through faith" (v. 17). The difficulty of explaining why the strengthening work of the Spirit is necessary for Christ to dwell in the readers' hearts may be one of the reasons that some commentators (e.g., Best 1998, 341; Arnold 2010, 210–11) treat the two infinitival clauses in vv. 16b-17 as parallel with one another (i.e., "that he may grant you . . . to be strengthened with power through his Spirit, in the inner person, and that Christ may dwell in your hearts through faith"), rather than reading the second as the desired effect of the first. This reading of the syntax is unlikely, however, given the distance between *hina dō* ("that he may grant . . .") and *katoikēsai ton Christon* ("that Christ may dwell") and the lack of a coordinating conjunction such as *kai* ("and") to connect the two infinitival phrases (cf. Hoehner 2002, 480–81; Thielman 2010, 229).

The main reason the indwelling of Christ in the heart that Paul describes in v. 17 may be viewed as depending on the strengthening work of the Spirit prayed for by Paul in the preceding verse is that it takes place "through faith" (*dia tēs pisteōs*). The faith Paul is referring to here is almost certainly, like the faith to which he refers elsewhere in the letter (1:15; 2:8; 4:13; 6:16, 23; probably also 3:12; 4:5): the human faith that believers exercise in God and in the Lord Jesus. This faith (as Paul implies in 1:15 and 6:23) is something that can only exist and persevere to the extent that it is enabled and strengthened by God.

The fact that Paul uses the aorist form of the infinitive *katoikēsai* ("may dwell") should not be read as implying that he is envisaging a one-time event in which Christ enters the heart and takes residence within it; he is, after all, praying the prayer for believers who are already "sealed" by the Spirit (1:13) and "being built . . . into the dwelling place of God" (2:22). The choice of the aorist form is probably best understood as a reflection of the fact that Paul is referring simply to the fact of Christ's indwelling, rather than to the extent of its duration (BDF §332; cf. Arnold 2010, 211). (Much the same can be said about the aorist form of the other various subjunctives and infinitives in vv. 16, 18, and 19.)

Paul's image of Christ dwelling in the hearts of believers should be read against the background of OT and Second Temple Jewish usage, in which language about the "heart" typically refers holistically to the inner being of a person, embracing cognitive, affective, and volitional elements (cf. NIDNTTE, "καρδία," 2.623–24). His prayer is that the whole orientation of the readers' inward lives, including their thinking, feeling, and choosing (and, therefore, the whole direction of their outward and visible lives, too) might be deeply and pervasively shaped by the influence of Christ (cf. Lincoln 1990, 207). For that to occur, given the human frailty of the readers and the constant pressure of rival claims and influences on their affections, beliefs, and behaviors (cf. 2:1-3; 6:10-17), requires exactly the kind of inward work of the Spirit that this prayer is asking for.

The clause that comprises the second half of v. 17 ("being rooted and grounded in love") joins together two perfect passive participles ("rooted" and "grounded"), both of which are plural in form and presumably referring to the readers. The fact that they are in the nominative case counts against attaching them to the dative *hymin* ("[to] you") of v. 16 or the genitive *hymōn* ("your") of v. 17. It is possible, as some commentators argue (Thielman 2010, 231–32; Best 1998, 342), that they may have been intended by Paul to be left dangling unattached, functioning as if they were indicative verbs in a freestanding parenthetical comment ("You are rooted and grounded in love!") along the same lines as the parenthesis in 2:5b. A more likely explanation, however, given the participial forms that Paul has chosen for the two verbs, is that they modify the "you" implied in the following verse as the subject of *exischysēte* ("might be strengthened"), and that—like the similar construction in 1:18—they have been fronted, ahead of the *hina* that introduces the new clause in v. 18, in order to give them prominence and form a bridge between the interrelated petitions contained within the two verses (Larkin 2009, 62–63). Verses 17-19 would thus read: ". . . so that Christ may dwell in your hearts through faith, in order that you, being rooted and grounded in love, might be strengthened to grasp, together with all the saints, what is the breadth and length and height and depth, and to know the love of Christ, which surpasses knowledge, so that you might be filled up to all the fullness of God."

If that is the case, then the picture Paul paints in v. 17b of the readers as "rooted and grounded in love" is a particularly important one, forming a bridge between the image in v. 17a of Christ dwelling in the readers' hearts, through faith, and the petitions of vv. 18-19, which ask that they might be empowered to know the love of Christ and thus be "filled" to the measure of God's own fullness. The combination of organic and architectural imagery is not unusual for Paul (cf. 2:21; 4:16; Col 2:7; 1 Cor 3:9). Here, as in Col 2:7, it functions to emphasize the groundedness and stability of believers in their relationship with God. The love Paul wants believers to know, and to be "filled" with in their own dispositions and conduct, is a love in which they themselves are grounded and secure (reading the "love" of v. 17b, like the "love" of v. 19, as a reference to the love that Christ has for them). The petition of v. 18 is, thus, something that Paul views as the desired outworking of the presence of Christ within the hearts of believers, in the center of their feeling, knowing, and choosing. Paul prays that Christ may occupy the focal point within the hearts of believers, in order that they might thereby be given the capacity to know the love of God, as it has been manifested in Christ, and to manifest that love in their own lives.

This knowledge is not something Paul pictures as being the possession of the individual, enlightened soul, in isolation from the community of believers. It is, rather, something that his readers will experience in communion with one another and, indeed, "with all the saints." Strictly speaking, the latter phrase modifies only the infinitive *katalabesthai* ("to grasp"), but in so doing it implies a corporate, communal context for all that follows in vv. 18b-19; both the "know[ing]" of the love of Christ and the "be[ing] filled" by it are implicitly represented as involving the social practices of a community who learn and manifest these realities together (cf. 5:18-21).

The four dimensions that Paul refers to in v. 18b as the objects of the readers' comprehension ("to grasp . . . what is the breadth and length and height and depth") have been much discussed by interpreters, who have found in them a wide variety of meanings including the four points of the cross (e.g., Irenaeus, *Haer.* 5.17.4; Augustine, *Doctr. chr.* 2.41), the dimensions of the wisdom of God (e.g., Bruce 1984, 327–28) or his saving plan (e.g., Theodoret, *PG* 82.532), and the vastness of his power (Arnold 2010, 215, citing PGM IV.964-74, 979-85).

The simplest interpretation, however, and the one best supported by the immediate context, is the one that reads the "breadth and length and height and depth" as referring to the vastness of the love of Christ (e.g., Calvin 1965, 168–69; Best 1998, 346; Lincoln 1990, 207–13), which, as Paul goes on to say in v. 19, "surpasses knowledge," or perhaps to the love of God, which—as Paul goes on to imply in the following verse—has been demonstrated and made knowable in the love of Christ (e.g., Moule 1914, 20). This interpretation has in its favor the fact that the petition in v. 18 is framed by references to the love of Christ in vv. 17 and 19, the close syntactical connection between v. 18b and v. 19a, and the way in which v. 19a offers a resolution to the "syntactical suspense" generated by the preceding verse (cf. Thielman 2010, 237).

3:19. On this reading, v. 19a functions in a way that is "climactically parallel" to the clause that precedes it (Lincoln 1990, 212). "To grasp" (v. 18b) becomes "to know" (v. 19a), with a slightly stronger implication of the kind of personal knowledge that goes beyond mere theoretical apprehension; and the powerful but unspecified implications of the "breadth and length and height and depth" referred to in v. 18b become explicit in the paradoxical assertion of v. 19a that the love of Christ, which Paul prays that believers will know, "surpasses knowledge."

Finally, in v. 19b, Paul states the ultimate end to which all of the petitions in the preceding verses are directed: "so that you might be filled up to all the fullness of God." The preposition *eis*, which Paul uses here, is most unlikely to carry the sense implied by the "with" that is used to translate it in the ESV and NRSV. God's fullness, that is to say, is not depicted here as the source from which believers are filled (though that idea is implied elsewhere in the letter, in 1:23), but as the—immeasurable!—measure toward which their fullness is to increase.

Abstracted from its present context, the idea of being "filled up to all the fullness of God" could be understood as referring to any or all of the communicable attributes of God. The earlier references to "fill[ing]" and "fullness" in 1:23 suggest a broad, all-encompassing image of the transformative presence of God, inhabiting the community of his people with his glory and power. Here, however, the repeated references to love in the immediately preceding context (vv. 17, 19) suggest that the accent falls on that particular attribute of God, and Paul's prayer is that it will become ever more pervasively present within the dispositions and actions of the readers (cf. 4:15-16; 5:2; Best 1998, 347–48).

To him be glory (3:20-21)

(20) To the one who is able to do beyond everything, exceedingly more than what we ask or imagine, according to the power that is at work within us; (21) to him be glory in the church and in Christ Jesus, to all generations, for ever and ever. Amen.

3:20. Chapter 3 concludes with a doxology, which arises out of the scope and content of the prayers in 3:14-19 and combines with the *berakah* in 1:3-14 to bracket the first half of the letter with outpourings of praise to God. The content of the doxology reflects the interrelated emphases on the power (cf. 1:19-23; 3:7, 14-19) and glory (cf. 1:6, 12, 14, 17, 18, 3:16) of God that have pervaded chapters 1–3. The desire that it expresses for God to receive "glory in the church" (v. 21) also anticipates the exhortations of chapters 4–6, in which the readers are urged to walk "worthily" (*axiōs*) of their calling as the community through which the wisdom of God is made visible in the world.

The immediate occasion for the doxology is the prayer report that precedes it, which Paul has framed in ostentatiously extravagant terms as a prayer that the readers will know "love of Christ, which surpasses knowledge" (v. 19a) and be filled to the measure of "all the fullness of God" (v. 19b). As if in answer to any possible doubts or questions that might be voiced in response to such an impossibly ambitious prayer, Paul follows it with a doxology that describes God as being able to do even more than the prayer has asked for: "To the one who is able to do beyond everything, exceedingly more than what we ask or imagine, according to the power that is at work within us; to him be glory in the church and in Christ Jesus to all generations, for ever and ever. Amen."

The language Paul uses here in the doxology to speak of the surpassing power of God heaps superlative upon superlative, offering praise to God as the one who is able to do *hyper panta* ("beyond everything"), *hyperekperissou* ("exceedingly more than") what we ask or even imagine. The latter expression is also used in 1 Thess 3:10; 5:13, but it appears nowhere else in the surviving literature from before Paul's time and may well be one that he himself coined. What God is able to do, through his power that is "at work within us," is left unspecified and unrestricted—the infinitive that complements the participial phrase, "the one who is able," is simply "to do" (*poiēsai*), leaving open a potentially infinite field of possibilities whose extent is quantified only by the claim that it is unquantifiable, beyond even what can be imagined.

3:21. The glory that the benediction speaks of God receiving is depicted as being manifest both "in the church" and "in Christ Jesus." Given the closeness of relationship Paul has earlier described between Christ as the head and the church as his body (1:22-23), it is natural that these two expressions should be joined together as they are here. The depiction of the church as a theater of God's glory is also consistent with the way Paul has previously outlined God's purpose for the church to be the community in which his wisdom is to be made known to the principalities and powers (3:10), and described God's work in raising and enthroning believers with Christ as being directed toward a day when he will "show the surpassing riches of his grace in kindness toward us in Christ Jesus" (2:7).

The double horizon implied by those earlier references to the purposes of God for the church, both "now" (3:10) and "in the coming ages" (2:7), is also reflected in the benediction at the end of 3:21. The glory that Paul ascribes to God is a glory that is to be given "to all generations, for ever and ever"—a double-barreled expression that rolls its way forward from generation to generation (*eis pasas tas geneas*) and from age to age, or—more literally—for an age of ages (*tou aiōnos tōn aiōnōn*), from the present into the infinite future. The benediction concludes with an Amen, in keeping with Paul's typical pattern of joining that expression to doxologies and blessings rather than to prayers (cf. Rom 1:25; 9:5; 11:36; 15:33; 16:27; Gal 1:5; 6:18; Phil 4:20; 1 Tim 1:17; 6:16; 2 Tim 4:18).

To walk worthily

Ephesians 4:1–6:20

I urge you therefore (4:1)

(1) I urge you therefore—I, the prisoner in the Lord—to walk worthily of the calling to which you have been called . . .

4:1. The opening verses of Ephesians 4 mark the beginning of a major new section in the letter. The main focus of chapters 1–3 is on the identity and calling of the readers as believers in Christ and members of the church, and its core (2:1–3:13) is composed of salvation-historical narratives that, from three different and mutually complementary angles, tell the story in which that identity and calling is grounded. In chapters 4–6, the accent shifts from reminder to exhortation, as Paul urges his readers to conduct their lives in a manner that is worthy of the calling that they have received.

Verse 1 thus serves as a hinge between the first half of the letter and the second: "I urge you therefore—I, the prisoner in the Lord—to walk worthily of the calling to which you have been called." Paul's self-description as "the prisoner in the Lord" recalls the references to his sufferings and imprisonment in 3:1, 13 and underlines the earnestness of the exhortations that follow (cf. Phlm 9). If there is a difference of meaning intended between "prisoner in the Lord" (4:1) and "prisoner of Christ" (3:1), it is the replacement of the emphasis of 3:1 on the sovereignty of Christ, under whose rule and in whose cause Paul has found himself imprisoned, with a reminder of the solidarity of Paul the prisoner with his readers in Ephesus, as members together of one people "in the Lord" (cf. Eph 5:8; Phlm 20).

In keeping with that solidarity, Paul commences the second half of the letter with an appeal in which he chooses to "urge" (*parakalō*) rather than command them (cf. Phlm 8–10). Paul's urgings to his readers, however, are not warranted solely by his own moral authority as a prisoner in the Lord; their more basic, explicit grounding is in the preceding chapters of the letter, as signaled by the "therefore" (*oun*) with which the exhortations that he commences in this verse are joined to what precedes them.

The pattern of life that he urges his readers to adopt and maintain is pictured here (as it is repeatedly in the following chapters; cf. 4:17; 5:2, 8, 15) as a way in which they are to "walk," in contrast to the previous way of life in which they walked (2:2) prior to their conversion. The metaphor is a traditional one within the OT and Second Temple Jewish literature (e.g., LXX 4 Kgdms 20:3; Prov 8:20) and is one Paul frequently uses within his letters (e.g., Gal 5:16; 1 Thess 2:12; 4:1, 12; Rom 6:4; 8:4; 13:13; 14:15; Col 1:10; 2:6; 3:7; 4:5).

As the "therefore" (*oun*) connecting this verse with the preceding context implies, the "calling" to which he refers is best understood in relation to the account Paul has offered his readers in chapters 1–3 of the saving work of God and its implications for both their present identity and purpose and the future hope that has been granted to them through their inclusion in God's plans. The close connection in 1:18 and 4:4 between "calling" and "hope" underlines the importance of the latter element in Paul's thinking; the focus on the church's unity in vv. 2-16, together with the image of the church as a "body" that "build[s] itself up in love" (4:16), makes it clear that the present identity of the church as the "one body" and "new humanity" created in Christ (2:15-16; cf. 1:10; 3:10) is also in view.

The original sense of the word "worthily" (*axiōs*), which Paul uses to describe the relationship that ought to exist between the readers' calling and their conduct, is a quantitative one; it derives from the verb *agō*, used to describe the way an item "draws down" the scales so as to balance out the weight that it is being compared with (cf. BDAG, s.v. "*axios*"). Frequently, however, within the New Testament and beyond, it can be used to describe a relation that is qualitative rather than quantitative. John the Baptist, for example, urges his hearers to bear fruit that is "worthy" (*axios*) of repentance (Matt 3:8)—i.e., fruit that fits with or corresponds to the nature of the repentance that they profess.

Paul has a relationship of that sort in mind here. His point is not so much a quantitative one, about the moral excellence of the life his readers are to lead, as measured against the quantity of the grace extended to them in their calling; it is, rather, a qualitative one, about the fittingness and correspondence that ought to exist between the identity and purpose that have been conferred on them by their calling, and the pattern of how they conduct their lives as members of Christ's people.

One body (4:2-16)

(2) . . . with all humility and gentleness, with patience, bearing with one another in love, (3) being eager to keep the unity of the Spirit in the bond of peace. (4) [There is] one body and one spirit, just as you were called in one hope that belongs to your calling. (5) [There is] one Lord, one faith, one baptism, (6) one God and Father of all, who is over all, and through all, and in all. (7) But to each individually grace has been given, according to the measure of the gift of Christ. (8) Therefore it says: "He ascended to the heights, and captured a body of captives; he gave gifts to people." (9) "He ascended": what does it mean but that he also descended, to the lower regions of the earth? (10) The one who descended is the same as the one who ascended, high above all the heavens, that he might fill all things. (11) And he gave some as apostles, some as prophets, some as evangelists, and some as pastors and teachers, (12) for the preparing of the saints for the work of ministry, for the building up of the body of Christ, (13) until we all attain to the unity of the faith and of the knowledge of the Son of God, to the mature man, to the measure of the stature of the fullness of Christ, (14) so that we might no longer be infants, tossed about and carried around by every wind of doctrine, in the trickery of humans, in craftiness directed toward a strategy of deception, (15) but that speaking the truth in love we might in all respects grow into him who is the head, Christ, (16) from whom the whole body, joined and held together through every assisting connection, according to the working in the measure of each individual part, accomplishes the growth of the body for the purpose of building itself up in love.

4:2. Accordingly, in vv. 2-3, when Paul expands on the exhortation of v. 1, he offers not a general list of virtues but a series of dispositions and practices that are more narrowly focused on preserving the unity and concord of the church: "with all humility and gentleness, with patience, bearing with one another in love, being eager to keep the unity of the Spirit in the bond of peace." The list closely resembles the list of items in which believers are urged to clothe themselves in Col 3:12-15—a list that is grounded, in part at least, in the fact that the readers were "called in one body" (v. 15).

"Humility" (*tapeinophrosynē*), the first item in the list, is a word that Greco-Roman writers used to name a quality they considered contemptible and weak. Josephus, for example, speaks of the way the brief reign of Galba as emperor was brought to an end by his soldiers, who despised him for his "pusillanimity" (*tapeinophrosynē*) (*J.W.* 4.9.2), and Epictetus repeatedly speaks of *tapeinophrosynē* as the attribute of those who lack self-respect and nobility of spirit, and are inappropriately overawed by their social superiors (e.g., *Diatr.* 3.24.54–58). In Jewish usage the word and its cognates acquired more positive connotations (e.g., LXX Ps 130:2; 1 QS 4.2) and were used to refer to the lowliness of spirit delighted in by God. Those positive connotations are further amplified in early Christian usage by the example of the *tapeinōsis* of Christ as the humble, suffering Servant (Isa 53:8; cf. Acts 8:33), and Paul elsewhere urges his readers to adopt a posture of humility in their dealings with one another, in imitation of Christ (Phil 2:3, 6-11).

Joined to that humility, in v. 2a, is the related attribute of "gentleness" (*prautēs*); Paul uses the same word elsewhere to speak of the "gentleness . . . of Christ" (2 Cor 10:1), which he claims to imitate in his dealings with fellow believers. The following attribute, "patience" (*makrothymia*), is not the same word as the one Paul uses elsewhere to speak of the "patience" (*hypomonē*) that waits for the fulfillment of God's promises (8:25) or the "endurance" that bears up under sufferings (Rom 5:3). Here, as is usually the case when Paul speaks of the *makrothymia* exercised by men and women (2 Cor 6:6; Gal 5:22; 2 Tim 4:2; Col 1:11; 3:12), the accent is on the forbearance that is shown within social relationships; this reading is confirmed in the remainder of the verse, where Paul unpacks the "patience" he has in mind as consisting in "bearing with one another in love" (4:2).

4:3. The focus on preserving the unity of the church that has been implied in v. 2 becomes explicit in v. 3, where Paul concludes the list with a final, more elaborately specified item: "being eager to keep the unity of the Spirit in the bond of peace." The "unity" that the readers are urged to keep is described as being "of the Spirit"—that is, a unity granted to them by the Spirit (Larkin 2009, 69–70), who has sealed them with the same seal (1:13) and granted them access together to the Father (2:18).

This unity is pictured by Paul as existing within, and held together by, the "bond" (*syndesmos*) of peace. The same word is used in Col 3:14 to speak of love as the fastener that holds together the various metaphorical garments that believers are to clothe themselves with—an indication that for Paul the metaphor of the *syndesmos* is a live one, and the original, literal sense of the word as a term for a buckle or fastener is not far from his mind. Here, however, the "bond" in Paul's metaphor is not love but peace (which Col 3:15 goes on to picture via a different metaphor). The peace Paul has in mind here in v. 3 is probably not (contra Lincoln 1990, 237; Thielman 2010, 255) to be understood primarily as an instrument that believers employ to guard and preserve their unity. It is true that Paul can, on occasion (e.g., Rom 3:17; 8:6; 14:17–19; 1 Cor 7:15; Gal 5:22; Col 3:15; 2 Tim 2:22), use the word *eirēnē* in a broad and active sense, referring not only to the "peace" that one is given or desires but also, by extension and inclusion, to the peace-loving dispositions and peace-making practices that foster and manifest it (cf. his use of the verb *eirēneuō* in Rom 12:18; 2 Cor 13:11; 1 Thess 5:13). Even on these occasions, however, it is impossible to reduce Paul's notion of peace entirely to an instrument or strategy. In this instance, in line with the way the word has already been used in 2:14-15, its primary reference is to the peace that has been accomplished in Christ and given to believers in him (Abbott 1897, 107)—"the peace of Christ," as Paul describes it in Col 3:15, which is both granted to believers and living and active among them.

Although the unity and peace that believers possess within the church are a gift that has already been given to them, they are a gift that should not be taken for granted and cannot be passively possessed. The readers are, Paul urges them, to be "eager" (*spoudazontes*) to maintain the unity they have been given—language that implies energy and effort on their part (cf. Gal 2:10; 1 Thess 2:17; 2 Tim 2:15; 4:9, 16), including the cultivation and exercise of the dispositions and behaviors listed in the preceding verse.

4:4. The focus on the church's unity continues in vv. 4-6, with a sevenfold list of items in which believers share, each of which is "one" in number: "[There is] one body and one Spirit, just as you were called in one hope that belongs to your calling. [There is] one Lord, one faith, one baptism, one God and Father of all, who is over all, and through all, and in all." Although the list commences abruptly, without a conjunction to specify the nature of its connection with the preceding verses, the strong connections of theme and language between vv. 1-3 and vv. 4-6 ("Lord"; "calling"; "unity"/"one"; "Spirit") make it clear that the reminders in the latter paragraph function as a warrant for the exhortations in the former one.

The list begins with two items ("one body and one Spirit") that reinforce the already implicit connections between the reference to the church's unity in 4:3 and the earlier references in chapters 1–3 to the "one body" in which Jews and Gentiles have been reconciled to God (2:15-16; cf. 3:6) and the "one Spirit" in whom they have together been granted access to the Father (2:18). In keeping with the way the image of "[Christ's] body" (1:23; cf. 2:16; 3:6) has functioned in the previous chapters, Paul's language here presupposes a unity that the readers share with all believers everywhere. The universal scope of Paul's imagery should not be overstressed, however, since both the virtue list in vv. 2-3 and the depiction of the church's upbuilding in vv. 15-16 are constructed in language that appears to imply the local community of believers, with its face-to-face relationships of love and interdependence, as the principal sphere in which the virtues are to be practiced and the mutual upbuilding is to take place.

A further connection between the exhortations in 4:1-3 and the identity-forming narratives and prayer reports of the preceding chapters is highlighted by the next item on the list: "just as you were called in one hope that belongs to your calling." Here, the juxtaposition of "hope" and "calling" recalls the prayer report of 1:15-23, in which Paul tells the readers that he prays God will grant them knowledge of "the hope that derives from his calling" (1:18), strengthening the echo of 1:18 that was already more faintly present in 4:1. Here, as in 1:18, the content of the "hope" in view is best filled out via the forward-looking references in chapters 1–3, which picture Jewish and Gentile members of the church as awaiting a common inheritance (1:13-14), look forward to the coming age as one in which God's kindness to the church will be displayed for all to see (2:7), and anticipate a day when the fullness of Christ, already filling the church, will fill the universe (1:23; cf. 3:19), so that all things are summed up in him (1:10).

4:5. The next three items on the list belong together as an interrelated triad: "one Lord, one faith, one baptism" (v. 5). Paul has already depicted himself in v. 1 as a prisoner "in the Lord"; here, he reminds his readers that the same can be said of all of them (cf. 2:21). The resurrection and enthronement of Jesus, as Paul has already emphasized in 1:21, place him "high above all . . . dominion (*kyriotēs*)." In a world in which there were (as Paul reminds the Corinthians in 1 Cor 8:5) "gods many and lords many," believers are united in their allegiance to "one Lord" (cf. 1 Cor 8:6). This allegiance (and the trusting dependence that underlies it) is probably what is in view in the second item of the triad: "one faith" (contra Thielman 2010, 258; Best 1998, 368–69, who read "faith" here as a reference to the body of doctrine that Christians unite in subscribing to).

The third item, "one baptism," is closely connected with the previous two, reminding believers of the rite in which they have all participated, enacting and representing their response of faith to the claims of Jesus as Lord (cf. Col 2:12; Gal 3:26-27). The shared experience of baptism into Christ and the exclusive allegiance that it represents are, as Paul stresses elsewhere, a powerful reminder of the unity and solidarity of believers with one another (cf. Gal 3:26-29; 1 Cor 1:12-15).

4:6. After the staccato brevity of items four through six, the seventh and final item stands out as the longest and most elaborate: "one God and Father of all who is over all, and through all, and in all." In both form and content, it is the climax of the list (cf. Lincoln 1990, 240), marked out from the others not only by the double naming of God as "God and Father of all" but also by the repetition with variation that follows, describing him as "over all, and through all, and in all."

The word "all" (*pantōn*), which occurs four times in the verse, takes a form in Greek that could be read as either masculine (and referring to people, i.e., the church) or neuter (and referring to things, i.e., the entirety of the universe). The first instance of the word stands apart somewhat from the other three; its closer connections are with the phrase that it concludes ("one God and Father of all"), which, in turn, comes at end of a series of seven items in vv. 4-6, all of which focus on the common experiences and possessions of believers. It is these connections, rather than the connection with the threefold "all" that follows, that the hearer encounters first as the verse is read.

These considerations, together with the way the language of fatherhood and adoption is used elsewhere in the letter to speak of the relationship God has with believers as his children (cf. 1:2-3, 5; 2:18; 5:1, 20; 6:23, though note the possible exception in 3:14-15), tip the scales in favor of reading the first "all" as masculine rather than neuter and of understanding it as referring to believers.

But a masculine reading of the first "all" does not rule out a neuter reading of the three instances of the word that follow. The threefold formula in v. 6b ("who is over all, and through all, and in all") has obvious affinities with similar formulations elsewhere in Paul's letters (esp. 1 Cor 8:6; Rom 11:36; Col 1:16-17) in which the word "all" refers unambiguously of the entire cosmos, viewed in its relationship to God (and/or to Christ)—a theme that has already been addressed within Ephesians (1:10-11, 22; 3:9, 15). Formulations of this sort can be found further afield, too, in the language of Hellenistic Judaism (e.g., Philo, *Spec. Laws* 1.208), Stoic panentheism (e.g., Marcus Aurelius, *Med.* 4.23; 7.9), and the magical papyri (e.g., PGM IV.2835–40). Given the likely familiarity of expressions such as this to the hearers and the possibility that they would have recognized the presence of a preexisting formula that Paul had borrowed and made use of (Thielman 2010, 256), it is by no means implausible to suppose that they would have detected a shift from the masculine gender (and ecclesial reference) of the first "all" to the neuter gender (and cosmological reference) of the last three. On this reading, Paul speaks first about the common relationship that all believers have with God as their father, and then he goes on to say that the one God who is their father is also the creator and ruler of all things, depicting him in a traditional formulation as sovereign ("over all"), providentially involved ("through all"), and everywhere present within his creation ("in all").

Alternatively (and somewhat less likely), if the first "all" is read, like the other three, as neuter in gender and cosmic in scope, the kind of fatherhood in view would be the sovereign, providential fatherhood that even Jewish writers in the Second Temple period could use as a way of describing the relationship between the creator and the cosmos (e.g., Philo, *Spec. Laws* 1.14; cf. Acts 17:28, quoting Aratus's *Phainomena*)—a relationship whose entailments are then spelled out in the three "all" statements that follow.

4:7. In v. 7 Paul's focus shifts from "all" to "each" and from the unity of the body to its diversity: "But to each of us individually grace has been given, according to the measure of the gift of Christ." Paul's language ("grace . . . given . . . gift") recalls his use of the same terms in the previous chapter (3:7-8) to speak of his own role in the unfolding purposes of God. Here, however, what was said of Paul is said of "each . . . individually" (*heni . . . hekastō*).

The scope of Paul's language is most naturally read as embracing the whole church and all of its members, rather than reading back into v. 7 the more limited range of gifts and ministers included in the list of v. 11 (as, e.g., in Schlier 1957, 191); not only does an inclusive reading of the "each" in v. 7 fit with the scope of vv. 1-6, but it is also consistent with the explicitly all-inclusive language with which Paul concludes his picture of the body building itself up in love in vv. 15-16.

The verbal parallels between 4:7 and 3:7-8, along with what Paul goes on to say in 4:11-16, make it clear that the "grace" in view here is not (or, at least, not directly) the saving grace of 2:5-8 but its overflow in the granting of responsibilities and empowerments to the people whom God has saved. This grace is given "according to the measure of the gift of Christ" (an expression that must almost certainly be read, in context, as a subjective genitive in which Christ is not the content but the giver of the gift). Although the gifts of Christ are drawn from the same well of "surpassing riches" (2:7), the particular assignments and enablings given to believers are measured out in accordance with the unique part each is to play within the plans and purposes of God (cf. Rom 12:6; 1 Cor 12:11, 18).

4:8-10. Paul follows his claim about the gifts given by Christ to believers with a modified quotation from Ps 68:18 and a discussion of the verse's meaning and entailments: "Therefore, it says: 'He ascended to the heights, and captured a body of captives; he gave gifts to people.' 'He ascended': what does it mean but that he also descended, to the lower regions of the earth? The one who descended is the same as the one who ascended, high above all the heavens, that he might fill all things."

The way the verse from the psalm is quoted and appropriated in Eph 4:8-10 is something of an interpretative *crux* (cf. the discussion in Starling 2014b, 149–55, from which the following paragraphs are abridged and adapted). Discussion has centered on two issues in particular:

1. Why does Ephesians 4:8 read "gave" when Ps 68:18 (at least in the textual traditions behind the MT and the surviving versions of the LXX) reads "received"?

2. When Paul draws the conclusion that the ascent spoken of in the psalm implies that the one who ascended "also descended, to the lower regions of the earth," what is the "descen[t]" to which he is referring?

In answer to the first question, a number of theories have been proposed:

1a. Paul simply misquotes the psalm to make the text fit his point (e.g., Fitzmyer 1961, 325). Without further elaboration, this theory is difficult to reconcile with the *gezera shava* method that Paul appears to have followed in introducing the quotation from the psalm, given that the key word "gave" is the very word Paul has had to insert into the verse to make it serve his purpose. If this theory is followed it requires another explanation to be given of why Psalm 68 is quoted at all, and why Paul felt at liberty to make the change to its wording.

1b. Paul is working from a variant form of the Old Testament textual tradition that reads "gave" rather than "received" (e.g., Taylor 1991, 319–36, citing evidence from the Peshitta and Targum).

1c. In the original context of the psalm, the "captives" are not Gentile enemies but Israelites, and the "taking captive" and "receiving" in the psalm are a reference to Numbers 8 and 18, in which the Levites are taken by the LORD as his own possession and then given back to Israel as servants and ministers (Smith 1975, 181–89). It is hard to reconcile this theory with the fact that the "gifts" and "spoil" and "tribute" elsewhere in the psalm (vv. 12, 29, 30, 31) are clearly material and not human, and the absence of any unambiguous clues in the psalm to the idea that the Levites are any more in view than the whole gathered congregation of Israel.

Three main theories have been proposed in answer to the second question, regarding the nature of the "descen[t]" spoken of in Ephesians 4:9:

2a. The descent Paul has in mind is a descent into Hades or into the grave (e.g., Thielman 2010, 271; Arnold 2010, 254). According to this theory, *ta katōtera* [*merē*] *tēs gēs* is to be read as "the lower parts of the earth" (cf. NRSV). This theory stumbles at a number of points, including the awkwardness of the comparative *ta katōtera* as a reference to the "lowest" regions of a three-story universe (references in the LXX to subterranean depths, e.g., LXX Pss 62:10; 138:15, use the superlative *katōtata* rather than the comparative *katōtera*), the fact that a two-step descent to Hades *via* earth is poorly balanced by the one-step ascent mentioned in vv. 8, 10, and the fact that the cosmology of the letter elsewhere speaks of "all things" as being made up of "heaven and earth," not "heaven, earth and things under the earth," and describes the current abode of the rebellious principalities and powers as "the heavenly places."

2b. The descent of Christ was his in his incarnation (and death/burial). According to this theory, *ta katōtera* [*merē*] *tēs gēs* should best be read as "the lower, earthly regions" (cf. NIV), treating *tēs gēs* as a genitive of apposition (Wallace 1996, 99–100; Barth 1974, 432–34).

2c. The descent was the descent at Pentecost of the exalted Christ in the Spirit (e.g., Harris 1996, 192–97; Lincoln 1990, 244–48). In support of this theory it is often pointed out that later rabbinic tradition associated the "ascent" of Ps 68:18 with Moses' ascent of Sinai and identified the thing that is "received" or "given"—depending on which text is followed—as the Torah. This rabbinic interpretation of the psalm correlated with the liturgical use of Psalm 68 in the synagogue as a Pentecost psalm and (it is argued) lies behind the reference to the ascended Christ "receiving" and "pouring out" the Spirit in Acts 2:33 (Lincoln 1990, 241–42). One significant weakness of this interpretation is the way it struggles to explain the logic of Paul's rhetorical question in v. 9. An ascent of God may well imply a *previous* descent, but why does an ascent imply a *subsequent* descent? (If the subsequent descent is necessitated by anything, it is necessitated by the *giving*—if one assumes that God needs to come down to earth in order to give—and not the *descending*.)

The simplest way through this maze of interpretive possibilities is to follow in the path of the hermeneutic implied in chapters 1–3 and chapter 6, in which the story of Christ is understood as a typological echo of the original exodus and a fulfillment of the OT hopes and promises of a new exodus (cf. Starling 2014b, 141–49; and the similar approach in Gombis 2005). Such an approach begins by reading Ps 68:18 in the original context of the psalm and noting the rich background of exodus and new exodus imagery surrounding it. Psalm 68 begins with a call to God to come and rescue his people (vv. 1-3). It goes on to address praises to God for his past acts of deliverance and provision, with clear allusion to the story of the exodus, the wilderness wanderings, and the conquest of the land (vv. 4-10). Before the triumphant progress of the LORD, the kings of the nations are scattered (vv. 11-14) and, having triumphed over his enemies, the LORD marches from Sinai to Zion, to ascend the holy mountain that he has chosen for his dwelling (vv. 15-18). There (v. 18) he receives gifts from (or, better, "among") people and takes up his dwelling place. The remainder of the psalm evokes the continuing significance of the story for the worshiping community of Israel. The God whose triumph is narrated in the exodus story and who now dwells among his people is "the God of salvation" (vv. 19-20) who has promised the overthrow of his enemies (vv. 21-23); the processing tribes of Israel reenact his triumphs and declare his praises (vv. 24-27), appealing to him to do once more what he did in the exodus (v. 28), so that the kings of the nations will be scattered and defeated (v. 30) and come to his temple in Jerusalem bearing gifts and singing praises (vv. 29, 31-35). Thus, against the backdrop of the psalm as a whole, we might read v. 18 as a picture—enacted, perhaps, in cultic procession—of the LORD ascending in triumph from his exodus victory to his dwelling on Mount Zion, a dwelling in the midst of his people that is gloriously enriched with the treasures of the nations (cf. vv. 29, 31-35).

If that is at least a plausible reading of Ps 68:18 in its original context, it is not difficult to see how Paul (whether or not he was aware of the textual tradition reflected in the Peshitta and the Targum) might have felt justified in altering "received gifts among people" to "gave gifts to people," given that the "people" among whom the gifts are received are not the defeated enemies giving the gifts but the Israelites who are indirectly enriched by them.

The exodus and new exodus imagery of the psalm also sheds some light on the interpretation of "he also descended" in Eph 4:9. On the one hand, there is an obvious exodus background for the interpretation that sees the descent as being a descent at Pentecost, viewed as a typological fulfilment of Moses' descent from Mt Sinai. This reading fits comfortably with at least one (apparently common and relatively early) strand of Rabbinic interpretation of the psalm, and with the liturgical use of the psalm in association with the festival of Pentecost. It struggles, however, to give any sort of coherent account of the original sense of the psalm, in which the LORD comes *from* Sinai *to* the holy place (v. 17), suggesting that the "high mount" in v. 18 is not Sinai but Zion. It also struggles (as I have argued above) to account for the logic of Ephesians 4:9-10, in which the descent is seen as a necessary implication of the subsequent or previous ascent.

If we follow the more plausible reading of Paul's logic in 4:9-10 and take the descent as being a reference to Christ's descent in the incarnation, this fits comfortably with the exodus imagery of the psalm. According to this reading, the previous "descent" implied by the LORD's victorious ascent of Zion is his descent as the warrior-redeemer in the events of the exodus (cf. the "coming down" of the LORD in Exod 3:8, Isa 64:1-3), suggested if not explicitly described in Psalm 68:7-8.

What emerges, then, when Eph 4:7-10 is read in the light of a hermeneutic in which the story of Christ is told as a typological echo of the exodus story, and a fulfillment of new exodus prophecies and hopes, is a coherent account of how Ps 68:18 is appropriated and understood by Paul. In the psalm, God's past triumph over the nations in the exodus led to his establishment of a glorious dwelling place in the midst of his people, enriched with the treasures of the nations (extracted as booty or willingly given as tribute). In the context of (cultic?) remembrance of that tradition, a prayer is uttered for a similar future deliverance, so that the nations may be scattered and defeated and that once more the dwelling of God may be enriched with their treasures. For Paul, this prayer has been answered in the new exodus salvation accomplished in Christ. In the incarnation, Christ has descended in power for the deliverance of his people; in his resurrection and ascension he has triumphed over the nations (and over the principalities and powers that stand behind their hostility); now, in the body of Christ, the fruits of that victory are being poured out, as grace is showered upon the people of God (v. 7) and as the body of Christ is being enriched and built up (vv. 11-16). Further, if the body of Christ, the church into which the Gentile believers of Ephesus are being built, is now the "temple" in which God dwells by his Spirit (2:21), and the "fullness" by which his eventual filling of the universe is anticipated (1:23), then it is not drawing too long a bow to suggest that Paul views the church as the sphere in which we see the eschatological vision of Ps 68:28-35 beginning to be fulfilled, as the men and women who are the spoils of Christ's victory are built into a temple to enrich the place of his dwelling.

Although the immediate beneficiaries of Christ's gifts are the church and its members, the boundaries of the church are not the outer limit of God's redemptive purposes: here, as is also the case in 1:22-23 (where it is Christ whom God "gave" to the church), the grace of God given to the church is part of a larger story in which the purposes of God extend beyond the church to the furthest extremities of the created universe: "The one who descended is the same as the one who ascended, high above all the heavens, that he might fill all things" (v. 10).

4:11. Having spoken in v. 7 about the grace of God given to his people, and having located that outpouring of grace in vv. 8–10 within the story of how Christ descended into the world in redemptive mission, ascended in triumph over his enemies, and ultimately plans to "fill all things," Paul goes on in vv. 11-16 to speak more specifically about the gifts Christ has given and the way they play their part in the upbuilding of the church, beginning in v. 11 with Christ's gift of "some as apostles, some as prophets, some as evangelists, and some as pastors and teachers."

The list in v. 11 is neither a complete enumeration of the gifts referred to in v. 7 nor a representative sample of the church's diversity, along the lines of 1 Cor 12:8-10. It is, rather, a focused list that concentrates exclusively on the agents through whom the risen and ascended Christ makes his word present within the church, preserving its health and life, participating in its mission, and equipping its members for the richly varied works of service that he goes on to refer to in vv. 15-16.

Its function is not (contra Hirsch 2016) to prescribe a timeless paradigm of the "fivefold ministry formula" that ought to be present in every congregation in every age; it is, rather, to narrate the risen Christ's outpouring of grace upon his church, commencing with the gift of the "apostles" and "prophets" to whom the mystery of the gospel was first made known (cf. 2:20; 3:5) and continuing with the work of the evangelists and the pastors and teachers who build on their foundation, extending and applying the word of Christ.

The "apostles" and "prophets," therefore, like the apostles and prophets of 2:20 and 3:5, are those of the New Testament church, given by Christ to his people upon his ascension. The New Testament writers use these same words, at times, to speak of a wide circle of "prophets" (e.g., 1 Cor 14:29-33), who speak words of upbuilding, encouragement, and consolation week by week in the church, and "apostles" (e.g., Acts 14:14; Phil 2:25; 2 Cor 8:23), sent out to extend the reach of the churches' speech and action in the name of Christ. The group Paul has in mind here, however, appears to be the somewhat narrower circle implied in 2:20 and 3:5, who play a pivotal role in the history of salvation and the establishing of the New Testament church.

The "evangelists" are identified with a word that occurs only three times in the New Testament and is rarely attested at all outside the literature of early Christianity. In the two other instances of the word within the New Testament, it is used in the context of a passing reference to Philip (described in Acts 21:8 as "the evangelist") and an encouragement from Paul to Timothy to "do the work of an evangelist" (2 Tim 4:5). Since both Timothy and Philip are elsewhere depicted as travelers, moving from place to place with the message of the gospel, and since the cognate terms, *euangelion* ("good news"; "gospel") and *euangelizō* ("bring/proclaim good news") are frequently used in contexts where a traveler brings good news from one place to another (e.g., 1 Sam 31:9; 2 Sam 18:19; Isa 52:7; Luke 4:43; Eph 2:17), Thielman argues plausibly that the "evangelists" are "probably those whom God has especially equipped to travel from place to place with the good news of peace through Christ" (Thielman 2010, 274).

The syntax of the list, which is structured by the initial *tous men* ("some") and the threefold *tous de* ("and some") that follows, suggests that the "pastors (*poimenes*) and teachers (*didaskaloi*)" are to be viewed not as the list's fourth and fifth items, respectively, but as constituting, together, its fourth and final item. It is impossible to say with certainty whether the two nouns should be taken as a hendiadys, referring to a single, undifferentiated group of "teaching shepherds" (Barth 1974, 438), or as a way of referring to two categories that were overlapping but not entirely coterminous (e.g., Wallace 1996, 284; Arnold 2010, 260). Usage of the two terms and their cognates elsewhere in Paul's letters, and in the New Testament more broadly, suggests a certain overlap of function between them: the task entrusted to elders/overseers of churches, for example, is described in some places using the language of "shepherding" (*poimainein*) the flock under their care (1 Pet 5:2; Acts 20:28-29) and in other places using the language of "teaching" (1 Tim 3:2; 5:17) or "exhorting in sound doctrine" (*parakalein en tē didaskalia tē hygiainousē*) (Titus 1:9). In view of the fluidity with which the New Testament writers use the various terms available to them to describe the functions and offices of teaching and oversight within the church, we would be unwise to assume that Paul has in mind a single, inflexible church order within which "pastors," "teachers," and "pastor-teachers" could be neatly categorized and distinguished.

4:12. Paul goes on in v. 12 to describe the combined effect of the work done by the groups named in v. 11, using three successive prepositional phrases: "for (*pros*) the preparing of the saints," "for (*eis*) the work of ministry," and "for (*eis*) the building up of the body of Christ." The syntactical relationship between the three phrases has been the subject of a long-running debate, stretching back at least as far as the mid-nineteenth century. The older view, which is still championed by some commentators (e.g., Lincoln 1990, 253) reads all three phrases in parallel, as descriptions of the tasks for which the members of the groups listed in v. 11 are given to the church. This view struggles to explain the absence of any coordinating conjunctions that would guide the readers to take the second and third phrases in parallel with the first; it also has difficulty with the fact that the work of "building up the body of Christ" appears to be explicitly depicted as the business of "the whole body" in v. 16.

The majority of more recent commentators, therefore (e.g., Thielman 2010, 277–80; Hoehner 2002, 547–49; Best 1998, 395–99), point to the shift of prepositions from *pros* to *eis* . . . *eis*, and the way in which *katērtismena* and *eis* work together in Rom 9:22 to convey the idea of being "prepared for," arguing that the second phrase is dependent on the first (and the third phrase expresses the combined effect of the first and second). On this reading, the function of the work done by the groups listed in v. 11 is "to prepare the saints for the work of ministry," and the outcome of this is the building up of the body of Christ.

The "work of ministry" for which the saints are to be prepared should not be defined too narrowly, as if the ministry of the saints were merely a carbon copy of the activities performed by the word-ministers of v. 11. There are, as Paul reminds the Corinthians in 1 Cor 12:5, "varieties of ministries," an idea that is implicitly confirmed here in Ephesians 4 by the language Paul uses in v. 7 ("to each individually . . . according to the measure of the gift of Christ") and v. 16 ("in the measure of each individual part"). Nor, on the other hand, should "the work of ministry" be understood too broadly, as if it were referring to all the good works that believers perform in every sphere of life. Important as that notion is for Paul (cf. Gal 6:10; Rom 12:17-21), his focus here is on the particular forms of service that are directed toward "the building up of the body of Christ"—a phrase whose content he goes on to unpack in vv. 13-16.

4:13. The temporal (and implicitly purposive) clause introduced by the *mechri* ("until") at the start of v. 13 makes best sense when read as subordinated not to the verb *edōken* ("he gave") in v. 11 but to the verbal idea implied by the noun *oikodomē* ("building up") in v. 12 (Thielman 2010, 280). The upbuilding that Paul pictures in v. 12 as the common task of the saints is to continue "until we all attain to the unity of the faith and of the knowledge of the Son of God, to the mature man, to the measure of the stature of the fullness of Christ."

The "unity" that is described here as a goal of the body's upbuilding is, by implication, the appropriation in faith and knowledge of the already accomplished unity that was spoken of in 2:14-18 and 4:1-6. The syntactically parallel construction in which *pistis* ("faith") and *epignōsis* ("knowledge") are placed, and their closely similar meanings, as nouns cognate with the epistemic/relational verbs *pisteuō* ("believe") and *ginōskō* ("know"), combine to suggest that the "faith" and "knowledge" in which believers are to become ever more deeply united are best understood in an active sense, with "of the Son of God" read as an objective genitive that belongs to both nouns. (The repetition of the article before *epignōsis* is not, as some commentators assert, sufficient reason to read "of the Son of God" as modifying only "knowledge" and not "faith"; cf. the similar constructions in Luke 20:20; 1 Cor 11:27; 2 Cor 8:4; Rev 12:10; 21:26.) What Paul is referring to here in v. 13, then, is the faith that believes in Christ (cf. the comments above on 3:12 and 4:5, above) and the knowledge that knows him (cf. Phil 3:8-11), rather than a body of doctrine that believers subscribe to and knowledge that believers possess. (He does, however, go on to say in v. 14 that a resistance to heterodoxy is one of the behavioral expressions of the mature, united faith and knowledge depicted in v. 13).

Two additional, parallel, descriptions of the goal toward which the body is built up are given in v. 13b-c: "to the mature man, to the measure of the stature of the fullness of Christ." The "mature man" of v. 13b, read within the larger context of the paragraph and the letter as a whole, is not the mature Christian individual but the mature community, depicted in 2:15 as the "new person" created in Christ and in 4:16 as the "body" that is "building itself up in love." The maturity toward which the body of the church grows is given a Christological definition in v. 13c, as "the measure of the stature of the fullness of Christ." Christ, according to Paul's use of the metaphor here, is both the body's head (v. 15) and the archetype of its maturity (v. 13c), with the implication that the growing maturity of the body will be seen in the increasing Christlikeness of the character and conduct of its members (cf. 4:20-24, 32; 5:1-2).

4:14. The (divinely intended) result of this growth toward maturity is expressed in the long, double-branched *hina* clause of vv. 14-15: "so that (*hina*) we might no longer be infants, tossed about and carried around by every wind of doctrine, in the trickery of humans, in craftiness directed toward a strategy of deception, but that speaking the truth in love we might in all respects grow into him who is the head, Christ." The focus of v. 14 is on the stability and resistance to deception that maturity gives rise to. It shifts metaphors momentarily to picture the church as a ship at sea, located among the waves and winds of heterodox teachings—a metaphor that conveys both the disordered and chaotic nature of the teachings to which the church is exposed and the disastrous consequences that they have for those who succumb to them.

4:15. This image of an immature church, wave-tossed and windblown and vulnerable to schemes of deception, is contrasted immediately in v. 15 with an image of the church's maturity, returning to the body metaphor of vv. 12-13. As in v. 13, the measure and goal toward which the church grows is Christ. In speaking of Christ as "him who is the head," Paul is probably not asking his readers to imagine the anatomical absurdity of a body growing into its head; rather, as Thielman argues, he is intentionally holding the possible Christological developments of the body metaphor in tension: "they are growing 'up to Christ' in the sense of verse 13, but Christ, they must not forget, is still the head of his body, the church" (Thielman 2010, 286).

This growth toward Christlikeness takes place as the members of the body play their part, "speaking the truth in love." It is tempting, given the way Paul's exhortations in 4:17–6:23 repeatedly encourage believers to pattern not just their speech but their behavior on the story of the gospel, to follow those commentators (e.g., Gombis 2010, 151; Hoehner 2002, 565;

Abbott 1897, 123) who argue that we should see in the participle *alētheuontes* not merely the "speaking" of the truth but a comprehensive picture of its performance, in action as well as in word. The way the same word is used elsewhere in Paul's letters (Gal 4:16) and in the LXX (e.g., Gen 20:16; 42:16), however, suggests that it should be understood straightforwardly as a verb of speech.

Although Paul goes on in 4:25 to commend the importance of truth-telling as a basic virtue of the new life believers have learned in Christ, the immediate context here in v. 15, in which the truth-telling of believers is contrasted with the "trickery," "craftiness," and "deception" of the propagators of false doctrine, suggests that it is not just generic truthfulness but the particular truth of the gospel and its entailments that Paul has in view (cf. 1:13; 4:21; 6:14). This truth is to be spoken "in love"—language that is capable of encompassing both the motive for which believers speak the truth and the manner in which it is spoken.

4:16. Finally, in v. 16, Paul draws the threads of the paragraph together, once again combining the images of the body and the building, and emphasizing both the dependence of the body on Christ and the active participation of all its members in the process by which it holds together and is built up: "from whom [i.e., Christ] the whole body, joined and held together through every assisting connection, according to the working in the measure of each individual part, accomplishes the growth of the body for the purpose of building itself up in love."

As the head of the body (v. 15), Christ is the one "from whom" the body accomplishes its growth. But this does not mean the members of the body are merely passive recipients of his grace. Paul goes out of his way to speak of the role played by "every assisting connection" in holding the body together (cf. 4:1-3), and the active involvement of the whole body, "in the measure of each individual part," in its upbuilding (cf. 4:7, 12-15). Read against the background of the earlier uses of "growth" and "building" imagery in the letter (cf. 2:21-22; 4:12-15), the picture in v. 16 implies both the quantitative growth of the building, as new members are added into the structure (2:21-22), and the qualitative growth of the body and its members, as they increasingly manifest in their character and conduct the Christologically defined maturity that Paul has described in the immediately preceding verses (4:12-15). This process of growth and upbuilding takes place "in love" (cf. 4:2, 15)—language that, once again, embraces both the motive and the manner of the actions the believers perform as part of the body's upbuilding.

No longer . . . as the Gentiles (4:17-24)

(17) Therefore I say this and testify in the Lord: that you should no longer walk as the Gentiles walk, in the futility of their mind, (18) being darkened in their understanding, separated from the life of God, because of the ignorance that is in them due to the hardness of their hearts, (19) who, having become despairing, have given themselves over to sensuality for the performing of all uncleanness, in greedy desire. (20) But you: it was not in this way that you learned Christ— (21) if indeed you have heard of him and were taught in him, as the truth is in Jesus, (22) that with regard to the former way of life, you should put off the old humanity which was being corrupted, according to the desires of deception, (23) and be renewed in the spirit of your mind, (24) and put on the new humanity, created according to the pattern of God in the righteousness and holiness of the truth.

4:17. In 4:17 Paul returns to the exhortative path on which he commenced in 4:1-3, before the extended depiction of the church's unity, giftedness, and mutual upbuilding that he provides in 4:4-16 as support for the exhortations in the chapter's first three verses.

While the exhortations of 4:1-3 focus exclusively on the internal dynamics of the relationships within the Christian community, as an expression of the unity to which believers have been called within the "one body" of the church, the longer series of exhortations in 4:17–6:9 combines a continuing emphasis on that theme with a series of reminders that the conduct of believers must differ from that of the pagan culture in which they live and from their own conduct before they came to know Christ. That note is struck, with solemn emphasis, at the outset of this new section of the letter, in 4:17a: "Therefore, I say this and testify in the Lord: that you should no longer walk as the Gentiles walk."

The "therefore" (*oun*) of v. 17 links the exhortation of that verse to the reminders in the preceding paragraphs: since the church is the grace-gifted community described in 4:7-16, growing toward a maturity that is measured by the stature of Christ, the lifestyle of its members cannot possibly continue to imitate the pattern of the surrounding pagan culture in its futility, darkness, and alienation from God.

Paul underlines the earnestness of his appeal by the redundancy of the language he employs in making it ("I say . . . and testify") and by the reminder that he makes the appeal "in the Lord" (cf. his self-depiction in 4:1 as "the prisoner in the Lord"). The content of the appeal ("that you should no longer walk as the Gentiles walk . . .") also recalls the imagery of 4:1, where Paul urged his readers to "walk worthily" of their calling, suggesting that the exhortations in 4:17–6:9 should be read as a continuation and extension of the line of thought commenced in the earlier verse.

Paul's call to his readers to "no longer walk as the Gentiles walk" reflects something of the complexity with which their collective identity has been constructed across the preceding chapters of the letter. They are, on the one hand, Gentiles, and Paul can still address them as such (2:11; 3:1; cf. 3:6, 8). But they are also, according to 2:1-22, a community whose story includes the radical discontinuities of having been "raised . . . up" (2:6) into a new life that God has prepared for them to walk in (2:10) and incorporated by God into the "one new person" that he has created in Christ (2:15). More than that: the surprising discontinuities in their story turn out, in retrospect, to have been the outworking of divine plans and purposes that are older even than the world itself (1:4-5; 3:9-11). Their continuing identity as Gentiles is now, therefore, something they are to view as being immersed within the larger and deeper identity that has been granted to them by their adoption as sons and daughters of God (1:5) and members of his household (2:19). It is those realities, rather than the formative influence of the cultures into which they were born, that should now determine the way they "walk" in their everyday conduct (cf. 2:1-3, 10).

To emphasize the urgency and importance of this point, Paul paints for his readers in vv. 17b-19 a dark and sobering picture of the way in which "the Gentiles walk": ". . . in the futility of their mind, being darkened in their understanding, separated from the life of God because of the ignorance that is in them due to the hardness of their hearts; who, having become despairing, have given themselves over to sensuality for the performing of all uncleanness, in greedy desire."

The picture that Paul paints here, like the similar depictions of the Gentile way of life elsewhere in his letters, should not be read as if it were an empirical report on the day-by-day behavior of the inhabitants of the Greco-Roman world or an exhaustive account of all that could be said about their beliefs and dispositions. The same Paul who paints the broad (and dark) brushstrokes of Rom 1:18-32 is also capable of the light and shade and careful nuance to be found, for example, in Rom 2:12-16 and 13:1-7 or (according to Luke's account) in Acts 17:22-31. What Paul is offering to his readers here in Eph 4:17b-19 is a deliberately stylized and theologically interpretive portrayal of what was characteristically and definitively pagan about the Gentile way of life, focusing on the mutually reinforcing interactions of idolatry, immorality, and misdirected desire.

He begins, accordingly, with reference in v. 17b to "the futility (*mataiotēs*) of their mind"—language that evokes the way Second Temple Jewish literature (e.g., LXX Jer 2:15; 8:19; Esth 4:17p; 3 Macc 6:11 cf. Rom 1:21; Acts 14:15) spoke of pagan idols as *mataioi*, i.e., as inauthentic and useless objects of worship. In ascribing this futility to "their mind" (cf. Rom 1:21), Paul signals that he has in mind not only the ritual practices of idol-worship, in and of themselves, but the total mindset that they express and reinforce—both the "threads of pagan religiousness" and the whole cultural fabric woven around them (cf. Rowe 2009, 51).

4:18. The "futility" of pagan religion and its pervasive effect on the mindset of the culture constructed around it are described in v. 18 as having their source in the ignorance and alienation of Gentiles outside of Christ: "being darkened in their understanding, separated from the life of God because of the ignorance that is in them due to the hardness of their hearts." Syntactically speaking, the participle "being" (*ontes*) probably does double duty, connecting periphrastically with the perfect passive participle "darkened" (*eskotōmenoi*) and implying a similar relationship with the participle "separated" (*apēllotriōmenoi*) in the following clause. The effect is to present the two participial clauses as functioning in parallel (Best 1997a, 418–19) and the whole complex of ignorance and alienation described in v. 18 as the reason the Gentiles conduct their lives according to the futile mind depicted in the preceding verse.

The passive construction, "darkened in their understanding," leaves unstated the agent by whose doing the pagans' understanding has been darkened. Paul is certainly capable of speaking, as he does elsewhere, about the role played by the will and action of God in hardening human hearts (Rom 9:18), making the wisdom of the world foolish (1 Cor 1:20), and handing people over to a debased mind (Rom 1:28). Here, however, his earlier depiction of the pagan predicament in 2:1-3 would suggest that the principal agent in view—to the extent that any agent is implied at all—is the spirit who has earlier been described in 2:2 as being "now at work among the sons of disobedience" (cf. the reference in 6:12 to "the cosmic powers of this present darkness"; note also the descriptions of the blinding work of "the god of this age" in 2 Cor 4:4 and "the spirit of anger" in T. Dan 2:4).

The agent of the following phrase, "separated from the life of God," is left similarly unstated. The earlier use of the same word in 2:12 places the readers' former alienation from God within a cluster of deprivations, the majority of which are most naturally taken as the consequences of divine preterition. The same idea may be in view here, though the double-barreled causal construction that follows ("because of the ignorance that is in them due to the hardness of their hearts") leaves open the question of whether their separation from God is to be viewed as the natural consequence of their ignorance and hard-heartedness or as a divinely imposed punishment for those same conditions of heart and mind. The absence of any explicit indication from Paul in either of these directions may be a clue that the choice is a false one: in the closely similar description of the fallen human predicament that Paul offers in Rom 1:17-25, the handing over of men and women to the natural consequences of their rejection of the truth is precisely the form that the revelation of God's wrath takes.

The fact that the "ignorance" (*agnoia*) Paul attributes to the Gentile mind is said to be "due to the hardness of their hearts" suggests that what he has in mind is not an innocent lack of knowledge but a culpable rejection of the truth, in line with his diagnosis in Rom 1:18-21. The "hardness of heart" from which this rejection of the truth derives is (like the "hardening" of Israel that Paul speaks of in Romans 11) primarily a way of speaking about the stubborn rejection of God and his messengers.

4:19. Having dug down in v. 18 into the causes of Gentile alienation from God, Paul returns in v. 19 to its consequences, with a further depiction of the Gentile mind and lifestyle: "who, having become despairing, have given themselves over to sensuality for the performing of all uncleanness, in greedy desire." The description of Gentiles as "having become despairing (*apēlgēkotes*)" uses a word that most English versions (and most commentators) translate as "having become callous," or "having lost all sensitivity." While it is true that the word can on occasion be used with this meaning (e.g., Polybius, *Hist.* 16.12.7, which could be interpreted in this way), in the great majority of instances the word implies something more like despair than insensitivity (e.g., Polybius, *Hist.* 1.35.5; Cassius Dio, *Hist. Rom.* 48.37.6). Given the way Paul has earlier emphasized the absence of hope as a defining feature of Gentile existence outside of Christ (2:12), and its presence as a key feature of the mindset he prays for in his readers (1:18), there is good reason to give *apēlgēkotes* its usual meaning here and translate it not as "desensitized" but as "despairing" (cf. Thielman 2010, 299).

In the absence of any secure hope beyond this world and this lifetime, Paul goes on to assert, the Gentiles have "given themselves over to sensuality for the performing of all uncleanness, in greedy desire." The word "sensuality" (*aselgeia*), to which Paul describes the Gentiles as having abandoned themselves, is frequently used in the Second Temple Jewish literature to refer to unrestrained sexual behavior (e.g., Philo, *Moses* 1.305), but it can also embrace a wider range of immoral pursuits (e.g., 3 Macc 2:25-26; T. Jud. 23.1), as can the "greedy desire" (*pleonexia*) with which the sentence concludes (cf. Luke 12:15). A broad reading of this sort may well be implied here, given the way Paul connects the sensuality and desire in view with the performing of "all" uncleanness. The Gentile lifestyle Paul has in mind is characterized, on this reading, not merely by its unrestrained sexuality but also, more comprehensively, by its insatiable quest for experiences and possessions that will provide immediate gratification, filling the void left by the absence of any well-founded hope.

4:20. In vv. 20-24 Paul draws a sharp line between this way of life and the new life to which believers have been called in Christ. The "but you" (*hymeis de*) with which v. 20 commences is doubly emphasized, given prominence by both the inclusion of the redundant "you" and its position at the start of the sentence. What is in view here is not merely a list of instructions about how to live but a new identity that is to be manifested in that lifestyle. What marks out the "you" to whom the letter is addressed from the "Gentiles" whose way of life they must no longer imitate is the fact that they have "learned Christ," and that they have done so in a manner ("not in this way") that is fundamentally incompatible with the way of life they once followed.

The expression Paul employs here to describe the readers' conversion and catechesis ("[the] way that you learned Christ") is a somewhat unusual one. It is, as most commentators point out, difficult to find analogous examples within the ancient Greek literature in which the verb *manthanō* ("learn") is used with a personal object, as is the case here. Perhaps the closest analogy, as Thielman argues (Thielman 2010, 300), can be found in the philosophers' notion of "learning God" (e.g., Chion, *Ep.* 16.6, 8)—a pursuit that involved not only the acquisition of theoretical understanding but also a transformation of values and affections: "receiving instruction on the proper veneration of righteousness and all the other virtues" (16.6) and "coming to despise . . . such things as ambition, wealth and the like" (16.8, as translated in Morales 2011).

In a somewhat similar manner for the readers of Ephesians, "learn[ing] Christ" involved not only becoming acquainted with a body of information about him but also being taught a new way of life. More than that: it meant the embrace of a whole new identity, as Paul goes on to stress in vv. 21-24.

4:21. The *ei ge* ("if indeed") that commences v. 21 functions in a similar manner to the way the same expression functions in 3:2—Paul is underlining the fact that the assertion he has made in v. 20 depends for its validity on the assumption that the readers have indeed been converted and catechized in the way that he goes on to describe. To have "learned Christ" involves both having "heard about him" (the accusative case of *auton*, "him," suggests that what Paul has in mind is not listening to Christ but hearing about him) and having been "taught in him"; this is the case because (as Paul reminds his readers) "the truth is in Jesus." The way Paul joins together the simplicity and kerygmatic focus of "hear[ing] about Christ" with the ongoing process of being "taught [the truth] in him" has similarities to the account Paul gives of his ministry in Col 1:28. The content of Paul's proclamation, as he reminds the Colossians in v. 28a, can be summed up in the one word, "him" (i.e., Christ); and yet, as he goes on to say in v. 28b, the content and entailments of that proclamation require a lifetime of ceaseless labors, "warning everyone and teaching everyone in all wisdom," since "all the treasures of wisdom and knowledge" are hidden in Christ (2:3).

Here, the content that Paul assumes the readers of Ephesians have been taught in Christ is summed up in a threefold formulation: "that with regard to the former way of life, you should put off the old humanity which was being corrupted according to the desires of deception, and that you should be renewed in the spirit of your mind, and that you should put on the new humanity, created according to the pattern of God in the righteousness and holiness of the truth."

4:22-24. The first and third parts of the formulation, in vv. 22 and 24, employ a clothing metaphor that depicts the readers as having been taught to "put off the old humanity" and "put on the new humanity." At the broadest, most general level of the metaphor's significance, it is not difficult to find a background for it in the life experience and cultural imaginary of the original readers. Arnold, for example, is content to find the background of the metaphor simply in "the daily experience of taking off and putting on clothing" (Arnold 2010, 287), and Sellin offers a list of examples of change-of-clothing motifs ranging from the Hymn of the Pearl (Acts of Thomas 108.9–15; 111.62, 72–3; 112.76–113.105) to the parable of the prodigal son, the story of Puss in Boots, and the wearing of designer-label clothes (Sellin 2008, 361). As a number of commentators grant, however (e.g., Lincoln 1990, 284; Dahl 2000, 392; Best 1998, 431), the particular use to which the change-of-clothing metaphor is applied here in vv. 22 and 24 (i.e., putting off and putting on a *person* or a *role*) is far less easy to find paralleled among the various kinds of clothing metaphors and customs that are typically cited as part of the background against which Paul's readers would have interpreted his language.

Among the various possibilities that have been proposed (cf. the survey in Starling 2019), the most promising candidate for a background against which Paul would have expected his readers to interpret the "putting off" and "putting on" metaphors of vv. 22 and 24 is the theatrical conventions of character and costume and the way they functioned as a metaphor in Greco-Roman discourse for transformation of identity or role (cf. Dionysius of Halicarnassus, *Ant. Rom.* 9.5; Libanius, *Ep.* 1048.2; Maximus of Tyre, *Diss.* 1.1, 4; Lucian, *Pisc.* 33). For the original readers of Ephesians, immersed as they were within a culture in which the theater was so prominent an institution and its practices so widely adopted as a metaphor for life, the conventions of the theater would have been an obvious background for Paul's "putting off" and "putting on" metaphors, without any necessary implication that what Paul had in mind was merely a matter of outward appearance or theatrical pretense. Believers are being reminded that their conversion involved them being clothed in the costume of the new humanity—the part that had been assigned for them to play within the drama of God's saving work in the world—and, in so doing, assuming a genuinely new identity (cf. Vanhoozer 2005, 363–97).

The "old humanity," which believers had been taught to put off, is described in v. 22 as "being corrupted (*phtheiromenos*) according to the desires of deception." The process of corruption that Paul describes is an ongoing one, tending inexorably toward the ruin of the self and the decay of human community (the latter idea implied by the corporate nature of the "new humanity" as it is depicted elsewhere in the letter, especially 2:15). The "desires of deception" (*epithymiai tēs apatēs*) that bring about this corrupting effect are presumably the same as the "sensuality" and "greedy desire" to which Paul has already referred in 4:19. Here, as there, Paul uses language that can frequently (e.g., *apatē* in Jdt 9:10, 13; *phtheirō* in Josephus, *Ant.* 4.252; *apatē* and *phtheirō* in 4 Macc 18:8) be used to refer to illicit sexual desires and their ruinous effects but need not be restricted to this meaning alone (Thielman 2010, 304–305). Although Paul is elsewhere (e.g., 1 Cor 15:42-54; 2 Cor 5:2-4) capable of using a similar clothing metaphor to describe the future, ontological transformation of the corruptible into the incorruptible, his interest here (in line with the focus throughout 4:17–6:9 on the new way of life in which believers are to walk) is on the present transformation of identity and lifestyle. Accordingly, in v. 22, he concentrates the attention of his readers on the way they were taught to put off the old humanity "with regard to the former way of life."

The "new humanity" (*ton kainon anthrōpon*) that believers have been taught to put on is described in v. 24 as having been "created (*ktisthenta*) according to the pattern of God in the righteousness and holiness of the truth." The language that Paul uses (both *ton kainon anthrōpon* and *ktisthenta*) is reminiscent of his earlier descriptions of believers as having been "created in Christ Jesus for good works" (2:10) and the purpose of Christ to "make . . . one new person" in himself, in the reconciled community of the church (2:15).

This new identity, with which believers are to clothe themselves, is described by Paul has having been created "according to the pattern of God"—language that suggests a correspondence in character and conduct between the lives of believers (and the culture of the church as a whole) and the character and action of God (cf. 5:1-2, 9). At the core of this correspondence between God and his people is the "righteousness and uprightness of the truth"—a collocation of concepts that is similar to the "goodness and righteousness and truth" in which Paul goes on in 5:9 to exhort the readers to walk, as "children of light." The image of believers being clothed with God's own righteousness recurs in 6:14, where the image of the "breastplate of righteousness" draws on the depiction of the battle-dress of YHWH in Isa 59:17.

The combination of "righteousness and uprightness (*hosiotēs*)" recalls Old Testament descriptions of the character and conduct of YHWH (e.g., LXX Deut 32:4; Ps 144:17); the same combination is also common in the Hellenistic philosophical literature (e.g., Arrian, *Epict. diss.* 3.26.32; Plato, *Apol.* 35d; *Theaet.* 176b), where it can be used variously to refer to the divine character, the proper conduct of men and women, or the correspondence that should existent between them (cf. Thielman 2010, 307). Although Paul would undoubtedly have assumed a significant overlap between the former understanding of righteousness and uprightness and the latter, the focus of his interest here is on the particular version of righteousness and uprightness that is "according to the pattern of God" and corresponds to "the truth"—i.e., the truth that is "in Jesus" (v. 21).

Between the putting off of v. 22 and the putting on of v. 24 is the reminder in v. 23 that the readers were taught in Christ to "be renewed in the spirit of your mind." Although the other uses of the word *pneuma* elsewhere in Ephesians all refer to a personal, spiritual being—either the Holy Spirit or (in 2:2) "the spirit that is now at work among the sons of disobedience"—the most natural reading of the genitive construction "of your mind" that follows the word in this instance is to take the phrase as referring to the (human) spirit that belongs to the mind and is the center of a person's self-knowledge and identity (cf. 1 Cor 2:11). The combined effect of v. 23 and the images of putting off and putting on in vv. 22 and 24 is to depict a transformation of identity that includes both the outward and visible change of allegiance signified by the clothing metaphors and the inward and ongoing renewal that corresponds to that change. Christian character, in other words, is constructed both from the outside in and from the inside out (cf. Starling 2019).

As beloved children (4:25–5:2)

(25) Therefore, putting off falsehood, speak the truth, each with his or her neighbor, for we are members of one another. (26) Be angry and do not sin; do not let the sun go down on your wrath, (27) or give a place to the devil. (28) Let the one who steals no longer steal, but let them labor, producing with their own hands what is good, so that they might have something to share with the one who has need. (29) Let not any bad speech come out of your mouth, but if there is something good for the building up of [the person who has] need, [let it be spoken], in order that it might give grace to those who hear. (30) And do not grieve the Holy Spirit of God, with whom you were sealed for the day of redemption. (31) Let all bitterness and wrath and anger and yelling and slander be removed from you, with all malice. (32) Instead, be kind to one another, compassionate, forgiving one another, just as God in Christ forgave you. (5:1) So then be imitators of God, as beloved children, (2) and walk in love, just as Christ loved us and gave himself for us, as an offering and sacrifice to God, as a fragrant aroma.

4:25. The summons in 4:17-19 to "no longer walk as the Gentiles walk" and the reminder in 4:20-24 of the way the readers were taught in Christ to "put off the old humanity" and "put on the new humanity" are followed in 4:25–5:2 by a series of brief admonitions, focusing on particular instances of the transformation of character and conduct that was described in general terms in 4:17-24.

The specific admonitions in 4:25-32 are strung together as a series of five clusters (v. 25; vv. 26-27; v. 28; vv. 29-30; vv. 31-32), without any conjunctions joining each new cluster to the one that precedes it:

> v. 25: Therefore, putting off falsehood, speak the truth, each with his or her neighbor, for we are members of one another.
> vv. 26-27: Be angry and do not sin; do not let the sun go down on your wrath, or give a place to the devil.
> v. 28: Let the one who steals no longer steal, but let them labor, producing with their own hands what is good, so that they might have something to share with the one who is in need.
> vv. 29-30: Let not any bad speech come out of your mouth, but if there is something good for the building up of [the person who has] need, [let it be spoken], in order that it might give grace to those who hear. And do not grieve the Holy Spirit of God, with whom you were sealed for the day of redemption.
> vv. 31-32: Let all bitterness and wrath and anger and yelling and slander be removed from you, with all malice. Instead, be kind to one another, compassionate, forgiving one another, just as God in Christ forgave you.

A loosely structured pattern can be seen in four of the five clusters, in which a negative admonition to avoid a certain behavior is followed by a positive admonition to embrace its opposite, and a reason to motivate obedience. The main exception to this pattern is in vv. 26-27, where the positive admonition ("be angry") comes first, and the emphasis falls on the three negative admonitions that follow (the last of which appears to take the place of the motivating reasons that conclude the majority of the other admonition clusters in the list). A partial exception, of a similar nature, can also be see in v. 30, which takes the form of a negative admonition but is joined by the conjunction "and" (*kai*) to the preceding verse and seems to perform the function of providing an extra motivation, in addition to the one given in v. 29b, for the admonitions in v. 29a (Arnold 2010, 305–306; Lincoln 1990, 307–308).

The "therefore" that commences v. 25 signals the connection between the specifics of these admonitions and the generalities of the previous one, as does the clothing metaphor implied by the picture of "putting off" falsehood (cf. vv. 22, 24). The positive admonition in v. 25b ("speak the truth, each with his or her neighbor") corresponds almost verbatim with the wording of LXX Zech 8:16 ("speak the truth, each to his or her neighbor"). There, as here in 4:25-32, the admonition stands at the head of a string of similar imperatives (cf. Zech 8:16-17), and the salvation oracles that precede it speak of the restoration of Israel and the return of YHWH to Jerusalem in terms that are similar to the second exodus and end-of-exile prophecies that are cited and echoed elsewhere in Ephesians. It is entirely possible that some among Paul's hearers would have been able (either of their own accord or with the help of others) to detect the presence of the scriptural quotation and its source in Zechariah and to discern its applicability to them within the pattern of typological correspondences implied in chapters 1–3 (cf. Starling 2014b). The significance of this possibility for interpretation should not be overstated, however; Paul's seamless integration of the words from Zechariah into the fabric of his own admonitions, without any citation formula to mark the quotation or identify its source, would suggest that he is not placing any great reliance on the ability of his readers to make the connection between his words and their origins in Zechariah. The meaning of his words can still be easily determined without reference to their original context, and their force derives more from the explicit warrants that Paul supplies (i.e., the "therefore" that links v. 25 to the preceding verses, and the immediately following reminder that "we are members of one another") than from their authority as words of Scripture.

Although the earlier statements about "truth" in Ephesians (cf. 1:13; 4:15, 21, 24) are probably best taken as references to the particular truth of the gospel and its entailments, the ethical focus of the immediate context here in 4:25-32 suggests that in this instance what Paul has in mind is not the truth of the gospel but truth-telling more generally (and that *to pseudos* in v. 25a should, correspondingly, be taken as a generic reference to "falsehood" rather than as a particular reference to false teaching as "the lie"). The "neighbor" to whom the truth is to be told is, according to the rationale supplied in v. 25c, the fellow believer with whom the speaker is united as "members of one another." This does not imply that Paul is encouraging his readers to think that they can lie with impunity to unbelievers, but it does suggest that his focus, even here in 4:17–6:9, is on the communal culture of the church rather than simply the ethical conduct of the individual Christian.

4:26-27. In vv. 26-27 the focus shifts from truth-telling to anger: "Be angry and do not sin; do not let the sun go down on your wrath, or give a place to the devil." As is the case in v. 25a, the words of the opening admonition ("Be angry and do not sin") derive from Scripture, corresponding precisely in this case to those of LXX Ps 4:5. Here, as in the previous verse, Paul does nothing to mark the presence of the scriptural quotation, though in this case there is perhaps a greater likelihood that hearers of the letter may have been familiar with the words and aware of their source through liturgical use of the psalm from which they are taken (cf. 5:19).

Commentators differ over the question of whether the opening imperative ("be angry") should be taken as a command (e.g., Arnold 2010, 300–302; cf. Wallace 1996, 491–92) or as a concession or condition ("if you are angry . . .") (e.g., Best 1998, 449–50). On the strictly grammatical question of whether the word can properly be translated as a "conditional imperative," Wallace is probably correct in his arguments against the applicability of the syntactical parallels that are sometimes alleged in texts such as John 1:46. But the larger context of the verse (in which the center of gravity is located not in the opening imperative but in the three prohibitions that follow) and the paragraph (which goes on in v. 31 to forbid "all bitterness and wrath and anger and yelling and slander") makes it difficult to sustain a reading such as Wallace's, in which the imperative at the start of the verse is taken as a strong and straightforward command to righteous anger, in situations when it is warranted by the sinful provocation of others. A more likely interpretation, given the emphases of the verse and the paragraph, is one that retains the form of the imperative but reads it as functioning principally to "set the stage" for the prohibitions that follow (Thielman 2010, 313).

The prohibition that follows ("and do not sin") is unpacked in vv. 26b-27: "do not let the sun go down on your wrath, or give a place to the devil." If we are to interpret Paul's elaboration on the words of the psalm on the assumption that he is aware of its original context (and may well have expected at least some of his readers to have been similarly aware), then the primary background in which his admonition against "let[ting] the sun god down on your wrath" should be understood is the immediately following lines of the psalm. There, the psalm's addressees are not urged to hurry out and pursue immediately resolution of the conflicts they have with those who have wronged them, but to "speak in your hearts, and on your beds be pricked" (presumably with contrition for their own sins), with the result that they "sacrifice a sacrifice of righteousness, and hope in the LORD" (LXX Ps 4:5-6, NETS). If it is this image of the reflective and contrite nighttime meditations urged in the psalm that stands behind Paul's admonition in v. 26b, then the *parorgismos* he is speaking of is almost certainly the "wrath" of his readers (cf. LXX 4 Kgdms 19:3; Jer 21:5) rather than the "provocation" (cf. LXX 3 Kgdms 15:30; 4 Kgdms 23:26; Neh 9:18, 26) that has occasioned it (contra Wallace 1996, 492), and the action he is urging is not the speedy resolution of the grievance but the choice to lay aside anger in the reflections on it that pass through one's mind after the sun has gone down.

The final prohibition of the cluster, in v. 27 ("[and do not] give a place to the devil") probably functions primarily as a motivation or warrant for the admonitions in the preceding verse. To brood on one's anger, refusing to lay it aside and reflect with contrition on one's own sins, is to open the door to the devil, granting him an opportunity to further his schemes for fostering division and disharmony among God's people (cf. 3:10; 4:2-3; 6:11).

4:28. The third cluster of admonitions, in v. 28, addresses the interrelated issues of theft, work, and the sharing of possessions. In form, it returns to the pattern established in v. 25, with a prohibition ("Let the one who steals no longer steal"), a contrasting, positive admonition ("but let them labor, producing with their own hands what is good"), and a concluding motivation ("so that they might have something to share with the one who is in need"). The "one who steals" is probably neither a slave (since slaves were hardly in a position to comply with the following injunction to find themselves some honest work to do with their hands as a source of income to share with others) nor a wealthy landowner (since the wealthy would not have needed to seek employment of this sort). The most likely scenario presupposed is that of the day laborers, tradespeople and shopkeepers, who would have been tempted to find easier profits in theft than in the hard work of their regular occupation (cf. Best 1998, 453).

In place of stealing, the positive admonition in v. 28b urges that the thief is to "labor, producing with their own hands what is good." Paul's picture of the reformed thief working with his or her "own hands" should not be read over-literally, as if the distinction he had in mind were between manual labor and other, less physical kinds of work; the more likely distinction that he wishes to stress is between using the hands to steal (cf. Pseudo-Phocylides, 153–54) and using them to do honest and productive work ("what is good"), or between dishonest exploitation of the work that other people's hands have done and honest labor (with one's "own" hands) to earn an income. Nevertheless, the verb "labor" (*kopiaō*) that he chooses to describe the work he has in mind still implies toil and effort and is frequently used in contexts of arduousness and exhaustion (e.g., Matt 11:28; Luke 5:5; John 4:6; 1 Cor 4:12), and Paul's words, along with his personal example as he describes it elsewhere, imply the dignity and value of labor of that sort.

The purpose that this labor is to serve is not only the intrinsic value of the "good" that the work produces or the ability, through the income that is earned, to provide for the worker's own needs; the end in view, according to v. 28b, is also to "have something to share with the one who is in need." The verb *metadidōmi* ("share") can sometimes be used to refer to the distribution of alms as an act of kindness to a stranger or dependent, but it can also be used to refer to "sharing" in the stricter sense of the word, within a relationship of mutual belonging and reciprocity (e.g., Rom 1:11-12; 12:8). It is the latter sense that is probably in view here, given the intra-communal context that is stated explicitly in vv. 25 and 32 and implied throughout the whole paragraph.

4:29. The fourth cluster of admonitions, in vv. 29-30, returns the focus to vices and virtues of speech (cf. v. 25). Once again, following the pattern established in v. 25, Paul commences with a negative admonition ("Let not any bad speech come out of your mouth"), follows it with a positive, contrasting one ("but if there is something good for the building up of [the person who has] need, [let it be spoken]"), and concludes with a motivating reason ("in order that it might give grace to those who hear") and a further command ("and do not grieve the Holy Spirit of God, with whom you were sealed for the day of redemption"), which is probably intended to function as an additional motivation for the admonitions of v. 29.

The word *sapros* ("bad") can be used in a literal sense to refer to objects that are rotten (e.g., Antiphanes, *Frag.* 218.4) or useless (e.g., Herm. *Sim.* 9.5–6), and its figurative senses range widely from faulty teachings (e.g., Epictetus, *Diatr.* 3.22.61) to immoral conduct (e.g., Menander, *Mon.* 722) and disingenuous speech (e.g., Marcus Aurelius, *Meditations* 11.15). The generality implied by "any (*pas*) bad speech" and the broad terms in which its opposite is described in v. 29b ("something good for the building up of [the person who has] need") suggest that it would be arbitrary to narrow down the range of possible ways in which speech can be "bad" to a single variety, such as the crassness and obscenity that are dealt with specifically in 5:4 (contra Arnold 2010, 303–304).

The positive, contrasting picture of "something good (*tis agathos*) for the building up of [the person who has] need (*pros oikodomēn tēs chreias*)" echoes the terminology of the preceding verse (*agathos . . . chreia*), suggesting that what Paul has in mind is something roughly equivalent in the realm of speech to what was encouraged in v. 28 in the realm of money and material possessions. The generality and indefiniteness of the expression "something good" (*tis agathos*) implies a wide range of ways in which words can be used constructively and generously, and the analogy between vv. 28 and 29 suggests that it would probably be a mistake to restrict the scope of the "grace" referred to in the purpose clause at the end of the verse to a narrowly defined notion of divine, saving grace (cf. Lincoln 1990, 306). Nevertheless, the image of "building up" the person who has need, read in the light of the earlier uses of the image in 2:22 and 4:12, 16, is a reminder that Paul's understanding of what constitutes the "good" of the fellow believer presupposes their membership within the community of Christ's people, and his notion of the growth and upbuilding of the body is directed not merely toward its material well-being but also, and supremely, toward its unity, maturity, and Christlikeness (cf. 4:12-16; 1 Cor 10:23-33).

4:30. The admonition in v. 30 ("and do not grieve the Holy Spirit of God, with whom you were sealed for the day of redemption")—linked as it is with a *kai* ("and") to the preceding verse, and lacking anything like the internal structure of the other admonition clusters in vv. 25-32—is probably not a free-standing command in its own right but an additional reason to motivate readers in their obedience to the admonitions of v. 29. As was the case in the earlier admonitions of vv. 25 and 26, Paul's wording draws on the language of Scripture, though in this case the verbal correspondence between his words and their source in Isa 63:10 ("they rebelled and grieved his holy spirit"; NRSV) is far from exact. Paul's "do not grieve" (*mē lypeite*) is closer to the sense of the MT's "they . . . grieved" (*'iṣṣᵉbû*) than it is to the LXX's "they . . . provoked" (*parōxynan*), suggesting either that he was working from a version of the Greek that is no longer extant or that he had the Hebrew original in mind as he composed his own paraphrase.

In all three versions (Paul's paraphrase here in v. 30 and the Hebrew and Greek versions of the text he is alluding to) the picture of "the Holy

Spirit of God" (or "your Holy Spirit," in the original) being "grieved" or "provoked" is a strikingly personal use of language. Although the clause that follows (*en hō esphragisthēte* . . .) is best understood, in light of 1:14, as a depiction of the Holy Spirit as instrument ("with which/whom") rather than as agent ("by whom . . ."), the intensely personal nature of the image in v. 30a makes it clear that the instrumental metaphor in the second half of the verse should not be read in a depersonalizing fashion; it is the *personal* presence of the Spirit—the Holy Spirit of God himself, who can be rebelled against and provoked and grieved—that constitutes the seal that marks believers as belonging to God and identifies them as the people whom he will vindicate and deliver on "the day of redemption."

The connection between the "bad speech" of v. 29 and the admonition against grieving the Holy Spirit in v. 30 probably lies in the close association between the Spirit and Christian speech (cf. Eph 5:18-19; 6:17; 1 Thess 5:18-19; also CD 5.11–12; Lincoln 1990, 307–308). The consequence of Israel's "griev[ing]" of the Spirit is depicted in Isa 63:10 in catastrophic terms: "Therefore he became their enemy; he himself fought against them." Paul's description of the Holy Spirit of God in v. 30b as the one "with whom you were sealed for the day of redemption" hints at a similar catastrophe: if the Spirit is the one whose presence with God's people is the mark and seal of their covenant relationship with God and the guarantee of their future inheritance (cf. 1:13-14), then to "grieve" the Spirit is to risk repudiating their very salvation (cf. 1 Cor 10:1-13). Paul does not dwell here on that dark possibility, or even state it explicitly; nor does he speculate on the metaphysical and theological issues concerning divine foreknowledge and predestination that are raised by the notion that the same Spirit who is the "guarantee" of believers' inheritance (1:14) might be so grieved as to become their enemy. It is worth noting, too, that the larger context of Isaiah 63 suggests a stubborn hopefulness that the same God who has turned and fought against Israel will eventually "turn back" (v. 17) and comfort them. But it is difficult nonetheless to avoid the implication of v. 30 that there is something at least hypothetically perilous lurking behind the admonition of v. 30, rather than merely an altruistic concern for the Spirit's emotional well-being (Witherington 2007, 301–302). Those whom God has foreknown and predestined will, one assumes, heed the warning and so be preserved from experiencing its fulfilment, but its full weight should be felt, nonetheless (cf. 1 Cor 10:12).

4:31. The final admonition cluster, in vv. 31-32, concerns issues of malice, compassion, and forgiveness. In keeping with the general pattern to be found in almost all the admonition clusters of vv. 25-32, it opens with a negative admonition ("Let all bitterness and wrath and anger and yelling and slander be removed from you, with all malice"), follows it with a contrasting, positive admonition ("but be kind to one another, compassionate, forgiving one another"), and concludes by reminding the readers of the forgiveness of God ("just as God in Christ forgave you"), which functions as both a pattern and a motive for their own.

Although the Greek and Hellenistic Jewish moral-philosophical literature could, on occasion, include attempts to parse out the lexicon of anger into a series of finely calibrated gradations (e.g., Chrysippus, *Frag.* 394–97; Ps.-Phoc., *Sent.* 63–64), the sequence Paul constructs here corresponds to none of their scales or progressions, nor is there anything in the context of vv. 31-32 to suggest that this sort of taxonomy is what he has in mind (cf. Thielman 2010, 318–19; contra Schnackenburg 1991, 211). The effect, rather, is simply one of accumulation, accented by the repeated "all . . . all" (*pasa . . . pasē*). Although Thielman is correct to point out (Thielman 2010, 319) that at least five of the six words Paul uses can be used on occasion to refer to verbal expressions of anger and hostility (for *pikria*, "bitterness," see Rom 3:14; LXX Ps 9:28; for *thymos*, "wrath," and *orgē*, "anger," see Pss. Sol. 2.23), if the words are taken in their commonest sense then the list appears to embrace a mixture of both malicious dispositions and the kind of "yelling" (*kraugē*) and "slander" (*blasphēmia*) that proceed from them. All of these things are to be "removed" (*arthētō*), language that recalls the clothing imagery of vv. 22, 24, and 25.

4:32. In place of all attitudes and utterances of this sort, Paul urges his readers to "be kind to one another, compassionate, forgiving one another." The word "kind" (*chrēstos*) echoes Paul's earlier reference to the "kindness" (*chrēstotēs*) that God has shown to believers (2:7; cf. Rom 2:4; 11:12; Titus 3:4). Like the word "compassionate" (*eusplanchnos*), it refers primarily to an inward disposition but is also frequently used so as to imply or include reference to the actions in which that disposition is made manifest. The former word is common and can be used with reference to a wide range of situations in which moral goodness and benevolence are displayed. The latter is less common and tends to be used in contexts that imply either a compassionate response to misery and need (e.g., T. Zeb. 9.7.2) or a merciful refusal to punish or exact revenge for a wrong that has been done (e.g., T. Sim. 4.4.2; Pr Man 7). It is probably this latter sense that is in the front of Paul's mind here, given the conflict situations implied in v. 31 and the focus on forgiveness in the remainder of v. 32.

The two references to forgiveness in the second half of v. 32 ("forgiving one another, just as God in Christ forgave you") make repeated use of a verb, *charizomai*, that can sometimes be used—even in the absence of a direct object—to mean "grant a favor" or "show grace" (e.g., Diodorus Siculus, *Bib. hist.* 14.11.1; Josephus, *Ant.* 17.222). Here, however, in light of the preceding context and in line with the similar exhortation in Col 3:13, it almost certainly carries the sense of "forgive," as it frequently does in Pauline usage (cf. 2 Cor 2:7, 10; 12:13; Col 2:13). The forgiveness of God, granted "in Christ" (probably, like the "in Christ" phrases of 1:3-14, a depiction of Christ as the metaphorical sphere in which the forgiveness of God is accomplished and experienced), is both the pattern believers are to imitate in their own forgiveness and a motive for them to do so. It is also, by extension, a motive for all of the preceding exhortations in vv. 31-32a.

5:1. Finally, in 5:1-2, Paul brings the paragraph to a close with a summary exhortation that draws together the threads of all the admonitions in the preceding verses: "So then be imitators of God, as beloved children, and walk in love, just as Christ loved us and gave himself for us, as an offering and sacrifice to God, as a fragrant aroma."

The conjunction *oun* ("So then") is probably not functioning here in a strictly inferential manner, though there is a logical relation of this sort that could be found between the picture of God's forgiveness in v. 32b and the summons to imitate God in 5:1-2. Given the broad and general nature of 5:1-2 and its position at the end of the paragraph, the conjunction is best read as marking vv. 1-2 as a summary conclusion of 4:25–5:2 (cf. Matt 5:48; 7:12; 1 Cor 10:31).

The command to "be imitators of God" recalls Paul's earlier reminder to his readers in 4:24 that the new humanity they were taught to put on is one that has been created "according to the pattern of God" (*kata theon*). The idea of being an "imitator" (*mimētēs*) of God can be found in the Greek philosophical literature (e.g., Sthenidas, *Frag.* 188.2; cf. Epictetus, *Diatr.* 2.14.12–13), and, although the language of "imitating God" cannot be found within the LXX, the notion of the ethical imitation of the character and action of YHWH is nonetheless implied (e.g., Gen 18:19; Lev 19:2; Deut 10:17-19; Pss 111–112; cf. Wright 2006, 363–67; Hood 2013, 19–40), and the Hellenistic Jewish literature makes frequent and unabashed use of the language of imitation to express it (e.g., T. Ash. 4.3; Philo, *Spec. Laws* 4.73).

While the language of *mimēsis* was frequently employed within the discourse of philosophy and moral instruction, it was equally at home in the world of the theater. At times (for example in Plato's famous discussion of the limits that should circumscribe theatrical performance in the ideal city) the two horizons converge and the theatrical background that lies behind some at least of the moral-philosophical discourse is laid bare (see especially Plato, *Resp.* 388a–388d; 394b–398b). A similar possibility is likely here, given the repeated uses of the costume metaphor as a structuring device in 4:22-24, 25, 32. The primary background of Paul's language here in 5:1, however, is not the imitation of a character by an actor but the imitation of a parent by a child, as he goes on to make explicit in v. 1b ("as beloved children"). This too was a frequently occurring motif in the Greco-Roman literature (e.g., Euripides, *Hel.* 940–43; Isocrates, *Demon.* 11) and one that Paul makes double use of in 1 Cor 4:14-17 as a metaphor for the way the Corinthians (as "beloved children") were to follow his example as they saw it reflected in the practices of his "beloved . . . child" Timothy. Like Timothy and the Corinthians in their relationship with Paul, the readers of Ephesians are to view themselves not only as children of God but as "beloved" children, an image that functions both (as it does in 1 Cor 4:14-17) to add emotional warmth to the call for imitation and also to recall the earlier description of the readers as "rooted and grounded in love" (3:17; cf. 2:4; 3:19) and to prepare the way for the exhortation that follows.

5:2. In keeping with God's love for them, the way the readers are to imitate him is by "walk[ing] in love." Here, as elsewhere in the letter (cf. 2:10; 4:1, 17; 5:8, 15), the language of "walk[ing]" has a summary function, serving as an umbrella term for the whole pattern of life to which the readers are called—gathering up, in this case, all the particulars of which they have been reminded in the admonitions of 4:25-32.

The call to imitate God is further concretized and focused in v. 2b, where the example of God is joined to that of Christ: "just as Christ loved us and gave himself for us, as an offering and sacrifice to God, as a fragrant aroma." It is tempting to read v. 2, in light of the reminder in 4:32 of the way that "God in Christ forgave you," as an account of the action of "God . . . in Christ" (cf. 2 Cor 5:19), but (contra Lincoln 1990, 311–12) the terms in which Christ's action is described ("just as Christ loved us and gave himself for us, as an offering and sacrifice *to God*" [emphasis added]) resist a reading of this sort. Although Paul is happy to speak in a direct manner elsewhere of the way God's love is manifested in Christ's (e.g., Rom 5:8; 8:39), that is not precisely his point here. Verse 2 is not a direct claim about the example of Christ as *constituting* the example of God; it is, rather, something more closely analogous to the way the Corinthians are to imitate Paul by imitating Timothy (Paul's "beloved . . . child") imitating Paul (1 Cor 4:16-17).

Paul's description of the action of Christ to be imitated by the readers focuses on the way he "gave himself for us (*hyper hēmōn*)"—language that recalls his summary in 1 Cor 15:3-4 of the primitive gospel that had been handed on to him as of first importance (". . . that Christ died for our sins [*hyper tōn hamartiōn hēmōn*] . . ."; 1 Cor 15:3) and the variations on that formula in which he describes Christ as the one who "gave himself" (e.g., Gal 1:4; 2:20; Eph 5:25; 1 Tim 2:6; Tit 2:14) and "died for all" (2 Cor 5:14-15). The appeal to Christ who "gave himself" as the paradigm of what it means to "walk in love" is reminiscent of Paul's appeal to the Corinthians in 2 Cor 8:5, where he urges his readers to imitate the example of the Macedonians, who "gave themselves first to the Lord and, through the will of God, to us."

The death of Christ, according to Paul's depiction of it in v. 2, was not only "for us"; it was also "an offering and sacrifice to God . . . a fragrant aroma." Paul's descriptions of Christ's death as an event in which he "gave himself" (*paredōken heauton*), as an act that was "for us" (*hyper hēmōn*), and as an "offering" (*prosphora*) and "sacrifice" (*thysia*), while not verbally identical to the terms used in LXX Isaiah 53, are nonetheless strongly evocative of that passage's depiction of the vicarious death of the servant, who was "given over" (*paredothē*) to death (53:12, twice) on account of the sins of others and suffered pain "for us" (*peri hēmōn*; 53:4). The image of Christ's death as "an offering and sacrifice to God" may also recall the way the MT depicts the life of the Servant as making (or being made) a "guilt offering" (*ʾāšām*). It should be noted, however, that neither of the words Paul uses (*prosphora*, "offering," and *thysia*, "sacrifice") is used for the guilt offering in LXX Leviticus, and the "fragrant aroma" that goes up before the Lord is typically associated in Leviticus with sacrifices other than the guilt offering. Paul's reason for making mention here of the aroma generated by Christ's sacrifice is probably not so much (contra Arnold 2010, 311–12) to underline the divine acceptance of Christ's sacrifice (and, therefore, its effectiveness for the forgiveness of sins) as it is to emphasize the pleasure of God in the costly love that it displays—a costly love that the readers of Ephesians are encouraged to imitate themselves, in anticipation of a similar pleasure that God will take in them (cf. Phil 4:18). On the question of how exactly the sacrificial death of Christ works to bring about salvation for believers, v. 2 is, as Fowl correctly emphasizes, "appropriately silent": "This silence is appropriate because the force of the verse is to describe a particular form of self-giving love that Christ has exemplified and that Paul wants the Ephesians to show to each other. No matter how well they achieve this, it would never accomplish the soteriological significance of Christ's death" (Fowl 2012, 162).

As children of light (5:3-14)

(3) But sexual immorality, and all impurity or greedy desire, let them not even be named among you, as is proper among saints. (4) Nor filthiness or foolish talk or crude joking, which are out of place, but rather thanksgiving. (5) For know this with certainty: that everyone who is sexually immoral or impure,

or who is greedy (that is, an idolater), has no inheritance in the kingdom of Christ and God. (6) Let no one deceive you with empty words, for because of these things the wrath of God is coming upon the sons of disobedience. (7) Therefore do not become partners with them; (8) for once you were darkness, but now you are light in the Lord. Walk as children of light (9) (for the fruit of the light is in all goodness and righteousness and truth), (10) discerning what is pleasing to the Lord, (11) and take no part in the unfruitful works of darkness, but instead expose them. (12) For it is shameful even to speak of the things that they do in secret. (13) But all things exposed by the light become visible, for everything that becomes visible is light. (14) Therefore it says,
Awake, O sleeper, and rise from the dead,
And Christ will shine on you.

5:3. After the summary exhortation of 5:1-2, Paul turns in v. 3 to a new paragraph that, like the preceding one, is a subsection of his larger appeal to the readers in 4:17–6:9 to "no longer walk as the Gentiles walk" (which is, in turn, an outworking and application of his appeal to them in 4:1 to "walk worthily of the calling to which you have been called").

The proportions of this paragraph are the reverse of the preceding paragraph's: whereas the bulk of 4:25–5:2 consists in the five admonition clusters in 4:25-32, which are followed by the brief, generalizing exhortation in 5:1-2, the concrete admonitions of 5:3-4 are succinctly stated, and the bulk of the paragraph consists in the supporting reasons and general exhortations that are offered in 5:5-14. In place of the imagery of costume (4:22-24, 25, 31) and imitation (4:20, 24, 32, 5:1-2), the rhetoric of 5:3-14 is dominated by the language of fittingness (5:3-4) and the imagery of light and darkness (5:8-14). Whereas the previous paragraph urged the readers to "be imitators of God . . . and walk in love" (5:1), this paragraph urges them to "walk as children of light" (5:8).

The opening admonitions in 5:3-5 focus on issues of impurity and covetousness: "But sexual immorality, and all impurity or greedy desire, let them not even be named among you, as is proper among saints; nor filthiness or foolish talk or crude joking, which are out of place, but rather thanksgiving."

Although all of the terms Paul uses can be used on occasion in connection with sexual immorality, misdirected sexual desire, or sexually suggestive speech, it is only the first word, *porneia* ("sexual immorality"), that is consistently and necessarily sexual in its meaning. In the Greco-Roman literature the word is rarely used, and it tends to refer narrowly to the practice of selling one's body as a prostitute (e.g., Demosthenes, *Fals. leg.* 200.7; Dionysius of Halicarnassus, *Ant. rom.* 4.24.4; cf. Harper 2011a, 366–69; Hippocrates, *Epid.* 7.122, which appears, on one possible reading, to use the word to refer to the visiting of prostitutes, is of uncertain date and may be influenced by later Jewish and Christian usage). In Hellenistic Jewish usage the range of meanings that it can carry widens significantly, so that it becomes in effect an umbrella term for all sexual activity that is outside of marriage or in some other way improper (e.g., T. Reu. 1.6; 6.1–2; T. Jos. 3.8; T. Benj. 9.1; T. Iss. 7.1–2; cf. T. Reu. 4.1) and can even be described as "the mother of all evils" (T. Sim. 5.3). Paul's use of the word has a similar breadth of meaning and is informed by a similar understanding of marriage as the sole context for legitimate sexual activity (cf. 1 Cor 6:16; 7:1-2). The prominent place that Paul gives to the warning against sexual immorality is consistent with the pattern of his teaching elsewhere (e.g., Gal 5:19; 1 Thess 4:1-8; 1 Cor 5:9; 2 Cor 12:21; Col 3:5; cf. Gupta 2012), suggesting that the call to a radically different understanding and practice of sexual morality was a core element of basic catechesis for Gentile converts to Christianity (cf. Acts 15:20).

Alongside *porneia*, Paul urges his readers to avoid "all impurity or greedy desire." While it is certainly true that both words (*akatharsia* and *pleonexia*) can be used to refer specifically to sexual impurity and illicit sexual desire, the range of possible meanings that they can carry in Paul's letters is somewhat broader than that (e.g., 1 Thess 2:3, 5; Rom 1:29), and the way Paul shapes his appeal suggests that it is a broad rather than a narrow range of meaning that they carry here. The function of the second and third words in this short vice list is not simply to accumulate a small pile of near similes; it is, rather, to generalize from the paradigmatic case of *porneia* to the whole field of all the different forms in which "impurity" or "greedy desire" can be manifested—hence the "all" that Paul joins to the first term and, by implication, the second.

The reason Paul gives for why the vices that he lists in v. 3 should not "even be named" among God's people is that this is what "is proper" (*prepei*) among saints. The verb he uses is an expression that can be used in the Stoic literature to speak of modes of conduct that are appropriate for particular social situations, as determined by the overarching principle of accordance with nature. Here, however, the criterion is not the norms of nature but the standard of what is fitting "among saints," i.e., what is in keeping with the distinctive ethos of the church as the holy people of God.

Paul's assertion that the vices in question must "not even be named" is almost certainly, in part at least, a hyperbolic way of saying that they must not be practiced or tolerated—otherwise, if Paul's words are read in a flatly literalist manner, he has broken his own rule even in the act of stating it. Nevertheless, the admonitions that Paul adds in the following verse about sins of speech do suggest that he views the concern he expresses in v. 3 for the distinctiveness of the church's culture as having implications for the way believers speak, as well as the way they think and act.

5:4. The three particular modes of speech that Paul singles out for censure in v. 4 are "filthiness" (*aischrotēs*), "foolish talk" (*mōrologia*), and "crude joking" (*eutrapelia*). The first of the three words, *aischrotēs*, used in its literal sense, refers to visual ugliness, as measured against conventional standards of beauty and decency. Used metaphorically, it can refer to a variety of shameful or obscene behaviors, but the present context, including both of the two vices of speech that follow, the preceding "must not even be named" (*mēde onomazesthō*), and the "thanksgiving" that follows by way of contrast, suggests that the primary form of ugliness Paul has in mind is probably the ugliness of obscene or otherwise disgraceful speech (Lincoln 1990, 322). The second and third words, *mōrologia* and *eutrapelia*, in their most basic sense, refer to talk that is simply foolish (in the case of *mōrologia*) or clever (in the case of *eutrapelia*); the context in which Paul uses the words here makes it clear that they are carrying the sense of moral disapprobation that they can sometimes have even in the Greco-Roman literature (e.g., Plutarch; Garr. 504b; Cic. 5.4; Vita Aesopi 32; cf. van der Horst 1978). The "or" between the two words suggests that they should be read as a connected and mutually complementary pair:

> One term is associated with dullness of mind, a dullness sometimes induced by drunkenness, the other with a quick wit, able to pinpoint precisely the weakness in an opponent that can be mocked and elicit laughter or able to turn an otherwise innocent phrase into a sexual allusion. Whether its source is wits dulled by wine or sharpened by rhetorical training, rude speech of a sexual nature or at another's expense has, Paul says, no place among God's people. (Thielman 2010, 331)

The reason given that these modes of speech are to be shunned is similar to the reason Paul supplies in v. 3 for the admonition in that verse. Here, the expression is even more succinctly articulated than in the previous verse; these ways of speaking are simply "out of place" (i.e., not in line with what is "proper among saints").

What is to take their place as the characteristic mode of Christian speech is "thanksgiving." While the thanksgiving spoken of in Paul's letters is always given to God (cf. 1 Cor 14:16; 2 Cor 4:15; Phil 4:6; Col 2:7; 4:2; 1 Thess 3:9; 1 Tim 2:1; 4:3-4), it would be a mistake to read his admonition as requiring the readers to replace ordinary human conversation with pious speech directed toward God. What he has in mind, rather, is a mode of human interaction that is framed and pervasively influenced by the words of thanks that are habitually offered to God, along the lines of the picture that he goes on to paint in vv. 15-21.

5:5. The brief rationales that conclude vv. 3 and 4 are extended and developed in vv. 5-14, commencing with the emphatic and earnest reminders of vv. 5-6:

> For know this with certainty: that everyone who is sexually immoral or impure, or who is greedy (that is, an idolater), has no inheritance in the kingdom of Christ and God. Let no one deceive you with empty words, for because of these things the wrath of God is coming upon the sons of disobedience.

The logical relationship between vv. 3-4 and vv. 5-6 hinges on the connection between people and practices. The reason that the people listed in vv. 5-6 are excluded from inheriting the kingdom is the fact that the practices to which they are habitually inclined are "out of place" among saints (vv. 3-4). And the fact that those who habitually and unrepentantly practice such vices are excluded from the kingdom (v. 5) and under God's wrath (v. 6) gives weight and urgency to the admonitions in vv. 3-4 (hence the *gar*, "for," connecting vv. 5-6 with the admonitions of the preceding verses).

The form of words that Paul uses to introduce v. 5 (*touto gar iste ginōskontes*; "For know this with certainty") is rhetorically forceful, with the word "this" brought to the front of the clause for emphasis and the imperative *iste* ("know") joined to the present participle form of its near synonym, *ginōskō*, to create a combined effect that places heavy stress on the truth of what is being asserted. The assertion that follows strings together three substantives—*pornos, akathartos,* and *pleonektēs*—corresponding to the three abstract nouns of v. 3 (*porneia, akatharsia,* and *pleonexia*), reminding the readers that there is no place for people who belong to any of these three categories within the kingdom of Christ and of God.

The first word, *pornos*, is used in the Greco-Roman literature to refer to a male prostitute, but in the literature of Second Temple Judaism and early Christianity its semantic range is a great deal broader, in line with the broadened range of meanings that could be covered by *porneia* (cf. Sir 16:17; 1 Cor 5–7). The second and third words, likewise, cover a wide range of possibilities, referring to people whose lives are characterized by the habitual practice of any of the various forms that the "impurity" and "greedy desire" of v. 3 could take.

The mention of the greedy person is supplemented by the parenthetical comment, "that is, an idolater." The function of the comment is not so much to define greed as it is to explain why it is a vice of character that is so starkly and fundamentally incompatible with the claim to be a worshiper of God. Behind Paul's words stands a long line of Old Testament and Second Temple Jewish teaching that highlighted the way the objects of covetous desire function as substitutes or rivals to God himself (e.g., Job 31:24-28; Philo, *Spec. Laws* 1.23) and the teaching of Jesus himself (e.g., in Matt 6:24; Luke 16:13) about money and greed (Rosner 2007, 69–100).

Paul's description of the realm from which such people are excluded as "the kingdom of Christ and God" (v. 5) is unique in his writings, and indeed the whole New Testament. It brings together the two interrelated ideas of the coming kingdom of God and the present reign of Christ, under whose feet all things have been subjected (1:20-22; cf. the similar though not identical formulation in 1 Cor 15:25-28). Although "kingdom of God" language can function, both in Paul's letters and elsewhere in the New Testament, to refer to the present experience of the reign of God among the community of his people (e.g., Rom 14:17; 1 Cor 4:20), this dimension of the phrase's meaning is brought into slightly sharper focus by the language of "the kingdom of Christ" (cf. Col 1:13). The joining of the two expressions here may be intended to convey a combined sense of the present and the future manifestations of the kingdom, and the exclusion of those who are "sexually immoral or impure, or . . . greedy" from both (Arnold 2010, 325)—an impression that is strengthened by the present tense form of the verb that Paul uses (contrast the future tense in of 1 Cor 6:9-10 and Gal 5:21) and the way "inheritance" language functions elsewhere in Ephesians (cf. 1:11, 14) to imply the present inauguration of a future reality.

5:6. The solemnity of Paul's reminder in v. 5 is further underlined in the verse that follows: "Let no one deceive you with empty words, for because of these things the wrath of God is coming upon the sons of disobedience." Although there is no conjunction joining this sentence to the previous one, the backwards-referring "these things" (i.e., the vices listed in vv. 3-4, and particularly those of v. 3, which are recalled in the list of people given in v. 5) suggests a close connection between them. The warning against deception, like the similar warning in 1 Cor 6:9, implies the dangerous possibility that some, even within the church, may seek to immunize believers against the threats of divine judgment by suggesting that some or all of the vices listed by Paul can be committed by believers with impunity. In response to ideas of this sort, Paul reminds his readers that it is precisely on account of vices such as these that "the wrath of God is coming upon the sons of disobedience" (i.e., the unconverted Gentiles already referred to by that label in 2:2). The present tense form of the verb "is coming" (*erchetai*) need not imply that Paul is depicting the wrath of God as already being experienced by unbelievers. Although an idea of that sort is certainly present in Rom 1:18-32, Paul's point here does not require it, and the verb *erchomai* can frequently be used in the New Testament to speak of a future event (e.g., the outpouring of God's wrath) that is on its way but has not yet arrived (e.g., 1 Thess 1:10; probably also Col 3:6) (cf. Larkin 2009, 113; Lincoln 1990, 326; contra Best 1998, 486).

5:7. If vices such as those listed in vv. 3-4 are the reason that God's coming judgment will fall upon unbelievers, then, the implied logic of the verse suggests, those who seek to lull believers into thinking that they can persist in the same practices are propagating a dangerous error (cf. the similar logic of the warning in Rom 11:19-22). "Therefore," Paul exhorts his readers in v. 7, "do not become partners with them." The context of the exhortation and its function as part of an extended elaboration on the admonitions in vv. 3-4 make it clear that Paul's intention here is not to rule out relationships and connections of any sort with unbelievers (cf. 1 Cor 5:9-10); his purpose, rather, is to warn against joining with unbelievers in practices such as those he has censured in the earlier verses, and so becoming "partners" with them in the sins that will incur God's wrath (cf. v. 11).

5:8. In v. 8a Paul offers an additional reason for the exhortation of v. 7, introducing a new pattern of imagery that becomes, in turn, the theme of a further series of reminders and exhortations in vv. 8b-15. If the negative reason for believers to separate themselves from the vices of sexual immorality and greed is stated in vv. 5-6, the positive reason is given in v. 8a: "for once you were darkness, but now you are light in the Lord." The transformation that Paul describes is not merely one of predicament ("once you were in darkness . . .") but one that goes to the core of the readers' very identity: "once you *were* darkness, but now you *are* light . . ." (Arnold 2010, 328). The form of the reminder, with its "once . . . now" contrast, is reminiscent of the identity-forming narratives of chapter 2 (cf. 2:2-4, 11, 13), and the location of believers' new identity "in the Lord" recalls the repeated references throughout chapters 1–3 to the metaphorical sphere "in Christ" within which believers now exist and enjoy the blessings of God's salvation.

The radical nature of the transformation of identity that believers have undergone is conveyed by Paul through the metaphorical contrast between light and darkness (cf. 2 Cor 4:6; 1 Thess 5:4-11; Rom 13:11-14) that he introduces in this verse, building on the earlier description in 4:18 of Gentiles outside of Christ as being "darkened in their understanding." Because this transformation of identity has now taken place, the readers are exhorted in v. 8b to "walk as children of light" (cf. 1 Thess 5:5), a conjunction of images that calls for a pattern of life in keeping with the new identity that believers have been given in Christ. The call to "walk" in this manner ties the exhortations of this paragraph to the earlier summonses in 4:17 and 5:2 and the one that follows in 5:15, connecting each major section of 4:17–5:21 with the overarching exhortation in 4:1.

5:9. The manner of life implied by the metaphor of "walk[ing] as children of light" is filled out somewhat in v. 9, with a parenthetical addition, "for the fruit of the light is in all goodness and righteousness and truth." The *gar* ("for") that connects v. 9 with v. 8 is probably explanatory in function, since the content of the verse that it introduces is more naturally read as an elaboration on the exhortation in the previous verse than as a reason that it should be followed. Although v. 9 does unpack the previous verse's metaphor somewhat, it still does not have the kind of concrete and specific content as vv. 3-4 or 4:25-32; one set of images (walking, children, light) is simply replaced with another ("the fruit of the light"), which is in turn identified by a string of broad and general abstract nouns: "all goodness and righteousness and truth." The metaphor of "fruit," used in an ethical sense, is used on a number of occasions in Paul's letters (cf. Rom 6:21-22; Gal 5:22; Phil 1:11) and implies the fittingness with which the lifestyle he is calling his readers to corresponds (by grace-transformed nature) with the new identity that they have been given. All three of the virtues Paul lists are used in the LXX to describe the character of God (e.g., *agathōsynē* in 2 Esd 19:25, 35; 23:31 [=MT Neh 9:25, 35; 13:31]; Pr Man 14; *dikaiosynē* and *alētheia* in 2 Esd 19:33 [=MT Neh 9:33]; Ps 95:13 [=MT 96:13]; Tob 1:3), and Paul's description of them as "the fruit of the light" is probably best read as, in part at least, an extension of the imitation of God motif that was more explicitly present in 4:24 and 5:1 (Thielman 2010, 341).

The "goodness" (*agathōsynē*) that is the first of the virtues listed by Paul is a word that is far less common than its English equivalent or the other cognate words (e.g., the adjective *agathos*) to which it is related. Outside of the New Testament, the only surviving instances of it are in the LXX and the Second Temple Jewish literature, where it tends to be used to refer to active benevolence (e.g., Judg 8:35; 2 Chr 24:16; 2 Esd 19:25, 35 [=MT Neh 9:25, 35]; Pr Man 14) rather than simply the absence of vice. If that is its meaning here (as it is in 2 Thess 1:11), then what Paul has in mind is not simply abstention from sexual immorality and greed but the replacement of these vices with the benevolent, generous goodness that is their opposite (cf. the pattern of "putting off" and "putting on" in 4:22-32). The "righteousness" (*dikaiosynē*) that comes next in the list is, similarly, the active, ethical righteousness that is manifested in grace-transformed human conduct (cf. Rom 6:13, 16, 18-20; 2 Cor 6:14; 9:9-10; 11:15; Phil 1:11) rather than the righteous status that Paul can elsewhere use the same word to refer to (e.g., Rom 4:11; Phil 3:9) (cf. Starling 2014a, 2012b). The "truth" (*alētheia*) that concludes the list is almost certainly, given the ethical focus of the context, a reference to the virtues of truthful speech and honest conduct (cf. 4:25) rather than to the content of the gospel and its entailments (as it is in 1:13; 4:15, 21, 24; 6:14). The word "all," which precedes "goodness," probably modifies "righteousness" and "truth" as well, implying a sense of comprehensiveness and consistency.

5:10. After the parenthetical comment of v. 9, Paul resumes in v. 10 the sentence that he commenced in v. 8b, adding to it the participial clause, "discerning what is pleasing to the Lord." The clause functions to modify the imperative "walk" in the earlier verse, and the process that it describes is represented by Paul as an essential part of what is required in order to "walk as children of light." The verb *dokimazō* ("discern") suggests a serious exercise of thought and judgment (cf. Epictetus, *Diatr.* 1.20.7; 2.23.6, 8; 4.5.16; 4.6.13; 4.7.40; 1 Thess 5:1; 1 John 4:1), focused on determining, in the midst of the complexities of circumstance, the path of conduct that pleases God (cf. Rom 12:2; 14:22).

5:11. The sentence that commenced in v. 8b now takes a new turn in v. 11. Having focused in vv. 8-10 on the positive command to imitate and please God, as "children of light," Paul now spells out its negative corollary, that the readers are to "take no part in the unfruitful works of darkness, but instead expose them." The command to "take no part" (*mē synkoinōneite*) reiterates the ideas of v. 7, where believers were warned against becoming "partners" (*symmetochoi*) with the sons of disobedience, and makes it clear that the kind of partnership Paul intends to rule out is active participation in the practices that he describes as the "works of darkness," not all personal connection and association with unbelievers (cf. Rom 13:12-14; 2 Cor 6:14–7:1; on the latter passage, see Starling 2012a). The description of the works of darkness as "unfruitful" contrasts with the image in v. 9 of "the fruit of light"; rather than constructing the contrast as one between the good fruits of the light and the bad fruits of the darkness, Paul chooses to highlight the asymmetry of the contrast between the "fruits of light" and the (barren, lifeless, sterile) "works of darkness" (cf. the contrast between "fruit" and works in Gal 5:19-23, and the studied mix of symmetry and asymmetry in Rom 6:21-23).

Rather than join in such practices, the readers are instead to "expose" (*elenchete*) them. The verb Paul uses is one that can frequently be used to refer to verbal correction and reproof (e.g., Matt 18:15; Luke 3:19; Titus 1:9), and some commentators (e.g., Best 1998, 492–94) argue that it carries that sense here. In other instances, however, it can refer to the exposure (literal or metaphorical) of things that would otherwise have remained hidden or in darkness (e.g., Aristophanes, *Eccl.* 485; Josephus, *J.W.* 3.512; Philo, *Names* 198); the fact that it is "works" rather than people who are the implied object of the verb in v. 11, together with the imagery of light and darkness in vv. 13-14, suggests that this is the more likely sense in which the word is being used here. Given the focus of the paragraph on the conduct of believers, and the fact that the "expos[ing]" of the works of darkness is presented as a contrast to joining in with them, it is probably best to envisage this exposing as taking place not primarily through argument or verbal censure (though note the effect that Paul envisages Christian prophecy as having in 1 Cor 14:25), but through the nonverbal impact of a visibly different Christian counterculture (cf. Phil 2:14-15).

5:12. Verse 12 supplies a reason for the injunctions of the previous verse (and v. 11a in particular): "for it is shameful even to speak of the things that they do in secret." It is likely (as was the case in v. 3) that Paul's assertion includes a degree of hyperbole, in line with the similar statements that can be found in the Greco-Roman literature (e.g., Dio Chrysostom, *In Cont.* [*Or.* 48] 16; Isocrates, *Demon.* 15; Quintilian, *Inst.* 1.2.8). But his point, in this instance, need not be taken as entirely hyperbolic: the description of the works in view here in v. 12 as things done "in secret" suggests that Paul has in mind the kinds of actions that transgress even pagan norms of what can be done by respectable people in the broad light of day. If these things (or some of them at least) are so disgraceful that they do not even bear mentioning, then the larger pattern of life to which they belong as particularly egregious examples is certainly not one in which believers should participating as "partners" (v. 11).

5:13. In vv. 13-14a, Paul paints a contrasting picture, which relates to v. 11b in a similar manner to the way v. 12 relates to the injunction in v. 11a, developing the metaphor suggested by the earlier verse's call to "expose" the deeds of darkness and relating it to the converting power of the gospel: "But all things exposed by the light become visible, for everything that becomes visible is light." In contrast with the "darkness" and "secrecy" referred to in vv. 11-12, the picture in vv. 13-14a is one of exposure and illumination. The dynamic described is a double one: things exposed to the light become visible (v. 13), and things that have been made visible are themselves a source of light (v. 14a).

5:14. Some translations (e.g., KJV; NIV84; NLT; HCSB) read *phaneroumenon* in v. 14 as a middle voice participle with an active sense that takes *pan* ("everything") as its object: "for the light makes everything visible" (NLT). The arguments made by some commentators (e.g., Arnold 2010, 333; Abbott 1897, 156) in favor of a translation such as this are unconvincing, however, since a middle voice form of *phaneroō* with an active sense is nowhere else attested in the New Testament, and the form of the verb in v. 13 is unambiguously passive.

Less easy to determine is the precise relationship between the dynamic described in v. 13 (light exposing things so that they become visible) and the dynamic depicted in v. 14a (things exposed being themselves a source of light). It is tempting to read the two pictures in sequence as a mini-narrative, in which the dynamic of v. 14a follows on as a consequence of the dynamic depicted in v. 13: "All things exposed by the light become visible, and everything that becomes visible in this way becomes, in turn, a source of light itself." Logical as the sequence imagined in this mini-narrative would be, it struggles to accommodate the conjunction *gar* ("for") that connects the two clauses, suggesting a relationship between them that is explanatory rather than sequential (see especially Runge 2010, 51–54). A more likely explanation of v. 14a would be that it offers an explanation of how believers (who are called on in v. 11 to "expose" the deeds of darkness) can function as the "light" that is depicted in v. 13 as performing that function. Since believers have themselves been brought out of darkness and made visible by the light of the gospel, they themselves are now a source of (reflected) light (cf. v. 8), even in their wordless conduct, which can thus function to shine with a potentially redemptive effect on the lives of those around them.

The transformative event in which the readers, who were once darkness, became light through the converting power of the gospel is, in turn, recalled in v. 14b: "Therefore, it says (*dio legei*), 'Awake, O sleeper, and rise from the dead, and Christ will shine on you.'" The citation in v. 14b has attracted almost as much scholarly discussion as the reference to Ps 68:18 in the previous chapter. The obvious issue that has attracted such attention is the fact that the quotation introduced by the *dio legei* formula (the same formula that introduces the quotation from Ps 68 in Eph 4:8) is nowhere to be found in the Old Testament Scriptures, at least in the verbatim form in which it is cited here. While some older commentators have suggested that the quotation is directly dependent on Old Testament sources or on a pre-Christian source from early Gnosticism or the mystery religions (cf. the survey of older scholarly views in Barth 1974, 574–75), the modern consensus has been that the source of the quotation is an early Christian hymn, perhaps associated with a baptismal context.

In recent years, Thorsten Moritz has helpfully refocused attention on two key Isaianic texts (Isa 29:16; 60:1) as the ultimate, if not immediate, source of the quotation (Moritz 1996a, 97–116). Without abandoning the hypothesis that the quotation's immediate source is a Christian hymn composed or inherited by Paul, Moritz has argued that the hymn's links with and dependence on the two Isaianic texts are stronger than has generally been conceded, and that the way the hymn is used in Ephesians reflects an awareness of the original context in Isaiah of the texts on which the hymn was based.

In the case of Isa 26:19, Moritz points out the similarities between the rhythmic pattern and vocabulary of the verse and that of Eph 5:14b, including the way both verses address (or, in the case of the LXX, prophesy concerning) the "sleeper" or the "dwellers in the tombs," with the language of "rising," "waking," and "the dead" (*egeirō*; *anistēmi*; *hoi nekroi*). In the case of Isa 60:1, the most significant links that Moritz points out are contextual ones. In both the Isaiah 59–60 context and the Ephesians 5 context, the text is embedded in an extended metaphorical discourse about light and darkness. In both cases, too, the light/darkness metaphor is used with predominantly ethical content. The Ephesians who "were once darkness" and "now . . . are light in the Lord" (v. 8) are to "walk as children of light," taking no part in the "secret" and "shameful" works of darkness. The children of Zion described in Isaiah 59 stumble about in the darkness and death of their transgressions, cut off from God by their iniquities and endeavoring in vain to cover themselves with the spiderwebs of deceit; it is to this community that the summons in Isa 60:1 is addressed, and the transformation is as much ethical as it is soteriological: the "salvation," "peace," "justice," and "righteousness" that are lamented because of their absence in chapter 59 are celebrated for their abundance in chapter 60.

It seems plausible, therefore, that Paul, when quoting the hymn or hymn-fragment that he makes use of in Eph 5:14, is thinking of the change in his readers' condition from "darkness" to "light in the Lord" not merely against the backdrop of the (putative) baptismal setting of the hymn but also against the wider scriptural horizon of the new exodus salvation to which they have been summoned in the gospel (as depicted, for example, in Isa 59–60). If that is the case, then the promise of the hymn that "Christ will shine on you" is understood by Paul (and presumably also the author of the hymn) as the fulfillment of the prophetic announcement that "the glory of the Lord has risen upon you" (LXX Isa 60:1; cf. 2 Cor 4:6).

Not as unwise . . . but as wise (5:15-21)

(15) Be careful, then, how you walk, not as unwise people but as wise, (16) redeeming the time, because the days are evil. (17) Therefore do not be foolish, but understand what the will of the Lord is. (18) And do not get drunk with wine, in which is debauchery, but be filled with the Spirit, (19) speaking psalms and hymns and spiritual songs among yourselves, singing and making melody to the Lord in your hearts, (20) giving thanks at all times and for everything in the name of our Lord Jesus Christ to God the Father, (21) submitting to one another in reverence toward Christ.

5:15. In v. 15 a new paragraph commences that, like the three before it (4:17-24; 4:25–5:2; 5:3-14), further elaborates on the call in 4:17 to "no longer walk as the Gentiles walk." In this instance, the contrast is not between putting off and putting on (4:17–5:2) or between light and darkness (5:3-14) but between "wise" and "unwise"—the latter exemplified in the concrete instance of being "drunk with wine" (v. 18a) and the former described as being "filled with the Spirit" (v. 18b).

The "therefore" (*oun*) that connects this paragraph with what precedes it is probably inferential in its function, presenting the call to wisdom as an implication of the exhortations in the previous paragraph to "walk as children of light" (v. 8) and "[discern] what is pleasing to the Lord" (v. 10). It may also, like the *oun* in 5:1, perform the additional function of marking the paragraph that follows as a kind of summation to the sequence of thought commenced in 4:17, preparing the way for the household code that follows.

The call to "be careful" (*blepete*) voices a concern similar to that expressed in the earlier call to vigilance in v. 6, though here the primary threat in view appears to be not the deceptions of others but the endemic sloth and folly to which the readers themselves may be prone. The question in view as the focus of the carefulness to which they are being urged is "how you walk" (cf. 4:1, 17; 5:2, 8)—which is the theme of the entire second half of the letter, introduced in 4:1. Here, the distinctiveness of the lifestyle that leaders are to follow is summed up in the contrast between wisdom and folly—"not as unwise . . . but as wise"—a contrast that is then unpacked across the remainder of the paragraph and applied to the relationships of the household in 5:21–6:9.

5:16. The elaboration on what it means to walk "not as unwise . . . but as wise" commences in v. 16, where Paul pictures wisdom as a matter of "redeeming the time, because the days are evil." The phrase "redeeming the time" (*exagorazomenoi ton kairon*) is a puzzling one, with few obvious parallels apart from the almost identical phrase in Col 4:5. A similar expression occurs in LXX Dan 2:8, where Nebuchadnezzar accuses his magicians of attempting to "buy time" through stalling tactics, but it is difficult to imagine how a scenario of this sort could be relevant to what Paul is saying here. If we are to guess at the meaning of Paul's metaphor (here and in Col 4:5) based on the ways the verb can be used in its literal sense, two main alternatives present themselves. One option is to read the verb as simply an intensified form of *agorazō* (i.e., "buy up" entirely, opportunistically, or urgently, as for example in Polybius, *Hist.* 3.42.2; Plutarch, *Crassus* 2.5.6); the other is to read the verb as meaning to "buy out of" a predicament of enslavement (e.g., Diodorus Siculus, *Bib. hist.* 15.7.1; Gal 4:5). Given the fact that Paul goes on to describe the days as "evil" rather than "short," the latter sense of the word is probably to be preferred over the former, and believers are to be pictured as rescuing back hours and days from the "present darkness" of this age (cf. 6:12), so as to make them occasions for goodness and truth.

5:17. Verse 17a ("Therefore, do not be foolish") reiterates the call of v. 15 to walk "not as unwise," with the "therefore" (*dia touto*) that introduces the verse suggesting that the evil days referred to in v. 16b provide an additional reason that wisdom is needed. The kind of wisdom that is held out as the opposite of the foolish thinking to be avoided is the practical and ethical wisdom that is focused on the task of "understand[ing] what the will of the Lord is" (17b; cf. 5:10), reflecting the fundamental orientation of Old Testament wisdom toward "fear[ing] the Lord" and "turn[ing] away from evil" (Job 28:28).

5:18. The command that follows in v. 18 ("And do not get drunk with wine, in which is debauchery, but be filled with the Spirit") has been the topic of much scholarly discussion and speculation. According to some interpreters, the presence of the prohibition (together with the negated present imperative form that it takes) implies a practice of habitual drunkenness among the readers, and the fact that it is contrasted with a command to be filled with the Spirit implies that the drinking culture of the readers was informed by the influence of the Dionysian *thiasoi* and their practice of cultic inebriation (e.g., Hengel 1983, 188; Rogers 1979; cited in Arnold 2010, 348). Both inferences are precarious. The negated present imperative does not necessarily imply a command to stop an action (Larkin 2009, 124), and the present context is one in which a general precept is much more likely than a reaction to reports of a problem among the readers. Nor is the hypothesis of a Dionysian-inspired quest for union with the divine through cultic inebriation a necessary one to explain the presence of Paul's injunction warning against drunkenness, or the contrast that he draws between being drunk with wine and being filled with the Spirit.

A far simpler explanation for the presence of the warning against drunkenness (and the contrasting injunction to be filled with the Spirit) lies in the contrast between wisdom and folly that is the theme of the paragraph. Pagan moral philosophy frequently drew the connection between drunkenness and folly (e.g., Plutarch, *Garr.* 503d–504b), and warnings against drunkenness were a common theme in Jewish wisdom literature and moral advice-giving (e.g., LXX Prov 23:29-34; T. Jud. 14.1, which both include the identically worded warning, "do not get drunk with wine"). Paul's letters contain warnings against drunkenness and exhortations to sobriety (e.g., Rom 13:13; Gal 5:21), and drunkenness can also serve in his letters as a kind of metaphor for sluggishness or folly (e.g., 1 Cor 15:34; 1 Thess 5:6-8). Here, the connection he draws between drunkenness and debauchery suggests that he has literal drunkenness in mind, though it is possible that it can also be functioning as a kind of synecdoche (i.e., that drunkenness is serving as both a specific instance of folly and a metaphor for it).

The word "debauchery" (*asōtia*), which Paul associates with drunkenness, can refer variously to financial profligacy, sexual promiscuity, or a combination of both of these vices. In all of these senses it is commonly associated in the Jewish and Greco-Roman literature with excessive consumption of alcohol, especially in the context of festivals and drinking parties (e.g., Athenaeus, *Deipn.* 4.59–67; 11.70; 1 Pet 4:4; Rom 13:13). It is difficult to say with certainty whether the antecedent of Paul's "in which" is the noun "wine" (cf. T. Jud. 16.1–2, which lists *asōtia* as one of the "four evil spirits" contained in wine) or whole idea of "get[ting] drunk with wine" (Larkin 2009, 124). The parallel with Testament of Judah 16.1–2 weighs in favor of the former alternative, though the intended meaning is probably much the same in either case.

Rather than getting drunk with wine, the readers are urged in v. 18b to "be filled with the Spirit." The present-tense form of the imperative should not be pressed for too much information about the nature of the action in itself (i.e., whether the filling in view is an instantaneous event or an ongoing process); like all of the other present imperatives in this section of the letter, it is probably best read as functioning simply to convey a general precept (Larkin 2009, 96–97). Nevertheless, the string of participles attached to the command in vv. 19-21 ("speaking . . . singing . . . making melody . . . giving thanks . . . submitting") does fit more readily with an ongoing process than an instantaneous event, and the equivalent command in the parallel passage in Col 3:16 ("Let the word of Christ dwell in you richly") is difficult to imagine in anything but an ongoing sense.

Commentators divide over whether the phrase *en pneumati* should be translated as "by the Spirit" (e.g., Hoehner 2002, 704; cf. Wallace 1996, 375), "in the sphere of the Spirit" (e.g., Thielman 2010, 359–60), or "with the Spirit" (e.g., Arnold 2010, 349–50, and most EVV). Critics of the third view frequently cite Abbott's assertion that " the use of *en* with *plēroō* to express the content with which a thing is filled would be quite unexampled" (Abbott 1897, 161). Arnold, in response, is able to point to several counter examples in which *en* is used with *plēroō* or *pimplēmi* to convey exactly this meaning (Ignatius, *Smyrn.* 1.1; LXX Ps 64:5 [=MT/Eng. 65:4]; 3 Bar. 15.2), and it is not difficult to supplement his list with several more (e.g., LXX 2 Chr 13:9; Pss. Sol. 4.12; Homer, *Odyssey* 12.417; Galen, *In Hippoc. epidem. comment.* 17a. 719.1). The parallel between the prohibition against being "drunk with wine" (*mē methyskesthe oinō*) and the positive command to "be filled with the Spirit" (*plērousthe en pneumati*), while admittedly not perfect or precise, does nonetheless offer support for an interpretation along these lines. Perhaps a decision between the first option ("filled by the Spirit") and the third ("filled with the Spirit") is unnecessary, given the way that both wine and the Spirit can be understood simultaneously as the (literal or metaphorical) substance with which one is filled and the instrument by which one is influenced (toward intoxication, in one case, or the fullness of Christ, in the other).

A second question that is debated by the commentators is the precise nature of the relationship between the command in v. 18b ("be filled with the Spirit") and the string of participles in vv. 19-21 ("speaking . . . singing . . . making melody . . . giving thanks . . . submitting"). According to some commentators (e.g., Arnold 2010, 351; cf. Gombis 2002, 269–70) the participles should be read as the means by which the command is to be fulfilled; according to others (e.g., Lincoln 1990, 345; cf. Wallace 1996, 639) they should be read as the results of the Spirit's filling. Neither alternative is entirely satisfying; the former makes better and more intuitive sense of the first three participles ("speaking . . . singing . . . making melody"), the latter makes better sense of the fifth ("submitting"), and "giving thanks" could sit equally well with either.

A better approach is to take an initial step back from the dichotomy between means and result and classify the common function of all five participles as elaborative—"spell[ing] out what the main action looks like" (Runge 2010, 262, 266–67). Within that broad, overarching function, which is common to all five participles, if we are to look for information in the text about the implied causal relationship between the action of the main verb and the actions described in the participles that follow, then the larger context of the sentence probably suggests a movement across vv. 19-21 from the means by which the Spirit's filling takes place toward its results. On this reading, the first three participles, and possibly also the fourth, function to fill the vacuum left by the (intrinsically paradoxical) form of the passive-voice imperative in v. 18b, supplying the readers with some guidance as to what it might mean for them to participate in the divine activity to which the command in v. 18b refers. The final participle in the list ("submitting") prepares the way for the paragraphs that follow in 5:22–6:9, which picture the outworking of the command in v. 18b (and, more broadly, the string of commands in vv. 15–18) within the relationships of the household.

5:19. The first three participles, in v. 19, all refer to Christian speech and song within the gathering of the assembly. Unlike the parallel passage in Col 3:16, which depicts the congregation members as "teaching and admonishing one another in all wisdom," the picture here focuses more narrowly on the speaking of "psalms" (*psalmoi*), "hymns" (*hymnoi*), and "spiritual songs" (*ōdai pneumatikai*). The first of these terms would have been understood by the readers as referring primarily to the LXX version of the canonical Old Testament psalms, though they may have also associated it with more newly composed songs that had affinities of genre and content with the songs contained in the Psalter (in line with the continuing practice within Second Temple Judaism of creating compositions such as the *Psalms of Solomon*). Although the placing of this word alongside the two others that follow probably implies a diversity of form and content, it would be a mistake to assume that there were watertight boundaries between the meanings of the three words Paul uses. The words "hymns" and "songs" can be used within the LXX and the Second Temple literature to refer to the psalms of David (e.g., LXX Pss 4:1; 6:1; Josephus, *Ant.* 7.305), and, conversely, the word "psalm" can be used by Paul with apparent reference to a song that is to be sung "in the Spirit" within the Christian assembly (1 Cor 14:15, 26). Taken together, the list implies a comprehensive reference to the songs sung in the Christian assembly, with the "psalms" in view not so much as subject matter for teaching and meditation (though the evidence of the New Testament, e.g., Hebrews 1–7, suggests that they did also function in that way within early Christianity) but as the content of congregational praise and lament.

With this in view, it is probably best to understand the "speaking" of v. 19a as (primarily at least) a reference to speech that takes the form of song (cf. Luke 1:46; LXX Deut 31:30; Judg 5:1; 2 Sam 22:1; Ps 17:1 for *laleō*, "speak," and *legō*, "say," used with apparent reference to the singing of a song). The fact that the congregation members are depicted as singing these songs "to one another" (assuming that *heautois* is functioning here as a reciprocal pronoun rather than with its more common, reflexive force) suggests that the formative, edifying effect of their singing is in view in v. 19a. But this depiction of the congregation members as singing their songs to one another is joined immediately in v. 19b by a complementary description of them as "singing and making melody to the Lord in [their] hearts"—presumably not as a separate and distinct activity but as a simultaneous, inward dimension of the singing described in the first half of the verse. The fact that "the Lord" (*ho kyrios*) is used everywhere else in Ephesians to refer to the Lord Jesus would suggest that it would be understood most naturally as functioning in the same way here, in line with Pliny's early second century description in *Ep.* 10.96 of the Christians of Bithynia as singing *Christo quasi deo* ("to Christ as to a god") (cf. Arnold 2010, 354).

5:20. A further layer of significance is added in v. 20: "giving thanks at all times and for everything in the name of our Lord Jesus Christ to God the Father." Just as songs addressed to fellow believers can function as expressions of the heart's praises to Christ, so also the praises offered up to Christ can serve as a way of "giving thanks . . . to God the Father" (cf. Phil 2:11). The comprehensive scope of Paul's language in v. 20 ("at all times and for everything") creates a bridge between the congregational focus of v. 19 to the whole-of-life orientation in 5:21–6:9; the offering up of thanks to God the Father includes but is not limited to the songs that believers sing within the assembly.

The first of Paul's qualifiers in v. 20 ("at all times") should not be pressed over-literally. Here as elsewhere in Paul's letters, language about prayer and thanksgiving "at all times" or "without ceasing" appears to function not to describe a form of wordless prayerfulness that continues through every waking (and sleeping!) moment but as a way of speaking about habitual, frequent, ordinary expressions of prayer and thanksgiving (Rom 1:9; 1 Cor 1:4; Col 1:3; 3:17; 1 Thess 1:2; 2:13; 5:18; Philm 4; cf. O'Brien 1977, 214).

The second qualifier ("for everything"; *hyper pantōn*) is somewhat more difficult to interpret. Its primary function is probably best understood as roughly equivalent to the encouragements that he offers in other letters to give thanks "in everything" (1 Thess 5:18; Phil 4:6; cf. Col 3:17). Whether the different form of words that he uses here is intended to go beyond that, implying that thanks should be offered not only "in" (and despite) adverse circumstances but also, in some sense, "for" them is a difficult question to answer briefly. The fact that Paul has already made mention of his own sufferings in chapter 3, encouraging the readers to view them as "your glory"

(3:13), and is capable in other letters of encouraging and modeling an attitude of "boasting in" sufferings because of the way God works through them (e.g., Rom 5:3-4; Col 1:24; 2 Cor 12:9-10; cf. Rom 8:28), would suggest that an idea of this sort would not be foreign to Paul's understanding. But the closer context of the exhortation within this paragraph does not include a discussion of Paul's sufferings or those of the readers, and the idea that the "all things" for which God is to be thanked includes even things that are painful or evil does not receive any emphasis or elaboration. Nor, in those places where that idea is in view elsewhere in Paul's letters, is there any suggestion that suffering and evil, in and of themselves (apart from the grace of God at work through them), are things for which believers should be glad or thankful, or that an attitude of thankfulness in all circumstances is incompatible with groanings of lament (Rom 8:22-27, 36; cf. Starling 2017) or prayers and plans directed toward the alleviation of suffering (cf. 2 Cor 12:8; 2:1-8).

5:21. The string of participles concludes in v. 21: "submitting to one another in reverence toward Christ." While there is an obvious syntactical and thematic relationship between v. 21 and the household code that follows (see comments on 5:21–6:9 below) it is initially encountered by hearers of the letter as a further elaboration on what it looks like for a community of believers to be "filled with the Spirit" (v. 18).

The expression Paul uses ("submitting to one another") raises an obvious question about the relationship between the participle "submitting" (*hypotassomenoi*) and the reciprocal pronoun "to one another" (*allēlois*) that follows. If the verb from which the participle is formed is to carry the same sense here that it has in every other instance of its use within the New Testament (where, in all cases, it implies an asymmetrical, ordered relationship in which a person or power has authority over another), then it is difficult to see how the submission in view can possibly be reciprocal in a strict and literal sense.

Commentators, therefore, tend to divide at this point and follow one of two paths. Those who take the first path (e.g., Chrysostom, *Hom. Eph.* 19; Calvin 1965, 204; Best 1998, 515–18; Thielman 2010, 372–74; Arnold 2010, 355–57) attempt to give the reciprocal pronoun *allēlois* its full value by assigning to *hypotassomenoi* a meaning more neatly compatible with a symmetrically reciprocal framework, such as "deferring to one another" or "being servants of one another." Support for an interpretation of this sort can be found in the reciprocal structure of the household code that follows, with alternating words addressed to wives and husbands, children and fathers, slaves and masters, and the admonitions that Paul gives elsewhere to believers to "serve one another in love" (Gal 5:13), to "outdo one another in showing honor" (Rom 12:10), and to "look not only to [their] own interests, but to the interests of others" (Phil 2:4). Critics of this view point out, however, that the household code, while strikingly reciprocal in its structure, is not *symmetrically* reciprocal (husbands are not told to submit to their wives, parents are not told to obey children, and masters are not told to obey slaves); furthermore, injunctions such as those in Gal 5:13, Rom 12:10, and Phil 2:4 communicate their meaning without ever making use of the verb *hypotassō*, and (as observed above) *hypotassō* is never used anywhere else in the New Testament in the modified sense proposed by these interpreters. (One text that comes close is 1 Cor 16:15-16, where Paul's readers are reminded that the household of Stephanas have "devoted themselves" [*etaxan heautous*] to the service of the saints, and urged to "submit" [*hypotassēsthe*] to people such as them. Another possible example from outside the New Testament is *1 Clem.* 38.1, where the Corinthians are urged to "submit, each to his neighbor"; here, however, our understanding of what Clement means by the phrase needs to be informed not only by the summons to mutual concern in 38:2 but also by the qualifying phrase in 38:1b, "according to the way in which he was appointed in his particular gift," and the exhortation in 37:1-3 to imitate the way in which soldiers respond "submissively" [*hypotetagmenōs*] and "in an orderly manner" [*eutaktōs*] to the authority of those who are over them [my translations].)

In view of these difficulties, other commentators (e.g., Theodoret in Hill 2001, 2.52; Talbert 2007, 130–32; Hoehner 2002, 717) opt for a second path, which gives *hypotassomenoi* its normal meaning and reads *allēlois* in a looser fashion, as a way of referring not to a strict and literal, case-by-case reciprocity but to a variety of ways in which believers submit to other believers, in accordance with the social roles in which their relationships with one another are structured (cf. the use of the reciprocal pronoun in passages such as 1 Cor 11:33; Gal 6:2; Matt 24:10; Luke 12:1). On this reading it is, strictly speaking, the instructions to the wives (5:22-24), children (6:1-3), and slaves (6:5-8) that flow directly out of the exhortation in 5:21; the instructions to husbands (5:25-32), fathers (6:4), and masters (6:9) derive from the broader concern that the conduct of believers be consonant with the gospel (cf. 3:10; 4:1), and urge dispositions and behaviors that function as a kind of counterpoint or complement to the submission exercised by wives, children, and slaves (cf. 1 Cor 11:11-12; 1 Pet 5:5b).

The latter option, though not without its difficulties, is probably on balance to be preferred over the former. The net difference between the two interpretations should not be overstated, however, since (regardless of how v. 21 is taken) it is the nuance and complexity of the paragraphs that follow rather than the one-line introduction in 5:21 that should have primacy in shaping our understanding of how Paul wishes to see believers interacting with one another within the relationships of the household.

On either reading, the submission that is called for in v. 21a is not represented by Paul as merely a pragmatic, fearful, or self-interested accommodation to the power structures of Greco-Roman patriarchy; it is, rather, to be an expression of "reverence toward Christ" (*phobos Christou*)— a Christologically inflected version of the Old Testament motif of the fear of YHWH, in keeping with the wisdom theme introduced in 5:15-17 (cf. the discussion of the social entailments of the fear of the Lord in Starling 2014c, 112–18), with a partial analogy in the way that "reverence" and "piety" were expected to regulate honorable household behavior in traditional Greek and Roman morality (cf. Pseudo-Aristotle, *Oec.* 3.120–49, and the discussion of *pietas* in Saller 1994, 105–14).

Submitting to one another in reverence toward Christ (5:21–6:9)

(21) . . . submitting to one another in reverence toward Christ: (22) wives to your own husbands, as to the Lord, (23) for the husband is the head of the wife just as Christ is the head of the church—himself the Savior of the body—(24) But as the church submits to Christ, so also the wives, in everything, to their husbands. (25) Husbands, love your wives, just as Christ loved the church and gave himself up for her, (26) in order to sanctify her by cleansing her with the washing of water by the word, (27) so that he might present the church to himself glorious, not having a spot or wrinkle or anything of the kind, but rather that she might be holy and unblemished. (28) In the same way, husbands ought to love their own wives as their own bodies. He who loves his wife loves himself. (29) For no one ever hated his own flesh, but he nourishes and cherishes it, just as Christ [nourishes and cherishes] the church, (30) because we are members of his body: (31) "For this reason a man will leave his father and mother and be joined to his wife, and the two will become one flesh." (32) This mystery is great, but I am speaking about Christ and the church. (33) You, however, each one of you, let each one love his own wife as himself, and the wife should respect her husband. (6:1) Children, obey your parents in the Lord, for this is right. (2) "Honor your father and mother"—which is the first commandment with a promise: (3) "in order that it might go well with you and you might live long in the land." (4) And, fathers, do not provoke your children to anger, but bring them up in the instruction and admonition of the Lord. (5) Slaves, obey your fleshly masters with fear and trembling, in singleness of heart, as to Christ; (6) not by way of eye-service, as people-pleasers, but as slaves of Christ, doing the will of God from the heart, (7) serving with goodwill, as for the Lord and not for humans, (8) knowing that each person, if they do something good, it will be repaid

from the Lord, whether they are slave or free. (9) And, masters, do the same things for them, refraining from threatening, for you know that their Master and yours is in heaven, and there is no favoritism with him.

5:21. Paul's depiction of the Spirit-filled congregation as "submitting to one another in reverence toward Christ" is not only (as I have argued above) the conclusion to the series of participial clauses in vv. 19-21 that elaborate on the commands of v. 18. It is also a kind of introduction to the household code that follows. The syntactical relationship between v. 21 and v. 22 is created by the lack of a verb in the latter verse, requiring readers to fill the gap with the participle "submitting" from v. 21 (assuming, as is most likely, that the version of v. 22 in $\mathfrak{P}^{46}$ and B is original, and that other MSS, such as ℵ and A, which include *hypotassesthōsan* after *andrasin*, represent an attempt to tidy up the grammar of the original). The thematic relationship between v. 21 and the household code as a whole is signaled by the recurrence of the verb *hypotassō* ("submit") in v. 24 and the related themes and vocabulary in 5:33, 6:1-3, and 6:5-8.

A good case could be made, therefore, for reading the section of the letter that commences in 5:15 as extending all the way to 6:9 and understanding the household code as an extended elaboration on the commands in 5:15-21 to "walk not as unwise . . . but as wise" (5:15) and "be filled with the Spirit" (5:18) (cf. Lincoln 1990, 338; Thielman 2010, 353–54). Nevertheless, the obvious structural features that can be observed within 5:22–6:9, with its series of six paired paragraphs addressed, respectively, to wives, husbands, children, fathers, slaves, and masters, mark it out as a subsection of its own, with 5:21 functioning as a kind of syntactical and thematic bridge between 5:15-21 and 5:22–6:9.

The sources drawn upon by Paul in the composition of the household code and its function within the pastoral and rhetorical strategy of the letter have been the focus of a great deal of scholarly discussion in the modern era (cf. Balch 1988; Hering 2007, 9–60 for useful overviews). The three relationships that function as the structural categories for the code undoubtedly (and unsurprisingly) correspond neatly with the categories that frame the discussions of household order in the political philosophy of Aristotle (e.g., the examination of "the proper constitution and character" of the relationships between "master and slave, husband and wife, father and children" that is introduced in Aristotle, *Pol.* 1.3) and the advice-giving of the Stoic moralists (e.g., the precepts on subjects such as "how a husband should conduct himself towards his wife, or how a father should bring up his children, or how a master should rule his slaves," the usefulness of which Seneca sets out to defend in his *Ep.* 94.1).

Nevertheless, the structure of the code, with its alternating, direct address to wives and husbands, children and fathers, slaves and masters, has no real parallel or precedent in either the Greco-Roman household management texts or the Hellenistic Jewish apologetic literature. (Partial analogies can be seen in the second-person advice that Plutarch gives to Pollianus and Eurydice in *Conj. Praec.* 145b–146a, and in the extended, third-person instructions on the responsibilities of wives and husbands in Pseudo-Aristotle, *Oec.* 3.1–198—though in the latter case the concluding words in 3.199–200 make it clear that the primary audience addressed is not a gender-mixed *ekklēsia* but the same reading community of freeborn male householders that is addressed elsewhere within the Aristotelian corpus.) Household management was certainly a standard *topos* within the Greco-Roman and Hellenistic Jewish literature, but it goes beyond the evidence to claim that the "household code" was an established, pre-Christian genre that determined the form in which the writers of the New Testament framed their instruction on conduct and relationships within the household (cf. the similar assessment in Gehring 2004, 230).

As far as the content of the code is concerned, there are obvious points at which the ethical norms that are taught within it coincide with elements of conventional pagan morality, as it was variously developed and reasserted by first century philosophers and moralists (e.g., Plutarch, *Conj. Praec.* 142e), and with the attempts made by Hellenistic Jewish writers to show the harmony between those values and the teachings of the Old Testament (e.g., Ps.-Phoc. 195–227; Josephus, *Ag. Ap.* 2.199–214; Philo, *Decalogue* 165–67).

Nevertheless, it is going beyond the evidence (and, indeed, pushing against it) to claim, as is frequently asserted, that the household code in Ephesians is simply "borrowed from Graeco-Roman cultural norms" and "adopted for Christian households for the purpose of promoting familial order and social cohesion" (Bird 2016, 64; cf. Schüssler Fiorenza 2017, 92), or that its principal function is an apologetic one, mitigating against pagan suspicions that the Christian movement posed a threat to the social order by requiring that believers comply with conventional social mores (e.g., Lincoln 1990, 360). Even where the injunctions of the household code overlap with the conventional morality of the time, the rationale that Paul offers as a warrant for those shared norms is a distinctively Christian rationale. At no point, either within the household code or in its surrounding context within the letter, does Paul offer any suggestion that the purpose of the code is an apologetic one; nor does the logic with which he supports its injunctions even remotely resemble the logic of Aristotle's *Politics* or the Stoic moral treatises. Instead, he accompanies the instruction with an elaborate and explicitly Christian account of the way it is grounded in the intentions of the creator, interpreted in light of Old Testament Scripture and its fulfilment in the gospel of Christ, and locates it within a section of the letter that is headed by a vigorous reminder that his readers must "no longer walk as the Gentiles walk, in the futility of their mind, being darkened in their understanding" (4:17) (cf. Wright 2013, 1108, 1375–76; Arnold 2010, 369–72).

It would be a mistake, however, to conclude from this that Paul intends the instructions of the household code to be read (as is sometimes assumed in popular-level treatments) as a timeless template of the will of God for the shape of relationships in the family and the workplace. Proponents of this approach (rightly!) struggle to maintain that assumption consistently, especially when dealing with the prescriptions for slaves and masters. For the majority of modern readers of the letter, who are neither slaves nor owners of slaves, the instructions in 6:5-9 are simply impossible to apply without at least some degree of translation and re-contextualization; nor (contra Aristotle, *Politics* 1260a) does the way Paul frames his instructions offer any suggestion that the institution of slavery is a permanent or necessary principle of the natural order.

A better approach to the household code (as I have argued elsewhere, in Starling 2016, from which the following paragraphs are adapted) is to read its instructions within the narrative-dramatic framework of the letter as a whole (cf. Gombis 2010, 15–17). Read within this framework, the function of the instructions in the letter's second half is not merely to outline an *ethical* pattern of action that the readers are to offer up to God in gratitude for the salvation described in the first three chapters but also, and more basically, to offer direction to the church for its performance of a pattern of *communicative* action that faithfully corresponds to and displays the divine wisdom that has been made known in the story of salvation. The practices and dispositions commended in the code are, in almost every case, given both warrant and theological meaning by the various ways in which they are said to correspond to aspects of the story of salvation.

On this reading of the household code, a crucial interpretive question—perhaps *the* crucial interpretive question—to be asked as we make sense of the instructions in 5:20–6:9 is how they relate to the various elements of the salvation history that Paul recounts in chapters 1–3, directing the conduct of the readers so that they faithfully perform that story in their own speech and action, within the sociopolitical context in which they find themselves.

Wives . . . and husbands (5:22-32)
5:22. The first and longest set of instructions, in 5:22-33, is addressed to wives and husbands, commencing with a word to wives in vv. 22-24:

> [submitting to one another in reverence toward Christ]: wives to your own husbands, as to the Lord, for the husband is the head of the wife just as Christ is the head of the church—himself the Savior of the body—But as the church submits to Christ, so also [are] the wives [to submit], in everything, to their husbands.

Wives who live out the exhortations in 5:15-21 are depicted in v. 22 as submitting "to [their] own husbands, as to the Lord." The word "submitting" (as discussed above, on v. 21) implies an asymmetrically ordered relationship within which wives are to recognize the particular responsibility that has been assigned to their husbands and relate to them accordingly. Although the participle, as it occurs in v. 21, is in a form that could be read either passive ("being subjected") or middle ("submitting [yourselves]"), the former is most unlikely, given the way the participle of v. 21 follows on from the string of active-voice participles that precede it: what is in view here, in line with the earlier participles of vv. 19-20, is a posture that wives themselves adopt as a free act of their own will, not a yoke that is to be imposed on them by their husbands (or anyone else).

The fact that Paul refrains from introducing the verb *hypakouō* ("obey") within these verses may be a hint at the distinction in his mind between the husband-wife relationship (in which the submission referred to in v. 21 is worked out in the context of a relationship in which both parties are adults and neither is the slave of the other) and the child-parent and slave-master relationships, in which submission takes the form (in part, at least) of obedience (cf. 6:1, 5). In going out of his way to specify that it is to "their own" husbands that wives are to submit, Paul also excludes any notion that all women, as a class, are to be in some way subject to or submissive to all men (cf. Schüssler Fiorenza 2017, lvii, 89).

The phrase "as to the Lord" (*hōs tō kyriō*), with which Paul concludes the verse, functions in part to anticipate the analogy that is introduced in the following verse, and at second hearing it makes good sense to read the typological correspondence of vv. 23-32 back into the logic of v. 22. But the primary and more basic point of Paul's "as to the Lord" in v. 22 is probably the same as that of the identically worded phrase in 6:5 (and its expanded form in 6:7), where it occurs in the absence of any equivalent to the elaborate analogy of 5:23-32: the submission of a wife to her husband is, at its heart, an expression and outworking of her submission to Christ.

5:23. The following verse supplies a reason for the exhortation in v. 22: "for the husband is the head of the wife, just as Christ is the head of the church—himself the Savior of the body." The claim made by a line of late twentieth century interpreters (e.g., Kroeger 1993; Mickelsen and Mickelsen 1986, 108–10) that the word *kephalē* ("head") is functioning here as a metaphor meaning "source," without any sense of authority implied, is not well supported by the evidence that is typically cited. It is true, for example, that Herodotus can refer to "the headwaters of the river Tearus" (*tearou potamou kephalai*) (*Hist.* 4.91), but the context of the metaphor in that instance is different from those places where it is a person that is referred to as "head." Closer to the mark is the frequently quoted Orphic fragment in which Zeus is acclaimed as "head" (*kephalē*) and "middle" (*messa*), and the one "from whom comes all that is" (*Dios d'ek panta tetyktai*) (e.g., Pseudo-Aristotle, *De Mundo* 401b). Even here, however, the relationship between Zeus and the cosmos that the hymn describes is one in which derivation (e.g., "root [*rhiza*] of the sea . . . root of the sun and the moon") and rule (e.g., "Zeus the king, ruler of all, ruling the thunder") are inextricably linked. In the LXX, although it is true that the Hebrew word *rōš*, used in the sense of "ruler," is more frequently translated as *archōn*, it is not difficult find examples of places in which *kephalē* does carry that sense (e.g., LXX Judg 11:11; 2 Kgdms 22:44), and it would have contributed to the range of possibilities that Paul and his readers would have had in mind for the metaphorical use of the word.

Within the closer context of Ephesians itself, Paul has already used the word *kephalē* to speak of Christ in relation to all things (1:22) and the church (1:22; 4:15). In the former instance (1:22), Christ is depicted as both "head over all things" and as the one whom God "gave . . . as head . . . to the church, which is his body, the fullness of the one who is filling all things in every way"; the fusing together of the two metaphors suggests an understanding in which the head is both a locus of authority and a source of fullness. In the latter instance (4:15), both of these ideas are also present in the surrounding context, which speaks of Christ as both the one who "ascended, high above all the heavens" (4:10) and the one who "fill[s] all things" (4:10) and is the source of the body's growth (4:16; cf. Col 2:19).

A similar combination of ideas can also be seen in 5:22-33. The exhortations to wives to "submit to" (v. 24) and "respect" (*phobētai*) (v. 33) their husbands imply the asymmetry of an ordered relationship in which husbands are charged with a particular authority or responsibility that wives are to recognize. At the same time, however, the way the analogy between marriage and Christ's relationship with the church is developed in vv. 25-33 suggests that the body/head metaphor has either been extended into or juxtaposed with an image of the way a person "feeds and cares for" their own body (vv. 29-30).

The dichotomy between "authority" and "source [of strength and fullness]" as rival senses of the metaphor in 5:23 is, therefore, best rejected as a false one. Although it is true that Paul can on occasion use the image to speak primarily of "authority over" (e.g., the depiction of Christ as head over the powers in Col 2:10), the lifegiving nature of Christ's rule as the one who "fills all things" is never far from Paul's thinking, whether he is speaking of Christ as head over the cosmos or as head of the church.

If, as v. 23b makes clear, it is the role of Christ as head of the church that is to shape our understanding of the role of a husband as the head of his wife, then v. 23, taken as a whole, offers a double reason for wives to "submit to" their husbands as they are encouraged to do in v. 22. In the first place (v. 23a) it is a reminder of the *fact* of the husband's headship; and in the second place (v. 23b) it is a reminder of the *nature* of that headship—or at least the nature of what that headship ought to be—as patterned on the strengthening, lifegiving headship of Christ over the church.

This last theme—the headship of Christ as a source of fullness (1:23) and growth (4:16) for his people—is further developed in v. 23b, where Christ is depicted not only as "head of the church" but as "Savior of the body." The point of the latter depiction is not to imply that husbands are somehow the brokers or guarantors of their wives' eternal salvation; those same wives, after all, are members of the very church that *Christ* is the savior of, and Paul can hardly be intending to displace Christ from that role. But it does imply an analogy of some sort between the self-giving, salvific love of Christ that Paul will go on to describe in vv. 25-27 and the manner in which husbands are called on to love their wives. While no human husband will ever succeed in fulfilling that vocation perfectly, the fact that they are called to do so is given by Paul as a reason that wives ought to receive the headship of their husbands not as an imposition or enslavement but as a source of blessing. (Conversely, where a husband's "headship" is functioning not as an imperfect copy of Christ's but as an ugly, abusive parody, the logic of vv. 22–23 would suggest that she should be urged in the strongest terms *not* to consider herself dutybound to continue as the victim of his abuse.)

5:24. The "but" at the start of v. 24 pulls the discussion back from the brief parenthesis in v. 23b ("himself the Savior of the body") to the topic more immediately at hand: "But as the church submits to Christ, so also the wives, in everything, to their husbands." The comprehensiveness with which that submission is depicted ("in everything") should not be pressed in a wooden, literalistic manner, as if it admitted no exceptions. Old Testament precedent (e.g., 1 Sam 25) and conventional Greco-Roman wisdom (e.g., Musonius Rufus, *Diss.* 16) would both have encouraged the assumption that there were situations in which a husband's folly or wickedness ought to be resisted rather than indulged or complied with (cf. Thielman 2010, 380–81); for Musonius Rufus (*Diss.* 16.23), a conclusion of that sort, in relation to the obedience that a son owed to his parents, was so self-evident that the question need hardly be asked. While the possibility of exceptions of this nature would almost certainly have been included among the taken-for-granted background assumptions that Paul and his readers brought to the text, his focus here is not on the exceptions but on the general pattern, in which the wife's submission to the Christ-imitating headship of her husband ought to pervade all aspects of their relationship.

5:25. The following paragraph continues the analogy and applies it in an extended series of exhortations to husbands. The gist of his exhortation, signaled in the opening verse, is not a word of advice to husbands about how they should "rule" (*archein*) or "control" (*kratein*) their wives (cf. Plutarch, *Conj. praec.* 142e) but a command that they should "love [their] wives, just as Christ loved the church and gave himself up for her" (v. 25).

The idea that husbands should love their wives would not have been an altogether novel one for first century Greco-Roman readers (e.g., the encouragement in Musonius Rufus, *Diss.* 13a for wives and husbands to cultivate *kēdemonia* ["solicitude" or "care"] for one another, Plutarch's picture in *Conj. praec.* 142f of the ideal marriage as "a marriage of lovers" [*gamos . . . tōn erōntōn*], and the injunction in Pseudo-Charondas [Stobaeus, *Anth.* 4.2.24.101] that "each one should love [*stergetō*] his lawfully wedded wife and beget children by her"). Nevertheless, the particular form of love that Paul urges husbands to have for their wives—a self-giving love, patterned on the love of Christ for the church—would have been understood by his readers as different in both kind and degree from what was typically advised and celebrated by the moralists and philosophers.

Paul has already, in 5:2, appealed to the example of Christ in his crucifixion as a paradigm of love as self-giving, and exhorted all believers to imitate that pattern in their love for one another. Here, however (without implying that wives are exempt from any need to love their husbands), the example is applied more particularly to the love that husbands are to have for their wives. One effect of this is that the "headship" of husbands, which Paul has already made reference to in the previous verse, is strikingly and counterculturally reframed so that it is defined not by the paradigm of Augustan imperial ideology or traditional notions of *monarchia* (cf. Augustus, *Res Gestae* 35; Aristotle, *Politics* 1255b) but by the cruciform politics of the gospel (cf. Mark 10:42-45).

5:26-27. Paul's appeal to the example of Christ in v. 25 gives rise to a digression in vv. 26-27, elaborating on Christ's purpose in loving the church and giving himself for her: "in order to sanctify her by cleansing her with the washing of water by the word, so that he might present the church to himself glorious, not having a spot or wrinkle or anything of the kind, but rather that she might be holy and unblemished."

Within this elaborated version of the analogy between the husband/wife and Christ/church relationships, the church is pictured not as the wife of Christ but as his bride, preparing for a marriage that is still to take place. Christ gave himself for the church, Paul reminds his readers, not only to save her (cf. v. 23) but also to "sanctify" her—that is, to set her apart as a holy people. While the death of Christ is pictured here as directed toward the goal of the church's sanctification, Paul's further elaboration on the image makes it clear that in his mind the kind of sanctification he has in view is not barely or one-dimensionally positional. Christ died in order to sanctify the church, but he accomplishes her sanctification "by cleansing her with the washing of water by the word," an image that would probably have carried connotations of Christian baptism but is constructed primarily as a metaphor for the cleansing effect of the gospel message (cf. 1 Cor 6:11; Eph 1:13-14), drawing on the image of the Levitical lustrations as it is refracted through Ezekiel (e.g., 36:25) and Zechariah (e.g., 13:1).

But even this is not the end of the story Paul has in mind. For the "cleansing" accomplished through the word of the gospel has a longer-term, eschatological purpose in view: "so that he might present the church to himself glorious, not having a spot or wrinkle or anything of the kind, but rather that she might be holy and unblemished." Although some commentators (e.g., Lincoln 1990, 377; Best 1998, 545–46) read v. 27 as referring to a purpose that has already been accomplished in the present existence of the church, it makes better sense to read it in light of the similar imagery and language that Paul employs elsewhere (e.g., 2 Cor 11:2; 1 Thess 3:13; 5:23; Col 1:22), as an anticipation of the day when Christ will "present" the church to himself at the parousia.

If that is the sense Paul has in mind in v. 27, then the earlier reference to Christ as having "cleansed" the church in v. 26 need not be viewed exclusively as a description of the instantaneous effect of believers' initial reception of the gospel but as a global, summary depiction of the gospel's effect in the lives of those who receive it, represented by Paul as the means by which the church's sanctification is accomplished (cf. Mathewson and Emig 2016, 122–23; 214–15; Wallace 1996, 557–58). The sanctification that Paul has in view, according to v. 27, includes not just a change in believers' status but the transformation of their conduct; the metaphorical depiction of the church in v. 27a as "not having a spot or wrinkle or anything of the kind" is unpacked in v. 27b in ethical terms ("holy and unblemished"), recalling the earlier, and similarly ethical, use of the same language in 1:4 (see comments above on that verse).

It would be a mistake to transfer the totality of what is said about Christ in vv. 26-27 to the role that husbands play in relation to their wives; Paul does not say that husbands "sanctify" their wives, "wash" them with the word, or "present" them to Christ at the last day. But it would also be a mistake to read vv. 26-27 as if they were entirely disconnected from the surrounding context of vv. 25-33. Paul's main point to husbands is that they are to love their wives and that the nature of their love is to be sacrificial and self-giving, modeled on the love of Christ for the church. But the elaboration in vv. 26-27 on the purposes of Christ in giving himself for the church does still serve indirectly to shed light on the way husbands are to love their wives, making it clear that the self-giving love of Christ was not, at its heart, a surrender to the projects and desires of the people for whom he died but a costly commitment to their good (and in particular, to their salvation and holiness). The love that husbands are to have for their wives is also, by implication, to be informed by the same desire—as, for that matter, is the love that all believers are to have for one another and for their neighbors (cf. 1 Cor 10:31–11:1; Rom 15:2).

5:28. The connection between what Paul has been saying about Christ and the church in vv. 25b-27 and the exhortation to husbands that is the main theme of the paragraph is made explicit in v. 28, where he tells his readers that "in the same way, husbands ought to love their own wives." The remainder of vv. 28-30 go on to extend and develop the analogy between marriage and the Christ/church relationship, *via* a reflection on the care a person takes for his or her own body, and the care Christ takes for his body, the church: "In the same way, husbands ought to love their own wives as their own bodies. He who loves his wife loves himself. For no one ever hated his own flesh, but he feeds and cares for it, just as Christ [feeds and cares for] the church, because we are members of his body."

Paul's encouragement to husbands to love their wives "as their own bodies" has an obvious background in Gen 2:24 (cf. 1 Cor 6:16), a connection that he will go on to make explicit in vv. 31-32. Broadly similar notions can also be found in the Greco-Roman literature (e.g., Plutarch, *Conj. praec.* 142e, though in that instance the picture is not of two people who are one flesh but of the soul in its relation to the body, and the simile is invoked as an image not of how the husband should love his wife but of how he should "rule" her). Here, however, the image is presented, at least initially, not as a direct implication of Gen 2:14 but as an outworking ("in the same way . . .") of the comparison in vv. 25-27 between the love to which husbands are called and the love of Christ for the church.

The exhortation in vv. 28-29, therefore, should not be read as a new and additional description of the way husbands are to love their wives, or a reason for them to do so. It is an elaboration on the Christ-church relationship and a further unfolding of its entailments as a model for the way husbands are to love their wives. The parenthetical comment in v. 28b ("He who loves his wife loves himself") serves the same purpose; its function within Paul's argument is not as a rhetorical appeal to advantage (though there is a certain common-sensical truth to the claim that the joy and flourishing of a man's wife will, in turn, contribute to his own well-being and happiness) but as a further underlining of the fact that husbands are tied to their wives with the closest of possible bonds, analogous to the bonds between Christ and his people.

5:29-30. Paul's exhortation in v. 28 receives further support in v. 29a, with its reminder that "no one ever hated his own flesh, but he feeds and cares for it." The point of v. 29a is not so much to ridicule the foolishness of a husband who fails to care for his wife but to expose the shamefulness of his failure: he would never neglect himself in this fashion, yet he is prepared to neglect his wife, who is "his own flesh." The terms that Paul uses (*ektrephei*, "feeds," and *thalpei*, "cares for"), applied to the way a person treats his or her own body, imply the provision of food in the case of *ektrephei*, and warmth or clothing in the case of *thalpei*; used in combination, and in the context of interpersonal relationships, they can refer to the kind of provision and care to which a wife was entitled from her husband (e.g., P.Cair. Masp. 1 67006; SB 18 13886, though the late date of these two texts should be noted), and can at times extend beyond the provision of material necessities to imply the kind of emotional tenderness that a mother shows to her children or a husband to his wife (e.g., 1 Thess 2:7; *Vita Aesopi* 250.13; cf. *thalpein* in CPR 1.30 frag. 2.20, also late).

In keeping with the fact that the ruling analogy throughout vv. 25-33 is not between marriage and the care that one shows for one's own body but between marriage and the relationship between Christ and the church, Paul returns to that relationship in vv. 29b-30: ". . . just as Christ [feeds and cares for] the church, because we are members of his body." The image of believers as "members of [Christ's] body" is one that he has already used earlier in the letter (cf. 1:23; 4:12, 16), as is the picture of Christ as providing for the body's fullness and growth (1:23; 4:16). Here, Paul's purpose is not simply to recapitulate that earlier idea but to apply it by analogy to the way husbands are to love their wives.

5:31. The threads that connect Paul's imagery in vv. 25-27 ("as Christ loved the church") and vv. 28-30 ("as their own bodies") are tied together more tightly still in vv. 31-32, which appropriate the words of Gen 2:24 about the one flesh unity of a wife with her husband as "mystery" pointing toward the unity of Christ and the church: "'For this reason a man will leave his father and mother and be joined to his wife, and the two will become one flesh.' This mystery is great, but I am speaking about Christ and the church."

Although the narrative of Genesis 2 about the creation of Eve and the inference drawn from it in Gen 2:24 have an obvious relevance to the topic at hand, Paul does not draw a straight line, applying them directly to the husbands and wives among his readers. Instead, he frames the quotation, both before (v. 30) and after (v. 32), with assertions about Christ and the church. Within this frame, the opening words of his quotation from the biblical text (*anti toutou*, "for this reason"—presumably Paul's adaptation of the similar expression, *heneken toutou*, in surviving versions of the Greek OT) are given a new function. Whereas in the original context of Genesis 2, the *heneken toutou* ("for this reason") with which the verse commences presents the depiction of marriage that follows as a consequence of the narrative in the preceding paragraph, in the verse's new context within Ephesians 5 Paul's *anti toutou* presents it as a consequence of the relationship between Christ and the church, as "members of his body" (for arguments in favor of this reading, see Thielman 2007, 826–28).

The assumption that appears to underlie Paul's assertion is that God the creator, who established the institution of marriage in the beginning, already had in mind its fittingness as an image for his own relationship with his people and, in particular, for the relationship between Christ and his body, the church. Paul's appeal to the creation story of Genesis 2 in this context does not, therefore, function as a philosophical argument, in Aristotelian fashion, to assert a particular view of the gendered roles of husbands and wives as a direct and necessary inference from the biological differences of nature (cf. the rationale Aristotle offers for the social roles that he prescribes in *Politics* 1260a.9–14). Rather, it suggests an understanding of marriage as an expression of the communicative purposes of God, designed to function as a sign of the relationship between Christ and the church, and an assertion that God had this purpose in mind at the beginning, when he created men and women in a manner that makes it fitting for them to be joined together as "one flesh."

The claim that Paul is making here about the (divinely intended) function of marriage as a sign of the union between Christ and the church is not something that can be drawn directly from the text of Gen 2:24, read within its immediate, original context. There is a partial precedent for the way Paul appropriates and applies the language of Genesis in the Old Testament's use of marriage as a figure for the relationship between YHWH and his people, Israel—either as a backward-looking image for Israel/Judah's covenant infidelities (e.g., Hos 1:2; Jer 2–3; Ezek 16, 23) or as a forward-looking image for YHWH's future mercies (e.g., Hos 2:14-20; Isa 54:5-10). But Paul goes beyond anything in the Old Testament, both by the way he converts an image of the exclusive relationship between YHWH and his people into an image of Christ and the (Gentile-inclusive) church and by the way he characterizes that relationship as a "one flesh" union, appropriating the words of Genesis 2.

5:32. Paul could not have been unaware of the extent to which his appropriation of the Genesis text goes beyond the meaning of the text within its original context or the way it is interpreted and appropriated within the Old Testament and in Second Temple Jewish interpretation. It is this awareness on his part that appears to lie behind his acknowledgment in v. 32a that "this mystery is great." The word *mystērion*, here as elsewhere in Ephesians, is best read as referring to a truth newly and specially revealed by God, which could not have been known or understood apart from that divine revelation. When Paul goes on in v. 32b to say, "but I am speaking (*egō de legō*) about Christ and the church," he is not (Lincoln 1990, 382) contrasting his interpretation of the Genesis text with the unspecified interpretations of others. He is, rather, signaling the distinction between the plain meaning of the text, read within its immediate, original context (or even within the larger, canonical context of the Old Testament) and the additional significance it carries when read in light of the eschatologically revealed mystery that Jews and Gentiles are "fellow members of the body (*syssōma*) . . . in Christ Jesus through the gospel" (3:6).

In appropriating the words of Gen 2:24 in this manner, Paul is not implying any desire to set aside the verse's original sense or reference (e.g., its applicability to ordinary human marriages, or its grounding in the preceding narrative of Gen 2:18-23). It is, after all, only because a husband and wife are "one flesh" with one another, in accordance with the ordinary and original meaning of Gen 2:24, that a typological parallel can be established between their union and the union that exists between Christ and the church. (Nor does Paul offer any suggestion that every detail of the verse should be read typologically, as if an antitype were to be found in the story of Christ and the church for the "leaving" of father and mother, or for the "father and mother" who are left.)

Accordingly, therefore, it is to the ordinary human marriages of his readers that Paul returns in v. 33, with the opening "you, however" (*plēn kai hymeis*) signaling a turn back from the Christ/church relationship that has been the focus in vv. 29b-32 to its application in the lives of the readers: "You, however, each one of you, let each one love his own wife as himself, and let the wife respect her husband."

The unusual syntax of the address to the readers that follows ("you . . . each one of you"; *kai hymeis hoi kath' hena*) has an effect that is both emphatic and individualizing, and should probably be read as directed to both the husbands and the wives (Larkin 2009, 142; Best 1998, 558; contra Thielman 2010, 390). What follows is a pair of short, summarizing statements addressed to husbands and wives respectively. Husbands are told that each of them is to "love his own wife as himself," echoing the ideas of vv. 25-32 (especially v. 28), though not in identical language. And wives, for their part, are told that they are to "respect" (*phobētai*) their husbands. The grammatical form that Paul uses in addressing this exhortation to the wives (*hina phobētai*) differs from the third-person imperative with which he addresses the husbands, and implies the ellipsis of a verb such as *thelō* ("I desire . . .") (Larkin 2009, 143). Although the verb *phobeō* can at times carry the sense of fear or even terror (e.g., LXX Exod 14:10; Matt 27:54), the sense in which Paul is using it here is better conveyed in English by a word such as "respect." It corresponds in an analogous manner to the "reverence" (*phobos*) that all the members of the congregation are to have toward Christ (5:31), but it is best translated with a verb other than "revere" to reflect the distinction (both in kind and degree) between the attitude that believers are to have toward Christ, as the one who is "high above all rule and authority and power and dominion" (1:21), and the attitude that wives are to have to their husbands. (On the complexities of *phobos* language in early Christian social and religious usage, see Starling 2014c, 112–18).

Children . . . and fathers (6:1-4)

6:1. The instructions to children and fathers in 6:1-4 are noticeably briefer than the preceding paragraphs addressed to wives and husbands. Although early Christians, in common with their pagan and Jewish neighbors, held a high view of the duties that adult men and women continued to owe to their parents (e.g., Mark 7:9-13; 1 Tim 5:4; cf. Cicero, *Off.* 1.58; Philo, *Decalogue*

116), the address to "children" (*tekna*) in vv. 1-3 should probably be taken as directed to a subset of the congregation rather than to the congregation as a whole, regardless of age (Arnold 2010, 415; Lincoln 1990, 403; contra the tacit assumption in Thielman 2010, 396–97). The "children" addressed, based on the content of the instructions that follow, are those who were old enough to be present within the assembly and listening to the letter as it is read out but young enough to still be in the process of being brought up (v. 4) by their parents.

Unlike wives, who are described in vv. 21-22 as "submitting" (*hypotassomenai*) to their husbands, children are told to "obey" (*hypakouete*) their parents, the variation in wording presumably reflecting the difference in Paul's thinking between the demands of the parent-child relationship and those of the relationship between a husband and a wife. The modifying phrase, "in the Lord" (*en kyriō*), is best interpreted as a reminder to children that their conduct in this respect, as in all others, ought to be understood as an expression of their own identity in Christ and their calling to speak and act as his people, in obedience to him (cf. 4:17, 5:8, and the discussion in Thielman 2010, 397; for text-critical arguments in favor of reading "in the Lord" as original see Metzger 1994, 541–42; Lincoln 1990, 395). The further warrant, "for this is right" (v. 1b), would probably have carried a certain self-evidentness in the light of the moral consensus of the time, but its context within Paul's exhortation, sandwiched between the reminder that Christian obedience is to be rendered "in the Lord" and the quotation from the Decalogue in the following verse, suggests that the primary source for believers' knowledge of what is right is the will of God (cf. 5:10), not the values of the surrounding culture (cf. the parallel exhortation in Col 3:20, and the brief comments in Arnold 2010, 416).

6:2-3. The quotation of the fifth commandment that follows in vv. 2-3 is interrupted by an editorial comment from Paul ("which is the first commandment with a promise"), focusing his readers' attention on the promise of blessing and inheritance that accompanied Moses' commandment to the Israelites and inviting them to identify their own situation as typologically equivalent to that of Moses's first hearers (cf. Starling 2014b, 155–58).

Two main hermeneutical questions arise out of the quotation of the fifth commandment that follows in v. 2 and the accompanying promise that Paul quotes in v. 3 (cf. Starling 2014b, 155–58, from which the following paragraphs are adapted). The first question (arising out of the commandment) is about whether and in what sense Paul viewed the Old Testament law as addressed to and authoritative for his Gentile Christian readers; the second question (arising out of the promise) is about how Paul understood that a promise of long life and blessing in the promised land might be fulfilled for those same readers.

The first question becomes particularly acute when Paul's quotation of the commandment in 6:2 is placed alongside his earlier assertion in 2:15 that Christ in his death has "abolish[ed] the law of commandments in the form of ordinances." The most natural reading of 2:15 (as argued in the discussion of that verse above) is that the only qualification intended by Paul is the one that he himself states—that what has been abolished is the law "of commandments in the form of ordinances" (*tōn entolōn en dogmasin*), i.e., the function of the law as a directly commanding covenantal authority over believers in Jesus. If that is the most natural reading of 2:15, then the tension between 2:15 and 6:2-3 remains, as long as the quotation from Exod 20:12 in Eph 6:2 is read as a commandment directly addressed to the Gentile Christian readers of the letter. The fact that this is the reading of 6:2-3 assumed by most commentators is, presumably, one of the reasons they feel compelled to hedge the bold statement of 2:15 around with additional qualifications, so that the law of Moses can still remain authoritative enough to command children in 6:2 to give honor to their parents.

The second hermeneutical problem raised by 6:2-3 is the question of how a promise of long life and blessing in the promised land addressed to Israel at Sinai was understood by Paul to apply to Gentile Christians in Ephesus. The assumption adopted by most commentators is that Paul intends his readers to hear themselves directly addressed in the words of the promise in v. 3. For this reason, it is argued, he abbreviates the quotation from Exodus 20 so that the final phrase *epi tēs gēs tēs agathēs, hēs kyrios ho theos sou didōsin soi* ("on the good land that the Lord your God is giving you") becomes simply *epi tēs gēs*, which would have been understood by the readers of Ephesians as meaning "on the earth." Almost all English translations (with the notable exception of the ESV) adopt this approach. This interpretation creates more problems than it solves, however, and leaves commentators clutching at straws to explain what Paul means when he promises his readers long life and earthly blessing in return for obedience to their parents. Lincoln, for example, suggests that the writer has simply failed to integrate the "Jewish this-worldly perspective" of the commandment with the way he has used "inheritance" language in the first half of the letter (Lincoln 1990, 405), and Mitton proposes that the promise should best be interpreted communally, to mean that "a society in which the aged are respected and cared for by their children is a healthy and stable one" (Mitton 1976, 213, as summarized in Lincoln, 405).

A better approach to resolving the hermeneutical issues raised by the command and the promise is to start by observing the way the word addressed to children in 6:1-3 is located not only within the immediate context of the household table (5:22–6:9) but also within the wider context of the eschatological ethic that Paul lays the foundation for in 4:17–5:21, which encourages the readers to think and act as people who have experienced a decisive transfer from the "darkness" of life under the powers of the present age into the "light" of life in Christ (e.g., 4:21-23, 5:7, 14).

Within 6:1-9 in particular, this latter connection is particularly prominent; thus, Snodgrass points out the connections between 6:1 and 5:3, 4, 9; between 6:4a and 4:26-27, 31; between 6:4b and 4:20-21; between 6:8 and 4:28-29; and between 6:8-9 and 5:5-6 (Snodgrass 1996, 320). What is "right" (6:1) is to be understood in these terms, as "the fruit of the light" (5:9), and the "darkness" and "light" themselves are to be understood as defined eschatologically by the coming judgement and salvation of God; the works of darkness are those things on which the wrath of God comes (5:6), and the things that are "proper" among the saints are the things that correspond with "an inheritance in the kingdom of Christ and of God" (5:5, cf. 4:30).

When the command to children is read against that backdrop, it seems almost inconceivable that Paul would have reverted in 6:3 to an ethic motivated by promises of this-worldly long life and blessing, forgetting the "inheritance" typology established in 1:13-14 and evoked as recently in the letter as 4:30 and 5:5. If that typological framework is still securely in place here in chapter 6, then there is no need for the promise about "life in the land" to be turned into a promise about "life on the earth"; "the land" is still "the land," but the readers are expected to know that the promise being quoted is a word addressed to Israel at Mount Sinai and that the corresponding promise for them, as the new exodus community, is a promise about life in the eschatological kingdom in which they have obtained an inheritance through Christ.

If that is the approach Paul would have expected his readers to take in appropriating the promise in v. 3, it is reasonable to assume that he expects a similar hermeneutical sophistication in the approach that they should take to the command in v. 2: like the promise, it is a word addressed to Israel at Sinai, a speech-event within the story of the original exodus, and not a word directly addressed to his Gentile Christian readers. For them, it still has instructive value and a normative function in teaching the way of wisdom (cf. 5:15, 17 and the discussion in Rosner 2013, ch. 6), but it is no longer encountered as if it were embedded within a covenant of law to which the readers are subject.

6:4. Fathers, for their part, are addressed in v. 4 and told not to "provoke [their] children to anger" but rather to "bring them up in the instruction and admonition of the Lord" (v. 4). While the instructions of vv. 1-3 presuppose a role for both fathers and mothers in the authoritative instruction of children, it is the fathers who are directly addressed in v. 4. This is probably, in part at least, a reflection of the particular responsibilities that were carried by fathers in both Old Testament teaching and Greco-Roman culture (cf. Gen 18:19; Deut 6:7, 20, and Prudentius, *C. Symm.* 1.197-214; Plutarch, *Cat. Maj.* 20, quoted in Lincoln 1990, 400); it may also reflect the unique way in which (for good or for ill) the care and discipline of fathers serves as a likeness of the care and discipline of God.

With this in mind, the warning of v. 4a ("do not provoke your children to anger") should be read as reflecting both the concerns about anger expressed earlier in the letter (cf. 4:26, 31) and the desire on Paul's part that fathers use the considerable power that they possessed within a first-century household in a way that faithfully represented the gentleness, patience, and justice of God, avoiding the harshness and unfairness that would provoke an understandable response of anger and bitterness in their children.

The likelihood that a concern of this sort is present within Paul's thinking is strengthened by the words he uses in v. 4a ("but bring them up in the instruction and admonition of the Lord") and their background in Old Testament texts such as Prov 3:11-12. If we are to read Paul's "of the Lord" as a subjective genitive, with the same force as the equivalent expression in LXX Prov 3:11 (cf. Thielman 2010, 402), then the most likely intended force of his words is to remind human fathers that their activity is meant to function as a vehicle for the Lord's own fatherly training and instruction of his children, with the implication that they ought to regulate the manner and conduct of their teaching accordingly.

The word *paideia* ("instruction"), in line with its use in both the Greco-Roman literature and the book of Proverbs (which is its primary background here), should best be understood as a comprehensive reference to the formative instruction that shaped the character and understanding of a child. While it can at times carry a narrower sense, referring to painful corrections of punitive discipline (e.g., LXX 2 Esd 7:26; 2 Macc 6:12; 7:33), the context here and the background in Proverbs suggest a broader understanding, including but not limited to the "discipline" that accompanied parental instruction (cf. Prov 15:5; 19:20). The accompanying word, *nouthesia* ("admonition"), can sometimes be used with a similar breadth of meaning, but it typically refers somewhat more narrowly to the warnings that anticipated bad conduct or the admonitions that responded to it (e.g., Wis 16:6; 1 Cor 10:11) and should probably be taken in that sense here.

Slaves . . . and masters (6:5-9)
6:5. Finally, in 6:5-9, Paul turns to slaves and masters. The direct address to slaves in v. 5, like the address to children in v. 1 and (to a lesser extent) the address to wives in 5:22, would have stood out as unusual in the first century context, presupposing as it does the moral agency and responsibility of slaves and their presence as full members in the *ekklēsia*. The masters whom they are urged to obey are described by Paul as "your fleshly (*kata sarka*) masters," a description that is unlikely to carry the negative connotations it can have elsewhere in Paul, when it is used of a "fleshly" mindset or conduct (e.g., Rom 8:4-5, 12-13; 2 Cor 1:17), but does, nonetheless, function to relativize the authority of earthly masters in comparison to the heavenly *kyrios* (cf. vv. 7, 8, 9) that slave and master have in common.

The obedience that slaves are to give to their masters is described by Paul in a series of phrases strung together in vv. 5b-7, which combine to show how the way they serve their earthly masters is transformed by the allegiance they have to Christ as their master in heaven. The first phrase, in v. 5b, describes their obedience as being offered "with fear and trembling" (*meta phobou kai tromou*). Within the Old Testament, the phrase Paul uses can sometimes refer to the terror that is felt before a human enemy (e.g., Deut 2:25) and on other occasions to the proper human response before God (e.g., Ps 2:11; LXX Dan 4:37a). Paul uses it in the latter sense in Phil 2:12 (and possibly also in 1 Cor 2:3; cf. Savage 1996, 73), and there is no compelling reason that it should not have that meaning here, given the repeated references to Christ and eschatological judgment in vv. 5c–9 and the explicit appeal to "the fear of Christ" in the closely similar context of Col 3:22 (cf. Witherington 2007, 340; Caird 1976, 90). Alternatively, if Paul is using the phrase to refer directly to the attitude slaves should have toward their masters, it is best taken as implying not a cringing fear of punishment but the sort of respectful conscientiousness that it is in view in 2 Cor 7:15, where it is used to describe the Corinthians' reception of Titus.

The second phrase, in v. 5c, describes the obedience slaves are to give to their masters as an obedience that is offered "in singleness of heart," language that implies sincerity and integrity (cf. 2 Cor 1:12; 11:3; LXX 1 Chr 29:17; Wis 1:1; T. Iss. 4:1-6). The reason such sincerity is required is the fact, third, that slaves are to perform their service "as to Christ" (v. 5c), an expression that is further unpacked in vv. 6-7 and depicts slaves' obedience to their earthly masters as a manifestation and outworking of their obedience to Christ.

6:6-7. Verses 6-7 further describe the obedience slaves are to give to masters, in the form of an extended *mē . . . alla* ("not . . . but") contrast. Slaves are not to obey their earthly masters "by way of eye-service, as people-pleasers" (v. 6a); instead, they are to serve "as slaves of Christ, doing the will of God from the heart, serving with goodwill, as for the Lord and not for humans" (vv. 6b-7). Paul's language here calls for an act of the moral imagination that involves both an element of fiction ("as if you were not working for humans, though in fact you are") and the recognition of a deeper truth ("in keeping with the reality that you are, in fact, slaves of Christ, and it is ultimately Christ whom you are serving"). Even the fictive element of the mindset that Paul calls for is, in a sense, made real by the way he has exhorted them to think and act in v. 6a: by choosing not to limit their obedience to the times and places when they are under human observation, they liberate themselves from a paradigm in which their conduct is determined entirely by the threats and rewards of their earthly masters (cf. the similar comments in Lincoln 1990, 421).

In place of the "eye-service" of "people-pleasers," they are to serve "from the heart (*ek psychēs*) . . . with goodwill (*met' eunoias*)." The latter expression is used nowhere else in the New Testament but occurs frequently in the Greco-Roman sources, both literary and non-literary. Used in relation to free people, it could describe either the generosity of a patron (e.g., Inschr. Eph. 233, 683a, 1537, 1547; cf. Judge 2008, 373) or the reciprocating goodwill of a client (e.g., IG VII, 2713, and the examples cited in Lendon 1997, 156); on the rare occasions when it is used of a slave, it describes the kind of ungrudging, enthusiastic disposition that was (understandably) both uncommon and highly valued (cf. P. Oxy. 494.6; Lucian, *Bis acc.* 16; Eccelus, *Frag.* 78.10-11, cited in Lincoln 1990, 422).

6:8. The exhortation to slaves concludes in v. 8 with a reminder that shifts the focus from the descriptions in vv. 5b-7 of the kind of obedience slaves are to give to their masters to the conviction that underlies and motivates it: "knowing that each person, if they do something good, it will be repaid from the Lord, whether they are slave or free." Although slaves who relate to their masters in the way that Paul has described in the preceding verses may not receive any earthly reward for their obedience and goodwill (especially the work that was done when no human eye was there to see it), they can be confident of an ultimate, eschatological reward from their true master, the Lord, who rewards the good works of all, regardless of whether the one who performs them is a slave or a free person.

6:9. The exhortations to slaves in vv. 5-8 are followed by a word to masters in v. 9: "And, masters, do the same things for them, refraining from threatening, for you know that their Master and yours is in heaven, and there is no favoritism with him." Two features of Paul's word to masters stand out when it is compared with the comparable words to husbands (in 5:25-33) and fathers (in 6:4). The first is the phrase "in the same way" (*ta auta*) that brackets the word to masters alongside the word to slaves in a relationship that is not only reciprocal (as are the wife/husband and child/father relationships) but also implicitly symmetrical or equivalent. The second, reinforcing the implication conveyed by the first, is the way Paul gives the actions of both slaves and masters the same meaning in relation to the story of salvation. Unlike husbands, who are to relate to their wives as Christ to the church, and fathers, whose training and instruction are represented as an extension or manifestation of the fatherly training and instruction of God, masters are not encouraged to interpret their role as a participation in the Lordship of Christ; rather, they are to remember that they, like the slaves who work within their households, are subject to the judgment of the same master and that "there is no favoritism with him."

Because that is the case, masters are to "refrain from threatening." This is an extraordinary exhortation, written as it is within a context in which beatings and whippings (and the threat of them) were generally assumed to be the primary way to maintain social control and to exhibit and perpetuate the distinction of status between slave and master (Bradley 1987, 113–38; Saller 1994, 133–53). In the absence of such threats, the form of the slave/master relationship could still, in theory at least, have been able to persist within a Christian household, but its nature would need to be radically transformed into a relationship of mutual benefaction and goodwill, along the lines that Paul has already hinted at in vv. 5-8 (cf. Phlm 16). The evidence that survives from the subsequent centuries suggests that the reality fell a long way short of this (Harper 2011b, 227–48).

Be strong in the Lord (6:10-20)

(10) In the time that remains, be strong in the Lord and in the might of his strength. (11) Put on the whole armor of God, so that you may be able to stand against the strategies of the devil. (12) For our struggle is not against blood and flesh, but against the rulers, against the authorities, against the cosmic powers of this present darkness, against the spiritual forces of evil in the heavenly places. (13) Therefore take up the whole armor of God, so that you may be able to withstand in the evil day, and having overcome all, to stand. (14) Stand therefore, having girded your waist with truth, and

having put on the breastplate of righteousness, (15) and having shod your feet with the readiness of the gospel of peace; (16) with all of these having taken up the shield of faith, with which you will be able to quench all the flaming arrows of the evil one. (17) And take the helmet of salvation, and the sword of the Spirit, which is the word of God, (18) praying in the Spirit at all times in every prayer and supplication, and with this purpose keeping alert in all perseverance and prayer for all the saints, (19) and also for me, that when I open my mouth, a message may be given to me to make known with boldness the mystery of the gospel, (20) for which I am an ambassador in chains—that I may declare it boldly, as I must speak.

6:10. The household code of 5:21–6:9 is followed in 6:10-20 by a new section in which the readers are urged to "be strong," clothing themselves with the armor of God (vv. 11-17) and devoting themselves to prayer (vv. 18-20).

Within the larger rhetorical strategy of the letter, this section functions both as the climax of the series of exhortations introduced in 4:1 and as a recapitulation of themes and motifs from chapters 1–3 (particularly the prayer in 3:14-19 for the strengthening of the readers and the reminders in 1:20-23; 2:1-6; 3:10 of the victory of Christ over the hostile spiritual powers under whose influence they once lived their lives). The battle against those powers that is in view within this section is not, therefore, to be viewed as an esoteric new theme, introduced into the letter for the first time here, or as a kind of Christian counter-magic, disconnected from the mundane realities of the preceding paragraphs. The battle against the cosmic powers that Paul describes in 6:10-20 is exactly the same struggle that has been in view throughout the letter (e.g., in the reminder of 1:20-23 that the ascension of Christ has placed him "high above all rule and authority and power and dominion, and every name that is named"; in the description of the pre-conversion life of the readers as one that was lived "according to the ruler of the realm of the air, according to the spirit that is now at work among the sons of disobedience"; and in the summons of 5:11 to the readers to "take no part in the unfruitful works of darkness, but instead expose them").

In keeping with the advice typically given by ancient rhetorical theorists about the strategies to be employed in the *peroratio* of a speech, this section is constructed around a vivid and powerful extended metaphor (cf. Cicero, *Part. or.* 15.53; Quintilian, *Inst. or.* 6.1.2), recapitulates major themes and ideas from earlier in the letter (cf. *Inst. or.* 6.1.7–8), reminds the readers of realities that incite powerful emotions such as fear and courage (cf. *Inst. or.* 6.1.7, 9, 12–13), and concludes with a pathos-laden reference to Paul as "an ambassador in chains," praying nonetheless for boldness in the midst of his imprisonment (cf. *Inst. or.* 6.1.46) (Witherington 2007, 346–47).

In addition to the conventions associated with the *peroratio* of a speech, commentators (e.g., Lincoln 1990, 433; Talbert 2007, 159) also frequently draw comparisons between Paul's rhetoric in this section (particularly vv. 11-17) and the kind of speeches that a military leader would make on the eve of battle. Apart from the obvious similarities of theme and function created by Paul's extended military metaphor and his desire to strengthen the courage and resolve of his readers, however, the similarities between the details of Paul's rhetoric and that of the pre-battle orations are not particularly striking (cf. Thielman 2010, 413–14). Neither Paul's repeated exhortation to "stand" (vv. 11, 13, 14) nor his elaboration on the armor with which believers are to clothe and equip themselves is a standard feature in the speeches that Jewish and Greco-Roman military leaders gave on the eve of battle, though a partial analogy for the latter can be found in the dream that Judas Maccabeus recounts to his troops in 2 Maccabees 15:15-16 (cf. Eph 6:16–17).

A much stronger and more direct literary influence on Paul's rhetoric in 6:11-17 is the language of the Old Testament, and Isaiah in particular. The description of the armor that his readers are urged to put on for this conflict is (as most commentators observe) laced with intertextual references to the language and imagery of Isaiah. The picture in v. 14 of the readers as "having girded [their] waist with truth" echoes the language of Isa 11:5 ("righteousness shall be the belt around his waist, and faithfulness [LXX: *alētheia*] the belt around his loins"); the "breastplate of righteousness" in v. 14 (cf. Wis 5:18) and the "helmet of salvation" in v. 17 echo the language of Isa 59:17 ("He put on righteousness like a breastplate and a helmet of salvation on his head"); and the exhortation of v. 15, "and having shod your feet with the readiness of the gospel of peace," echoes the language and imagery of Isa 52:7 ("How beautiful upon the mountains are the feet of the messenger who announces peace, who brings good news").

The armor spoken of in 6:14-17 (and in most of the Isaianic texts that stand behind that passage) is thus the armor of God (Isa 59:17; cf. Wis 5:16-23) and of his Messiah (Isa 11:5) before it is the armor of his people. In doing battle against the powers that oppose them, the readers are to see themselves as a community who exist and act "in the Lord" (cf. v. 10) and, consequently, as participants in the conflict and triumph of God himself (see especially Gombis 2010, 155–80).

Paul commences in v. 10 with an exhortation that is framed in broad and general terms: "In the time that remains, be strong in the Lord and in the might of his strength." The opening phrase, *tou loipou* ("In the time that remains"), is replaced in some manuscripts with the accusative-case *to loipon* ("Finally"), but the manuscript support for *tou loipou* (e.g., 𝔓⁴⁶, ℵ*, A, and B) is strong, and the variant reading is easily explained as a scribal assimilation to the easier reading of *to loipon*, which frequently appears toward the end of Paul's letters. Although some commentators (Lincoln 1990, 441) treat the meaning of the two expressions as the same (i.e., "Finally"), *tou loipou* is a well-established idiom that carries the meaning (depending on context) of either "in the remaining time" (e.g., Sophocles, *El.* 817; Hermas, *Sim.* 9.11.3) or, more loosely and open-endedly, "from now/then on" (e.g., Herodotus, *Hist.* 1.189; Josephus, *Ant.* 1.96). Although it is probably the latter of these two senses that the phrase carries in Gal 6:17, its meaning here in v. 10 is best understood in light of the eschatological references that precede (v. 8, and implicitly v. 9) and follow it (v. 13): a future day is coming when the faithful obedience of believers will be rewarded, but in the meantime, in anticipation of the "evil day" that must be endured before then, believers are to be strong and to arm themselves for conflict (cf. Barth 1974, 759–60).

The call to "be strong" (*endynamousthe*) is expressed in a form that could be taken either as passive ("be strengthened") or middle ("strengthen yourselves"); the former is more likely, given the explicit references to "the Lord" and "the might of his strength" that follow. Nevertheless, the fact that the verb is an imperative implies that there is still an initiative to be taken on the part of the hearers. Something similar can be seen in the description of David in LXX 1 Kingdoms 30:6 (=1 Sam 30:6), where the passive verb form of the LXX ("David was strengthened [*ekrataiōthē*] in the LORD") is clearly intended to carry the same meaning as the Hebrew original, which uses the hithpael form of the verb (*wayyithazzēq*) to say that "David strengthened himself in the LORD"—presumably by calling to mind and leaning upon the LORD's strength (cf. Lincoln 1990, 441). "The Lord," here in Eph 6:10, is the Lord Jesus, in line with the way in which "Christ" and "the Lord" have been used interchangeably in 6:5-9.

6:11. The way believers are to go about this is spelled out in an extended metaphor in vv. 11-17, commencing the command to the readers in v. 11 to "put on the whole armor of God, so that you may be able to stand against the strategies of the devil." The verb "put on" (*endysasthe*) recalls the earlier use of the same verb in 4:24 and may carry some of the same theodramatic connotations here as it does there. The "whole armor of God" in which believers are to clothe themselves is not only armor from God, supplied by him, but also (at least in the case of the belt, the breastplate, and the helmet, as they are depicted in Isa 11:5 and 59:17) armor that belongs to and is worn by

God and his Messiah. To put on that armor is not only to be fitted for battle but also to step into character, as members of Christ and participants in the warfare and victory of God. (For a famous example in the Greco-Roman literature of the way armor could function to signify identity, see the request that Patroclus makes to Achilles in *Iliad* 16.1–45 that he might dress in his armor so that the Trojans will take him for Achilles.)

The purpose for which believers are to clothe themselves with this armor is "so that you may be able to stand against the strategies (*methodeias*) of the devil." The language of "stand[ing]," here and in vv. 13-14, should not (contra Witherington 2007, 349) be taken as an indication that the part believers are to play in the battle is a purely defensive one. As Talbert rightly points out, the idea of "standing" in battle, when read against the background of ancient Roman and Greek military tactics, implies "neither an offensive nor a defensive posture per se" but rather "a resolve to remain in the battle," in expectation that the opponents' ranks will break and their troops flee (Talbert 2007, 160–61).

In keeping with a background understanding of that sort, the armor that Paul goes on to describe appears to envisage a community who are both assailed by the attacks of the devil and actively engaged in the advancement of the gospel, wearing footwear that symbolizes "the readiness of the gospel of peace" and wielding "the sword of the Spirit, which is the word of God." The "strategies" of the devil should therefore be taken, by implication, as embracing not only his attempts to tempt, divide, and discourage the church (cf. 4:27) but also his efforts to prevent it from fulfilling its mission in the world.

6:12. Verse 12 supplies the reason that believers, if they are to "stand" in the battle, need to be clothed with the divine armor referred to in v. 11: "For our struggle is not against blood and flesh, but against the rulers, against the authorities, against the cosmic powers of this present darkness, against the spiritual forces of evil in the heavenly places." Paul's rhetoric here, as Thielman observes (Thielman 2010, 420), moves in the opposite direction from the arguments commonly employed in pre-battle speeches by military leaders, who emboldened their troops by stressing the weakness and vulnerability of the enemy. The Athenian general Chabrias, for example, is represented by Polyaenus as having motivated his troops by reminding them that they were fighting not against gods but against "men who have blood and flesh" (*Strat.* 3.11.1); Paul, on the other hand, stresses to his readers that (despite the human hostility and ridicule they will no doubt encounter at times) their real opponent is *not* "blood and flesh" but spiritual rulers and authorities that he goes on to describe in the remainder of the verse.

The list that follows ("the rulers . . . the authorities . . . the cosmic powers of this present darkness . . . the spiritual forces of evil in the heavenly places") commences with two terms that have already been used, in combination with each other, in 1:21 and 3:10. The two terms that follow ("cosmic powers" and "spiritual forces") are presumably added for the sake of rhetorical amplification, without any necessary implication that four distinct ranks or species of spiritual beings are in view (cf. Witherington 2007, 350).

The term *kosmokratores* ("cosmic powers") cannot be found in any surviving texts from before Paul's time, but in the surviving examples of its use from the second century and later it can refer variously to heavenly bodies such as the sun and the moon (e.g., Vettius Valens, *Anth.* 9.16.12), fate-controlling deities (e.g., IGUR I 194), and evil spirits associated with heavenly bodies (e.g., T. Sol. 18.3, the wording of which is possibly influenced by that of Eph 6:12). The most likely background against which the original readers of Ephesians would have understood Paul's use of the term is the magical-astrological tradition, viewed through the lens of first century Jewish polemics (cf. Arnold 1997, 65–68). By characterizing them as the rulers of "this present darkness" Paul both acknowledges the power that they hold (cf. 2:1; 4:18) and relativizes it by locating its sway within an age that is destined to be superseded by the coming kingdom of God (cf. 1 Cor 2:6; Rom 13:12). The final item in the list, "the spiritual forces (*pneumatika*) of evil," is probably intended as kind of catch-all for whatever other hostile, non-human powers and beings there may be (Best 1998, 594), operating within the same invisible realm of "the heavenly places" that Paul has referred to elsewhere in the letter (1:3, 20; 2:6; 3:10).

6:13. The command of v. 11 to "put on the whole armor of God" is reiterated in v. 13: "Therefore, take up the whole armor of God, so that you may be able to withstand in the evil day, and having made all preparations, to stand firm." The "evil day" (*hē hēmera hē ponēra*) referred to here is best understood, within the larger framework of the letter's inaugurated eschatology, not as a potentially distant future crisis (e.g., Meyer 1884, 331) or an occasional experience of egregious hardship (e.g., Calvin 1965, 219) but as a way of characterizing the whole era in which the readers already find themselves (cf. the "evil . . . days" of 5:16), without excluding the possibility of a further escalation of evil and suffering before the final consummation of Christ's victory (cf. Dan 12:1; 2 Thess 2:3-12; Barth 1974, 804–805; Lincoln 1990, 446).

The participle *katergasamenoi* ("having overcome") is formed from a verb that is typically used by Paul in a broad, general sense, meaning "to do" or "to perform" (e.g., Rom 1:27; 2:9; 1 Cor 5:3), or with the somewhat more specialized sense of "to prepare" (e.g., 2 Cor 4:15; 5:5). The fact that Paul is describing the process of arming for battle leads some commentators (e.g., Lincoln 1990, 446) to understand it in the latter of those senses here, as "having completed preparations." As Meyer points out, however (Meyer 1884, 331–32), the verb can also be used in military contexts to refer to the completion of battle and attainment of victory (e.g., Herodotus, *Hist.* 6.2.6; Thucydides, *Hist.* 4.85.3), and if it is read in that sense here then it is easier to follow the implied narrative suggested by Paul's otherwise awkward "so that you may be able to withstand in the evil day, and . . . stand." On this reading, the picture of the believer "stand[ing]" in v. 13b is not merely a reiteration of the picture of the believer in v. 13a, "withstand[ing]" in the midst of battle in v. 13a, but rather a picture of the believer as (still) standing, unconquered, at the end of the battle (Meyer 1884, 331–32). (If the alternative interpretation is adopted, and *katergasamenoi* is understood as "having completed preparations," then the *kai* ["and"] that links v. 13a with v. 13b is best understood as epexegetical in function, introducing v. 13b as an elaboration or explanation of v. 13a rather than as the next event in a narrative sequence.)

6:14. The focus in v. 14 returns from the victorious future envisaged in v. 13b to the present struggle, in which the readers must "stand," embattled, against the adversaries listed in v. 12. The armor that was referred to in general terms in vv. 11 and 13 is now enumerated in detail, commencing with the belt ("having girded your waist with truth [*alētheia*]") and breastplate ("and having put on the breastplate of righteousness"). As discussed above, both of these items evoke intertextual connections with Isaiah—the belt with Isa 11:5 ("righteousness shall be the belt around his waist, and faithfulness [LXX: *alētheia*] the belt around his loins"), and the breastplate with Isa 59:17 ("He put on righteousness like a breastplate").

Given the fact that the armor described is *both* armor that is worn in battle by God and his Messiah *and* armor that is to be worn by his people, it is best to avoid dichotomizing interpretations that attempt to force a choice between "truth" and "righteousness" as references to the character and action of God in Christ and "truth" and "righteousness" as references to the virtues to be cultivated by believers. Read against the verses' original, Isaianic horizon, the "truth" in view is the covenant-keeping faithfulness of YHWH, as manifested in the character and action of his Messiah, and the "righteousness" is the divine character of uprightness and justice, as manifested in his activity of judgment and salvation. For believers to "put on" these realities as armor is for them to become participants in God's activity in the world. They are, therefore, to be speakers of "the word of truth" that proclaims and enacts God's covenant-keeping faithfulness (1:13; cf. 4:15, 21, 24) and, by extension, to be people of integrity and truthfulness in their own speech and action (cf. 4:25; 5:9; also 2 Cor 4:2; 6:7; 13:8). And they are to be bearers and agents of the just and salvation-creating righteousness of God, acting uprightly in the world (cf. 4:24; 5:9) and furthering the progress of salvation and justice in the lives of others (cf. Rom 6:13; 2 Cor 6:7).

The function of the breastplate to protect the chest of a soldier against the weapons of the enemy is not something that Paul draws any attention to here; nor is there even the remotest hint that this is an issue in the surrounding context of his source text, Isa 59:17; tempting as it may be to find in this verse a reference to the imputed righteousness of God or the status conferred by his verdict of justification, as a defense against the accusations of the evil one, that is probably not (contra Barth 1974, 796) the sense in which the image is intended to function.

6:15. Verse 15 continues the enumeration of the items of armor that believers are to wear, adding "and having shod your feet with the readiness of the gospel of peace." Once again an allusion of some sort to Isaiah seems likely—in this instance, to the image in Isa 52:7 of the "beautiful . . . feet" of the one who "publishes peace" and "proclaims good news." It is difficult to say whether the footwear Paul has in mind here is that of the human herald implied in the Hebrew original or of God himself, as implied by the LXX's "I am here . . . like the feet of one bringing glad tidings of a report of peace" (LXX Isa 52:7, NETS). Either way, in a mixing of metaphors that is presumably deliberate, the soldier in battle is being implicitly represented as a messenger of peace, "stand[ing]" in the conflict by "bringing" the good news of the gospel. The accent of the image is not so much on the Christian as a believer in the gospel, inwardly prepared for battle by internalizing its truth (contra Lincoln 1990, 449), but on the Christian as a speaker of the gospel, characterized by "readiness" to make it known when opportunity arises (cf. Rom 10:15; for *hetoimasia* as "readiness," see LXX Ps 9:38).

6:16. The list continues in v. 16: "with all of these having taken up the shield of faith, with which you will be able to quench all the flaming arrows of the evil one." The opening phrase ("with all of these taking") functions as a kind of syntactical seam between the first three items in the list and this next one, connecting it to them but also leaving room for it to be distinguished in some way from them. One obvious point of difference lies in the fact that the shield in v. 16 is the first item of the armor Paul describes that is not derived from a source-text in Isaiah or (if the LXX reading of Isa 52:7 is taken as the source of the image in v. 15) referring to an aspect of the character and action of God and his Messiah. It is not out of place, therefore, to take the "faith" (*pistis*) in view in this verse, like the other instances of *pistis* within Ephesians

(1:15; 2:8; 3:12, 17; 4:5, 13; 6:23), as the faith exercised by believers, which Paul describes here as functioning like a shield to protect those who exercise it against the "flaming arrows" of the evil one.

By referring to "all" (*panta*) the flaming arrows, Paul may be hinting at the diversity of attacks that the evil one may employ—"not just temptation to impure or unloving conduct but also false teaching, persecution, doubt, and despair" (Lincoln 1990, 450). The incendiary effects of all of these, Paul assures his readers, can be quenched by the persevering exercise of faith in God and his promises (cf. the function of faith as a "breastplate" in 1 Thess 5:8).

6:17. Verse 17 completes the list with a fresh imperative: "And take the helmet of salvation, and the sword of the Spirit, which is the word of God." The first of the two items referred to in the verse, the "helmet of salvation," is (like the "breastplate of righteousness" in v. 14) an allusion to Isa 59:17. It is difficult to decide whether this image should be read in parallel with the earlier one and in line with the function of the image in Isa 59:17 (i.e., as a way of referring to the participation of believers in the saving activity of God in the world) or in the same sense as the closely similar image in 1 Thess 5:8 ("having put on . . . as a helmet the hope of salvation"), i.e., picturing believers as the recipients of God's salvation, placing their confidence in that truth as a protection against the attacks of the devil. On balance, the former option is probably to be preferred over the latter as the primary sense of the metaphor, in view of the difference of wording between the formulation here and in 1 Thessalonians (particularly the change from "the hope of salvation" to "salvation"), the presence of the additional allusion to Isa 59:17 in the earlier image of the "breastplate of righteousness" in v. 14 (which is much closer to the language and ideas of Isa 59:17 than the reference in 1 Thess 5:8 to "faith and love as a breastplate"), and the fact that Paul's readers in Ephesus would have been more likely to have access to Isaiah than to 1 Thessalonians. All of these factors combine to suggest that Paul is freshly reworking the image he has earlier used in writing to the Thessalonians and not simply reproducing it with the same meaning and function here, and that Isa 59:17 should be given priority over 1 Thess 5:8 as the primary intertext for the image in v. 17a. (On the helmet as an emblem of identity, see *Iliad* 11.41-42; 16.337-339, 793-890, and the brief comments in Fowl 2012, 208.)

Nevertheless, in view of the obvious protective connotations that the helmet metaphor also carries, the earlier descriptions of the readers in 2:5, 8 as recipients of salvation, and the immediately preceding image of "the shield of faith, with which you will be able to quench all the flaming arrows of the evil one" (v. 16), there is good reason to assume that Paul would have also intended the metaphor to carry, as its secondary sense, a reminder of the protection that believers themselves experience in God's salvation.

The last item in the list, in v. 17b, is "the sword of the Spirit, which is the word of God." Unlike the genitive constructions used in earlier items in the list ("the breastplate of righteousness"; "the shield of faith"; "the helmet of salvation"), the intended meaning of effect of this one is not to imply that the Spirit *is* the metaphorical sword wielded by believers; the sword, as Paul goes on to say, is not the Spirit but "the word of God." The most likely force of the genitive construction in this case is to represent the sword as being supplied by the Spirit (cf. Thielman 2010, 429) or (perhaps) wielded by the Spirit through the agency of believers who speak the word.

The "word of God" (*rhēma theou*), which the sword represents, is understood by some commentators (Best 1998, 604; Hoehner 2002, 853) as a Spirit-inspired retort to the temptations of the evil one, along the lines of Matt 4:1-11/Luke 4:1-13. The more likely interpretation, however (in view of the fact that the readers have been depicted in v. 15 as having shod their feet with "the readiness of the gospel of peace"), is that the word in view is the message of the gospel (Lincoln 1990, 451; Thielman 2010, 429) and that the readers are depicted as not only receiving and internalizing it but speaking it to others (cf. the use of *rhēma* to refer to the gospel in Eph 5:26; Rom 10:8, 17-18).

6:18. In vv. 18-20, Paul offers a further elaboration on what is involved in or entailed by the command of v. 17 to "take the helmet of salvation, and the sword of the Spirit, which is the word of God." (On the elaborative function that is typically served by present participles following an imperative, see Runge 2010, 262; Wallace 1996, 652.) The encouragements to prayer in vv. 18-20 should thus be read neither as a new, disconnected thought, independent of the commands in vv. 10-17, nor as simply a further piece of armor to add to the list. The prayers of vv. 18-20 are the prayers that should accompany the taking of the helmet of salvation and the sword of the Spirit.

Paul's description of the prayers that believers ought to pray places heavy emphasis on the constancy and perseverance by which it should be characterized, in keeping with the context of battle that has been evoked in vv. 10-17. Believers are to pray "at all times," "in every prayer and supplication," and "with this purpose keeping alert in all perseverance and prayer." As with the earlier reference in 5:20 to thanksgivings offered "at all times," it would be a mistake to interpret Paul's language here as if he were requiring a practice of prayer that was literally ceaseless; it does, however, imply a commitment to frequent, earnest, and persevering prayer, requiring endurance and self-discipline on the part of the readers. This will involve "keeping alert" (*agrypnountes*)—a word that can carry the literal meaning of "staying awake" but can also have an extended, metaphorical sense, in which wakefulness serves as a way of speaking about alertness and concentration (cf. Mark 13:33; Luke 21:36).

Read within this context, Paul's encouragement to his readers to pray "in the Spirit" is unlikely to be meant as a reference to a particular, specialized form of Spirit-informed prayer; it is, after all, "at all times in every prayer and supplication" that they are to pray in this manner, and Paul has already reminded them in 2:18 that their access to the Father is "through Christ . . . in one Spirit," with the implication that, in that sense at least, all Christian prayer is prayer "in the Spirit." The further reminder of that fact here in 6:18 is probably intended to function as an encouragement to persevere in the struggle and self-discipline described in the rest of the verse, relying on the empowering presence of the Spirit to motivate and enable their prayers (cf. Rom 8:26).

The prayers that they are to pray are to be not only for themselves but for "all the saints" (v. 18)—an encouragement that echoes the language of Paul's earlier prayer in 3:18 that the readers will be granted empowerment and understanding "with all the saints," and functions to counteract any tendency toward self-absorption that the circumstances of their own context might give rise to and to remind them of their solidarity in mission, suffering, and prayer with all of their fellow believers.

6:19-20. Within the larger scope of their prayers for all the saints, Paul asks specifically in vv. 19-20 that they offer prayers for him. Although the content of the prayers that the readers are to pray for themselves and for their fellow believers is left unspecified, Paul offers a lengthy description of the prayers that they are to pray for him: "that when I open my mouth, a message may be given to me to make known with boldness the mystery of the gospel, for which I am an ambassador in chains—that I may declare it boldly, as I must speak." The exclusive focus of the prayer on enabling and emboldenment for the proclamation of the gospel is framed by Paul as a reflection, in part at least, of his unique vocation as apostle to the Gentiles and his situation in prison, as "an ambassador in chains" (cf. 3:1-13); it is probably reasonable to assume that the implied content of the prayers the readers are to pray for "all the saints . . . at all times in every prayer and supplication" includes a somewhat broader range of concerns. Nevertheless, the syntactical connection between this prayer request and the command to the readers in v. 17 to "take the helmet of salvation and the sword of the Spirit, which is the word of God" strengthens the case for reading the imagery of that verse as a way of describing the participation of the readers in the saving mission of

God and their active involvement in the progress of the gospel. The prayers they are to pray for themselves and their fellow believers will, therefore, be informed by the same vision for the gospel's advance that is reflected in the content of the prayers that Paul asks them to pray for him. (Also worth noting at this point is the juxtaposition between the similar prayer request that Paul makes for himself in Col 4:3-4, the more general exhortation to prayer in 4:2, without any specified content, and the encouragement to the readers in 4:5-6 to "walk in wisdom in relation to outsiders, redeeming the time," suggesting a connection in Paul's mind between the readers' prayers for themselves, their prayers for him as a messenger of the gospel, and their own interactions with "outsiders," in speech and in action.)

Tychicus . . . peace . . . and grace (6:21-24)

(21) So that you also may know how I am and what I am doing, Tychicus will tell you everything. He is a beloved brother and a faithful minister in the Lord, (22) whom I have sent to you for this very purpose: that you might know our circumstances, and that he might encourage your hearts. (23) Peace be to the brothers and sisters, and love with faith, from God the Father and the Lord Jesus Christ. (24) Grace be with all who love our Lord Jesus Christ incorruptibly.

6:21-22. The letter closes in vv. 21-24 with a commendation of Tychicus as the letter carrier (vv. 21-22) and a final prayer wish for the readers (vv. 23-24). The wording that Paul uses in commending Tychicus to the readers is closely similar, though not identical, to the wording of his commendation of Tychicus in Col 4:7-8. (The differences between the two passages increase a little if, as I advocate below in the comments on Col 4:8, we follow the variant reading of that verse to be found in manuscripts including $\mathfrak{P}^{46}$, C, and D^1.) The simplest explanation for this close correspondence of wording is that Ephesians and Colossians were written and sent from the same place, at the same time, with Tychicus serving as the letter carrier for both. (A similar phenomenon can be seen in the identical commendations of the letter carrier, Burrhus, which Ignatius includes in *Phld.* 11.2 and *Smyrn.* 12.1, as Thielman observes in Thielman 2010, 439).

If Ephesians is taken to be a pseudepigraphical letter (constructed by reworking an authentically Pauline Colossians, or composed in parallel with a pseudepigraphical Colossians), then the rhetorical function of the commendation is presumably to add verisimilitude to the letter and provide an explanation for its lack of specific information about Paul's circumstances (cf. Lincoln 1990, 465). A hypothesis of this sort places significant strain on the claim (made, for example, in Lincoln 1990, lxxii) that Ephesians is best understood as a transparent form of pseudepigraphy, written on the assumption that the readers were as aware as the writer of the device that was being employed.

The phrase "you also" (*kai hymeis*) in v. 21 has been variously understood by the commentators. Some (e.g., Schnackenburg 1991, 288; Gnilka 1977, 321) argue that the phrase (or, more particularly, the *kai* with which it commences) functions to shift the focus from the doctrinal and ethical concerns of the letter body toward the more personal issues alluded to in the conclusion. An interpretation of this sort is unlikely, however, since the *kai* is so closely attached to the (otherwise redundant) *hymeis*; Paul does not say, "so that you may know also *how I am* and what I am doing" but "so that *you also* may know . . ." (emphasis added). Equally unsatisfying is the argument made by some that the *kai* has no particular function at all, apart from (possibly) serving "very loosely to emphasize the following pronoun *hymeis*" (Lincoln 1990, 465; cf. Best 1998, 615). It is true that Paul is capable of using *kai* as a mark of emphasis (e.g., *kago*, "I in particular," in 1:15), without any implication that what is emphasized is placed alongside or in addition to something or someone else. Here, however, it is difficult to see anything in the context that would warrant why it is "you especially" or "you in particular" that Paul has in mind. And if the *kai* has no function at all, then the same must be said of the (otherwise redundant) *hymeis* that follows it, adding to the unlikeliness of this reading.

The more likely and more natural reading, giving the *kai* its commonest force in a construction of this sort, is to read this verse as an allusion to the fact that it is not only the readers of this letter but others as well (including the Colossians and possibly also the Laodiceans) who are on Paul's mind as he thinks about the function of Tychicus as a bearer of news about his circumstances (cf. Schlier 1957, 305–306; Thielman 2010, 442; Sellin 2008, 490–91; Sellin regards Ephesians as pseudonymous and reads the phrase as part of the pseudepigrapher's attempt to add verisimilitude to the letter frame). It is true that there is nothing within Ephesians equivalent to the explicit references to other churches in Col 2:1; 4:13, 15-16, which would make it obvious to the readers that the *kai* performs a function of this sort (Abbott 1897, 190). Nevertheless, the fact that the phrase occurs in immediate proximity to a reference that Paul is making to Tychicus (who will also be carrying letters to the Laodiceans and Colossians) makes it plausible that an idea of this sort would have been on his mind. The presence of Tychicus among the readers of the letter, who would no doubt have been aware of the fact that he was passing through *en route* to other destinations, would have suggested the same idea to them, almost as effectively as an explicit reference to those other churches within the letter.

The task that Tychicus has been entrusted with is described in vv. 21a and 22b. It has two main components: to let the readers know about the details of Paul's circumstances, to which he has just alluded in the immediately preceding prayer request (6:19-20; cf. 3:1, 13), and to "encourage [the] hearts" of the readers. The former purpose is consistent with what was commonly the task of letter carriers in antiquity (cf. Head 2009, 296–98); here, the provision of additional information about Paul's circumstances is presumably related, in part at least, to Paul's request for prayer and implies that he is hoping their prayers will be informed and specific, relating the general request of vv. 19-20 to the particulars of Paul's situation. The latter purpose ("and that he might encourage your hearts") is probably best understood in close connection with the former. The verb to "encourage" (*parakaleō*) can be used in a variety of senses in Paul's letters, including the urging of a particular course of action (e.g., 1 Cor 16:12), the consoling of the anxious or the downcast (e.g., 2 Cor 7:6-7, 13), and the exhorting function of a letter or a word of prophecy spoken in the assembly (e.g., 1 Cor 1:10; 14:31). Here, used as it is in close proximity to Paul's repeated references to the information that Tychicus will bring about his circumstances, it probably functions primarily to anticipate the reassurance that Tychicus will provide to those who have been disheartened by the news of Paul's imprisonment (cf. 3:13), without implying that Tychicus will be expected to provide expert commentary on the doctrinal content of the letter or deliver a formal homily to the readers.

Tychicus himself (cf. Acts 20:4; Col 4:7; 2 Tim 4:12; Titus 3:12) is warmly commended in v. 21 as "a beloved brother and a faithful minister in the Lord." The words Paul uses imply both affection and trust (cf. the similar combinations in 1 Cor 4:17; Col 1:7). The word *diakonos* ("minister") can sometimes be used by Paul as a technical or semi-technical term for a formally recognized office-bearer within the church (cf. Phil 1:1). Its use here, however, does not require that meaning and is probably best understood in a sense that is roughly equivalent to its use in Col 1:7, where Epaphras is described as a "faithful minister" of the Colossians in his fulfilment of the mission entrusted by them to him.

6:23. In vv. 23-24, Paul concludes the letter with a double prayer wish for the readers, expressed in more elaborate terms than he more typically employs in the prayer wishes at the end of his letters, and in the third person rather than the second person. The first prayer wish, in v. 23, is expressed as being for "the brothers and sisters" (*hoi adelphoi*), a common Pauline description of believers and a way of referring to the readers that reinforces his earlier description of them in 2:19 as *oikeioi tou theou* ("members of the household of God").

Paul's prayer is that they will be blessed with "peace . . . and love with faith." All three of the words that Paul joins together here have been used repeatedly within the letter, primarily to refer to the "peace" (1:2; 2:14-15, 17; 4:3; 6:15), "love" (1:4, 15; 4:2, 15-16; 5:2), and "faith" (1:15; 2:8; 3:12; 4:5, 13; 6:16) that believers possess through the work of God in Christ, uniting them to him and to one another, and they are used in that same sense here. The syntax of the verse gives particular prominence to "peace," which functions (as it does in 1:2; cf. 6:15) as a kind of umbrella term for the benefits of the gospel, including both "vertical" reconciliation with God and the "horizontal" reconciliation that is experienced within the community of the church. The additional two terms, "love with faith," are also paired together in 1:15, where they are expanded as "faith in the Lord Jesus" and "love for all the saints." Paul probably has something similar in mind here in 6:23. In describing that "peace," "love," and "faith" as coming "from God the Father and the Lord Jesus Christ," Paul echoes the language of the letter's opening prayer wish in 1:2, and the phrase should be understood in a similar sense (see comments above on 1:2).

6:24. The final verse of the letter expresses a second prayer wish, adding a prayer for "grace" to the prayer in v. 23 for "peace" (and love with faith), to create a kind of chiastic echo of the "grace and peace" wished for the readers in 1:2. Here, as there, the "grace" that is prayed for is almost certainly a reference to the grace of God himself, as the source of all the blessings Paul prays for the readers (cf. 1:6-7; 2:5-8; 4:7).

The prayer of v. 24 is prayed for "all who love our Lord Jesus Christ incorruptibly"—an expansive description that should probably be taken as including not only the readers of the letter but all believers everywhere (cf. Col 2:1). The phrase *en aphtharsia* ("incorruptibly") is understood by some (e.g., Arnold 2010, 482; Lincoln 1990, 467–68) as qualifying *eirēnē*, so that Paul is taken to be praying that the readers (and all who love the Lord Jesus) will receive "grace . . . with immortality." The syntax of the verse, however, is such that the phrase is more readily connected with the immediately preceding description of the beneficiaries of the prayer as "all who love our Lord Jesus Christ." On this reading, the phrase functions to describe the love that believers have for the Lord Jesus as undying (e.g., NIV; NRSV) or sincere and pure (e.g., ESV; NASB). The latter of these two senses is probably more likely, given the moral sense that *aphtharsia* and its cognates can have in the New Testament (e.g., 1 Pet 1:4; 3:4) and other early Christian literature (e.g., Ignatius, *Eph.* 16.1–17; *Magn.* 6.2). One possible influence on the structure and content of Paul's prayer wish is the liturgical formulations of the Psalms of Solomon, which pray (e.g., Pss. Sol. 4.25) that the mercy of God will be extended to those who love him *en alētheia* ("in truth"; Pss. Sol. 6.6; 10.3; 14.1) (Thielman 2010, 445–49).

The language Paul uses here to describe the beneficiaries of his prayer wish should not be read as if he were backing down at the last minute from his assertions in the earlier chapters (esp. 2:1-10) about the free and unconditioned character of the saving grace of God. Read in light of the earlier chapters of the letter, the prayer wish is not a picture of a God who holds back his grace, waiting for a people who merit it by the quality of their love for him. It is, rather, a prayer that the God who has already rescued his people from the corruption and death that once held them captive, granting them a new life and a new and incorruptible love for him, will continue to be gracious to them, dwelling with them and empowering them in this age and the age to come.

Introduction to Colossians

Authorship

Like Ephesians, the letter to the Colossians commences with an explicit claim to Pauline authorship—a claim that is doubled down on in the closing verse of the letter, with an emphatic assertion of authenticity (Col 4:18; cf. 2 Thess 3:17; Phlm 19). Nevertheless (like the authorship of Ephesians), the authorship of Colossians has been a question of considerable scholarly debate— in the case of Colossians, since the first half of the nineteenth century (cf. Wilson 2005, 9, citing E. T. Mayerhoff, writing in 1838, as the first to call the authenticity of Colossians into question).

Many (though not all) of the reasons for which the authorship of Ephesians is debated also apply in the case of Colossians. Here, as in Ephesians, we encounter features of style including the heaping up of seemingly redundant synonyms (e.g., 1:9, "praying . . . and asking" [*proseuchomenoi kai aitoumenoi*]; "in all . . . wisdom and understanding" [*en pasē sophia kai synesei*]; and 1:22, "holy and unblemished and blameless" *[hagious kai amōmous kai anenklētous]*) and the linking together of chains of genitive-case nouns and pronouns (e.g., 2:2, "riches of full assurance of understanding" [*ploutos tēs plērophorias tēs syneseōs*]; 2:12, "through faith in the working of God" [*dia tēs pisteōs tēs energeiōs tou theou*]). Rhetorical questions, too, are thin on the ground (just two, in 2:20-21), and outside of the section of the letter in which they occur (2:8-23) the rhetorical strategy is noticeably similar to that of Ephesians, with a preference for liturgically fortified reminder and exhortation over diatribe and argument (cf. the analysis in Lohse 1971, 84–91).

Many of the theological emphases that set Ephesians apart from the undisputed Pauline letters are also present in Colossians. As in Ephesians, the image of the body of Christ is applied, in at least some instances, not to the local assembly or community of believers but to the one universal or heavenly church, with Christ as its head (1:18, 24; 2:19). As in Ephesians, too, a heavy emphasis is placed on the present participation of believers in the resurrection and ascension of Christ (3:1-4). And as in Ephesians, the language of righteousness and justification that is so prevalent in the soteriology of letters such as Galatians and Romans is largely replaced by the language of rescue and redemption (1:13-14), forgiveness (1:14; 2:13; 3:13), and reconciliation (1:20-22).

In addition to these theological tendencies that are shared with Ephesians, Colossians goes even further than that letter in the expansiveness and explicitness of its Christological claims, celebrating in hymnic form the preeminence of Christ over the entire cosmos, his preexistence before all things, and his instrumentality in the making and sustaining of the universe (1:15-20). Hand in hand with these assertions about Christ and the cosmos go a series of related, and equally enormous, assertions about Christ's participation in the identity and nature of God, as the one in whom "all the fullness" dwells bodily (1:19; 2:9), and the consequent assurance the readers can have that "all the treasures of wisdom and knowledge" are hidden in him (2:3). None of these considerations is, however, sufficient in itself to disprove the Pauline authorship of the letter; nor is their combined weight sufficient to overturn the presumption in favor of authenticity that can reasonably be adopted in view of the letter's own emphatic claims and the unanimous acceptance of them in the early history of its reception.

Many of the stylistic features that Colossians shares with Ephesians can (as argued above in the introduction to that letter) be plausibly be explained by the hypothesis that Paul adapted its style to the Asiatic conventions that would have been familiar to the letter's intended audience (Witherington 2007, 4–6, 24–25, 104), with the possible assistance of Timothy as the letter's amanuensis (note the explicit reference in 1:1 to Timothy as co-sender and perhaps co-author). Some at least of its more distinctive vocabulary (especially in 2:16-23, where terms found nowhere else in Paul are thickest on the ground) is likely to have found its way into the letter from the language of the philosophy against which Paul is warning the Colossians (cf. Kümmel 1975, 341; Pao 2012, 20).

The theological emphases of the letter, too, are not as sharply divergent from those of the undisputed Pauline letters as is sometimes claimed and (as will be discussed below) can convincingly be explained as a development and contextualization of the theology articulated in Paul's earlier letters. Nor should the theological emphases of earlier letters such as Galatians or 1–2 Corinthians be taken as an expression of "pure," non-contextualized Pauline thought; in all of his letters, the theological categories he employs and the themes he emphasizes are shaped in important ways by the context he is addressing (cf. the classic discussion in Beker 1991), and the scholarly habit of privileging of a subset of his correspondence as the *Hauptbriefe* that define his authentic theology and style runs the risk of obscuring that fact or underplaying its significance.

When all the relevant factors are taken into consideration, therefore, the assertion of Pauline authorship (with Timothy as co-sender) that the letter makes in its opening verse should be taken at face value and the letter read as an authentically Pauline text.

Destination

If the letter is accepted as authentically Pauline, then there is no serious reason to doubt that its originally intended readers were, as the opening verse suggests, "the saints and faithful brothers and sisters in Christ in Colossae," along with the fellow believers in Laodicea with whom they are urged in 4:16 to share its contents. (If the letter were a later, pseudonymous composition, then all of the elements of the letter's epistolary frame, including its Colossian destination, the reference in 4:7 to Tychicus as letter carrier, and the string of commendations and greetings in the following verses, would need to be regarded as at least potentially fictive in nature.) In contrast to the situation with Ephesians, there is no evidence in the manuscript tradition of variant versions lacking the reference to Colossae within the opening greetings, and the letter contains a wealth of specific references to people and places of the Lycus valley (1:7; 2:1; 4:7-17), including almost all of the cast of characters named within the letter to Philemon.

The ancient city of Colossae was located a little over 100 miles inland from Ephesus, in the fertile Lycus river valley. Although Colossae had once been "a great city" (Herodotus, *Hist.* 7.30.1; see also Xenophon, *Anab.* 1.2.6), its significance within the region had by the first century AD been thoroughly eclipsed by the much larger and wealthier nearby city of Laodicea. Strabo, writing late in the first century BC, calls it a "town" (*polisma*) (*Geogr.* 12.8.13); Pliny the Elder, similarly, writing a decade or so after Paul's letter to the Colossians, refers to it in Latin not as an *urbs* but as an *oppidum* (*Nat.* 5.145) (cf. Wilson 2005, 4).

The region of Phrygia, in which the town of Colossae was located, was an area in which, according to the testimony of Josephus (*Ant.* 12.149), a considerable Jewish population had been resettled during the time of Antiochus the Great (223–187 BC), and there is evidence of a continuing and sizeable Jewish minority in the towns and cities of Roman Asia during the first century AD (cf. Trebilco 1991, 5–6; Dunn 1996, 21); Philo, for example, asserted that Jews were "very numerous in every city" of the region (*Legat.*

245). The very fact that a community of Christians sprang up there is in itself, given the pattern of earliest Christianity's expansion, indirect evidence of the likelihood that there was a Jewish community present in the town.

Within a context such as that, the emergence of the kind of teaching against which Paul warns in the second chapter of the letter (deriving its practices and its moral authority primarily from Old Testament and Jewish sources but commending them as a "philosophy" through which adherents could wisely order their lives and attain mastery over the passions) is an entirely unsurprising development. It is true, as Arnold has stressed, that the environment of a provincial town in first century Asia Minor would probably not have been one in which there was a pool of literate and educated people sufficient to sustain a "philosophy" that required close and detailed study of the writings of (say) the Middle Platonist tradition (cf. Arnold 1996, 4–5). But a philosophy that was propagated in a primarily oral form among those who had sufficient leisure to attend the lectures of local or visiting orators and teachers is not difficult to imagine as a feature of the cultural life of a town such as Colossae; the city of Prusa in Bithynia, for example, would not have been much larger or more cosmopolitan than Colossae—Dio Chrysostom, a native of that city, felt compelled to admit that it was "not the largest of our cities" (*Or.* 44.9)—but it was still large enough to provide an audience for the kind of orations that Dio wished to present on his return there late in the first century. And there is ample evidence in the literature of first century Hellenistic Judaism (e.g., 4 Maccabees and the writings of Philo) that Jewish and Old Testament teachings could be promoted as a "philosophy," in various forms of synthesis with categories and ideas drawn from popular Stoicism and other philosophical traditions.

Situation and Date

If the letters to the Colossians, the Ephesians, and Philemon are all authentic Pauline compositions and arise from the same period of imprisonment, then (as argued in the introduction to Ephesians, above) the most likely candidate for the place and time from which they were written is Paul's period of house arrest in Rome in the early 60s. At some point during that imprisonment, it appears that Epaphras had arrived in Rome bringing news from Colossae, including both the good news of the Colossians' continuing faith and love (1:8) and, presumably, the unsettling news about the influence that the philosophy to which Paul refers in chapter 2 was gaining among some of them (cf. Dunn 1996, 65).

It is impossible to say with any certainty when exactly Epaphras's arrival in Rome took place and how long the period was between his arrival and the composition of Paul's letters to the Colossians, the Ephesians, and Philemon. (The composition and sending of a letter would presumably have had to wait until the emergence of an opportunity for Tychicus to travel from Rome to Colossae.) Nor can we say with certainty whether the writing of Colossians, Ephesians, and Philemon occurred before or after Paul received the news of the earthquake that (according to Tacitus, *Ann.* 14.27) shook Laodicea and its environs in AD 60. The description in 4:12 of Epaphras as "always wrestling" in prayer for the Colossians suggests that some time had elapsed between his arrival in Rome and the writing of Paul's letter to the Colossians. The urgency of Paul's warnings in chapter 2, on the other hand (while not as white-hot as the urgency of his warnings to the Galatians), suggests that the interval was not a particularly long one. A similar impression is conveyed by the reassurances Paul gives to the readers in 1:24–2:5, which suggest that (in Paul's mind at least) the news of his imprisonment was sufficiently fresh to still be potentially unsettling to the Colossians.

Within that set of circumstances, the two main issues that required a response from Paul (aside from the return of Onesimus, which is addressed largely in a separate letter to Philemon and the church that met in his house) were Paul's imprisonment at the hands of the Roman authorities and the pressure that was being exerted on members of the church in Colossae to conform to the beliefs and practices being advocated by the teachers against whom Paul warns in 2:8. These two circumstances combine to form the occasion for the letter and the background to most of its encouragement and instruction.

The former of these two developments—about which Tychicus would presumably have been able to inform the Colossians more fully on his arrival (4:7-9)—is addressed directly and indirectly, in various ways, throughout the letter (cf. Seitz 2014, 32–35). In the companion letter that Paul sends to the Ephesians, Paul expresses his concern that the believers to whom he is writing might have become "discouraged" (3:13) by the news of his sufferings, interpreting his arrest and imprisonment as a sign that the religio-political powers that dominated their world (and the invisible, spiritual forces that stood behind them) had proved victorious over Christ and the cause of his gospel. A similar concern can be inferred from the encouragements that Paul gives to his readers in Colossians, reminding them repeatedly of Christ's victory over the powers (e.g., 1:13, 15-20; 2:10, 13-15; 3:1-4) and assuring them that his own sufferings are not a frustration or impediment to his apostleship but are precisely the form in which he enacts his vocation as a servant of Christ, of his gospel, and of the church (1:23, 24–2:5).

The latter development—the emerging influence of the "philosophy" to which Paul refers in 2:8—is the topic to which Paul turns in the first major section of the letter body (2:6-23). The precise content and origins of the "Colossian philosophy" has been the subject of considerable scholarly conjecture and debate. Proposals vary widely, with some (e.g., DeMaris 1994; van Kooten 2003; Martin 1996) arguing for a predominantly pagan background to the philosophy, some (e.g., Beetham 2008; Bevere 2003; Smith 2006) for a predominantly Jewish background (with emphasis either on nomistic or mystical elements of Jewish tradition), and many (e.g., Arnold 1996; Pao 2012; Wilson 2005) for a kind of syncretism of the two, with either Jewish or pagan elements forming the basic substrate.

Another, related debate is over the question of whether Paul's warnings were occasioned by an identifiable philosophy that was being actively promoted within the circles of the church at Colossae at all. According to some (e.g., Hooker 1973), the warnings of chapter 2 are of a general and hypothetical nature, and not a reaction against any particular group or movement that was already exerting influence on the Colossians; others (e.g., Dunn 1996) have proposed that the philosophy Paul is describing in chapter 2 is not a group within the boundaries of the early Christian community but simply the self-confident apologetic of a standard, mainstream, diaspora synagogue; and still others (e.g., Copenhaver 2018) that the oppositional rhetoric of Colossians is not directed against any single group but functions instead as a warning to both Jewish- and Gentile-Christian readers against returning to the religious customs of their pre-conversion lives, whatever they may have been.

Given the plethora of possible options and the paucity of evidence within the letter itself (Paul is, after all, making reference to a set of circumstances that the readers are already well aware of), certainty at twenty-one centuries' distance is an elusive goal. The bulk of the evidence within the most closely relevant section of the letter (i.e., 2:8-23), however, points in the direction of a predominantly Jewish background to the teaching that Paul is referring to, with matters such as circumcision and uncircumcision (2:11, 13), food laws, festivals, new moons, and Sabbaths (2:16) all featuring prominently in either Paul's description of the philosophy's practices and rules or his argument for why believers have no need to submit to such teachings. A passing reference in 2:18 to "the worship of angels" raises intriguing possibilities regarding the kind of mystical practices (Jewish or otherwise) in which the proponents of the philosophy were participants, but it does not appear to have been the primary focus of the demands they made on the Colossians or of the critique with which Paul responded to them (see the comments on that verse, below).

The heart of the philosophy, at least as Paul interpreted it, appears to have been the regulations that its proponents attempted to impose on the Colossians (2:20-22) and the mastery over the passions that they promised to those who lived by them (2:23). The latter was entirely consistent with what was commonly expected of a "philosophy" within the first century Greco-Roman context (cf. Stowers 2016; Rowe 2016, 31, 23–33, 40) and with the way that the apologetic and morally formative literature of Hellenistic Judaism spoke about the traditional Jewish practices that they advocated to their readers as a "philosophy" to be embraced along the path to devout wisdom. The author of 4 Maccabees, for example, commences his discourse by informing his readers that the subject he will be discussing is the "most philosophical" (*philosophōtaton*) question of "whether devout reason is sovereign over the emotions," before going on immediately to advise them to "pay earnest attention to philosophy (*philosophia*)" (4 Macc 1:1, NRSV). This subject remains in focus throughout the entirety of the book, with the "devout reason" that the author advocates frequently finding concrete, behavioral expression in the practices and abstentions that he derives, via Jewish tradition, from the law of Moses.

While teachings of this sort were entirely in line with the ethos and practices of mainstream first century Hellenistic Judaism (in line with the claims of scholars such as Dunn), the fact that the philosophy's proponents had become so influential within a predominantly Gentile-background community of believers, together with the way Paul frames his critique of them for "not holding fast (*mē kratōn*) to the Head," suggests that they were probably within the relational sphere of the Colossian believers and had at some point in the past identified themselves as believers in Christ.

Purpose

Given the prominence of those two factors within the situation that Paul is addressing in Colossians, it is not surprising that the letter has a double purpose. Negatively, it warns the readers not to submit to teachings that are framed "according to human tradition, according to the elements of the world, and not according to Christ" (2:8). Positively, like the accompanying letter to the Ephesians, it aims to strengthen and encourage the readers, reinforcing their sense of identity and their confidence in the supremacy and sufficiency of Christ, and urging them to frame their lives in keeping with these realities. In the face of an intimidating array of powers that stand against them (a situation that can only have been exacerbated by the news of Paul's imprisonment and the sense of insufficiency inculcated by the boasts and judgments of the teachers against whom Paul is warning in 2:16-23), the readers are reminded in the strongest possible terms of Christ's supremacy over all the powers, and they are encouraged to continue to walk in line with their original confession of Christ as Lord.

Relationship to Philemon and Ephesians

As noted above, the list of people named in Colossians as present with Paul in his imprisonment (4:10-14) is almost identical to the list of those named in that category in the final greetings of Philemon (Phlm 23-24). This fact, combined with the mention in Col 4:9 of Onesimus as accompanying the letter carrier, Tychicus, makes it highly probable that if Colossians is an authentically Pauline letter, then the two letters originated in the same circumstances and were sent simultaneously to Colossae. Both letters, too, are addressed to the whole church (or at least, in the case of Philemon, to all those who gathered as "the church in [Philemon's] house," which may or may not have been the only house church in Colossae).

The combined effect of these circumstances surrounding the two letters' composition and reception is to create an inevitable interpretive relationship between them. Not all the original hearers of Colossians would also have heard Philemon (the believers in Laodicea, it seems, would not have had the letter to Philemon read among them; nor would those in Colossae who belonged to other house churches than Philemon's), but all the original hearers of Philemon would have heard Colossians. Paul's brief and pointed comments to Philemon, therefore, can and should be read within the larger frame provided by the letter to the Colossians, including its theology of cosmic and personal reconciliation and the transformation of relationships that is required and accomplished by the saving lordship of Christ.

The question of the literary relationship between Colossians and Ephesians is discussed above, in the introduction to Ephesians. As argued there, the simplest and most convincing explanation for the kind of similarities and differences that the two letters exhibit is that they originated from the same author, under the same circumstances, and were sent with the same letter carrier, Tychicus (cf. 4:7; Eph 6:21). Although it is difficult to say with certainty which of the two letters was dictated first, the most likely scenario is that the letter to the Colossians was the first composed, addressing head-on the problems in Colossae that Paul was compelled to respond to, and the letter to the Ephesians was composed second, replacing some of the material that was more narrowly relevant to the situation in Colossae with a more broadly relevant set of reminders and exhortations, and transforming the epistolary form of Colossians into the more homiletic genre of Ephesians.

Introduction to Colossians

If (as argued above in the introduction to Ephesians and below in the comments on 4:16) the "letter from Laodicea" to which Paul refers in 4:16 is the circular homily that we call Ephesians, then Paul's instruction in that verse suggests an interpretive relationship between Colossians and Ephesians that is loosely analogous to the interpretive relationship between Philemon and Colossians. In this instance, as in that, the relationship is an asymmetrical one; while not all those who received Ephesians would also have had access to Colossians, all those who received Colossians would also have had access to Ephesians. Ephesians, consequently, can be read without any necessary reference to Colossians (though comparisons between the two may at times be illuminating), but Colossians should be read with a habitual sideways glance toward Ephesians, so as to be alert for the various ways that the contents of the latter at times reinforce, at times complement, and at times expand on the former.

Structure

Structurally speaking, Colossians is far closer than Ephesians to the form of a typical Pauline letter. It begins in the standard fashion with initial greetings in 1:1-2, a thanksgiving report in 1:3-8, and a report on the prayers of intercession that Paul prays for the readers in 1:9-12a.

The prayer report in 1:9-12a is followed by a series of soteriological and Christological elaborations in 1:12b-23, cascading down from the picture in v. 12a of the believers in Colossae "joyfully giving thanks to the Father." The longest and most substantial of these elaborations is the prose hymn in 1:15-20, celebrating Christ as the one who fulfills and surpasses everything that could be said about the wisdom of God and declaring him to be the one in whom the entire cosmos was made and through whom God has acted to reconcile all things to himself. The introductory section of the letter concludes in 1:24–2:5 with a series of assurances about Paul and his ministry as an apostle, encouraging the readers to understand his sufferings not as a defeat of God's plans and purposes but as the divinely intended form in which Paul's servant vocation is playing out, extending and completing the sufferings of Christ.

The letter body commences in 2:6-7 with a command (the first in the letter) that functions structurally as a kind of hinge. The first part of the sentence ("So then, just as you received Christ Jesus as Lord . . .") looks back to the reminders in chapter 1 of the supremacy of Christ as head over all things and the readers' reception of the gospel that proclaims his saving lordship. The command in v. 6b ("so walk in him") sets the direction for the remainder of the letter, encouraging the readers to continue living in line with these realities.

This command is then unpacked across the following chapters, first negatively (in 2:8-23), with a warning against the teachings they have been exposed to that would divert them from that path, then positively (in 3:1–4:6), with a section that applies the heavenly realities of Christ's ascension and rule to the conduct and relationships of believers within the church (3:5-17), in the household (3:18–4:1), and in their prayers and their relationships with those outside the community of believers (4:2-6). Finally, in 4:7-18, Paul brings the letter to a close with a series of commendations, greetings, and instructions, followed by a plea to the readers to remember his chains and a benediction commending them to the grace of God.

Theological Emphases and Contemporary Significance

While Colossians is a letter that is rich with theological content, none of it is purely abstract, theoretical, or speculative in nature; it is, rather, a deeply pastoral piece of communication, unpacking the entailments of the gospel and applying them to the situation in which the Colossians find themselves and the issues that face them.

The high-water mark of the letter's theology is undoubtedly the Christ hymn in 1:15-20. The core of the hymn's assertions is the basic confession of Christian faith—that Jesus, the Christ, is Lord of all—a confession that Paul unpacks in categories that borrow from (and go far beyond) the wisdom traditions of the Old Testament and Jewish tradition. The theology that Paul articulates is sweeping and explicit in its claims but entirely in keeping with the briefer but no less bold assertions that can be found in the undisputed Pauline epistles (e.g., Rom 9:5; 1 Cor 8:6; Phil 2:6, 9-11). Even here, in ascribing to Christ all that the Jewish tradition says about the wisdom of YHWH (and more besides), Paul's purpose is pastorally oriented, preparing the way for the warnings in chapter 2 against a teaching that offers a substitute wisdom, not deriving its substance from the one "in whom are hidden all the treasures of wisdom and knowledge" (Col 2:3).

The letter's heavy emphasis on realized eschatology, too, including the reminders to the readers that in Christ they have already been "filled" (2:10) and "raised" (3:1), is in keeping with Paul's pastoral purposes. Some commentators have found in verses such as these a contradiction with the reminders Paul gives to his readers in the undisputed letters that fullness, glory, and resurrection are a future hope, not a present privilege (e.g., 1 Cor 4:8-13; 15:23; Rom 8:17b-18, 24-25), but the contradiction is more apparent than real. Colossians, like the undisputed Pauline letters, contains strong elements of futurist eschatology (e.g., 1:5, 23, 27; 3:6, 24-25), and even in 3:1-4, where Paul makes his assertion about the present participation of believers in the resurrection and ascension of Christ, he immediately goes on to make it clear that the realities he is speaking of are still "hidden" to present human sight, awaiting their revelation on the future day "when Christ, who is your life, is revealed" (3:4) (see especially Still 2004).

The soteriology of Colossians, likewise, is consistent with the soteriology of Paul's earlier letters, contextualizing it in relation to the issues that his imprisonment and the teaching that Paul is warning against have raised for the readers. The idea of salvation as a story of victory over and rescue from hostile powers is hardly absent from Paul's earlier letters (e.g., Rom 6:5-14; 1 Cor 2:6-8; 15:24-28; Gal 1:3); nor is the thought that this rescue story is somehow bound up with the forgiveness of sins and the canceling of the law's condemning power (e.g., Rom 8:33–39; 1 Cor 15:17, 56–57). In emphasizing these dimensions of the gospel to the Colossians, Paul is not departing from the soteriology of his earlier letter; he is merely highlighting perennial and centrally important elements of his gospel, applying them to a context in which his readers are at risk of feeling overawed by the powers arrayed against them or intimidated by the rhetoric of teachers who are attempting to bring them back into subjection under the "basic principles" of the present age and its religio-political order (2:8).

Although the theology of the letter is consistently framed in relation to the issues raised by the circumstances that occasioned it, it is nonetheless rich with continuing relevance for Christians reading it within our own context today. The sweeping breadth of Paul's claims about the universal scope of Christ's cosmic lordship and his reconciling work make it clear that, in his mind at least, this is not a letter with a narrow field of applicability. The circumstances in which we labor in the cause of the gospel as early twenty-first century Christians are not identical to those in which Paul's readers struggled to make sense of the unsettling news of his arrest and imprisonment, but they are not without their share of reasons that we, like they, might find ourselves intimidated, silenced, or discouraged. And the teachings and patterns of ministry that exert influence in the church in our own time are not the same as those against which Paul warns the Colossians, but they are no less likely, in many instances, to undermine the confidence of believers in the centrality and sufficiency of the gospel, replacing its wisdom and power with some other substitute package of piety, technique, or controlling and heavy-handed religious authority structures. We need the reminders and encouragements of Colossians no less than its originally intended readers, and we are as blessed as they were to have the opportunity of reading and digesting its contents and helping one another work out how to live in light of the vision it establishes for life as a community shaped by the saving lordship of Christ.

The gospel which you heard
Colossians 1:1–2:5

To the saints (1:1-2)

(1) Paul, an apostle of Christ Jesus through the will of God and Timothy our brother; (2) to the saints and faithful brothers and sisters in Christ in Colossae. Grace to you and peace, from God our Father.

1:1. The prescript of Colossians, like the prescript that commences most of Paul's letters, follows the conventional form of a Greco-Roman letter in identifying the sender ("Paul, an apostle of Christ Jesus through the will of God and Timothy our brother") and the recipients ("to the saints and faithful brothers and sisters in Christ in Colossae"), then adding a greeting ("Grace to you and peace, from God our Father").

It differs from the prescript of Ephesians in four main ways: the inclusion of "Timothy our brother" as co-sender; the description of the recipients as not only "saints" and "faithful" but also as "brothers as sisters" (*adelphois*); the somewhat smoother syntax in which the description of the recipients is couched (with "in Colossae" placed before "saints," and no "who are" following it); and the slightly shorter greeting, wishing the recipients grace and peace "from God our Father," and not also "[from] the Lord Jesus Christ."

Paul's overt reference to his apostleship within first line of the prescript does not imply that his authority and authenticity as an apostle are under challenge among the believers to whom he is writing (cf. Gal 1:1; 1 Cor 1:1; 2 Cor 1:1); rather, as is the case in Rom 1:1 and Eph 1:1, it appears to reflect the fact that the majority of the letter's intended recipients will not be his converts or acquainted with his ministry firsthand. It also anticipates the later references to his vocation and ministry within the letter (e.g., 1:23, 24-29; 2:1-3) in which, in a manner somewhat similar to the treatment of these themes in Eph 3:1-13, Paul's calling and labors as a servant of the gospel are referred to in connection with his sufferings (1:24) and the inclusion of the Gentiles as beneficiaries of his ministry and recipients of the revelation entrusted to him (1:27).

The inclusion of Timothy as co-sender is not an unusual phenomenon within the Pauline corpus; indeed, the majority of Paul's letter prescripts make reference to co-senders in various combinations (Sosthenes in 1 Cor 1:1; Timothy in 2 Cor 1:1, Phil 1:1, and Phlm 1; Silvanus and Timothy in 1 Thess 1:1 and 2 Thess 1:1; and "all the brothers and sisters with me" in Gal 1:1). Although the references to Timothy (and Silvanus, in the case of the Thessalonian letters) in some cases anticipate a role that he plays in the subsequent chapters of the letter (Phil 2:19, 22; 1 Thess 3:2, 6; 2 Cor 1:19; see also 1 Cor 4:17; 16:10) here in Colossians (as is also the case in Philemon and 2 Thessalonians) he plays no subsequent part in the letter. The main effect of his inclusion as co-sender is to position Paul, the letter's apostolic author, as "a Christian among Christian brothers [and sisters]" (Seitz 2014, 60), in keeping with the depiction of the recipients in the immediately following verse as "faithful brothers as sisters" (1:2) and the subsequent references to Tychicus as "beloved brother . . . faithful minister, and . . . fellow slave in the Lord" (4:7); Onesimus, "the faithful and beloved brother" (4:9); and "the brothers and sisters in Laodicea, and Nympha and the church in her house" (4:15).

The fact that Timothy is mentioned in Philemon and Colossians but not in Ephesians (which, if we adjudge all three letters to be genuinely Pauline and accept Col 4:7-9 and Eph 6:21-22 at face value, was written at the same time and under the same circumstances) is a curious phenomenon with no obvious explanation. It may perhaps be a reflection of the difference of genre between Colossians and Philemon (as letters addressed to particular communities and replete with greetings and personal references) and Ephesians (as a letter intended to function as a circular homily, sent to a multiplicity of churches and containing little by way of personal greetings and information).

1:2. The letter's recipients are identified in v. 2 as "the saints and faithful brothers and sisters in Christ in Colossae." Although it is syntactically possible that *hagiois* is functioning as an adjective, in parallel with *pistois*, to qualify the noun *adelphois* (so that the verse would read "to the holy and faithful brothers and sisters in Christ in Colossae"), the more likely reading, in line with the way that *hagioi* normally functions in Pauline letter prescripts, is to take *hagiois* as a noun, referring to the letter's recipients as "saints." As is the case in Eph 1:1, the syntax (which in this instances joins together *hagiois* and *pistois adelphois* with a single article) suggests that a single group is in view rather than two distinct communities composed of (Jewish) "saints" and (Gentile) "brothers and sisters." The *kai* ("and"), on this reading, functions epexegetically to say that "the saints" addressed in the letter are also "faithful brothers and sisters" (Harris 2010, 9). As "saints" they belong to the chosen and consecrated people of God (cf. 1:22; 3:12) and possess privileges originally restricted to the people of Israel (cf. 1:12, 26-27). The additional description of them as "faithful brothers and sisters" reminds them that their possession of this status and its associated privileges is a consequence of the trust and fidelity with which they have responded (and continue to respond) to the message of the gospel (cf. 1:23; 2:7) and that they share it with one another as "brothers and sisters" within the fictive kinship network into which they have been brought as fellow believers in Christ (cf. 3:11, 12-17; 4:7-18). Their whole existence as "saints" and "faithful brothers and sisters" is depicted at the end of the sentence as being "in Christ"—language that (as is the case in Eph 1:1) is probably best read not as a reference to Christ as the object of their faith but rather as a depiction of Christ as the metaphorical sphere within which they are set apart as saints and exercise their trust and fidelity as believers. The phrase that identifies them as the recipients of the letter is thus bracketed by references to their geographical location "in Colossae" and their spiritual and social location "in Christ."

The greeting in v. 2b that concludes the letter prescript wishes the readers "grace . . . and peace, from God our Father." The background and meaning of the greeting's wish for "grace" and "peace" are discussed in the comments on Eph 1:2. Here, in Colossians, the language of "grace" (*charis*), used with reference to the favor of God and the gifts that he bestows, is less frequently employed than in Ephesians. Nevertheless, the way the word is employed (in keeping with Pauline custom) in the greeting that opens the letter and the benediction that concludes it (4:18) is suggestive of the foundational significance of the grace of God for Christian existence—so much so that in 1:6, where the conversion of the readers is described as the day on which they "truly heard and came to know the grace of God," the phrase "the grace of God" can function as a shorthand for the gospel itself (Anderson 2016, 278–79). The idea of salvation by divine grace, if not the word itself, is also fundamental to the reminder and polemic in 2:6–3:4, and the exhortations of 3:5–4:6 repeatedly depict the Christian life as a pattern of practices framed and pervaded by gratitude and thanksgiving to God (3:16-17; 4:2; cf. 1:12; 2:7).

The language of "peace," similarly, occurs less frequently than in Ephesians but is still given some prominence in the description of Christ's death on the cross as an event through which he "ma[de] peace" (1:20), reconciling both the cosmos (1:20) and the readers (1:22) to himself, and the exhortation to the readers in 3:15 to "let the peace of Christ rule in your hearts, to which indeed you were called in one body" (cf. the similar language and ideas in Eph 2:14-18).

The grace and peace that are wished for the readers are described as proceeding "from God our Father," in keeping with the customary language of Paul's letter greetings, in which God is represented as the "Father" of the readers. The omission of the additional phrase, "and the Lord Jesus Christ" (present in Rom 1:7; 1 Cor 1:3; 2 Cor 1:2; Gal 1:3; Eph 1:2; Phil 1:2; 2 Thess 1:2; Phlm 3; cf. 1 Tim 1:2; 2 Tim 1:2; Titus 1:4), should not be taken as implying any diminution of the role Christ plays within the letter as the one through whom (and in whom) the grace and peace of God are extended and received. The immediately following verse, after all, identifies the God to whom thanks is to be given as "the Father of our Lord Jesus Christ," and the letter goes on to place the heaviest possible emphasis on the fact that Christ is the one through whom all of the creating and reconciling work of God is accomplished (esp. 1:15-23); thanksgiving directed to the Father is, therefore, to be offered by the readers "through him" (3:17).

We always thank God . . . when we pray for you (1:3-8)

> (3) We always thank God, the Father of our Lord Jesus Christ, when we pray for you (4) because we have heard of your faith in Christ Jesus and the love which you have for all the saints, (5) because of the hope that is stored up for you in heaven, which you heard about previously in the true message of the gospel, (6) which has come to you, just as it is also bearing fruit and growing in all the world as it has been among you too from the day when you truly heard and came to know the grace of God, (7) just as you learned it from Epaphras, our beloved fellow slave, who is a faithful servant of Christ on our behalf, (8) and who has also made known to us your love in the Spirit.

1:3. As is the case in almost all of Paul's letters (cf. Rom 1:8-10; 1 Cor 1:4-9; Phil 1:3-11; 1 Thess 1:2–2:13; 2 Thess 1:3-12; 2 Tim 1:3; Phlm 6-7), the initial greeting in 1:2 is followed immediately in 1:3-8 by a report of the prayers of thanksgiving (vv. 3-8) and intercession (vv. 9-14) that he prays for the readers.

Both the thanksgiving report and the report of Paul's prayers for the readers are couched in the first-person plural. This could either be simply an epistolary plural, referring to Paul as the letter's author (Lohse 1971, 14, citing Rom 1:5 and 1 Thess 3:1 as examples of a Pauline epistolary plurals) or a reflection of the role played by Timothy as co-sender of the letter (McKnight 2018, 89–90). In support of the latter option it can be argued that Timothy would have likely been present when the report from Epaphras referred to in v. 8 was received and would, therefore, have joined with Paul in the thanksgivings and prayers that the report occasioned. Against it, however, is the difficulty of imagining a sense in which Epaphras's ministry could be thought of as having been conducted on Timothy's behalf as well as Paul's (v. 7; assuming, as argued below, that "our" [*hēmōn*] rather than "your" [*hymōn*] is original) and the fact that there is no obvious correlation between named co-senders and first-person plurals in Pauline letter introductions. (First Corinthians, Philippians, and Philemon all refer to co-senders but have thanksgivings and/or prayer reports in the first-person singular.)

The thanksgivings that Paul describes in v. 3 are offered "always . . . when we pray for you"—language that suggests a consistent, habitual offering of thanks to God, along with the prayers of intercession that Paul prays for the Colossians (cf. 2:1 and the description of Epaphras in 4:12 as "always wrestling on your behalf in his prayers"). (See Pao 2012, 50; Moo 2008, 83; Harris 2010, 14, for arguments in favor of reading "always" as modifying "give thanks" rather than "pray" and taking the participial phrase, "praying for you," as a temporal frame elaborating on and restricting the preceding "always.") Paul's prayers of thanksgiving are offered up to "God, the Father of our Lord Jesus Christ"—language that grounds the description of God in 1:2 as "our Father" in a reminder of his prior and more basic identity as the Father of the Lord Jesus (cf. the similar expressions in Rom 15:6; 2 Cor 1:3; 11:31; Eph 1:3).

1:4. The reason Paul gives for the prayers of thanks that he describes in v. 3 is the fact that he has heard of the readers' "faith in Christ Jesus" and their "love . . . for all the saints" (v. 4; cf. the reference in v. 8 to Epaphras's report of their "love in the Spirit," which is, by implication, at least the most recent occasion for Paul's thanksgiving). The description of these realities as something that Paul has only "heard of," not witnessed firsthand, is consistent with the fact that (as Paul goes on to make reference to in v. 7) they heard the gospel not from him but from Epaphras. The "faith" of the Colossians, for which Paul gives thanks to God, implies both the belief and trust within which they initially received the message of the gospel (cf. vv. 5-7) and the continuing dependence on and allegiance to Christ that they have demonstrated since then (cf. 1:23; 2:6-7).

As a number of commentators point out, a good argument can be made for taking the following phrase, "in Christ Jesus," as a reference to Christ as the sphere in which the readers' faith has been exercised rather than as the object of it (cf. Harris 2010, 14; McKnight 2018, 92, and the similar use of the phrase "in Christ" two verses earlier, in 1:2). On the other hand, the parallelism between "faith in Christ Jesus" and "love . . . for all the saints" lends itself to a reading in which "Christ Jesus" is understood as the object of their faith and "all the saints" as the objects of their love (cf. Morgan 2015, 311; Campbell 2012, 171). The closely similar language that Paul uses in Philemon 5, where "faith toward [*pros*] the Lord Jesus" refers unambiguously to the Lord Jesus as the reference point or object of Philemon's faith, also supports that interpretation (cf. the concession in Thielman 2010, 94–95, with reference to the similar phrase in Eph 1:15).

Closely connected with the Colossians' faith in Christ (cf. Gal 5:6; Eph 1:15; 6:23; 1 Thess 3:6; 5:8; 2 Thess 1:3; 1 Tim 1:14; 2 Tim 1:13; Phlm 5) is their "love . . . for all the saints." Here, as elsewhere in Paul's letters, "love" functions as a kind of summary term for the whole constellation of dispositions and practices that believers ought to manifest toward one another (see esp. 3:12-14; Rom 13:8-10; 1 Cor 13:1-13), grounded in and modeled on the love that God has shown toward them (3:12; cf. Eph 4:33–5:2). The inclusion of "all the saints" within the embrace of the Colossians' love is a reflection of the new social identity that they have in common as members of Christ's people, among whom "there is no Greek and Jew, circumcised and uncircumcised, barbarian, Scythian, slave, free; but Christ is all and in all" (3:11). The fact that Paul, here and elsewhere in his letters, gives thanks to God for faith and love that have been exercised by the believers to whom he is writing is an expression of his conviction that the grace and power of God are the ultimate source of both (cf. 1 Cor 15:10; Phil 1:6; 2:13).

1:5. The faith and the love of the Colossians are depicted in v. 5 as deriving from "the hope that is stored up for you in heaven, which you heard about in the true message of the gospel." Unlike the "faith" and "love" of the previous verse, both of which refer to dispositions and practices of the Colossians themselves, the "hope" to which Paul refers in v. 5 is used in an objective sense to refer to the promised future held out to the readers in the message of the gospel (cf. 1:23). It is, therefore, a hope that can be spoken of by Paul as having been "stored up" (by God) for them "in heaven." This latter expression should not be taken as implying that the readers' own eternal future will be a disembodied existence somewhere in the heavens; rather, it directs their attention in the present to heaven as the place "where Christ is, seated at the right hand of God" (3:1) and encourages them to look to the risen and glorified Christ as the guarantor and paradigm of the future that God has promised and stored up for them (3:2-4; cf. Phil 3:20-21).

The Colossians' knowledge of (and possession of) this hope has come about through "the true message of the gospel" (v. 5b). The Greek expression that this phrase translates connects "the message" (*tō logō*) with two genitive modifiers: "of truth" (*tēs alētheias*) and "of the gospel" (*tou euangeliou*).

How exactly the three components of the phrase relate to one another is not entirely clear. Among the various possibilities, the most likely option is to take the first genitive (*tēs alētheias*) in a qualitative sense ("the true message") and the second (*tou euangeliou*) as epexegetical ("the true message, i.e., the gospel") (cf. Harris 2010, 16; Campbell 2013, 4, and the similar though not grammatically identical expression in Eph 1:13). The Colossians "heard about [it] previously" (*proēkousate*) through the ministry of Epaphras, as Paul goes on to spell out in v. 7.

1:6. Having made reference to the gospel in v. 5, Paul goes on in vv. 6-8 to elaborate on the way it came to the Colossians, its effects among them (and in the whole world), and the credentials of Epaphras who first brought it to them. This elaboration on the gospel as "the true message" and the reliability of Epaphras as a minister of it anticipates, without yet making explicit, Paul's later warnings against other messages that are not to be believed (cf. 1:23; 2:4, 8, 16-17, 20-23) and other teachers who are not to be trusted (cf. 2:18-19).

The description of the gospel that Paul gives in v. 6 represents it as the subject of a string of active or middle-voice verbs ("has come" [*parontos*] . . . "bearing fruit" [*karpophoroumenon*] . . . "growing" [*auxanomenon*]). The first of these personifies the gospel message as the subject of a verb that Paul frequently uses elsewhere to speak of his own personal presence (e.g., 1 Cor 5:3; 2 Cor 10:2, 11; 11:9; 13:2, 10; Gal 4:8, 20); the second and third implicitly represent the gospel metaphorically as a growing plant or spreading vine, full of life and power, benefit and blessing. Although some interpreters (e.g., Beale 2007, 842–46; Beetham 2008, 41–60) hear in the language of "bearing fruit and growing" an echo of the blessing pronounced over humankind in Gen 1:28, the likelihood of this being an intentional allusion on Paul's part is diminished by the inexactness of the correspondences between Paul's language and that of the LXX (which in extant versions of Gen 1:28 uses *plēthynō* ["multiply"] rather than *karpophoreō* ["bear fruit"]). The case for an allusion to Gen 1:28 is further undermined by the fact that Paul goes on in v. 10 to unpack the "bearing fruit" metaphor in terms of good works, not progeny or converts (which would have fitted more neatly with a typological fulfillment of the Genesis 1 blessing through the growth of the word, as manifested in the expansion of the Christian community).

The powerful effects of the gospel message (manifested in terms of both the numerical growth of the Christian community and the fruit that the message bears in the good works its believers perform) are described by Paul has having been manifested "in all the world" and, on a smaller scale, as witnessed by the readers, in Colossae itself ("as it has been among you too").

Both of these realities function, in the larger context of the letter, to reinforce the Colossians' confidence in the version of the gospel message that they were taught by Epaphras, which has (in contrast with the high-sounding but ultimately ineffectual alternative that Paul goes on to warn against in 2:8-23) had a good and powerful impact amongst the Colossians and has demonstrated its validity by having the same effect in numerous other communities (cf. Moo 2008, 89; Abbott 1897, 197).

The gospel message has had this good effect among the Colossians (as Paul goes on to remind them in v. 6b) "from the day when [they] truly heard and came to know the grace of God." This reminder at the close of the verse has several functions. In the first place, it adds to the point previously made about the effect of the gospel among the Colossians by highlighting the fact that it had this impact from the beginning of their acquaintance with the message (cf. the similar point made in Phil 1:6 about the Philippians' partnership in the gospel). In the second place, it foregrounds the grace of God as a fundamental presupposition and entailment of the gospel message (anticipating the criticisms that Paul will go on to make in 2:8-23 regarding alternative philosophies and spiritualities that promise spiritual progress and self-mastery on some other basis). And in the third place, underlining that point, it emphasizes that the Colossians "truly" heard and came to know God's grace in the gospel message. (The phrase *en alētheia* ["in truth"] is probably best taken adverbially, as modifying "came to know"; the basic idea is not much different, however, if it is taken adjectivally, as modifying "grace"—either way, the net effect is [implicitly] to contrast the content of the teaching that they received from Epaphras with the darkened understandings that they had previously been gripped by [1:21] and the "empty deceit" [2:8] that they continue to be exposed to.)

1:7. The focus shifts in v. 7 to Epaphras as the messenger from whom the Colossians originally received the gospel: "just as you learned it from Epaphras, our beloved fellow slave, who is a faithful servant of Christ on our behalf." The *kathōs* that commences the verse is probably best taken in something that approximates its usual, comparative sense (Harris 2010, 19), in loose continuity with the function that it has already performed twice in the previous verse: just as the gospel (by implication) came to others through Paul and his various fellow workers, so also the Colossians came to learn it through Epaphras (vv. 6, 7); and just as the gospel has been bearing fruit and growing in all the world, so also it has among the Colossians (v. 6).

Although Paul occasionally uses the verb *manthanō* ("learn") to refer simply to the receiving of a discrete piece of information that has been passed on (e.g., Gal 3:2), he more typically uses it to refer to the learning of a larger pattern of teaching and/or conduct (e.g., Rom 16:17; Eph 4:20; Phil 4:9). Its use here in v. 7, in keeping with language of the previous verse ("when you truly heard and came to know the grace of God"), is consistent with the later content of the letter, in which the message of the gospel that was originally received by the Colossians is presented as containing within it a latent wisdom that is to be taught and learned across the whole of life (esp. 1:28; 2:2-3, 6; 3:16).

Epaphras, the original teacher of the gospel to the Colossians, is warmly endorsed in the remainder of the verse, as "our beloved fellow slave, who is a faithful servant of Christ on our behalf" (v. 7). The difference in meaning between "slave" (*doulos*) and "servant" (*diakonos*) is a fine one, with the latter word tending to be used in a slightly wider range of contexts in which one person provides services for another, and the former—when used in its literal sense—typically reserved for contexts that refer more narrowly and specifically to men and women who belong as chattel slaves of another (e.g., 3:22; 4:1). An additional difference in early Christian usage, including Paul's letters, is that *diakonos* can occasionally function in a semi-technical sense, referring to a person who serves in the office of deacon within the church (e.g., Rom 16:1; Phil 1:1). When Paul uses the word *doulos*, therefore (or, in this instance, *syndoulos* ["fellow slave"]), there is a slightly greater likelihood that a live metaphor is in play, and Paul is expecting his readers to be conscious of the paradoxical relationship between the low status of a slave (which Paul, in this instance, shares with Epaphras as his *syndoulos*) and the high honor of being a slave/servant of Christ.

Epaphras's ministry among the Colossians is an expression of two interconnected relations of agency and representation: he is a servant "of Christ" (probably best understood as an objective genitive, specifying Christ as the one whom Epaphras, ultimately and most basically, serves), and he also performs this service "on our behalf," as one whose service of Christ extends Paul's ministry and is carried out under his aegis. (The better-attested *hēmōn*, "our," is more likely to be original than the *hymōn*, "your," that is preferred in the UBS5 and NA28 text; the latter is presumably the consequence of a scribal emendation that, if it was consciously made, could perhaps have been an assimilation to what is said of Epaphras in 4:13). In both of these relations (to Christ and to Paul), Epaphras is described as being "faithful" in his ministry, an affirmation that probably has the primary function, within the larger context of the letter, of underlining the reliability of the teaching that he passed on to the Colossians.

1:8. The thanksgiving report concludes in v. 8, continuing the focus on Epaphras but shifting the focus from his role as the original teacher of the gospel to the Colossians (v. 7) to the more recent past, in which he has brought to Paul a report of their "love in the Spirit" (a report that was presumably one of the occasioning circumstances for the writing of Colossians). The reference here in v. 8 to the Colossians' love does not specify its object (Paul? God? their neighbors? one another?), but the most likely candidate, given the focus of the thanksgiving that Paul reports a few verses earlier, is the love they have for their fellow believers ("all the saints"; v. 4), manifested primarily in the mutual love they show for one another within the local community of believers in Colossae (cf. 2:2; 3:14). The phrase "in the Spirit" that Paul uses to describe this love (the only reference to the Spirit within the letter) is probably best understood in an instrumental sense (Campbell 2013), identifying the Spirit as the one through whom God has stirred up and sustained their love (cf. Gal 5:22).

Asking that you may be filled with the knowledge of his will (1:9-14)

(9) For this reason, we too, from the day when we heard, have not stopped praying for you, and asking that you may be filled with the knowledge of his will, in all spiritual wisdom and understanding, (10) in order that that you may walk worthily of the Lord, to please him in all things, bearing fruit in every good work, and growing in the knowledge of God, (11) being strengthened with all power according to the might of his glory, for the sake of all endurance and patience, joyfully (12) giving thanks to the Father, who has qualified you for a share in the inheritance of the saints in the light; (13) he has rescued us from the dominion of darkness and transferred us into the kingdom of the son of his love, (14) in whom we have redemption, the forgiveness of sins.

1:9. The thanksgiving report in vv. 3-8 is followed in vv. 9-14 by a report of the prayers that Paul prays for the Colossians. The precise boundaries of this section of the letter are not easy to delineate (cf. McKnight 2018, 105). There is certainly a clear transition at the start of v. 9 ("For this reason . . .") from the thanksgiving to the prayer report. But the prayer report, once commenced, moves by a series of steps, almost imperceptibly, from a statement of the primary content of Paul's prayer ("that you may be filled with the knowledge of his will, in all spiritual wisdom and understanding"; v. 9) to an account of the purpose for which he requests it ("in order that that you may walk worthily of the Lord, to please him in all things"; v. 10), to a series of participial clauses that paint a picture of the kind of community life that "walk[ing] worthily" entails ("bearing fruit in every good work, and growing in the knowledge of God, being strengthened with all power according to the might of his glory, for the sake of all endurance and patience, joyfully giving thanks to the Father"; vv. 10b-12a). The final item in this list ("joyfully giving thanks to the Father") is, in turn, followed by an amplified description of the Father to whom they direct their thanksgivings, "who has qualified you for a share in the inheritance of the saints in the light" (v. 12b)—a description that also functions by implication as a reminder of the content at the heart of their thanksgivings. A pair of relative clauses follows, further elaborating on the work of the Father (v. 13) and the Son (v. 14) and their consequences for Paul and the readers, and indeed for all believers.

This last elaboration in v. 14 is then followed by another, much longer elaboration in vv. 15-23, which commences, like 14, with a relative pronoun referring to Christ and falls neatly into two halves: an exalted account of the preeminence of Christ and his role in the creation and reconciliation of all things (vv. 15-20) and a return to the story of the readers in vv. 21-23, locating them within that larger narrative of cosmic reconciliation.

In the broadest sense, therefore, the prayer report should be read as extending all the way to v. 23 (cf. the similar analysis in McKnight 2018, 105–106), with the soteriological and Christological elaborations contained in vv. 12b, 13, 14, and 15-23 all functioning as codas to the account of Paul's petition (v. 9) and its purposes (vv. 10-12a).

But the gravity and complexity of the material in vv. 15-20, the twists and turns that are involved in following the thread of Paul's syntax all the way to v. 23, and the tight structural and thematic links that tie vv. 15-20 and vv. 21-23 to one another as a subunit in their own right all suggest that the report in vv. 9-12a of Paul's petition and its purposes should first be read within its most immediate context, in vv. 9-14, and only subsequently placed within the larger frame of vv. 9-23.

The opening words of v. 9, "for this reason," suggest a connection of some sort between Paul's prayers for the Colossians, which he is about to describe, and some portion of the contents of the preceding paragraph. The fact that Paul goes on immediately to say that his prayers have been offered "from the day when we heard" suggests a connection with either v. 8 ("who has also made known to us your love in the Spirit") or v. 4 ("because we have heard of your faith in Christ Jesus and the love which you have for all the saints"). Paul's language, like the language he has used in v. 6 to describe the impact of the gospel among the Colossians, implies a period of some duration, and the evidence of the greetings in chapter 4, together with the accompanying letter to Philemon, suggests that the report Paul has received from Epaphras is by no means the first time he has heard about the existence of a community of believers in Colossae. It seems most likely, therefore, that the reference in v. 9 is to the whole of the preceding paragraph (Moo 2008, 92–93; Campbell 2013, 6; Pao 2012, 68), with a particular focus on the reports that Paul has received over the years (including, but not limited to, the most recent report from Epaphras) as a stimulus to his prayers.

Although some commentators (e.g., Lohse 1971, 24) read the *kai* ("also") as attached to the verb that comes later in the verse (i.e., "not only do we give thanks, but we also do not stop praying"), the syntax of the sentence ties the *kai* more closely to the *hēmeis* ("we") that follows immediately after it. The effect is to signal a switch in the subject of the verbs, either from Epaphras in v. 8 (Wilson 2005, 99; Pao 2012, 68) or, more broadly, from the gospel as ministered by Epaphras, and the Colossians in their response to it, in vv. 6-8 (Abbott 1897, 201), to Paul in v. 9. The gospel, from the day the Colossians first heard it from Epaphras, has been growing and bearing fruit among them; and Paul also, from the day he heard of their faith, has been joining his prayers to Epaphras's labors (and Epaphras's prayers; 4:12) and asking God to do the very things that the gospel has been doing and Epaphras's ministry has been aiming at.

It is not surprising, therefore, that the description of Paul's intercessions and their goal in vv. 9-10 contains a string of parallels with the report of what Paul thanks God for in vv. 4-6 (as pointed out by Lohse 1971, 24; Moo 2008, 92): "from the day when we heard" (v. 9) echoes "from the day when you . . . heard" (v. 6); "knowledge" (*epignōsin . . . epignōsei*; vv. 9, 10) echoes "came to know" (*epegnōte*; v. 6); "bearing fruit . . . and growing" (v. 10) echoes "bearing fruit and growing" (v. 6). Paul's prayer, in other words, is not that God would begin to do something new and different among the Colossians but that he would continue doing the same things that he has already begun to do—an encouragement that anticipates the warnings and exhortations that follow later in the letter (esp. 2:4, 6-7).

A further way that Paul's prayer report anticipates the subsequent content and emphases of the letter is in its focus primarily on matters of knowledge, wisdom, and understanding. If the emphasis of the thanksgiving has been on the mutual love that is already (according to Epaphras's report) richly evident in the Colossians' conduct toward one another (1:4, 8), the emphasis of the prayers is on the wisdom they will need to navigate the challenges that Paul turns to in the following chapter (which were also, one presumes, referred to in the report he had received). The initial, and genuine, understanding that the Colossians were granted when they "truly heard and came to know the grace of God" (v. 6) must continue to be confirmed and deepened, so that they are "filled with the knowledge of [God's] will, in all spiritual wisdom and understanding" (v. 9). This emphasis is also echoed in the subsequent reports of Paul's labors (including, by implication, his prayers) in 2:2-3 and Epaphras's prayers in 4:12.

The "knowledge of (God's) will" with which Paul prays that the Colossians will be filled is not the kind of knowledge that consists in a series of piecemeal oracular revelations concerning particular events that are to take place or tasks that are to be performed. It is, rather, the kind of knowledge that consists in "all spiritual wisdom and understanding," as Paul goes on to elaborate in the remainder of the verse, and is directed toward the purpose of "walk[ing] worthily of the Lord, to please him in all things, bearing fruit in every good work" (v. 10; cf. 4:12; Rom 12:2; Eph 6:6; 1 Thess 4:1-3).

It is possible, as some commentators speculate (e.g., Moo 2008, 93), that the language of Paul's request that the Colossians might be "filled" with such knowledge (along the similar references to "filling" and "fullness" later in the letter, e.g., 1:19; 2:9-10) may be a deliberate appropriation of language used by the teachers of the kind of philosophy that Paul warns against in the following chapter. But this is not a necessary inference to draw from Paul's use of these words. His use of the language of "filling" and "fullness" occurs only in his positive statements about Christ and about God's work in believers, not in the (admittedly brief) sketches he offers in 2:4, 8, 16-23 of the teachings and practices that he is warning the readers against—the closest he comes to the language of "fullness" in describing the philosophy that is in view in these verses is to denounce it, by contrast, as "empty" (*kenos*, 2:8). Of relevance, too, is the similar language he uses in Ephesians (e.g., 1:23; 3:19; 4:10; 5:18) without anything in that letter to suggest a polemical context equivalent to that of Colossians.

Irrespective of whether the language of "fill[ing]" that Paul uses here is borrowed from and used against the teachers of a rival philosophy, its immediate context here in the prayer report suggests an obvious function that it serves: to point toward the kind of ever-broadening, ever-deepening grasp of God's will that he desires for the Colossians, manifested in "all" spiritual wisdom and understanding, aimed at walking so as to please Christ in "all" things, enabled by the strengthening of the readers with "all" power so that they might persevere with "all" endurance. In keeping with the divine agency implied by the passive forms Paul employs to speak of the readers being "filled" (v. 9; and "strengthened," v. 11), it is probably best to understand the "spiritual" (*pneumatikos*) nature of the wisdom and understanding that Paul desires for the Colossians as a way of referring to its origins in the work of the Spirit (cf. esp. the close connection between the Spirit, wisdom, and understanding [*epignōsis*] in Eph 1:17).

1:10. Verse 10 expands on Paul's report of the prayers he prays for the Colossians by specifying the moral and practical purpose of the wisdom that he prays they will be filled with: "in order that you may walk worthily of the Lord, to please him in all things, bearing fruit in every good work, and growing in the knowledge of God."

The purpose clause that opens the verse ("in order that you may walk worthily of the Lord") is closely similar to the language Paul uses in Eph 4:1 to introduce the exhortations that make up the majority of the second half of that letter. (As a sidenote, it is worth pausing to observe the insight this offers into the closely related functions of prayer report and exhortation within the rhetoric of Paul's letters.) The image of "walk[ing]" functions as a metaphor for the pattern of life that the readers are to adopt and maintain as believers in Christ (2:6; 4:5; cf. Gal 5:16; 1 Thess 2:12; 4:1, 12; Rom 6:4; 8:4; 13:13; 14:15; Eph 4:17; 5:2, 8, 15), in contrast to the pattern of life that they formerly followed when they lived in ignorance of him (3:7; cf. Rom 13:13; Eph 2:2). The kind of correspondence expressed by the word "worthily" (here, as also in the similar expressions that Paul employs in 1 Thess 2:12; Eph 4:1; Phil 1:27; Rom 16:2) is best understood in a primarily qualitative rather than quantitative sense—Paul's desire is not so much that the moral excellence of the readers will match that of Christ but that the shape of their lives will faithfully reflect their identity as his people.

Following closely on the heels of this first purpose clause comes another expression suggestive of purpose or, perhaps, result: "to please him in all things" (*eis pasan aresekeian*). The phrase is not an easy one to translate. Its syntactical function is probably here to modify the infinitive *peripatēsai* ("to walk"), as a purpose construction specifying the goal that characterizes the kind of "walk[ing]" that is worthy of Christ (Harris 2010, 28; Campbell 2013, 7–8, reads it as indicating result rather than purpose). The word *areskeia*, here translated as "please," is, properly speaking, a noun that generally carried the sense of "desire to please," frequently with the negative connotation of obsequiousness (cf. BDAG, s.v. "*areskeia*"). On occasion, however, the word can be used in a non-pejorative sense to refer to a legitimate attempt to please or (as here) to the pleasure of the person whose approval is sought (cf. Philo, *Creation* 144; *Spec. Laws* 1.300, in both instances also using the expression *eis areskeian*).

The two participial clauses that complete v. 10 ("bearing fruit in every good work, and growing in the knowledge of God") elaborate on the kind of community life that "walk[ing] worthily" entails. (On the elaborative function that is typically served by present participles following the main verb, see Runge 2010, 262–63.) The language of "bearing fruit . . . and growing" (like the similar language in v. 6) is probably not intended to be heard as an allusion to Gen 1:28 (see the discussion above on v. 6). It does, however, reflect the common Old Testament and early Jewish image of "fruit" as a metaphor for outwardly visible moral conduct (e.g., Isa 5:1-7; Jer 17:10; 21:14; 32:19; Amos 6:12; Sir 27:6; Philo, *Cherubim* 84; Odes Sol. 11.23; Matt 7:16-17), a meaning that is already confirmed in the word order of the original Greek by the immediately preceding phrase, which specifies the referent of the metaphor as consisting "in every good work" (with the anarthrous "every" probably best taken here in the sense of "every kind of"; cf. Harris 2010, 27–28). The "growing" that is in view here (unlike the "growing" spoken of in v. 6, where the metaphor appears to refer to the growth of the gospel as manifested in the numerical expansion of the Christian community) is specified as consisting in the readers' increasing knowledge of God—assuming that the dative-case construction, *tē epignōsei tou theou*, translated here as "in the knowledge of God," should be read (in parallel with the earlier phrase, "in every good work") as a dative of respect, specifying the content that the growth consists in, rather than an instrumental dative indicating that the knowledge of God is the means by which it takes place (Harris 2010, 29). The earlier references to the time when the Colossians "came to know the grace of God" (v. 6) and the "knowledge of his will" that Paul prays the Colossians will be filled with (v. 9) create a context in which it is clear that the genitive "of God" (*tou theou*) should be read as an objective genitive, representing God as the object of the readers' understanding. The close connection between the two clauses in v. 10b ("bearing fruit in every good work and growing in the knowledge of God"), their combined relationship with the preceding purpose clause ("in order that that you may walk worthily of the Lord"), and the reference in v. 9 to "the knowledge of [God's] will" all combine to suggest that the kind of knowledge in view is relational and transformative, not merely speculative or theoretical (cf. the way that "knowledge of God" [LXX: *epignōsis theou*] is framed in Prov 2:5 within the chapter's larger depiction of a cluster of interrelated concepts including wisdom, understanding, and righteous conduct).

It is tempting, given the way the account in vv. 9b-10 of the content and purpose of Paul's prayers begins and ends with *epignōsis* ("knowledge"), to postulate a kind of virtuous epistemic circle, in which "the very thing for which Paul and Timothy are praying, knowledge of the divine will, produces a transformed mode of life, which in turn makes members of the Colossian community more open to growing in the knowledge of God" (Foster 2016, 159–60), but a construction of that sort would require an overly neat account of the causal relationships between the various clauses and phrases in vv. 9b-10. Certainly Paul prays in these verses for the kind of knowledge, wisdom, and understanding that will lead to a transformed way of life, and it is by no means foreign to his thought to speak of moral dispositions and patterns of conduct having epistemic consequences (cf. 1:21; Eph 4:18; Rom 1:18-23), but the knowledge of God that is referred to in v. 10b is depicted as growing in parallel with, not as a consequence of, the transformed life described in the previous clauses of the verse. Nor does Paul's unfolding of the entailments of the prayer that he describes in v. 9b conclude at the end of v. 10, as if to close a neatly drawn circle in which knowledge leads to virtue and, in turn, deeper knowledge; the picture continues in vv. 11-12 with a series of further elaborations that focus on the divine strengthening that enables it and the thankfulness that accompanies it.

1:11. Verse 11 commences with a picture of the readers "being strengthened with all power according to the might of his glory." The present participle that introduces the clause is, like the two preceding participles in v. 10b, elaborative in function, further filling out the picture of what "walk[ing] worthily" (v. 10a) entails. Although the grammatical construction itself does not imply a causal relationship between the participle ("being strengthened") and the preceding infinitive ("[to] walk worthily"), the meanings of the respective verbs suggest that the part played by the strengthening work of God within the picture Paul paints is as the enabling that makes it possible for believers to "walk worthily," in the manner that Paul describes in v. 10. That the agent implied by the passive-voice "being strengthened" in God is implied by both the fact that the strengthening is "with *all* power" and the fact that it takes place "according to the might of [God's] glory." The former phrase, "with all power" (*en pasē dynamei*), is probably best understood, like the two similar phrases in v. 10, as a reference not to the instrument by which the strengthening is performed (contra Campbell 2013, 8; Harris 2010, 29) but to the sphere or commodity in which it consists (cf. Abbott 1897, 204; also, by implication, Wilson 2005, 107; cf. BDAG, s.v. "en," 12); the depiction of the believers as furnished with "all" power is not implying that they are made literally omnipotent but that their empowerment by God is amply sufficient for their needs (cf. the earlier references to "all" all spiritual wisdom and understanding, pleasing Christ in "all" things, and bearing fruit in "every" good work, and the subsequent reference to "all" endurance and patience). The latter phrase, "according to [*kata*] the might of [God's] glory," suggests the standard or measure to which their strengthening takes place (cf. Campbell 2013, 8; Abbott 1897, 204, and the similar use of "according to" in Eph 1:7, 19; 3:16, 20; 4:7, 16), which is, in this instance, the limitless might of God's glory.

Although most modern English versions assume a qualitative understanding of the genitive construction "of his glory" (e.g., NIV: "his glorious might"), the pervasive presence of references to the personal glory of God in the Old Testament and early Jewish literature is probably sufficient reason to opt for a translation in which "glory" is understood first in relation to "his"—i.e., as an attribute of and metonymy for God himself—and only second in relation to "might"—i.e., as serving to identify the might in question as the might that is possessed and exercised by God, in his glory (Moo 2008, 98; Wilson 2005, 109).

The idea conveyed in v. 11a—that the pattern of life depicted in v. 10 (and, by implication, the knowledge and understanding prayed for in v. 9) can only take place through the strengthening work of God—closely parallels the thinking expressed in the prayer report of Eph 3:14-19. The assumption underlying it, here as in Ephesians, is that the life to which believers are called is a struggle in which believers are pitted against powerful opponents and must persevere through trials and hardships. Although the notion of opposing powers is not as prominent in Colossians as it is in Ephesians, it is still implied here in the prayer report by the reference in v. 13 to "the dominion of darkness," and it is further developed in the letter's subsequent references to the "thrones," "dominions," "rulers," and "authorities" (1:16; cf. 2:10, 15) that are subject to Christ and have been defeated by him at the cross.

The assumption that the life Paul describes in v. 10 requires perseverance through trials is immediately confirmed in v. 11b, which speaks of the strengthening of v. 11a as being granted "for the sake of all endurance and patience." The two words are closely similar in meaning, the former (*hypomonē*) tending to be used to refer to perseverance in the face of sufferings and adverse circumstances (e.g., Rom 5:3-4; 8:25; 2 Cor 1:6; 2 Thess 1:4, always referring to an attribute exhibited by humans) and the latter (*makrothymia*) to refer to patience in the face of provocations and incitements from others (e.g., 3:12; Rom 2:4; 9:22; Eph 4:2, referring on some occasions to human patience and on other occasions to the patience of God). Both attributes are required if the Christian community is to maintain its solidarity and faithfulness over time and under pressure (cf. Phil 1:27-30), and both require divine power for their enablement (cf. Paul's inclusion of both of these attributes as part of his account of how the power of God is manifested in his own ministry, in 2 Cor 6:4-7).

The last two words of the verse, "with joy" (*meta charas*), are read by some (e.g., Barth and Blanke 1994, 183; cf. AV; RSV) as qualifying the "endurance and patience" that have just been spoken of, most (e.g., Pao 2012, 73; Wilson

2005, 110) link them with the "giving thanks" that follows, pointing out that each of the preceding participles in vv. 10-11 is modified by a prepositional phrase (or, in the case of the second participle, "growing," the closely similar dative-case expression, "in the knowledge of God") and drawing attention to the connection between joy and thankfulness in Phil 1:4.

1:12. The thanksgiving that Paul goes on to speak of in v. 12, as a further elaboration on the pattern of life depicted in v. 10 as "walk[ing] worthily of the Lord," is probably best thought of not as an additional and occasional activity (though it will involve frequent and explicitly voiced prayers and songs of thankfulness) but as a pervasive disposition of the heart (cf. 2:7; 3:17). The prominence that Paul gives to thankfulness as a basic Christian disposition reflects both a background conviction regarding the indebtedness that all creatures have to God as their creator (cf. Rom 1:20-21) and the additional and particular reasons that Christians in particular have for giving thanks, based on the deliverance that they have experienced in Christ and the inheritance that has been promised to them—realities that Paul goes on immediately to foreground in vv. 12b-14. The knowledge of God that they have been granted and are to grow in is therefore, at its heart (as Paul has already described it in v. 6), a knowledge of God's grace, calling for a fitting response of gratitude to their divine benefactor. (On the larger cultural background to Paul's understanding of thanksgiving, see especially Barclay 2015, 11–65; Pao 2003, 165–73.)

Paul's unfolding of these particular, Christian reasons for thanksgiving commences in v. 12b by identifying the Father to whom thanks are to be given as the one "who has qualified you for a share in the inheritance of the saints in the light." The verb "qualified" (which here takes the form of a dative particle, *tō hikanōsanti*) is not one that Paul characteristically uses in soteriological contexts—the only other instance of the verb in Paul's letters (and, indeed, in the New Testament as a whole) is in 2 Cor 3:6, where it is used in reference to the divine authorization of Paul and his fellow workers as ministers of the new covenant. There, as here, Paul's decision to opt for the verb may be a reflection of a context in which credentials are being questioned, albeit implicitly or subtly—in one instance, by the adverse comparisons that some are making between Paul and rival teachers who come furnished with impressive letters of recommendation (cf. 2 Cor 2:16–3:5; 10:12) and in the other by the (implicitly?) "disqualify[ing]" tendency of the elitist spirituality that Paul warns against in 2:6-23 (see especially 2:18; the verb in that verse instance is *katabrabeuō*).

What the readers have been qualified for by God is "a share in the inheritance of the saints in the light." Although the saving work of God will be depicted in the immediately following verses in terms that are inclusive of Jews as well as Gentiles, here in v. 12 (assuming, with the UBS5 and NA28 editors, that the better-attested "you" [*hymas*] is to be preferred as original over the less well attested "us" [*hēmas*]—presumably a scribal assimilation to vv. 13-14) the focus is on the particular experience of the readers as Gentile converts who have entered into the inheritance originally promised to Israel (cf. Gal 3:29; 4:7; Eph 3:6). The fact that the readers have already been addressed in 1:2 as "saints" is probably a sufficient reason to read the word in its broader sense here, as referring inclusively to the whole people of God, not just Jewish believers or the nation of Israel, but the reminder to the readers of how they ("you") were "qualified" to receive a share in the saints' inheritance suggests that the word should be heard here with a conscious awareness of its prehistory as a term for the people of God when, in the not-too-distant past, that category was reserved for the nation of Israel. The words "share" (*meris*) and "inheritance" (*klēros*) have overlapping domains of meaning, and on occasion (e.g., Acts 8:21; LXX Deut 10:9) they can be used synonymously, but the background notion of Gentiles as *sharing* in the inheritance with the Jews (cf. the depiction of the Gentiles in Eph 2:6 as *synklēronoma* ["fellow heirs"] and *symmetocha tēs epangelias* ["sharers in the promise"]) is of sufficient importance in Paul's thought to warrant reading the genitive construction here as partitive (i.e., "a share in the inheritance") rather than epexegetical ("a share, i.e., an inheritance") (see especially the discussions in Harris 2010, 31; McKnight 2018, 120–21). The final phrase, "in the light," is best read in connection with the contrast in the following verse between "the dominion of darkness" and "the kingdom of the son of his love"; "the light," as implied by this contrast, is a reference to the kingdom of Christ as the metaphorical realm in which the inheritance of believers is situated.

1:13. This picture of God the Father as having qualified believers to receive an inheritance in the light is unpacked across the following two verses: "he has rescued us from the dominion of darkness and transferred us into the kingdom of the son of his love, in whom we have redemption, the forgiveness of sins." This elaboration achieves two main effects: (i) to reinforce what has been said in v. 11 by making explicit the fact that the God to whom Paul looks to strengthen the Colossians in the face of trials and conflicts is the one who has already delivered them from the powers of darkness; and (ii) to reinforce what has been said in v. 12 by pointing the readers to Christ as the one in whom the inheritance they have received is granted and secured.

Verse 13 points the readers back to the same event as the one described in v. 12, narrating it this time as involving not only the granting of an inheritance but also the overcoming of an enemy. The life that the readers lived before their conversion and incorporation into Christ is characterized as one that was lived in "the dominion of darkness"—language that draws on the traditional image of conversion as a movement into the light from out the darkness of ignorance and/or evil (cf. Jos. Asen 8.2; 15.13; Acts 26:18; 2 Cor 4:6; Eph 5:8; 1 Pet 2:9) and combines it with an implied reference to the powers by which that existence was dominated and controlled (cf. Rom 6:17-18; Eph 2:1-3; 6:12). (In and of itself, the expression "the dominion of darkness" could be merely an instance of personification, like the references in Romans 6 to personified sin as exercising dominion, paying wages, etc.; it is only in combination with the letter's subsequent references to the "thrones," "dominions," "rulers," and "authorities" [1:16; cf. 2:10, 15] defeated by and subjected to Christ that the expression hints at something more personally malevolent than that.)

Reverberating beneath the story Paul tells of God as having "rescued" (*errysato*) the readers from the powers that previously enslaved them is the paradigmatic Old Testament salvation story of the exodus (e.g., Exod 6:6-8; 14:30) and its echoes in psalms and prophetic oracles concerning Israel's rescue from Babylon and return from the darkness of exile (e.g., Ps 107:1-16; Isa 42:7, 16; 49:9) (cf. Moo 2008, 103–104).

The verb that follows, "transferred," is typically used in contexts that imply a literal or metaphorical removal (e.g., the removal of the people of Israel from before God's presence into exile in Assyria [2 Kgs 17:23], or the removal of Jehoahaz from Jerusalem to Riblah [2 Kgs 23:33]). Here, the movement that is described is a metaphorical one, the destination of which is "the kingdom of the Son of his love" (v. 13b). References to the kingdom of God are a good deal rarer in Paul's letter than they are in the Gospels (particularly the Synoptic Gospels). When they do occur, like the references to the kingdom in the Gospels, they refer sometimes to a future reality that believers "inherit" in the age to come (e.g., 1 Cor 6:9, 10; 15:50; Gal 5:21) and sometimes to a present experience of the reign of God that believers enter into in this lifetime, as a foretaste and anticipation of the coming age (e.g., Rom 14:17; 1 Cor 4:20); here, the reference is clearly to the latter rather than the former. The special metaphor of transfer reinforces the likelihood that Paul has in view here not only a *reign* but also the (metaphorical) *realm* of the church, in which the first fruits of its inauguration are experienced in the present age (see especially McKnight 2018, 127–29; Wilson 2005, 117–18).

Anticipating the high Christology of vv. 15-23, Paul refers to the kingdom here as "the kingdom of the son of his love" (cf. 1 Cor 15:24; Eph 5:5; 2 Tim 4:1). The genitive expression, "the son of his love," is best read as a qualitative genitive (i.e., "his beloved son"; cf. Harris 2010, 32–33) rather than as a genitive of origin (Lightfoot 1879, 140, citing Augustine). The expression carries an echo of 2 Sam 7:8-17, suggesting that its primary reference is to Jesus as Messiah rather than (explicitly) to Jesus as the eternal Son (though the latter idea quickly comes into view in vv. 15-23).

1:14. The prayer report concludes in v. 14 with a further expansion on the soteriological reminders of vv. 12-13. The focus this time is on Christ, the "son" of the previous verse, who is now further identified as the one "in whom we have redemption, the forgiveness of sins." Like the similar expression in Eph 1:7, and for similar reasons, the "in" that commences the verse reads most naturally in a locative rather than an instrumental sense (Campbell 2013, 9): life in Christ is depicted here as a kind of metaphorical sphere or domain in which the readers exist and experience the outcome of the liberating divine actions narrated in summary in the previous verse. The shift from the aorist verb forms of vv. 12-13 to the present tense "we have" (*echomen*) marks v. 14 as not merely the next event in the story but a kind of arrival point at the end of the paragraph, directing the readers' focus back to the situation in which they now stand (Moo 2008, 33).

In keeping with the depiction of the readers in v. 12 as having been "rescued" from the dominion of darkness, their present situation is described here as being one of "redemption" (cf. the use of that word with reference to the Exodus events in Deut 7:8; 9:26; 13:5; 15:15; 21:8; 24:18; also Exod 6:6; 15:13). As in Eph 1:7 (though here with the word "sins" rather than "trespasses"), the image of "redemption" is immediately unpacked as consisting in "the forgiveness of sins"—a juxtaposition implying the closest of connections between the readers' pre-conversion plight as victims of the oppressive power of darkness and their situation as sinners needing divine forgiveness. Although in this instance (unlike Eph 1:7) there is no explicit reference to the blood of Jesus as the means of redemption or the price of forgiveness, the later references to the saving work of Christ in the letter explicitly connect his death on the cross with the reconciliation that he has accomplished (1:20) and his defeat and disarming of the powers (2:13-14). (The latter verses are probably the best clue we have within the letter to how "redemption" from hostile powers can consist in "forgiveness" of sins committed against God; the relationship between those two dimensions of the soteriology of Colossians will be further explored in the comments on those verses, below.)
Although the effects and outworking of the former reality that Paul refers to ("redemption" from the tyranny of darkness) spill over beyond the latter ("forgiveness of sins"), it is nonetheless grounded securely in it. Its ultimate goal and destination, too, are inseparable from the relational fruits of forgiveness, in the form of a restored and reconciled relationship with God: believers

. . . for in him all the fullness was pleased to dwell (1:15-20)

> (15) He is the image of the invisible God, the firstborn of all creation, (16) for in him all things were created in heaven and on earth, the visible things and the invisible things, whether thrones or dominions or rulers or authorities; all things have been created through him and for him, (17) and he is before all things, and in him all things hold together; (18) and he is the head of the body, the church. He is the beginning, the firstborn from among the dead, in order that in all things he might be supreme, (19) for in him all the fullness was pleased to dwell, (20) and through him to reconcile to himself all things, making peace through the blood of his cross—through him—whether the things on earth or the things in heaven.

1:15. In v. 15 the flow of the passage takes a noticeable turn from the direction in which it has previously been traveling. Although, syntactically speaking, the relative pronoun with which it commences (*hos*, translated here as "He") signals a further elaboration on the prayer report, in parallel with the relative clause in the preceding verse, it quickly becomes apparent that the elaboration that follows differs markedly from v. 14 (and the preceding elaborations of vv. 10-13) in both content and scope. Whereas the elaborations of vv. 10-12a are thick with verb forms (mostly participles) whose subject is the readers of the letter, and those in vv. 12b-14 contain a string of pronouns referring to Paul and/or the readers, both of these features disappear entirely in vv. 15-20 (cf. the analysis in Moo 2008, 108). By the time Paul and the readers reappear in vv. 21-23, their story has been located against a vast Christological and cosmological horizon that is even grander in its proportions than the horizon implied by the transfer-of-kingdoms story in v. 13.

The genre, origin, and background of vv. 15-20 have been the topic of enormous and long-running scholarly debate. (For useful summaries of the main issues, see Gordley 2007, 1–26; McKnight 2018, 133–43; Pao 2012, 89–93.) On the question of genre, Matthew Gordley has made a strong case for the claim that the form and content of these verses fit within the range of what a first century Greco-Roman reader would have understood as a "hymn," according to the definition that he proposes based on a survey of examples in the surviving Jewish and Greco-Roman literature (especially those identified explicitly as *hymnoi* ["hymns"]):

(The text above being liberated from their prior enslavement to the dominion of darkness in order that they might be "transferred" into the community of Christ's people, to live out a new life under his rule and in fellowship with him.)

> A hymn is a self-contained composition of relatively short length (most are between 4 and 35 lines, though longer hymns are attested as well) whose contents are primarily centered on praise of the divine in a descriptive or declarative style, which may be expressed in direct address (e.g., You alone are . . .) or in the third person (e.g., She shows mercy . . .), whether in poetry or prose, and whose primary purpose may have been liturgical or instructional (i.e., cultic or didactic). (Gordley 2007, 32–33)

One crucial feature of this definition is its focus on content (descriptive or declarative praise of the divine) rather than form as the primary determinant of whether a text belongs within the boundaries of what first century readers would have classified as a hymn: it thus allows room for a wide variety of sub-genres distinguished from one another by form and function, including "prose hymns, metrical hymns, cultic hymns, didactical hymns, liturgical hymns, philosophical hymns, and so on" (Gordley 2007, 33), without stretching the boundaries of the category to breaking point or imposing arbitrary restrictions on it.

The praises of Christ in vv. 15-20 are, admittedly, expressed in language that is *about* him rather than addressed *to* him, and although the lines of the paragraph are artfully composed and exalted in register (cf. Witherington 2007, 130–33; Reyes 1999), it is debatable whether they exhibit the kind of metrical features that would suggest the paragraph's use as a song in the context of gathered worship, especially when measured against the kind of criteria that distinguished poetry and song from prose in the Greek tradition (Gordley 2007, 36–39, 181–98). It does not, therefore, appear to have been the kind of text that Pliny's informants had in mind when they spoke of the early second century Christians in Bithynia assembling on the first day of the week to sing "a hymn to Christ as to a god" (Pliny, *Letters* 10.96); nor, closer to home, would it necessarily have been one of the "psalms, hymns, and spiritual songs" that the Colossians sang to one another in their gatherings (3:16). But there are other subgenres within the spectrum of possibilities that can accommodate it comfortably, warranting Gordley's conclusion that it should be viewed as "a hybrid of Jewish and Greco-Roman expressions of praise that can be considered a philosophical prose-poem" (Gordley 2007, 39).

Closely related to the question of the paragraph's genre is that of its origin. This question is a more complicated one, to which it is difficult to provide a definitive answer. The presence of explicitly Christian concepts and terms (e.g., "the head of the body, the church"; "the firstborn from among the dead"; "making peace through the blood of his cross") is certainly enough to rule out the possibility that the original source of the paragraph was a non-Christian text, transplanted into the letter without alterations or additions. But choosing between the remaining options (e.g., that the paragraph was an original composition created in the process of dictating the letter; that it was a preexisting Christian text [e.g., a hymn in praise of Christ] borrowed by Paul for use in the letter; or that it was a rewritten version of a preexisting Jewish or Greek philosophical text with Christian alterations and additions) is an unavoidably speculative exercise. Nor does the decision have much bearing on the exegesis of the paragraph; if it was borrowed without alteration from a preexisting Christian poem or hymn, it was clearly chosen with care, and if adaptations to the original have been made, they have clearly been executed with sufficient skill for the end result to be both a coherent unit, in and of itself, and a carefully integrated contribution to the larger architecture of the letter.

What can be sketched with a good deal more confidence is the paragraph's conceptual background and (in particular) the extent to which it reflects the vocabulary and ideas of Jewish wisdom literature (e.g., Philo, Sirach, and Wisdom of Solomon), its roots in the Old Testament wisdom tradition and creation accounts, and (to a lesser extent) its conversation partners in the Greek philosophical literature (cf. Gordley 2007, 155–69).

A string of key concepts and terms in 1:15-20 (especially vv. 15-17) can be found in the literature of the Jewish wisdom tradition, in which the personified word or wisdom of YHWH is frequently described as the "image" (*eikōn*) of God (e.g., Philo, *Alleg. Interp.* 1.43; 3.96; *Spec. Laws* 1.81; *Flight* 101; *Dreams* 1.239; 2.45; cf. Wis 7:26), the "beginning" (*archē*) of all things (e.g., Philo, *Alleg. Interp.* 1.43; *Confusion* 146), the "firstborn" (*prōtotokos*, or its near-synonym, *prōtogonos*) of God's works (Philo, *Who is the Heir?* 117–19; *Confusion* 146; *Dreams* 1.215; *Agriculture* 51; cf. Prov 8:22, 25; Sir 1:4; 24:9), the one with whom or by whom all things were made (e.g., Prov 3:19; 8:22-31; Ps 104:24; Wis 7:22a; 9:1-2, 9; Philo, *Alleg. Interp.* 3.96), and the one in whom all things hold together (e.g., Sir 43:26; cf. Wis 1:7; 7:24, 27; 8:1) (cf. Lamb 1998; McKnight 2018, 133–45). In close connection with these texts about the personified word or wisdom of God are texts that speak about Adam as created in God's image (e.g., the discussion in Philo, *Alleg. Interp.* 3.96, where the words of LXX Gen 1:27, "God made humankind according to the image of God [*kat' eikona theou*]," are taken to mean that the Word, God's true and eternal Image, is the pattern or archetype after which humans were created; cf. *Spec. Laws* 3.83; *Confusion* 147). Also relevant, and an important part of the background of the hymn in Second Temple Jewish thinking, is the close connection or identification frequently made between wisdom and Torah (e.g., Bar 3:9–4:4; cf. the survey and analysis in Schnabel 1985, 69–92; 93–226).

To point out these parallels is not to argue that Paul was consciously drawing on particular Jewish wisdom texts as he composed the words of this paragraph (or—if the paragraph was a preexisting hymn borrowed by Paul—that the original author was doing the same). Nor is it to claim that the vision of God and the world projected by the hymn in 1:15-20 is simply a reproduction of the already existing theological and cosmological vision projected in the Jewish wisdom literature. It is one thing to predicate the things that are said in Col 1:15-17 of the personified Wisdom or Word of God; it is another thing altogether to predicate them of the crucified and risen Jesus (cf. Pao 2012, 92). But it does help to confirm the fact that, even though the word "wisdom" is nowhere used in 1:15-20, the hymn is saying of Christ all that could be said of wisdom (and a good deal more!), preparing the way for the assertions and warnings about true and false wisdom that the letter will go on to make in the subsequent chapters.

One final issue to be broached before we turn to the details of the paragraph is the question of its basic structure. As most commentators agree, the paragraph's architecture is essentially bipartite, with a series of words and phrases in its first half ("he is . . ." [*hos estin*]; "firstborn" [*prōtotokos*]; "in him" [*en autō*]; "all things" [*ta panta*]; "in heaven and on earth" [*en tois ouranois kai epi tēs gēs*]; "through him" [*di' autou*]; "for him" [*eis auton*]) mirrored precisely or approximately by a series of similar terms in its second half.

There is debate, however, over the exact point at which the first stanza concludes and the second commences. Some commentators (e.g., Harris 2010, 38; Abbott 1897, 217; Beale 2019, 98) locate the point of transition at the start of v. 18 ("and he is the head of the body, the church"), which is read as signaling a shift from the first stanza, focusing on Christ's relation to the cosmos, to the second, focusing on his relation to the church. There are strengths in this analysis, given the close connections in the theology of Ephesians and Colossians between the church and the work of God to reconcile and fill the cosmos (cf. Eph 1:20-23; 2:14-18; 4:7-13; Col 1:23b; 2:10; 3:11). It also has in its favor a kind of symmetry between the sentence that, according to this structure, ends the first stanza ("And he is before all things . . ." [v. 17]) and the sentence that commences the second ("And he is the head of the head of the body . . ." (v. 18a]).

The majority of commentators, however (e.g., Foster 2016, 193; Dunn 1996, 84; Lohse 1971, 41–46), see the point of transition as being the second "he is" (*hos estin*), which comes at v. 18b; a variation version of this approach is to read vv. 17-18a as a kind of hinge or transition from the first stanza to the second (e.g., Wilson 2005, 126–27; Moo 2008, 115–16). On this reading, the movement from the first stanza to the second is not from the cosmos (vv. 15-17) to the church (vv. 18-20) but from the Son's role in the creation and coherence of all things (vv. 15-18a) to his role in their reconciliation (vv. 18b-20). This second approach has in its favor the syntactical parallelism between the "he is" (*hos estin*) that commences v. 15 and the "he is" (*hos estin*) that commences v. 18b, and the fact that the cosmos is still as much in view in the second stanza as it is in the first (though as the object of Christ's reconciling work, not his creating and sustaining activity). For these reasons it is probably the second approach that is to be preferred, though with the rider that the sentence in v. 18a clearly plays a pivotal role as a new and climactic thought at the end of the first stanza and as the launch pad from which the second takes flight (especially if the immediate antecedent of the "he is" [*hos estin*] in v. 18b is taken as being the "he" [*autos*] of v. 18a, rather than "the Son" in v. 13).

The paragraph commences in v. 15 with a pair of parallel assertions about Christ: "He is the image of the invisible God, the firstborn of all creation." An obvious Old Testament background to the first assertion is the pronouncement in Gen 1:27 that humans were created "according to the image of God" (LXX: *kat' eikona theou*), but the history of that verse's interpretation in the literature of Second Temple Judaism and the way the statement is unpacked in vv. 15b-16 (and further developed in 3:10) both make it clear that much more is being claimed for the Son than merely that he fulfills the same image-bearing function as all human beings. In Philo's interpretation, for example (as we have already seen), the fact that humans were created "*according to* the image of God" is read as implying a prior template (the eternal Word of God) that informed the creation of the first humans (cf. *Spec. Laws* 3.83; *Confusion* 147). Something similar appears to be in Paul's mind here, though in this case it is being said not of the (personified) Word but of the (personal) Son.

The fact that Paul goes on almost immediately, in v. 16, to unpack the assertions of v. 15 by speaking about the active involvement of the Son in the creation of all things suggests that he has in mind, at least in part, a story that includes the Son's preexistence (and one that vastly transcends human identity and vocation). The story of the Son goes on, however, to include the events of his incarnation, death, and resurrection (cf. vv. 20, 22); in the wake of these events Paul's description of him as the "image" of God carries connotations of physicality and visibility that go beyond what Second Temple Jews would have understood by the use of similar language to speak of God's Wisdom or Word of God, even for readers such as the Colossians whose sole knowledge of the Son was mediated through the testimony of the gospel (1:23; 3:1-4; cf. 2 Cor 4:6).

In parallel with the description in v. 15a of the Son as "the image of the invisible God" is the description of him in v. 15b as "the firstborn of all creation." Although the term is frequently used in a literal sense to refer to the oldest child born to a mother (e.g., Luke 2:7; Heb 11:28), it can also carry a figurative sense of preeminence—for example, when used in the Old Testament to refer to the nation of Israel (Exod 4:22) or the Davidic king (Ps 89:27). The way the claim is unpacked in the verses that follow makes it clear that this second, figurative sense is in view here, along with the rights of inheritance that go with the position of the firstborn. The preeminence of the Son is manifested in part in his temporal priority as the one who was "before all things" (v. 17), but it is not reducible to that; it is a comprehensive preeminence, unpacked in a multiplicity of ways across vv. 16-20. Nor is his temporal priority to be understood as if he were simply the first created being, chronologically prior to the others that followed; Paul goes out of his way in vv. 16-17 to stress that "all things" (not merely "all other things" or "all earthly things") were created through him and for him (cf. Dunn 1996, 90–91).

1:16. The lines that make up the middle portion of the hymn's first stanza, in vv. 16-17, go on to offer an elaboration and substantiation of the assertions in v. 15 (particularly the assertion in v. 15b that the Son is "the firstborn of all creation"). Verse 16a ("for in him all things were created") functions as a kind of headline statement that is unpacked across the remainder of vv. 16-17.

The precise meaning of the phrase "in him" is much debated, with most scholars opting for either an instrumental sense (roughly equating to "by" or "by means of") or a spatial metaphor (broadly similar to the spatial-metaphorical sense carried by Paul's "in Christ" language in vv. 2, 14). The former option has in its favor the closely similar idea that Paul goes on to state in v. 16b ("all things have been created through him") and the instrumental sense that similar phrases appear to carry at times within the Jewish wisdom tradition (e.g., Prov 3:19; Wis 9:1-2). But even in the wisdom literature, the role that wisdom (and especially personified Wisdom) is depicted as playing in the creation of the world goes beyond one that can adequately be characterized as instrumental (cf. Prov 8:22-31; Wis 9:9), without neatly and cleanly crossing the boundary from instrument to agent (since YHWH himself is still, ultimately, assumed or depicted as the creator in these texts). And if the phrase "in him" carries an instrumental sense in v. 16a, it is difficult to see what is added by the additional phrase, "through him," in v. 16b (Moo 2008, 120–21). It seems best, therefore, to understand the phrase in a spatial-metaphorical sense, with the precise meaning of the metaphor initially left broad and undefined (implying something like "in connection with" or "in dependent relation to"; cf. Acts 17:28), before its dimensions and entailments are progressively unpacked in vv. 16b-17 (cf. Pao 2012, 95–96, who suggests that the phrases "through him" and "for him," in particular, should be read as "explicating the meaning of 'in him.'")

The assertion in v. 16a that "in him all things were created" is unpacked across the remainder of vv. 16-17, beginning with a series of three phrases, each of which makes explicit the universal scope of "all things." The first two phrases ("in heaven and on earth, the visible things and the invisible things") consist of paired sets of polar opposites, joined together to signify in each case the totality of created things (Pao 2012, 96). The first pair, "in heaven and on earth," is reminiscent of the language of Genesis 1, where the phrase "the heavens and the earth" refers to the two distinct realms that add up to the created order. Here, a similar meaning is implied, in line with the subsequent references to "heaven" within the letter (1:20, 23; 4:1). Although the similar phrase "in the heavenly [places]" (*en tois epouraniois*) can be used in Ephesians to refer to the invisible, spiritual realms that impinge upon the experience of believers in their present, earthly lives, the phrase that is used here, "in heaven" (*en tois ouranois*), does not appear to carry that meaning; the repeated contrast between "in heaven" and "on earth" (1:16, 20), together with the reference in 1:23 to "all creation under heaven," combine to suggest that the "heaven" in view is to be thought of as a spatially distinct domain within the created cosmos.

Nor does the juxtaposition of the first phrase ("in heaven and on earth") with the second ("the visible things and the invisible things") necessarily imply a neat correlation between "in heaven" and "invisible," or between "on earth" and "visible." The fact that the risen and ascended Christ is presently (by implication) "hidden" from human view (3:1-3) does not seem to place him, in Paul's view, within the category of things that are "invisible" by their own, intrinsic nature; he will, after all, one day "appear" (still glorified) and be seen by all (3:4). And, on the other side of the ledger, the reminders that Paul gives to his readers in passages such as Eph 2:1-3; 6:12 imply the existence of realities that are "invisible" but nonetheless present and powerfully active "on earth."

The final phrase ("whether thrones or dominions or rulers or authorities") is probably best read in light of the previous two and of the sense of comprehensiveness that the whole of v. 16 is intended to convey. Thus, rather than force an artificial choice between a one-dimensionally visible/political interpretation of what Paul has in mind by "thrones," "dominions," "powers," and "authorities" and a one-dimensionally invisible/supernatural interpretation, it is best to allow the phrase to do its intended work, leaving open a wide field of possibilities that embraces both the visible, earthly powers that dominate human existence within the social world of the readers and the invisible, spiritual powers and forces (both personal and impersonal) that operate in part, at least, through them (cf. the similar list in Eph 1:21, and the discussions in Wright 1986, 71–72; McKnight 2018, 151–52; Thompson 2005, 34–39).

The assertion that concludes v. 16 ("all things have been created through him and for him") functions partly as a recapitulation of the assertion at the start of the verse ("in him all things were created"). In two important ways, however, it further develops or expands on the previous statement. The first way it does so is, as argued above, by beginning the work of unpacking the spatial metaphor "in him" by introducing two new prepositional phrases, "through him (*di' autou*) and for him (*eis auton*)." These two phrases speak of the Son as both the agent through whom God's creative work was accomplished and the purpose toward which the universe's existence is directed (cf. the similar things that are said of God himself in 1 Cor 8:6; Rom 11:36). The second way the sentence at the end of v. 16 develops or expands on the sentence at the start is the shift it makes from the aorist tense ("were created") to the perfect tense ("have been created"); the effect is to redirect our attention from what happened in the beginning to the state of affairs that is the case in the present as a consequence (cf. Campbell 2013, 12).

1:17. Verse 17 adds two more assertions regarding the relationship between Christ and all things: "and he is before all things, and in him all things hold together." Although the preposition *pro* ("before") can refer in some contexts to preeminence rather than preexistence (e.g., 1 Pet 4:8; Jas 5:12), its use by Paul consistently carries a temporal meaning (Moo 2008, 125), and the present context, with its assertions regarding the Son's involvement in the creative work of God in the beginning, suggests that the preexistence of the Son is at least part of the meaning that Paul has in mind here (Wilson 2005, 143).

The second line in v. 17 ("in him all things hold together") completes the process of unpacking the entailments of the claim at the start of v. 16 that "in him all things were created." Not only is the Son the one "through" whom the creation was made and "for" whom it exists; he is also, in consequence, the one "in" whom it has been put together and possesses its order and coherence. Similar things are said in the Second Temple Jewish literature regarding the divine word and wisdom, sometimes with a focus on cosmological and doxological themes (e.g., Sir 43:26) and sometimes with a focus on the role played by wisdom in attaining mastery over undisciplined and unholy urges (e.g., Wis 1:7; 7:24, 27; 8:1). Both domains of thought are relevant to the context Paul is addressing in Colossians, in which the "philosophy" being held out before the readers as an alternative to Christ involves both devotional practices and ascetic disciplines (cf. 2:16-23), and Paul's depiction of Christ here in chapter 1 as the one in whom "all things hold together" prepares the way for the exhortations and warnings that will follow in chapter 2.

1:18. The first stanza of the hymn concludes in v. 18a with a climatic statement that moves from the Son's role in relation to creation to his role as "the head of the body, the church" (cf. the depiction in 2:10 of Christ as "head of every ruler and authority," and the similar move from cosmos to church in Eph 1:22-23). If we are to work on the assumption that the way Paul uses the metaphor of headship here in Colossians is consistent with its use in Ephesians, particularly on those occasions when it is used to describe the relationship between Christ and the church, then its meaning includes elements that transcend the dichotomy that is sometimes assumed between headship as "source" and headship as "authority" (cf. the comments above on Eph 1:22-23 and Eph 5:23). A similar set of interrelated meanings is implied by the juxtaposition within the hymn itself between Christ's relation to the church and his relation to the cosmos, as both the "firstborn" over the creation and the source of its existence and coherence. Christ's headship, according to the metaphor as Paul employs it here, is multidimensional: he is "the locus of the church's unity and coherence, the source of the church's sustenance and direction" (Fowl 1990, 112–13; quoted in Moo 2008, 128). As is the case with the preceding lines of the hymn, what is said here, in the form of doxology, prepares the way for what is said later in the letter as warning and exhortation: since Christ is the head of the body, the Colossians are to be wary of those who claim to teach a pattern of wisdom and piety without "holding fast to the Head, from whom the whole body, nourished and held together through its joints and ligaments, grows with a growth that is from God" (2:19).

The remainder of v. 18 constitutes the beginning of the hymn's second stanza: "He is the beginning, the firstborn from among the dead, in order that in all things he might be supreme." Building on what has been said in the first stanza regarding the Son's role in the creation and coherence of all things, the second stanza goes on to speak of his role in their reconciliation. Not only is Christ "the firstborn of all creation"; he is also "the beginning, the firstborn from among the dead." The terms "beginning" (*archē*) and "firstborn" (*prōtotokos*) both frequently carry a meaning that includes temporal priority, and there is an obvious sense in which that is the case here (cf. 1 Cor 15:20). But, in keeping with what Paul goes on to say in the final line of the verse, both words also carry an implication of supremacy in rank and dignity: Christ is the first one raised from the dead "in order that in all things he might be supreme."

While Christ's supremacy over all things is depicted in vv. 15-17 as a primordial fact, deriving from his preexistence, his identity as "the image of the invisible God," and his role in the creation of the cosmos, it is depicted in v. 18b as a future goal toward which God's reconciling work is directed. It is no doubt true that Christ's resurrection from the dead was a *consequence* of his primordial supremacy, but that is not quite the point Paul is making here; his point, rather, is that Christ was raised *in order that* his rightful supremacy might be manifested and accomplished through his victory over death and every hostile power (cf. the similar idea in 1 Cor 15:20-28).

1:19. The (twofold) reason that Christ was raised from the dead to be the one supreme over all things is stated in vv. 19-20: "for in him all the fullness was pleased to dwell, and through him to reconcile to himself all things, making peace through the blood of his cross—through him—whether the things on earth or the things in heaven."

The first part of the reason is supplied in v. 19: "for in him all the fullness was pleased to dwell." The grammar of the verse in the original Greek can support two possible translations: the one shown above, in which "all the fullness" (*pan to plērōma*) is read in the nominative case, as the subject of "was pleased" (cf. NRSV, ESV), or an alternative translation in which "all the fullness" is read in the accusative case, as the subject of the infinitive "to dwell," and "God" is taken as the implied subject of "was pleased" (cf. NIV: "for God was pleased to have all his fullness dwell in him"). The former translation is probably to be preferred as the slightly more natural reading of the Greek, especially if "all the fullness" is read as a metonymy for "God in all his fullness" (Moo 2008, 131). The fact that Paul speaks of God's fullness as dwelling in Christ in consequence of a divine decision or decree ("was pleased") is probably not (or, at least, not directly) to be taken as a statement about the eternal relationship between the Father and the Son. When Paul returns to this thought in 2:9, he makes it explicit that what he has in mind is the *bodily* form in which Christ bears the fullness of God, suggesting that (to borrow the categories of the systematic theologians) v. 19 should be read as a statement about the incarnation, not as a statement about the eternal generation of the Son.

The language of "fullness" implies a sense of comprehensiveness (an implication that is further reinforced by the word "all" that is appended to it); it would therefore be a mistake to try to identify too precisely which particular attribute or attributes of God Paul has in mind as being present in

Christ. The Old Testament echoes carried by the language Paul uses suggest that at least part of what Paul had in mind would have been the image of the visible glory of God, dwelling in Christ as in a sanctuary (cf. Beale 2019, 108–10 on the multiple echoes of LXX Ps 67:17-18 in Col 1:19, along with the various places in which the temple or tabernacle is spoken of as being "filled" with the divine glory). To the extent that this idea is present in or implied by the text, the resurrection of Christ from the dead can be understood as the restoration of the temple that is to be the focus of universal worship in a reconciled cosmos.

An additional (and somewhat simpler) connection between the statement in v. 18 and the twofold warrant that is provided for it in vv. 19-20 may lie in the repeated word "all" ("everything," v. 18; "all the fullness," v. 19; "all things," v. 20). The particular, historical event of Christ's resurrection from the dead, as proclaimed in Paul's gospel, contains within it a wisdom that is of universal significance, because the Christ who was raised from the dead is (i) the one in whom all the fullness of God's glory dwells (v. 19) and (ii) the one through whom God has purposed to reconcile all things to himself (v. 20).

1:20. The purpose of God to restore all things to himself through Christ is the theme of v. 20. Although, strictly speaking, the word *auton* would normally be translated as "him" rather than "himself," the fact that the reconciliation Paul is speaking of is accomplished "through" Christ suggests that, in line with the language of reconciliation is used elsewhere in Paul's letters, the sentence should be understood as a story about God reconciling all things "to himself" (i.e., to God) not "to him" (i.e., to Christ) (Beale 2019, 111).

The scope of the reconciliation purposed by God is expressly all-embracing: "all things . . . whether the things on earth or the things in heaven." What Paul has in mind is not merely the redemption and forgiveness of individual men and women (though that in itself is no small thing!) but the reordering of the entire cosmos. The picture that he paints does not, however, imply that each and every personal being within the cosmos is to become a forgiven and reconciled friend of God; the next paragraph contains a warning that the reconciliation of the readers is contingent on their continuing faith in the message of the gospel. What Paul does encourage his readers to look forward to is a vision of universal *shalom*, in which all hostile powers (whether on earth or in heaven) have been defeated (cf. 2:15) and the universal harmony of God's creation has been restored (cf. Beale 2019, 111–12).

The fact that it is *through Christ* that this universal reconciliation is to be accomplished is given additional emphasis in the twofold *di' autou* ("through him") that he includes within the verse. The phrase is both brought forward to the start of the sentence for emphasis and then reiterated at the sentence's halfway mark (if, as seems likely, the original wording of the verse is the strongly attested and syntactically more difficult reading that is found in $\mathfrak{P}^{46}$, ℵ, A, C, and D¹). The epicenter of God's reconciling work is specified even more particularly than that: the reconciling work of God in Christ, Paul reminds his readers, took place by "making peace through the blood of his cross." The reference to "his cross" anchors the story of universal reconciliation in the historical event of the crucifixion; the focus on the "blood" that was shed in that event offers a hint in the direction of the Old Testament sacrificial system as the framework within which its meaning is to be understood (cf. Lev 16:15-16; Rom 3:25).

The total effect of the hymn, with its exalted prose, its relentlessly repeated "he," "in him," "he himself," "through him," and its expansive embrace of "all creation," "all things," and "all the fullness" is to draw the strongest of connections between the unique, particular, historical message of the gospel that the Colossians have believed and the universal themes and concerns that were the subject matter of first century theology and philosophy. In so doing, it paves the way for the exhortations of the following chapters, in which Paul urges the readers to order the totality of their lives and their worship in accordance with a wisdom that is rooted and grounded in Christ (see especially Wright 1990; Gordley 2007, 231–69).

And you . . . he has now reconciled (1:21-23)

(21) And you, who were once alienated and enemies in your mind, in evil deeds, (22) he has now reconciled in the body of his flesh, through death, to present you holy and unblemished and blameless before him, (23) if indeed you continue in faith, firmly grounded and steadfast, not shifting from the hope of the gospel which you heard, which has been proclaimed in all creation under heaven, of which I, Paul, became a servant.

1:21. Within the architecture of the letter as a whole, the hymn in 1:15-20 functions as a theological foundation for the exhortations in the following chapters. Within the closer context of chapter 1, however, as a digression within the prayer report in 1:9-23, its more immediate function is to act as a kind of bridge between the account in 1:12-14 of the readers' salvation (as the theme of the thanksgiving that Paul prays they will be offering up to the Father) and the return to that story in 1:21-23 (retold this time in new categories and with additional emphases that derive in part, at least, from the intervening hymn).

The return to the readers' story is signaled immediately in v. 21 by the words "And you . . ." (*kai hymas*) with which the sentence commences. The principal verb, "reconciled" (*apokatēllaxen*), of which *hymas* is the object, does not appear until v. 22, where it creates an obvious link between the story of the readers and the larger story of cosmic reconciliation that Paul has just told in v. 20. But before that, in v. 21, Paul pauses to draw a picture of the readers' prior existence—the "once" (*pote*) that he goes on to contrast with the "now" that he describes in v. 22.

The prior existence that he wishes his readers to recall in v. 21 is one in which they were "alienated and enemies in [their] mind, in evil deeds." The alienation and enmity that Paul depicts as characteristic of the readers' pre-conversion lives no doubt had concrete and visible manifestations in their alienation as Gentiles from the people of Israel (cf. Eph 2:12) and, more generally, in the mutual hostilities and dysfunctions of their social relationships (cf. Titus 3:3). The primary focus here, however, given the frame story of cosmic reconciliation to God that Paul has already established in v. 20, is on their alienation from God (cf. Eph 4:18) and their enmity toward him.

The enmity toward God that characterized and shaped their prior existence was manifested in both their inward attitudes ("in your mind" [*tē dianoiā*]) and their outward conduct ("in evil deeds" [*en tois ergois tois ponērois*]). The precise nature of the relationship between these two elements in the syntax of the sentence (and in Paul's understanding of the pathology of human alienation from God) is open to debate. The preposition *en* that connects them (translated here as "in") can carry a variety of meanings in Greek. It is possible that Paul could simply be saying here that the hostility of their mind was manifested or expressed in the evil of their behavior (Moo 2008, 140; Campbell 2013, 18). Alternatively (in line with the way Paul depicts the relationship between evil conduct and darkened understanding in Rom 1:18), the *en* could be taken causally and the phrase translated "because of evil deeds" (cf. NIV), depicting a state of affairs in which Gentiles are "hostile to the God of Israel due to their idolatry and immorality" as the outworking of a dynamic in which "doing evil deeds engenders hostility of mind against the one who resists and opposes such deeds" (Witherington 2007, 138; cf. Harris 2010, 52). The text itself gives us merely the juxtaposition between a hostile mind and evil deeds, without specifying the precise causal relationship between them, leaving room for an understanding that the interrelationship between the two is a complex one in which "thought and act are both tainted, each pushing the other into further corruption" (Wright 1986, 81).

1:22. Having sketched in v. 21 the pre-conversion lives of the readers, Paul turns in v. 22 to narrate their salvation: "And you . . . he has now reconciled in the body of his flesh, through death, to present you holy and unblemished and blameless before him." The verb "reconciled," as we have already observed, locates the story of the readers' reconciliation, accomplished by Christ, within the larger cosmic story of God's work, through Christ, to reconcile all things to himself (v. 20). Although some commentators (e.g., Beale 2019, 114–15; Moo 2008, 141) take the unstated subject of the verb, "reconciled," to be God in order to preserve consistency with v. 20, a decision of this sort is hardly necessary since the active participation of Christ in God's work of reconciliation is already implied by the twice-repeated "through him" of that same verse. The fact that Paul can go on to speak in v. 22 of "his flesh," without needing to specify that it is "Christ's flesh" that he has in mind, makes it more likely that the subject of the verb in v. 22 is Christ rather than God (Pao 2012, 107). The description of Christ's reconciling work as having been accomplished "in the body of his flesh, through death" (v. 22) recalls the earlier reference of v. 20 to "the blood of his cross." The phrase "of his flesh" accentuates the fragility and mortality of Christ's body and contributes to Paul's continuing emphasis on the unique, historical-material, personal form in which the saving wisdom of God has been made known (cf. 1:19-20; 2:9). It also anticipates the reference Paul goes on to make in v. 24 to the sufferings he undergoes in his own flesh as a completion and extension of the fleshly sufferings of Christ.

The goal of Christ's reconciling work is stated in v. 22b: "to present you holy and unblemished and blameless before him." Paul's language here is similar to the language of Eph 5:27, and here, as is the case in that passage, the picture he paints is an eschatological one: Paul is not speaking here of an imputed, positional holiness that is accomplished immediately at the point of Christ's death or the readers' conversion but of a holiness of character and conduct, revealed in the presence of Christ when they stand "before him" at the final judgement (Moo 2008, 143). Although the words "holy" and "unblemished" both have cultic connotations, and the thought of Gentile believers as "an offering . . . sanctified by the Holy Spirit" is an authentically Pauline idea (cf. Rom 15:16), a one-dimensionally cultic meaning is unlikely in this instance. Both words can also be used by Paul in an ethical sense (e.g., Eph 1:4), and cultic and ethical categories are closely interconnected in Paul's thought. The third term, "blameless" (*anenklētous*), tips the scales decisively in favor of reading the combined meaning of three terms as including an ethical/behavioral dimension (Pao 2012, 108). The focus of v. 22b on the last day is consistent with the "eschatological climax" that is typically present in the closing verses of Paul's prayer reports, as an outworking of the way in he views the Christian life and his own ministry as directed toward the day of Christ (cf. Wiles 1974, 158, though Wiles himself overlooks v. 22 and focuses on the "eschatological emphasis" in v. 28, connecting it with the implied prayer report in 1:29–2:4).

1:23. The future timeframe implied in v. 22b is confirmed in that following verse, where Paul makes it clear that the fulfillment of Christ's purpose for the readers is contingent on their perseverance as believers: "if indeed you continue in faith, firmly grounded and steadfast, not shifting from the hope of the gospel which you heard, which has been proclaimed in all creation under heaven, of which I, Paul, became a servant." The "faith" that the Colossians are to continue in is probably best understood as a reference to their own faith (cf. the similar expressions in Rom 11:20, 23) rather than to "the faith" as an objective body of truth; a reference to the latter is supplied in the second half of the verse, where Paul describes it as "the hope of the gospel which you heard" (cf. Pao 2012, 109). Built into the concept of faith, as Paul uses it here and elsewhere, are elements of both trusting reliance and continuing fidelity; the fact that it is here described as being oriented toward "the hope of the gospel" (cf. 1:5) suggests that it is reliance rather than reliability that is at the forefront of Paul's thought in this instance, but the reliance he has in view is still a steady, unwavering, loyal reliance that is an expression of the believers' devotion and allegiance to the one in whom they have put their trust.

The triple description of such persevering faith as "firmly grounded," "steadfast," and "not shifting" borrows from the language of architecture to depict the believers as a metaphorical building, resting on the hope of the gospel as its foundation (cf. the similar image in 2:7); if, as is likely, Paul is writing to the Colossians in the aftermath of the earthquake of A.D. 60, and he is aware of that event, it is possible that his language here is an intentional allusion to the earthquake and its effects (cf. Kreitzer 2004).

The fact that the Colossians' final salvation is contingent on their continuing faith does not imply that their faith and perseverance must be generated from within their own autonomous resources; in other contexts (e.g., 1 Cor 1:8; Rom 8:29-30), he is happy to speak about the work of God in supplying the grace that is needed to make such perseverance possible (and indeed, for those whom God has foreknown and predestined, to make it certain). But his confidence in the enabling presence of the Spirit does not detract from the urgency of his warnings about the danger of apostasy (cf. 1 Cor 10:1-13; Col 2:8, 18) or diminish the responsibility of believers to labor and endure in the strength that the Spirit supplies (cf. 1 Cor 15:10; Phil 2:12-13).

The reference to "the gospel which you heard" as the source of the hope on which the Colossians are to continue relying becomes the occasion for two brief elaborations in the second half of the verse, where Paul describes the gospel as having been "proclaimed in all creation under heaven" and reminds the readers that it is of this gospel that he, Paul, has become a servant. The first of these two elaborations provides another connection between the Colossians' experience of hearing and believing the gospel and the story of cosmic reconciliation in the final verse of the hymn in 1:15-20. Paul's language here need not be read as a hyperbolic claim about the extent of the territory covered by his missionary journeys (and those of his fellow missionaries); it is, rather, an expression of the fact that in the mission to the Gentiles that has been commissioned by the risen Jesus and commenced by his apostles, the publication of the gospel to the entire world has, at least in principle, already taken place (cf. Eph 4:10-11; 1 Tim 3:16) (Pao 2012, 111).

The second elaboration ("of which I, Paul, became a servant") closely resembles the language of his self-description in Eph 3:7. As is the case in that passage, it expresses a thought that is closely connected in Paul's mind to the role he has been given in making known the mystery of the gospel to the Gentiles and the sufferings he experiences in consequence of that commissioning—themes to which he turns in the following paragraph.

Now I am rejoicing in my sufferings for your sake (1:24–2:5)

> (1:24) Now I am rejoicing in my sufferings for your sake, and filling up in my flesh the things that are lacking in the afflictions of Christ for the sake of his body, which is the church, (25) of which I became a servant, according to the commission from God, given to me for you, to fully proclaim the word of God, (26) the mystery that was hidden from the ages and from the generations, but has now been disclosed to his saints, (27) to whom God willed to make known what are the riches of the glory of this mystery among the Gentiles, which is Christ in you, the hope of glory; (28) whom we proclaim, admonishing everyone and teaching everyone in all wisdom, in order that we may present everyone mature in Christ, (29) to which end I toil, struggling according to his energy, which is working in power within me.
>
> (2:1) For I want you to know how great a struggle I have for you, and for those in Laodicea, and for all those who have not seen my face in the flesh, (2) that their hearts may be encouraged, having been brought together in love, and in the quest for all the riches of full assurance of understanding, for the sake of the knowledge of God's mystery, which is Christ, (3) in whom

are hidden all the treasures of wisdom and knowledge. (4) I say this in order that no one may deceive you with plausible arguments. (5) For though I am absent in flesh, yet I am with you in spirit, rejoicing to see your good order and the firmness of your faith in Christ.

1:24. Paul's reference at the end of v. 23 to his own calling as a servant of the gospel marks the end of the series of soteriological and Christological elaborations in vv. 12b-23 that have expanded on the report in vv. 9-12a of Paul's prayers and their purpose. In bringing Paul and his ministry back into focus it also functions as a transition into the last part of the letter's introductory section, where Paul speaks (by implication) about the circumstances of imprisonment in which he is writing (cf. 4:3), encouraging the Colossians to understand them not as a tragic interruption to his activity as an apostle but as a fitting extension of the sufferings of Christ and as a context in which Paul continues to labor in fulfillment of his calling.

Accordingly, this section begins and ends with references to Paul's rejoicing: Paul rejoices in his sufferings (1:24) and he rejoices in the good order and firmness of the Colossians' faith (2:5), which have continued (and, Paul prays, will continue) undiminished, in spite of his absence and imprisonment. The rhetorical strategy of this section of the letter is similar to the strategy Paul follows in the equivalent section of Philippians (Phil 1:12-26), implicitly encouraging the readers to channel their concern for Paul away from any discouragement or dismay that they may have been feeling in consequence of his imprisonment, and toward the pursuit of the kind of "good order and firmness" (or, in the case of the Philippians, "progress and joy in the faith"; Phil 1:25) that will give him continuing reason to be joyful. In both cases, the account that Paul gives of his sufferings, ministry, and joy in the closing section of the letter's introduction prepares the way for the exhortations in the immediately following section of the letter.

The sufferings in which Paul is rejoicing are, he says, sufferings that he endures "for your sake" (*hyper hymōn*). What he has in mind by this claim is unfolded in the (somewhat cryptic) elaboration he gives in the remainder of the verse: "and filling up in my flesh the things that are lacking in the afflictions of Christ for the sake of his body, which is the church."

Foundational for Paul's understanding of his role as an apostle, and the place that suffering occupies within that vocation, is the "servant" (*diakonos*) language he uses in vv. 23 and 25, framing the description in v. 24 of the relationship he sees between his own sufferings and those of Christ. Standing behind that language is the figure of the Isaianic Servant, whose mission was fulfilled by Christ as "a servant (*diakonos*) to the circumcised" (Rom

15:8) and continued by Paul as "a minister (*leitourgos*) of Christ Jesus to the Gentiles" (Rom 15:16). Christ's work through Paul, his minister, is thus an extension and completion of the mission of the Servant (Rom 15:21, cf. Isa 52:15; also Gal 2:5, cf. Isa 49:1)—a mission that includes arduous labors (Isa 49:4), sufferings (Isa 53:4-11), and intercessions (Isa 53:12 [MT]) and participates in the work of God to restore Israel and extend salvation to the ends of the earth (Isa 49:5-6, cf. Acts 13:47).

This dimension of Paul's self-understanding helps to explain what he has in mind when he speaks in v. 24 of his sufferings as "fill[ing] up" what is "lacking" in the afflictions of Christ. Paul's claim is not that the meaning and efficacy of his sufferings are identical with the meaning and efficacy of Christ's—he has, after all, in the immediately preceding section of the letter, spoken of the unique role that the crucifixion of Christ plays in the work of God to reconcile the world (including, by implication, both Gentiles and Jews) to himself (cf. 1:20, 22). But the mission of Jesus to Israel and his death on the cross do not, in themselves, accomplish the immediate repentance and restoration of the nations; there is still a part (and a costly, suffering part) to be played by Paul, as Christ's servant, in proclaiming the gospel of Christ among the nations so that "those who were not told about him will see, and those who have not heard will understand" (Rom 15:26 [NIV], quoting from LXX Isa 52:15). Paul's missionary sufferings thus add to was accomplished by the sufferings of Christ in a distinct and complementary manner, so as to bring their purpose to completion—a meaning that is consistent with the usual sense of the rare, doubly prefixed verb *antaplērō* ("I am . . . filling up") that Paul employs here (cf. White 2016).

1:25. As a servant of the gospel (v. 23), Paul is also a servant of the church (v. 25; cf. 2 Cor 4:5), charged with a specific "commission" (*oikonomia*), given to him by God. The word Paul uses here is one that is typically employed in contexts of delegated responsibility (e.g., the stewardship entrusted to the dishonest manager in the parable Jesus tells in Luke 16:1-9). The picture Paul paints here is similar to the one he gives to the Corinthians in 1 Cor 4:1, where he describes himself and Apollos as "servants of Christ and stewards (*oikonomoi*) of God's mysteries" (NRSV), and in Eph 3:2, where the word *oikonomia* refers to the responsibility that has been given to Paul through the grace and call of Christ.

Paul's account of his ministry in Ephesians 3 goes on to define that responsibility in terms of his commissioning "to proclaim to the Gentiles the good news of the immeasurable riches of Christ, and to enlighten all with regard to what is the plan of the mystery that was hidden from ages past in God" (Eph 3:8-9). Here in Colossians, the content of his commissioning is described in similar terms: "to fully proclaim the word of God, the mystery that was hidden from the ages and from the generations, but has now been disclosed to his saints." The phrase "to fully proclaim" translates the single Greek word, *plērōsai* ("fill up," or "fulfill"), which recalls the language of the previous verse, in which Paul describes his sufferings as "filling up" the sufferings of Christ (Bormann 2012, 114). If the two images of "filling up" are to be read in conjunction with one another, then Paul's commission to "fully proclaim" the gospel should probably be read in a sense that is analogous to the way his sufferings complement and complete the sufferings of Christ: that is to say, Paul is to "fulfill" the proclamation of the word of God (i.e., the message of the gospel) by extending its reach to the Gentiles (cf. the similar language and ideas in Rom 15:19) so that it can truly be said to have been "proclaimed in all creation" (v. 23).

1:26. The message that Paul has been given to proclaim (referred to in v. 25 as "the word of God") is further described in the following verse as "the mystery that was hidden from the ages and from the generations, but has now been disclosed to his saints." The word "mystery" (*mystērion*) is used here (as is the case in Eph 3:3-5, 9 and Rom 16:25) to refer to a truth that was once concealed from human knowledge, and would have remained so but for the revelatory intervention of God (cf. the similar use of the term in LXX Dan 2:28-30). The word *aiōnes* (here translated as "ages") can sometimes be used to refer to supernatural beings (cf. the examples listed in BDAG, s.v. "*aiōn*," 4), and the construction "hidden from" (*apokekrymmenon apo*) is most commonly used with a personal object following the preposition (Moo 2008, 156); here, however, the parallel with "generations" and the contrast that follows with what has "now" taken place suggest that the "ages" from which the mystery was kept hidden should probably be understood in a chronological rather than a personal sense (cf. "for long ages" [*chronois aiōnois*] in Rom 16:25; for *apo* used in this sense, see BDAG, s.v. "*apo*," 2.b.). The people to whom the mystery has now been disclosed are described in v. 26b as "the saints"—a term that (in line with its use in 1:2, 4, 12) probably includes Gentile as well as Jewish believers, though (given the content of the mystery that was revealed to them, regarding the eschatological novelty of Gentile incorporation) the way the term is used here carries the memory of a time when "the saints" referred to an exclusively Jewish people of God (McKnight 2018, 197).

1:27. These people, Paul goes on to say in v. 27, are those to whom God has willed to make known "what are the riches of the glory of this mystery among the Gentiles, which is Christ in you, the hope of glory." The initial string of genitives ("the riches of the glory of this mystery") is probably best read epexegetically ("the riches that consist of the glory that consists of this mystery"). (For "riches" that consist of "glory," and are to be "known" or "made known," see Eph 1:18; Rom 9:23.)

The phrase "among the Gentiles" follows immediately after "the mystery" in the word order of the original and is best understood in close connection to it (Harris 2010, 64). It is not so much the proclamation of the coming of Christ, *per se*, that is the mystery once hidden but now revealed; it is the proclamation of Christ *among the Gentiles* and their inclusion in him. (Cf. the way "the mystery of Christ" [Eph 3:4] is unfolded in the following verses as consisting in the fact that "the Gentiles are fellow heirs, fellow members of the body, and sharers in the promise in Christ Jesus, through the gospel" [Eph 3:6].) This point is underlined when Paul goes on to spell out the content of the mystery at the end of the verse: "which is Christ in you, the hope of glory." The "you" to whom Paul is referring here, read in light of the preceding "among the Gentiles," is probably best taken not as a generic Christian "you" but as a specifically Gentile "you." In possessing Christ, the Gentiles now possess "the hope of glory" (i.e., the expectation that they will one day be witnesses and participants in the revelation of God's glory that will take place in the coming age; cf. 1:5, 23; 3:4; Rom 5:2; 8:18, 30).

1:28. Since it is Christ himself who is the hope that is held out to Gentiles in the message of the gospel, and Christ himself—proclaimed and believed among the nations—who is the center of the mystery that Paul has been charged with making known, it comes as no surprise when Paul goes on to say in v. 28 that it is "him" (i.e., Christ) that Paul proclaims as the preeminent and unchanging focus of his message. The "we" in which Paul includes himself may simply be an editorial we or a reference to Paul's fellow workers, though the first-person singular pronouns in the preceding and following verses (vv. 24, 25, 29) make both of these explanations somewhat less likely. A third possibility, and perhaps the best explanation of why Paul switches for this one verse from the first-person singular to the first-person plural, is that he is speaking in this verse of all the apostles (cf. 1 Cor 15:11) or, more broadly still, of all who take part in the gospel's proclamation (Pao 2012, 131), in keeping with the universal scope of the picture he paints in the remainder of the verse ("everyone" . . . "all wisdom" . . . "everyone" . . . "everyone").

The participial phrases that follow immediately after the main verb ("admonishing everyone and teaching everyone") are probably best understood in an elaborative sense, painting a picture of the kinds of activities that are involved in "proclaim[ing] [Christ]" (Runge 2010, 262) and making it clear that, in Paul's mind at last, the proclamation of the gospel is not an activity that can be confined narrowly to the evangelization of unbelievers. The first of the two terms that Paul uses (*nouthetountes*, "admonishing") can sometimes (e.g., Rom 15:14) be used in a broad and general sense, without any necessary implication that an error is being corrected or a danger warned against, but in the majority of cases an element of warning or correction is implied by the context, and it is probably present here, too, given the prominent place that warnings occupy within the following paragraphs.

Both the "admonishing" and the "teaching" are described as being exercised "with all wisdom"—language that recalls the prayer in v. 9 that the readers will be "filled with . . . all spiritual wisdom and understanding," and anticipates the remainder of the letter's continuing focus on matters of wisdom—both the true wisdom that Paul urges the readers to teach and practice (3:16; 4:5) and the spurious wisdom of the "philosophy" that he warns them against (2:8, 23). Because Christ is the one in whom "all things hold together" (1:17) and "all the treasures of wisdom and knowledge" are hidden (2:3), Paul can envisage the work of proclaiming Christ as including within it the task of a wisdom teacher, imparting to believers a way of understanding all things in their relation to Christ so that they might order their lives accordingly.

The goal of this work is understood by Paul in eschatological terms: "in order that we may present everyone mature in Christ." As in v. 22, the verb "present" anticipates the day of Christ, when the outcome of Paul's ministry (and the outcome of the ministry of all who have, like him, labored in the work of the gospel) will be revealed. Paul's hope is that on that day the people whom he has taught and admonished will be "mature in Christ," language that he unpacks in Eph 4:13-16, where he depicts it as the outcome of a communal process in which the whole body works together to foster the growth of all (and of the community as a whole) into the likeness of Christ.

1:29. This common goal, shared by all who participate in the work of proclaiming Christ, is the end toward which Paul's own labors as an apostle are directed, as he goes on to state in v. 29: "to which end I toil, struggling according to his energy, which is working in power within me." The verb "toil" (*kopiaō*) is typically used in contexts that imply wearisome labor (e.g., Luke 5:5; John 4:6; 1 Cor 4:12) and is frequently used by Paul to speak of the work done by servants of the gospel (e.g., 1 Thess 5:12). Given the repeated use of "servant" language in the preceding verses (vv. 23, 25) and the way it functions as a frame within which Paul draws connections between his sufferings and the sufferings of Christ (v. 24), it is possible that Paul may have viewed his labors through a similar lens, as an aspect of his participation in the work of the Isaianic servant (cf. Isa 49:4; 1 Cor 4:11-13; 2 Cor 6:5;

11:23). Paul's description of himself as "struggling" (*agōnizomenos*) evokes the image of an athlete (cf. 1 Cor 9:25) engaging a sustained and strenuous effort directed toward the attainment of a goal. This element of toil and struggle is enabled, rather than eliminated, by the empowering presence of Christ within him, as he goes on to stress in the final line of the verse: "struggling according to his energy, which is working in power within me" (cf. 1 Cor 15:10; Phil 2:12-13; 4:13).

2:1. The broad, sweeping statements of 1:24-29 about Paul's sufferings and ministry zoom in a little closer in 2:1-5 to focus on the intensity and purpose of his present labors "for you, and for those in Laodicea, and for all those who have not seen my face in the flesh." The "for" (*gar*) that links the statement in 2:1 to the preceding sentence suggests that the function of the more focused claims in 2:1-5 is to offer support of some kind for the broad and general description of his ministry that he has offered in the previous paragraph (1:24-29). Lest the Colossians think that absence and imprisonment have brought an end to Paul's missionary labors, he insists emphatically that those labors have continued regardless.

In particular, he wants his readers in Colossae to know "how great" (*hēlikon*) those labors continue to be and to be assured that the scope of his concern includes not only the congregations that he himself has planted but also those congregations such as the Colossian and Laodicean house churches that were planted by others, most of whose members he has never met in person. In describing his ongoing missionary labors as "struggles" (*agōna*), he continues the athletic imagery of 1:29 ("struggling"; *agōnizomenos*), reinforcing the links between the general statement in 1:28-29 and the more specific claim in 2:1. In the present circumstances of his imprisonment, the most obvious form that this struggling could be envisaged as taking is his prayers, and the same image of "wrestling" is used in 4:12 to refer specifically to the prayers of Epaphras. Here, however, following immediately after the broad and general description of his ministry in 1:24-29, the "struggles" of Paul for the Colossians (along with the various others whom he has not met in person) should be taken in a slightly broader sense, referring comprehensively to all that he continues to do for the strengthening of their faith, contending against the adverse circumstances of his own imprisonment and the "plausible arguments" that are threatening to undermine the Colossians' trust in and allegiance to Christ; they thus include not only his prayers but also the writing of this letter to the Colossians and the sending of Tychicus as his emissary to them. The bracketing together in here in 2:1 of "you, and . . . those in Laodicea and . . . all those who have not seen my face in the flesh" anticipates the later reference in 4:16 to another letter that has been sent to the Laodiceans, and it is consistent with the hypothesis that the letter to the Laodiceans is the one that came to be known as Paul's letter to the Ephesians, sent as a circular homily to "all those [in Asia] who have not seen my face in the flesh."

2:2. Having spoken in v. 1 about the intensity and scope of his struggles for the Colossians (and the various others who are on his mind in his imprisonment), Paul turns in vv. 2-3 to the goal toward which his labors are directed: "that their hearts may be encouraged, having been brought together in love, and in the quest for all the riches of full assurance of understanding, for the sake of the knowledge of God's mystery, which is Christ." His desire that the Colossians' hearts might be encouraged (restated in 4:8 when he describes the purpose of Tychicus's visit) presupposes a context of struggle and adverse circumstances, within which the readers will need resolve and fortitude if they are to persevere and be fruitful (cf. 1:11).

The encouragement that Paul prays the Colossians will experience is through a dynamic that he envisages as taking an explicitly communal form, as the believers are joined with one another in a double bond—knitted together in mutual love and united in a shared quest for "all the riches of full assurance of understanding." The word Paul uses to express that interconnectedness (*symbibasthentes*: "brought together") is the same one he uses in Col 2:19 and in Eph 4:16 to speak of the community of believers as a body "held together" by its joints and ligaments, united in love and growing into maturity; a similar image is probably in the back of Paul's mind here.

His emphasis in v. 2 on love as the bond by which the community is held together is consistent with the role he describes it as playing elsewhere in Colossians (esp. 3:14) and in his other letters (e.g., Rom 12:10; 1 Cor 8:1; Gal 5:13-14; Eph 4:2, 16; Phil 2:2). The second bond that he envisages the Colossians as being held together by—their shared quest for "assurance of understanding"—is an expression of the more particular concerns of Colossians; having told the readers in 1:9 about his prayer that they will be "filled with the knowledge of his will, in all spiritual wisdom and understanding," he now returns to that theme, in preparation for a warning against an alternative wisdom that is elitist, destabilizing, and divisive in its social outworking, propagated by teachers whom he describes as "not holding fast to the Head, from whom the whole body, nourished and held together through its joints and ligaments, grows with a growth that is from God" (2:19).

2:3. The true understanding that Paul works toward seeing the Colossians united in is not a small, thin, static orthodoxy; the goal of his labors is not simply to hold the Colossians back from exploring the alternative wisdom that is being propagated among them but to unite them in the pursuit of an expansive, dynamic, ever-growing wisdom that he pictures here as "all the riches of . . . understanding." Expansive and dynamic as it is, however, the understanding that he pictures as the goal of their quest is still firmly grounded in the "full assurance" (*plērophoria*) of solid, lived conviction (cf. 1 Thess 1:5) and focused on the quest for an ever-deepening grasp of "the knowledge of God's mystery, which is Christ, in whom are hidden all the treasures of wisdom and knowledge."

The mystery that Paul has in view here is the same mystery that he has spoken of a few verses earlier, in 1:26-27: Christ himself, as the once-hidden-but-now-revealed climax of God's plans and purposes, proclaimed among the nations as the fulfillment of God's self-revelation to Israel. What the wisdom traditions of the Old Testament and the Second Temple Jewish literature had said about the treasures of wisdom possessed by YHWH and made accessible to his people in the sayings of the wise (e.g., Isa 33:5-6; Prov 2:1-6; Job 28; Sir 1:24-25; Wis 7:13-14), Paul says here about Christ.

Although the once-hidden counsels of God are now made known in Christ, there is a sense, too, in which they remain "hidden" in him; those who look elsewhere than in Christ do not find them, and the form that God's revelation takes in him is not one that is immediately recognizable by all for what it is. The traditions and practices of the philosophy that Paul is about to warn the Colossians against look much more like what their neighbors, peers, and social superiors would have regarded as wisdom (cf. 2:23; 1 Cor 2:6-8); but in the age to come, the full glory of Christ (and of the Colossians who have believed in him) will be made manifest for all to see (cf. 3:3-4).

2:4. The presence of an alternative wisdom in Colossae, which has already loomed unstated in the background behind Paul's description in 2:2-3 of the goal at which he aims in his labors for the Colossians, comes into explicit focus in v. 4, where Paul spells out the reason he frames the goal of his struggles in the way that he has: "I say this in order that no one may deceive you with plausible arguments." If we were judging solely on the basis of what Paul says here in this verse, it might be possible to draw the conclusion that his concern is merely hypothetical, and some commentators (e.g., Hooker 1973) have followed that path. The tone and content of what follows in 2:8-23, however, do suggest that the danger Paul sees the Colossians as being exposed to is a real and present one, and that the propagators of the alternative wisdom to which the Colossians might find themselves attracted include some at least who are (or have been) closely connected with the community of believers in Christ. Paul's description of their teachings as "plausible arguments" (*pithanologia*) is reminiscent of the language used by Plato (*Theaetetus* 162e) to refer to speciously presented philosophical claims that appeal to the crowd but are not firmly grounded in cogent logical and empirical proof (*apodeixis*) (cf. McKnight 2018, 213, and the similar connection between pithanologia and appeal to the crowds in Vitae Aesopi, Vita W 88a), reinforcing the impression that the battle Paul is waging here is (at least partly) a battle between rival wisdoms or philosophies.

2:5. The introductory section of the letter concludes in v. 5 with a reference to Paul's bodily absence from the Colossians (and, by implication, to the imprisonment that has kept him from them), his presence with them in spirit, and the joy he finds in their "good order" and the firmness of their faith. The shadow of Paul's imprisonment has hung across the entire section from 1:24 to 2:5, but here at the end of the section, as was the case in 1:24 at its start, Paul wants the Colossians to know about the joy that he feels in his imprisonment and to be confident (as he is) that his connection with them has not been broken or his ministry to them brought to an end. Despite being absent from them in flesh, he is (as he goes on to assure them) present with them "in spirit," language that echoes the similar claim in 1 Cor 5:3-4, albeit under somewhat different circumstances. Here, as there, the most obvious form in which he is likely to have imagined his presence as being mediated to the readers is through the reading of the letter (Pao 2012, 141), though his words may also carry an additional, underlying sense similar to the one conveyed (in slightly different language) by his assurance to the Thessalonians that during the time of his absence he was separated from them "in person, not in thought" (*prosōpō ou kardia*; 1 Thess 2:17).

Paul's presence in spirit with the Colossians is not, at heart, an anxious or censorious presence but a joyful one, encouraged by the reports he has received of their "good order" (*taxis*) and the "firmness" (*stereōma*) of their faith. The rival philosophy that Paul has alluded to in the previous verse has not yet, it seems, made significant inroads into the community of believers, though—judging from the exhortations and warnings that follow in vv. 6-23—the continuance of that encouraging state of affairs is not something Paul takes for granted. The "good order" that Paul rejoices in is probably best taken as a reference to the social structures of church and household within which the Colossians are living out their faith (McKnight 2018, 214; cf. 3:5–4:1). Their "faith in Christ" that remains firm is likely to carry the same meaning as the similar language in 1:4 and 2:7, referring in all three cases to the steadfast trust that they continue to place in Christ and the allegiance that they continue to show to him.

So walk in him

Colossians 2:6–4:18

Just as you received Christ Jesus as Lord . . . (2:6-7)

(6) So then, just as you received Christ Jesus as Lord, so walk in him, (7) rooted and being built up in him and established in the faith, just as you were taught, abounding in thanksgiving.

2:6. After an extended, theologically rich introduction in 1:1–2:5, Paul now commences the body of the letter, which consists of the warnings, reminders, and instructions in 2:6–4:6. Grammatically speaking, the encouragement in v. 6 to continue to "walk" in a manner that is consistent with their acknowledgment of Christ Jesus as Lord is the first imperative-mood verb in the letter, and it is followed by a string of subsequent commands that dominate the content of every major section from 2:6 to 4:6 (see the full list in Moo 2008, 174–75).

The opening command, in 2:6-7, functions as a kind of hinge. The first part of the sentence ("So then, just as you received Christ Jesus as Lord . . .") sums up the content of the various passages within the introductory section that speak about the readers' reception of the gospel (e.g., 1:5-8, 21-23), their salvation and transference into the kingdom of Christ (e.g., 1:13-14), and the supremacy of Christ himself as the Lord of the universe and head of the church (1:15-20). The command in v. 6b ("so walk in him") establishes the trajectory of everything that will follow, urging the readers to frame the manner of their lives in accordance with their reception of Christ as Lord. And the string of participial phrases in v. 7 ("rooted and being built up in him and established in the faith, just as you were taught, abounding in thanksgiving") begins the process of unpacking that command, offering a series of metaphors to assist the readers in picturing what it will look like to walk "in him," living their daily lives as a people who have received Christ as Lord and been incorporated into him.

The verb "received" (*parelabete*) is frequently used by Paul to speak about the reception of a message or tradition (e.g., Gal 1:9; 1 Thess 2:13; 2 Thess 3:6), and that sense may be in the background of Paul's thinking here. In this instance, however (uniquely in Paul), the object of the verb is a person, "Christ Jesus," and the primary sense in which it used is to speak of their acceptance and acknowledgment of him (cf. John 1:12). The fact that the word "Christ" (*Christos*) is used before the personal name Jesus and is preceded in the Greek by an article (*ton Christon*) suggests that it should probably be taken as a title or honorific ("the Messiah, Jesus," or "King Jesus") rather than simply as a personal name. The word "Lord" that follows (again with an article: *ton kyrion*) could either be functioning in apposition to "Christ Jesus" (i.e., "Christ Jesus, the Lord") or, more likely, as a predicate ("Christ Jesus as Lord"), echoing the basic confession of the Christian faith ("Jesus is Lord") as it reverberated through Paul's letters in a variety of similar, though not identical, grammatical forms (e.g., Rom 10:9; 1 Cor 12:3; 2 Cor 4:5; Phil 2:11). In calling Jesus "Lord," Paul recalls and encapsulates what has already been said in 1:1–2:5 about his agency in the creation and reconciliation of all things, his supremacy over all powers, and his sovereignty over the dominion into which believers have been transferred. Against this background, the acknowledgment of Jesus as Lord implies a claim that stands over and (at least potentially) collides with the political and religious claims of Roman imperial propaganda; it also implies the full participation of Jesus in the identity and authority of Israel's God, YHWH, whose name was translated as "Lord" (*kyrios*) in the Greek versions of the Old Testament.

Having received Jesus on those terms at their conversion, the Colossians are, in keeping with that confession and commitment, to "walk in him." As was the case in the earlier use of the same verb in 1:10, the verb to "walk" functions as a metaphor for the pattern of daily living that believers are to follow. To walk "in him" suggests a pattern of life that is decisively and comprehensively shaped by their allegiance to Jesus and their membership of his people. The spatial metaphor implied by the preposition "in" recalls the claim made several verses earlier, in 2:3, that "in [him] are hidden all the treasures of wisdom and knowledge," and it anticipates the similar claims that are repeated in 2:9-11 as reasons that believers have no need to look outside of Christ for any alternative or supplementary wisdom to shape the way they live their lives.

2:7. The encouragement to the readers in v. 6b to "walk in him" is unpacked in v. 7 through a series of four participial phrases: "rooted and being built up in him and established in the faith, just as you were taught, abounding in thanksgiving." The grammar and content of v. 7 are both strikingly reminiscent of language that Paul has already used in 1:10-12, where a reference to Paul's hope that the Colossians might "walk worthily of the Lord" is followed by a series of four participial phrases that picture them as "bearing fruit in every good work" (cf. the horticultural metaphor implied by "rooted" in 2:7), "growing in the knowledge of God" (cf. "being built up"; 2:7) "being strengthened with all power" (cf. "established in the faith"; 2:7), and "joyfully giving thanks to the Father" (cf. "abounding in thanksgiving"; 2:7).

The first two participles, "rooted" and "being built up," are tied closely together (cf. the similar combination, "rooted and grounded," in Eph 3:17) and jointly govern the phrase "in him." The former of the two focuses primarily on the stability that the believers possess through their connection to Christ. The latter (a present passive participle, suggesting an ongoing process) focuses on the ongoing formation of believers as members of Christ's people (cf. Eph 4:14-16, where the image is placed in explicit contrast with the instability and immaturity of a community that is "tossed about and carried around by every wind of doctrine").

The third participial phrase, "established in the faith, just as you were taught," further reinforces the sense of firmness and stability that was implied by the previous two, grounding it this time in the pattern of teaching that the believers were taught when they were inducted into Christ. (The elaboration, "just as you were taught," suggests that what Paul has in mind by *tē pistei*, in this context, is not the subjective, personal faith of believers but the body of teaching regarding the gospel and its entailments that believers were initiated into when they first received Christ.) The final phrase, "abounding in thanksgiving," suggests an overflowing, habitual disposition of gratitude as a pervasive and characteristic sign of a community created and shaped by the generosity of God.

See to it that no one takes you captive (2:8-23)

(8) See to it that no one takes you captive through philosophy and empty deceit, according to human tradition, according to the basic principles of the world, and not according to Christ. (9) For in him all the fullness of deity dwells bodily, (10) and you have been filled in him, who is the head of every ruler and authority. (11) In him you were also circumcised with a circumcision made without hands, by the stripping off of the body of flesh in the circumcision of Christ, (12) by being buried with him in baptism, in which you were also raised with him through faith in the working of God, who raised him from the dead. (13) And you, though you were dead in your trespasses and the uncircumcision of your flesh, God made you alive together

with him, having forgiven us all [our] trespasses, (14) by canceling the written document that stood against us with its legal demands; and he set it aside, nailing it to the cross. (15) Having stripped of their armor the rulers and authorities, he made a public spectacle of them, triumphing over them in it. (16) Therefore let no one pass judgment on you in matters of food and drink, or with regard to a festival or a new moon or Sabbath, (17) which are a shadow of the things to come, but the substance belongs to Christ. (18) Let no one disqualify you, delighting in self-humiliation and worship of angels, going into detail about the things he has seen, puffed up without reason by the mind of his flesh, (19) and not holding fast to the Head, from whom the whole body, nourished and held together through its joints and ligaments, grows with a growth that is from God. (20) If you died with Christ to the basic principles of the world, why, as if you were still living in the world, submit to regulations: (21) "Do not handle! Do not taste! Do not touch!"—(22) which are all referring to things that perish with use, according to human precepts and teachings? (23) These, while having a reputation for wisdom in self-made religion and self-humiliation and harsh treatment of the body, are of no value in dealing with the indulgence of the flesh.

2:8. The command in vv. 6-7 is followed immediately by a warning in v. 8 that sets the direction for the paragraphs that make up the remainder of the chapter. Within these paragraphs, Paul addresses the readers with a series of commands and prohibitions ("see to it that no one takes you captive . . ." [v. 8a]; "let no one pass judgment on you . . ." [v. 16a]; "let no one disqualify you . . ." [v. 18a]) and a sharply worded rhetorical question that functions with a similar effect ("why, as if you were still living in the world, submit to regulations?" [v. 20]). The remaining content of vv. 8-23 surrounds and undergirds these commands and prohibitions (and the rhetorical question of v. 20) with reminders of gospel tradition (vv. 8b-15, 19b, 20a) and descriptions and critiques of the teaching that Paul is warning the Colossians against (vv. 16b-17, 18b-19a, 21-23).

The tone of the warnings is set in v. 8: "See to it that no one takes you captive through philosophy and empty deceit, according to human tradition, according to the basic principles of the world, and not according to Christ." The opening verb, *blepete* ("see to it"), places on the readers a responsibility to be vigilant and to resist the efforts made by proponents of the teaching Paul is warning against to "take [them] captive"—an image that combines with the language of the following paragraphs ("pass judgment" [v. 16]; "disqualify" [v. 18]; "submit to regulations" [v. 20]) to suggest an overbearing or dictatorial approach on behalf of the teaching's proponents. Here in v. 8 (as is also the case in v. 16), Paul makes use of the indefinite particle *tis* ("[no]

one"; "anyone") in referring to the people against whom he is warning. This is probably not to be taken as an indication that the warning is a merely hypothetical one—the rhetorical prominence and urgency of the warnings Paul gives across vv. 8-23 suggest that he views the philosophy as a real and present threat—but it does have the effect of giving a certain flexibility or generality to the warning that he gives. Paul may not give us enough information to say with any certainty what was the precise content of the "philosophy" that was present in Colossae and influential among the readers, but he does elaborate at some length on the reasons he warns against it, and his warning is framed in a manner that suggests its applicability is not narrowly limited to the particular circumstances in which the Colossians find themselves.

Paul's description of the teaching as a "philosophy" should not be taken as implying that its content is abstract or theoretical in nature, or that its primary source is in the Greco-Roman intellectual tradition. The verses that follow suggest a strongly Jewish cast to the philosophy's content and a behavioral rather than speculative or theoretical focus to its teachings. The closest analogies we have to the use of the word "philosophy" in a context of this sort are in the literature of Hellenistic Judaism, in which the precepts of Moses (and their further development in Jewish tradition) are held out as resources for the wise man to draw upon in his quest for attaining mastery over the passions (e.g., 4 Macc 1:1-3; 5:22-23).

In Paul's view, however, the "philosophy" being propagated by the teachers against whom he is warning is not a true and life-giving wisdom but a teaching that consists in "empty deceit," unable to establish what it asserts and unable to accomplish what it claims to achieve (cf. v. 23). The reasons for this strongly negative judgment are offered in the remainder of the verse, where Paul goes on to describe the merely human origins of the philosophy ("according to human tradition, according to the basic principles of the world") and the absence of Christ at its core ("and not according to Christ")—an absence that he goes on to contrast in vv. 9-15 with the Christocentric pattern of teaching in which "all the fullness of deity" has been made known to the Colossians.

Paul's description in v. 8 of the philosophy as being framed *kata to stoicheia tou kosmou* ("according to the basic principles of the world") has generated much discussion and debate among interpreters. Because the word *stoicheia* can sometimes be used to refer to personal, transcendent powers that control the elements of the universe (e.g., Stobaeus, *Flor.* I.409; Philo, *Contempl. Life* 3), and Paul makes reference here in Colossians 2 to "worship of angels" (v. 18) and speaks of the *stoicheia* elsewhere (in Gal 4:3, 8) in personal or personified terms, some commentators interpret the word as referring here to "elemental spirits" as the origin of the philosophy or the authority to which it appeals (e.g., Lohse 1971, 96–99; Pao 2012, 160–61). The more likely interpretation, however, given the close juxtaposition to "human tradition" and the primary focus of the paragraph on teachings and rules of conduct, is that Paul is using the word in one of the other senses that it could commonly carry, to refer to "basic principles" (e.g., Xenophon, *Memorabilia* 2.1.1)—in this case, basic principles of human piety and religion (cf. Witherington 2007, 154–55; McKnight 2018, 227–28). (This may well be the sense in which Paul uses the word in Galatians 4, too, though in that instance those "basic principles," like the Law of Moses itself, are being personified as agents of the Galatians' pre-conversion slavery to the pagan gods and the enslavement of Paul and his fellow Jews to the Law.)

2:9. Verses 9-10 supply the reason that the Colossians should be on guard against a teaching that is "not according to Christ" and view it, contrary to its grand-sounding claims, as "empty deceit": "For in him all the fullness of deity dwells bodily, and you have been filled in him, who is the head of every ruler and authority." In both content and wording, these verses are closely reminiscent of the hymn in 1:15-20, and in function they serve to bring the Christology of the hymn to bear on the situation in which the readers find themselves as they determine their response to the philosophy that is being advocated to them by the teachers Paul is warning against.

The opening assertion, in v. 9, is in essence a restatement and expansion of the claim that Paul has already made in 1:19: "for in him all the fullness was pleased to dwell." Here, as there, the scope of the claim is explicitly universal—"all the fullness"—leaving no remainder of the divine nature that is to be understood in disconnection from Christ. Here, too, as in 1:19, the primary background of Paul's "fullness" language is probably the Old Testament image of the visible glory of God that filled the tabernacle or the temple (e.g., Exod 40:34-35; Isa 6:13; Ezek 43:5; 44:4), and the presence of God's fullness in Christ is pictured not as a fleeting moment of glorification but as a permanent indwelling. The main expansions on the assertion of 1:19 that Paul makes here in 2:9 are the adverb "bodily," which makes explicit the incarnational focus of the idea that Paul has in mind, and the phrase "of deity" (*tēs theotētos*). The latter addition has the double effect of making it clear that the fullness Paul is speaking of is *God's* fullness (not some sort of undefined and impersonal cosmic essence) and, at the same time, by using the abstraction "deity" (*theotēs*), bringing the particular assertions that Paul is making about the God of Israel and the person of Christ into connection with the universal claims and questions that were the common subject matter of "philosophy," in its various first century forms.

2:10. The "fullness" of God that dwells bodily in Christ contrasts starkly with the "empty deceit" of the philosophy that is being propagated among the Colossians. The stake that they have in Christ's fullness is further emphasized in v. 10, where Paul goes on to assure the readers that they themselves, by virtue of their inclusion in Christ, have been "filled in him." If the language of "fullness," as Paul uses it here in v. 10, is to be interpreted in continuity with the sense that it carries in the immediately preceding verse, then the most likely candidate for the primary idea it conveys is that of presence and indwelling. Believers do not, in themselves, contain already the completeness of all that is in God—that is for Paul a goal to be sought and prayed for, not a reality that is already accomplished (cf. Eph 4:16-21). But they are, nonetheless, authentically indwelt by his presence and granted access in him to "all the treasures of wisdom and knowledge" (2:3)—and hence have no need to be overawed or enticed by the claims being made for the Christ-less philosophy that is being promoted among them.

An additional echo of the Christ hymn in 1:15-20 is sounded in v. 10b, where Paul reminds his readers that the Christ in whom they have been granted access to the fullness of God is "the head of every ruler and authority" (cf. 1:16, 18). It is difficult to say with certainty what precise role (if any) the "rulers and authorities" of the cosmos played within the message of the Colossian philosophy. The reference to "worship of angels" in 2:18 may offer a hint in the direction of mystical practices that accompanied and validated their ascetic disciplines and abstentions, suggesting that the rulers and authorities in view are invisible, supernatural cosmic powers. On the other hand, the depiction of Christ's death in 2:15 as an event in which he "stripped of their armor the rulers and authorities" and "made a public spectacle of them" reads most naturally as a reference to the earthly, political powers who (incited and emboldened by invisible, supernatural powers of evil) conspired to have him crucified. And the assertion in 1:16 that "in him all things were created . . . whether thrones or dominions or rulers or authorities" explicitly includes within its scope the earthly and visible as well as the heavenly and invisible. It is possible, if we rely primarily on 2:15, that the "rulers and authorities" spoken of by the teachers of the philosophy were angelic beings whose veneration required elaborate ascetic preparations and purifications; it is also possible, if we rely primarily on 2:18, that the "rulers and authorities" in view are the guardians of the religio-political order that was disturbed by the message of the gospel and could be put back together again by proper adherence to Jewish halakhic tradition. One way or another (regardless of whether the goal in view is a comfortable relationship with the existing social order, an empowering ascent into transcendent, visionary experience, or some combination of both), the philosophy that is being advocated to the Colossians amounts to a demand that believers yield obedience to rules that originate with authorities other than Christ, without any acknowledgment of his overarching supremacy, and a promise of benefits and blessings that lie outside and beyond the benefits that believers already possess in him. And for those reasons, as Paul sees it, the philosophy is to be rejected as illegitimate in its demands and deceptive in its promises.

2:11. In vv. 11-13 Paul adds to the reminder of v. 9 that the readers have been "filled" in Christ a further reminder that they have also been "circumcised" in him. The idea of a metaphorical circumcision that is a work of God, not of human hands, is not in itself original; the image of a circumcised heart, for example, is a recurring one in the Old Testament (e.g., Deut 10:16; 30:6 Jer 9:24-25) and the Second Temple Jewish literature (e.g., Jub. 1:22). Paul's initial reference in v. 11a to the metaphorical "circumcision" that believers have experienced, "with a circumcision made without hands," is consistent with this conventional use of the image and reminiscent of the way he speaks in Rom 2:28-29 about a circumcision that is not "outward, in the flesh" but "of the heart, by the Spirit," along with the contrasting reference in Eph 2:11 to "what is called 'circumcision' (done in the flesh by hands)."

Some commentators (e.g., Moo 2008, 198–200; Harris 2010, 102–103) read the further development of the metaphor in v. 11b as equally conventional, interpreting "the circumcision of Christ" as a subjective genitive construction, in which Christ is understood to be the one performing the circumcision, and taking "the putting off of the body of [the] flesh" as a reference to the excision of the old, unregenerate nature in Christian conversion/baptism by the work of the Holy Spirit.

Several features of the text point in a different direction, however. In the first place, there is the fact that Paul refers to the stripping off of "the body of flesh" (not the stripping off of "the flesh")—language that closely resembles his earlier reference to "the body of his flesh" in which Christ died to reconcile believers to himself (1:21). In the second place, there is the verbal parallel between the reference in v. 11b to the "the stripping off (*apekdysis*) of the body of flesh" and the description in v. 15 of Christ in his crucifixion as "having stripped of their armor (*apekdysamenos*) the rulers and authorities." And in the third place, there is the way the image in v. 11b is followed immediately in v. 12 by a description of believers as having been "buried with him in baptism, in which you were also raised with him through faith in the working of God, who raised him from the dead." These three features of the text combine to suggest an alternative and more contextually fitting interpretation of v. 11b, in which "the circumcision of Christ" is read as an objective genitive construction, speaking of a (metaphorical) circumcision that Christ himself underwent, and "the stripping off of the body of flesh" is understood as a graphic description of the violent, shameful death that Christ endured on the cross (cf. McKnight 2018, 237–38; Pao 2012, 165–66).

Paul's other references to a metaphorical circumcision experienced by Gentile believers occur in the context of polemics directed against those who attempt to argue for the sufficiency of physical circumcision as a guarantee of covenant membership for Jews (Rom 2:25-29) or its necessity for Gentiles who wish to be counted among God's people (Phil 3:2-3). Given the close proximity of this verse to a description of the philosophy's content that includes the observance of Torah-derived traditions regarding "matters of food and drink . . . festival[s], . . . new moon[s], . . . and "Sabbath[s]" (v. 16), which Paul describes as "a shadow of the things to come" (v. 17), it seems likely that here, too, Paul's emphasis on the spiritual circumcision undergone by believers and the metaphorical circumcision endured by Christ on the cross are a response, in part at least, to the prominence of physical circumcision within the teachings and practices of the philosophy.

2:12. The event experienced by believers that dramatizes the relationship between their own conversion (recalled in v. 11a) and the death of Christ (alluded to in v. 11b) is the ritual of Christian baptism, which Paul goes on to remind the readers of in v. 12: "by being buried with him in baptism, in which you were also raised with him through faith in the working of God, who raised him from the dead." The aorist participle, *syntaphentes* (here translated as "by being buried"), is probably best understood as indicating the means by which believers have experienced the spiritual circumcision spoken of in the previous verse (Campbell 2013, 37), rather than an event chronologically prior to it ("having been buried"). In Paul's mind, the event of baptism dramatizes and signifies the whole process of Christian conversion, understood as an initiation into fellowship with Christ (cf. Gal 3:27) and into the experience of participation in his death, burial, and resurrection (cf. Rom 6:1-4); a reference to the one event (Christian baptism) can imply the other (Christian conversion/initiation).

Despite the closeness of the relationship in Paul's mind between the event of Christian baptism and the conversion and initiation into Christ that it signifies, it would be a mistake to conclude that the ritual, in and of itself, effects what it signifies. The link between the believer and Christ is not effected quasi-magically by the event of immersion in the water but (as Paul goes on to make clear in v. 12b) by the faith that believers give expression to in their baptism. (Cf. the similarly close relationship between "faith" and "baptis[m] into Christ" in Gal 3:26-27.)

The object of the faith that Paul speaks of here is "the working of God, who raised [Christ] from the dead"—a formulation that suggests that the primary sense carried by the word *pistis* in this context is trust or reliance, rather than the closely related notion of fidelity or allegiance that the word can carry as an additional or alternative sense in some instances in Paul's letters. Here, as elsewhere in Paul, the resurrection of Christ is held out as the principal demonstration of the power of God (cf. Eph 1:19-20), and the God in whom believers are called upon to put their trust is identified as the one "who raised Christ from the dead" (cf. Rom 4:17, 24; 8:11; 10:9; 1 Cor 5:14-15).

2:13. Having spoken in v. 12 of baptism into Christ as an event that involves believers being "buried with him" and "raised with him," Paul goes on in vv. 13-15 to elaborate on what it is about Christ's death by crucifixion that makes it such a powerfully salvific and transformative event. He begins in v. 13 with a picture of the pre-conversion condition of the readers, as "dead in your trespasses and the uncircumcision of your flesh." The first part of the image ("dead in your trespasses") is reminiscent of the similar description Paul uses for the pre-conversion state of the Ephesian readers in Eph 2:1; the second part ("and the uncircumcision of your flesh") brings into the foreground their Gentile origins and exclusion from the covenant people of God, echoing the parallel description of the Ephesian readers' pre-conversion plight in Eph 2:11. Here, those two descriptions combine to produce a composite picture of death and alienation (or, more precisely, a picture of a single, overarching plight of "death" that was the consequence and manifestation of two parallel and interrelated factors—the "trespasses" that were a pervasive feature of their way of life and the "uncircumcision" that emblematized their alienation from the people of God).

Having explicitly included the readers' uncircumcised, Gentile origins within the picture of their pre-conversion plight, however, Paul goes on in the second half of the verse (and in the verse that follows) to describe a solution that embraced not only them but also the Jewish believers with whom they had come to be united in Christ. Where exactly the transition from "you" to "us" takes place within v. 13 depends on whether we follow the manuscripts in which the second half of the verse begins with *synezōopoiēsen hymas* ("made you alive" [with "you" repeated from earlier in the verse]; cf. ℵ*, A, C) or *synezōopoiēsen* ("made [you] alive" [with you understood from earlier in the verse]; cf. ℵ², D, F), or the manuscripts in which the verse's second half begins with *synezōopoiēsen hēmas* ("made us alive"; cf. 𝔓⁴⁶, B). The first of the three options has reasonable manuscript support, and it best explains how the other two readings could have arisen as scribal alterations (to improve the grammar by removing the redundant *hymas* or to alter it to *hēmas* to match the *hēmin* that follows). Whichever of these three is the original, however, by the end of the verse it is unambiguously "us" (Jews as well as Gentiles) whose trespasses have been forgiven, uniting Gentiles with Jews in a common solution and, by implication, in a common plight of sin and death that was the shared predicament of circumcised and uncircumcised outside of Christ (cf. Eph 2:1-3; Rom 3:9-20).

2:14. The closest Paul comes to explaining how the crucifixion of Christ resolves this predicament is in the following two verses (vv. 14-15): "by canceling the written document that stood against us with its legal demands; and he set it aside, nailing it to the cross. Having stripped of their armor the rulers and authorities he made a public spectacle of them, triumphing over them in the cross."

The word Paul uses in speaking of the "written document (*cheirographon*) that stood against us" occurs nowhere else in Paul's letters or in the New Testament as a whole. It is frequently used in the surviving papyri, however, where it typically refers to a legal record of indebtedness or a written confession of guilt (Moulton and Milligan 1997, 687; Pao 2012, 170; cf. Tob 5:3; 9:5), and it is probably that sense of the word that would have been uppermost in the minds of Paul and the original readers of Colossians. In the immediately following phrase, Paul further specifies the image that he has in mind by describing it as a document that stood against us "with its legal demands" (*tois dogmasin*). The language he uses here closely resembles the way he refers in Eph 2:15 to "the law of commandments in the form of ordinances (*en dogmasin*)," and it anticipates the question put to the readers in Col 2:20 as to why they would "submit to regulations (*dogmatizesthe*)" imposed on them by the proponents of the philosophy he is warning against. The combined effect of these phrases, therefore, is probably to evoke the image of a bond of indebtedness that stands against all people, Jew and Gentile alike, as a consequence of the ways they have transgressed against the righteous requirements of God as they are spelled out in the ordinances of the Torah (cf. the interpretation of this passage and the larger argument regarding Paul's views on law and Gentiles in Blazosky 2019). Since it is on the ordinances of the Torah that the regulations and requirements of the Colossian philosophy are ostensibly based, an event that nullifies the condemning power of the former will simultaneously have the effect of undercutting the moral authority of the latter (an implication that Paul goes on to draw in vv. 16-23).

The "canceling" of the record of indebtedness that once stood against the readers did not take place simply by divine edict, as if the wrongs that men and women have done could be simply erased with the stroke of a pen.

What Paul has in mind is something infinitely more costly than that; as he goes on to say in the second half of v. 14, Christ "set . . . aside" the record of our indebtedness by "nailing it to the cross." In and of itself, the image of nailing the written record to the cross does not imply a theory of atonement, but when the image is read against the background of the custom in which the accusation against a crucified criminal was nailed as a *titulus* to the cross on which they hung (and in combination with the earlier reference in 1:20 to the peace that Christ has made "through the blood of his cross"), the strong implication is that the condemnation did not simply evaporate but was absorbed vicariously by Christ's own sufferings and death (cf. Gal 3:13; Rom 8:3): "The innocent one . . . assumes the charges against the guilty ones so that the guilty ones might become innocent. We thus have here vicarious, substitutionary atonement. Jesus shoulders the accusations against us so we need not experience their consequences in death" (McKnight 2018, 251).

2:15. But there are other, additional participants in this story, alongside God the judge and lawgiver, the men and women who have transgressed his commandments, and Christ who has taken upon himself their condemnation. Also active in the crucifixion of Christ were the human, religio-political authorities under whose jurisdiction Christ was condemned and executed, and the invisible, supernatural powers who were acting upon and through them in rebellion against God. The "rulers and authorities" that Paul goes on to refer to in v. 15 appear to include within their scope the former as well as the latter. The likelihood that the former are included among the "rulers and authorities" that Paul has in view is strengthened by the military-imperial connotations of the language Paul uses to describe Christ's triumph over them. Just as they "stripped off" the body of Christ's flesh in crucifixion (having previously "stripped [*exedysan*]" him of the purple robe that they had dressed him in as an act of calculated mockery; cf. Mk 15:20) so God, in Christ, has now "stripped [them] of their armor [*apekdysamenos*]." And just as the Roman imperial powers routinely "triumphed" over their enemies in elaborately choreographed processions (the account of Aemilus Paullus's triumph over Perseus of Macedon, in Plutarch, *Aemilius Paullus*, 32.2–34.5, quoted at length in McKnight 2018, 257–59), so God, in Christ, has "made a public spectacle of them, triumphing [*thriambeusas*] over them." Less obviously implied by Paul's language but still probably present in his thought (and that of his readers) are the invisible, supernatural powers, to whom he has already referred in 1:16 and whom he explicitly identifies in Eph 2:2; 6:12 as the principal opponents of the warfare that God wages in the world.

Although Paul frequently speaks elsewhere of the resurrection and ascension of Christ as events in which the power of God was displayed and his triumph over his enemies accomplished (cf. Eph 1:19-21; 4:8-10), the immediate focus here is on the event of the crucifixion itself (assuming, as seems most likely, that the phrase *en autō* at the end of the verse should be translated as "in it" [referring to its closest antecedent, the cross] rather than "in him" [referring to Christ]). The subsequent vindication of Christ in his resurrection can hardly be far from Paul's mind (cf. 2:12; 3:1), but the picture here in v. 15 is of the ironic, subversive victory already accomplished in the crucifixion itself (cf. 1 Cor 1:18–2:16). (A similar claim can be made about the ironic appropriation of the *titulus* image in Col 2:14, in which the accusations written against Christ become a metaphor for the accusations against his people, "nail[ed]" to the cross and thereby "set . . . aside.") The triumph described in v. 15 and the forgiveness described in vv. 13b-14 are, therefore, not unrelated events. If the "rulers and authorities" over which Christ has triumphed are, among other things, accusing and condemning powers, then the exhaustion of their condemnation in the death of Christ is both a facet of his triumph over them and a sufficient basis for the forgiveness and deliverance of his people (cf. Rom 8:31-39; 1 Cor 15:54-57; Rev 12:10-11).

2:16. The reminders in vv. 9-15 provide a platform for the reiterated warning in v. 16: "Therefore let no one pass judgment on you in matters of food and drink, or with regard to a festival or a new moon or Sabbath." The third person prohibition, *mē . . . tis hymas krinetō* ("let no one pass judgement on you"), with which the verse commences, does not focus on the judgments that the readers themselves might pass on others but on the judgments that others might pass on them. By directing the imperative to the readers, Paul implies that they can play a part in resisting or disregarding such judgments. As was the case in the similar injunction Paul gives to the readers in v. 8, the construction is an indefinite one, ruling out of court the judgments on matters such as these that "[any]one (*tis*)" might make, though here, as there, this should not be taken as implying that the threat is merely a hypothetical one.

The matters on which the judgment Paul seeks to exclude are focused are described in the remainder of v. 16: "in matters of food and drink, or with regard to a festival or a new moon or Sabbaths." Although some of the items in the list (e.g., "matters of food and drink") are elements that feature pervasively as the focus of regulations and prohibitions in a wide variety of religious and philosophical systems, the list as a whole clearly suggests a set of practices that derive, ostensibly at least, from the Torah (cf. the similar lists in Gal 4:10 and Romans 14, and the statement in v. 17 that these things are "a shadow of the things to come"—language that is strongly suggestive of an Old Testament source for the practices).

Within that framework, "matters of food and drink" is most naturally read as a reference to disciplines of abstention and purity based on the Mosaic food laws (cf. 4 Maccabees 5) and/or the desire to avoid the possibility of consuming food and drink that may have been offered to idols. The threefold expression, "festival[s], new moon[s], and Sabbath[s]" is used in the Old Testament to refer to Jewish calendrical observances (e.g., 1 Chr 23:31; LXX 2 Chr 2:4), the proper observance of which was a preoccupation of many within Second Temple Judaism (e.g., *Jub.* 6:34-38; 4Q326). The longer treatment of these themes in Romans 14 makes it clear that Paul is by no means opposed outright to the observation of Sabbaths and the celebration of Jewish calendrical feasts, to the maintenance of ritual purity through abstention from foods that were unclean, or to the kind of scrupulous abstentions that would remove any risk of consuming food and drink that may have been offered to idols. In the same passage, however, he makes it clear that there is no place for "judging" others over whether they follow the same practices (Rom 14:3-4, 10, 13), and here in Colossians 2 he urges the readers not to submit to judgments of this sort when they are made by others.

2:17. The reason matters such as these are not a proper basis for determining the inclusion or exclusion of men and women from the people of God is the fact that (as Paul goes on to say in v. 17) these things are "a shadow of the things to come, but the substance belongs to Christ." The distinction Paul draws between "shadow" (*skia*) and "substance" (*sōma*) is not the distinction drawn in Platonic dualism between ephemeral, earthly "shadows" and the immutable and eternal "realities" (*pragmata*) or "forms" (*eikones*) (e.g., Plato, *Resp.* 514a–518b); it is, rather, the distinction between Old Testament anticipations and their New Testament fulfilments—which were, viewed from within the timeframe of the Old Testament, "the things to come" (cf. Heb 10:1). The reality of these things "belongs to Christ"— an expression that leaves room for a plurality of New Testament antitypes, including not only the person of Christ himself and the events of his death and resurrection but also the various practices and experiences that belong to him as part of the life of his people. By imposing the "shadows" of the Old Covenant as mandatory practices for the people of the New Covenant community, the teachers of the philosophy show that their teaching is, at its heart, "according to human tradition, according to the basic principles of the world, and not according to Christ" (v. 8).

2:18. The warning of v. 8, already reiterated in v. 16, is repeated a third time in vv. 18-19, this time with a further elaboration on the pattern of religion within which the judgments and demands of the philosophy were embedded: "Let no one disqualify you, delighting in self-humiliation and worship of angels, going into detail about the things he has seen, puffed up without reason by the mind of his flesh, and not holding fast to the Head, from whom the whole body, nourished and held together through its joints and ligaments, grows with a growth that is from God."

Here, as in v. 16, the warning is expressed as a third person prohibition—"Let no one . . . disqualify you"—once more with the implication that the part for the readers to play is to resist any impulse they may feel to acquiesce to the disqualifying verdict passed by others (or, by implication, to bend their behaviors into compliance with the philosophy that is being promoted among them so as to avert the risk of incurring the disqualifying judgment of its teachers). The verb "disqualify" (*katabrabeuō*) that Paul uses here is, if etymology is any guide, originally derived from an athletic context (as the antonym of *brabeuō*, "to award a prize"), but the surviving instances of its use suggest that it could frequently carry a more generic sense of censure or exclusion without a specifically athletic metaphor being evoked (cf. NIDNTTE, 1.530–32, s.v. "*brabeion*"); the absence of any developed or extended athletic imagery here in Colossians 2 suggests that this slightly broader sense may be the meaning here, too.

The remainder of vv. 18-19 elaborates on the posture and practices of the teachers whom Paul envisages as pronouncing or threatening a verdict of this sort. (Grammatically speaking, the four participial clauses that make up the majority of vv. 18-19—"delighting in self-humiliation . . ."; "going into detail . . ."; "puffed up without reason . . ."; "and not holding fast to the Head . . ."—are adverbial rather than adjectival in function, modifying *katabrabeuetō* ["let no one disqualify"] rather than *mēdeis* ["no one"], but their content suggests that they paint a picture of accompanying circumstances rather than specifying the means by which the disqualification is conveyed.) The description is vivid and clearly disapproving, even if the precise meaning of some of the words Paul uses is somewhat difficult for us to determine.

The first of the four participial clauses depicts the teachers of the philosophy as "delighting in self-humiliation and worship of angels." Almost every word of this description is the subject of scholarly debate. The first word, *thelōn*, is translated by some as "insisting," presumably on the understanding that the proponents of the philosophy are demanding ascetic exercises and visionary experiences as a compulsory requirement of true religion. This may perhaps have been a part of their message, but if it is, this is the only place in the letter where Paul makes mention of the fact that the Colossians themselves were being pressured into participating in practices of angel-worship. The accent of the following three clauses, too, is not on what the philosophy's proponents demand from the Colossians (that comes next, in vv. 20-23) but on the boasts they make about their own observances and experiences. It seems best, therefore, to interpret the phrase *thelōn en* as conveying the same sense it typically carries elsewhere in the NT and LXX, translating it as "delighting in" rather than "insisting on" (cf. BDAG, s.v. "*thelō*," 3.b).

The word "self-humiliation" that the teachers delight in is described by Paul using a word (*tapeinophrosynē*) that he typically uses in a positive sense, to speak of the humility to which Christians are called in imitation of Christ (cf. Eph 4:2; Phil 2:3). Here, however, the context strongly suggests that the word is being used in a negative sense, presumably carrying the same meaning as it does in v. 23, where it is used in close connection with "self-made religion" and "harsh treatment of the body," suggesting that what Paul has in mind is a pattern of ascetic practices designed to cultivate self-humiliation through denial of bodily appetites and desires.

Within the philosophy that Paul is describing here, these practices of self-humiliation are connected with visionary and/or cultic experiences of some sort, which he refers to by the phrase "worship of angels" (*thrēskeia tōn angelōn*). The principal issue over which commentators on this verse divide is the question of whether the construction should be understood as a subjective genitive (i.e., "the worship that angels perform" [in which the teachers participate through their visionary experiences]) or an objective genitive (i.e., "worship directed toward angels").

Those who argue for the subjective genitive interpretation (e.g., Dunn 1996, 179–82) point to instances in which Old Testament and Second Temple Jewish writers speak about the participation of humans in the worshiping activities of angels (e.g., Isa 6:2-3; Apoc. Ab. 17–18; T. Job 48–50) and the unbending opposition of Old Testament and Second Temple Jewish texts to the idea that angels themselves, or any other celestial beings, should be the recipients of human worship (e.g., Deut 4:19; Jer 8:2; Apoc. Zeph. 6:15).

Proponents of the objective genitive interpretation point out in response that none of the depictions of heavenly worship appealed to in the Second Temple Jewish literature make use of *thrēskeia* in a subjective genitive construction to speak of the worship offered by angels (or any other celestial beings); they also point to instances in which *thrēskeia* can be used to refer to acts of invocation and conjuration, without any necessary element of cultic devotion, opening up the possibility of a scenario in which the proponents of a philosophy derived principally from a Jewish source have incorporated elements of local Phrygian folk religion into a syncretistic pattern of mystical practice (see especially Arnold 1996, 8–102).

It is difficult to decide between the two alternatives, but the arguments in favor of the subjective genitive interpretation are marginally stronger. Further support for this interpretation can be found in the analogies it allows us to draw with passages in the extant writings of Hellenistic Jewish authors in which ascetic practice and devotion to Torah (framed as a pathway to wisdom and self-mastery) are combined with accounts of heavenly ascents and visionary experiences, all within an integrated pattern of religious practice and rhetoric (e.g., Philo, *Dreams* 1.25-36; *Moses* 2.67-70, quoted in McKnight 2018, 273–74). Whichever alternative is decided on, however, the main point of Paul's description of the teachers of the philosophy as "delighting in . . . the worship of angels" does not appear to be that they were seeking to recruit the readers into the experience that is being referred to; Paul's focus, rather, appears to have been on the role that "worship of angels" played within the boasts the teachers made about their own experiences and credentials, reinforcing their authority to impose upon the Colossians the ascetic disciplines that they advocated.

Paul's focus on the boasts of the philosophy's proponents continues in the second and third participial clauses of that make up the remainder of v. 18. The second clause depicts the teachers as "going into detail about the things [they have] seen"—a description that almost certainly refers to the things that have been seen in visionary experiences, given the immediate context with its reference to "the worship of angels." The participle *embateuōn* (translated here as "going into detail") is formed from a verb whose primary sense is "enter into." Some commentators (e.g., Arnold 1996, 104–57; Lohse 1971, 114) point to the fact that it (or other similar verbs such as *eiserchomai*) can on occasion be used to speak of initiation into a mystery cult or the entry of a seer into the realm in which their visions took place (e.g., 1 En. 14:13; Apuleius, *Metam.* 11.23). Tempting as that theory is, it does not sit neatly with the present-tense form of the participle or the function of the clause as an elaboration on the principal clause, "Let no one disqualify you. . . ." For that reason, the more likely meaning of the word in this context is the idiomatic sense that can it can sometimes have as a way of speaking about a person "going into detail" about a subject that they are describing at length (Moo 2008, 227–29; Harris 2010, 108).

The verse concludes with a third participial clause, "puffed up without reason by the mind of his flesh," which uses a favorite image of Paul's for the unwarranted boasting of those who are "puffed up" (*physioumenos*) with a sense of self-importance based on the special knowledge and spiritual experience that they claim (cf. 1 Cor 4:18-19; 8:1; 13:4). Despite the pretensions of the teachers to exalted spiritual experiences, their claims are dismissed by

Paul as "without reason" (*eikē*), deriving not from the Spirit but from "the mind of [the] flesh."

2:19. The fourth participial clause, in v. 19, points to the fundamental deficiency in the pattern of spirituality modeled by the teachers of the philosophy: "and not holding fast to the Head, from whom the whole body, nourished and held together through its joints and ligaments, grows with a growth that is from God." Here, as was the case in the threefold series of descriptions of the teachers in v. 8 ("according to . . ."; "according to . . ."; "and not according to Christ"), the culminating description of the teachers themselves focuses on the Christological deficit at the heart of their philosophy. The language Paul uses in describing that deficiency ("not holding fast [*kratōn*] to the head") makes use of a verb (*krateuō*) that is frequently, though not invariably, used to speak of a person continuing to hold on firmly to something (e.g., LXX Song 3:4; Mark 7:3; 2 Thess 2:15; cf. BDAG, s.v. "*krateō*," 6.a). If that is the sense in which it is used here (and the head/body image that follows seems to fit better with "hold fast" than with "seize hold"), the implication would appear to be that the teachers at one point were people who professed faith in Christ and belonged to the community of the church—a scenario, if true, that would help to explain the extent to which the philosophy they advocated had captured the attention and interest of the Colossian believers.

The failure of the teachers to hold on to Christ is no small thing: Christ, as Paul goes on to remind the readers, is "the Head, from whom the whole body, nourished and held together through its joints and ligaments, grows with a growth that is from God." The way the image of Christ as "head" (*kephalē*) functions here is closely similar to the way it functions in Eph 4:15-16, with the accent falling on the role of the head as a source of nourishment and strength to the rest of the body. Here too, as there, the description of the body that is joined to the head highlights not only its growth but also its unity and coherence—"held together through its joints and ligaments." The impact of the philosophy advocated by the teachers is therefore doubly injurious—it diverts its adherents away from the indispensable source of life and growth on which the people of Christ depend, and it tears apart the unity of the body, undoing the unifying work that the gospel performs.

2:20. The final paragraph of the chapter, in vv. 20-23, draws to a fitting conclusion the warning section that was introduced in v. 8. Having addressed the readers with a threefold series of commands/prohibitions warning against the philosophy and its teachers ("see to it that no one takes you captive . . ." [v. 8a]; "let no one pass judgment on you . . ." [v. 16a]; "let no one disqualify you . . ." [v. 18a]), Paul reinforces his point with a rhetorical question that underscores the incompatibility of the philosophy with their identity as believers in Christ: "If you died with Christ to the basic principles of the world, why, as if you were still living in the world, submit to regulations?"

Here, as was already implied earlier in vv. 11-12 by the image of the readers as having been "circumcised . . . in the circumcision of Christ" and "buried with him in baptism," the conversion/baptism of believers is pictured as an event in which they "died with Christ." The additional element of the significance of that event that is made explicit here is the fact that this participation in the death of Christ involved dying "to the basic principles of the world (*apo tōn stoicheiōn tou kosmou*)." As was the case in the previous reference to the *stoicheia tou kosmou* (v. 8), the primary focus of the context is on teachings and rules of conduct, suggesting that the *stoicheia* are to be understood not as personal, transcendent powers ("elemental spirits") but as the "basic principles" of the world order under which Christ was crucified. Because the death of Christ exhausted the penal claims and religio-political demands of that world order, believers, through their union with Christ and participation in his death, have "died to" (or, to translate the phrase more literally, "died from") those basic principles and are no longer under their jurisdiction. (Cf. the similar logic in Rom 6:1-14; 7:1-6.)

The form in which Paul poses the question (*ti . . . dogmatizesthe*) is capable of being understood and translated as a question predicated on the assumption that they are already complying with the rules of the philosophy ("why . . . do you submit to regulations?") (cf. Rom 3:7, where the word *eti* ["still"] makes it clear that this is the sense in which the question is being asked). This reading of the verse is difficult to square with the absence of a stronger and more sustained rebuke directed at the Colossians themselves; it also sits uncomfortably with the way the warning in v. 8 is framed, not as a call for the Colossians to separate themselves from a false teaching but as an encouragement to vigilance against a risk of being "take[n] . . . captive"— language that implies a scenario in which the threat is real and imminent but has not yet eventuated. The more likely function that the rhetorical question is intended to perform, then, is not as an expression of incredulity about a stance the Colossians have already adopted but as a preemptive assertion of the incongruity of adopting it ("why . . . submit to rules?"). (Cf. the hypothetical premise of the rhetorical questions in 1 Cor 10:29-30 and the reading of this verse in Hooker 1973, 317; Dunn 1996, 188, though it should be noted that a translation along these lines does not necessitate agreement with the larger reconstruction that Hooker and Dunn propose for the scenario that Paul is addressing.) For the Colossians to acquiesce in this manner to a pattern of religion that is shaped according to merely "human tradition" and "the basic principles of this world" (v. 8) would be to behave as if they were still "living in the world," with their allegiances and identity tethered to the authorities and systems of the present age, and not determined by their incorporation into Christ.

2:21. The content of the regulations advocated by the teachers of the philosophy is summed up by Paul in v. 21: "Do not handle! Do not taste! Do not touch!" Although rules and taboos against touching and eating are commonplace in a wide variety of cultural and religious contexts, the information about the Colossian philosophy that has already been conveyed in the preceding paragraphs suggests that the primary background of the prohibitions is in Torah-derived Jewish traditions. Within the context of the philosophy, regulations such as these appear to have performed multiple functions: safeguarding the purity of the philosophy's adherents, inscribing the boundaries of communal membership (cf. v. 11), preparing worshipers for visionary experiences (cf. v. 18), and paving a path toward mastery over the passions. The fact that Paul introduces this section of the letter by describing the teaching he is warning against as a "philosophy" (v. 8) and concludes it by asserting that "these, while having a reputation for wisdom . . . are of no value in dealing with the indulgence of the flesh" (v. 23) suggests that it is the last of these functions—prohibitions and abstentions as a strategy for attaining mastery over the passions—that is uppermost in his mind as he describes and warns against the pattern of rule-keeping that is being advocated to the Colossians.

2:22. Verses 22-23 offer three interrelated reasons that the Colossians should not acquiesce to the judgments of the philosophy's teachers and submit themselves to their rules. The first two reasons, in v. 22, focus on the merely physical and perishable matters and the merely human origins and structures from which the rules derive their authority: "which are all referring to things that perish with use, according to human precepts and teachings." On both of these issues Paul's criticism is similar to the criticism leveled by Jesus against Pharisaic purity customs in Mark 7:1-23. Jesus' criticism of the Pharisees for elevating human tradition over the commands of God is buttressed by a quotation from Isa 29:13, and the final phrase of that quotation (*didaskontes didaskalias entalmata anthrōpōn*, "teaching [as] doctrines the precepts of humans"; Mk 7:7b) closely resembles Paul's language in v. 22b (*kata ta entalmata kai didaskalias tōn anthrōpōn*, "according to human precepts and teachings"). The preceding paragraphs, the larger, surrounding context of the letter as a whole, and the still larger context of the rest of his letters make it clear that Paul's problem is not with the desire for a life of everyday, embodied holiness (3:5–4:1; cf. Rom 12:1-2; Gal 5:13-26; 1 Cor

6:12-20); nor is he opposed to the idea of granting a place for human agency and responsibility in the pursuit of that goal (3:5, 8, 12; cf. Phil 2:12-13; 1 Cor 9:24-27). The focus of his criticism is on the idea that the mere regulation of outward and visible patterns of contact and consumption, through a system of rules and prohibitions, is sufficient in itself to accomplish the renewal of the heart, and on the claim that a system of humanly invented (or humanly elaborated and codified) regulations, organized around a center other than Christ (cf. v. 8b), can be imposed on others as a framework for judgment and exclusion.

2:23. Paul's third point of critique, in v. 23, focuses on the efficacy (or, rather, the inefficacy) of the regulations that the teachers of the philosophy are advocating: "These, while having a reputation for wisdom in self-made religion and self-humiliation and harsh treatment of the body, are of no value in dealing with the indulgence of the flesh." The syntax of this sentence is complicated and has been the subject of a good deal of scholarly debate. Some proposals can be easily dismissed (e.g., the grammatically impossible reading proposed in Foster 2016, 302–306), but deciding between the remaining options is difficult. The two strongest contenders are as follows:

(i) the interpretation that reads the main clause as a claim that the regulations *lead to* fleshly indulgence ("These . . . are [something that leads] to the indulgence of the flesh") and interpret what comes between as a concessive clause ("while having a reputation for wisdom in self-made religion and self-humiliation and harsh treatment of the body"), followed by a free-floating interjection ("—they are of no value—"); and

(ii) the interpretation that reads the main clause as a claim that the regulations fail to guard against fleshly indulgence ("These . . . are of no value in dealing with the indulgence of the flesh"), interrupted by a single concessive clause ("while having a reputation for wisdom in self-made religion and self-humiliation and harsh treatment of the body"), followed by a parenthetical extension of the concessive clause ("without any honor").

Option (i) has in its favor the fact that it reads the word *pros* in its commonest sense, as "to" or "toward" (understood here in a causative sense) and *timē* in its commonest sense as "honor" (Hollenbach 1979; Arnold 1996, 199–200). Those who argue for it can also point to the fact that Paul has already described the teachers of the philosophy in v. 18 as "puffed up . . . by the mind of their flesh." Syntactically speaking, however, the proposal that *ouk en timē tini* should be read as a parenethesis["parenthesis"?] ("without any honor") subordinated to the preceding concessive clause is somewhat forced and places additional strain on the already stretched syntax that connects *hatina estin* ("these are . . .") at the start of the verse with its complement at the end. For these reasons, among others, the majority of translations and commentaries favor option (ii), with *timē* understood as "value" (cf. BDAG, s.v. "*timē*," 1) and *pros* as "against" (cf. BDAG, s.v. "*pros*," 3.d.α) (cf. Pao 2012, 197). On this reading, the primary contrast conveyed by the syntax of the verse is between the "reputation" (*logos*) for wisdom that the regulations have and the "value" (*timē*) that they lack in reality (Pao 2012, 197). This reading of the verse also fits well with the widely held understanding in the Greco-Roman world that the primary function of "wisdom" and "philosophy" was to foster self-mastery, enabling a person to exercise control over bodily desires and appetites (cf. Rowe 2016, 31, 23–33, 40; Stowers 2016, and the references to philosophical remedies for indulgence in Philo, *Sobr.* 2.2; *Her.* 297.4; *Somn.* 1.122.7; *Contempl.* 37.6); the philosophy being promoted to the Colossians may cultivate a reputation for achieving that goal, through its practices of "self-made religion and self-humiliation and harsh treatment of the body," but its value in reality falls far short of its claims.

Therefore, if you have been raised with Christ . . . (3:1-17)

(1) Therefore, if you have been raised with Christ, seek the things above, where Christ is, seated at the right hand of God. (2) Set your minds on the things above, not on the things that are on the earth, (3) for you died, and your life is hidden with Christ in God. (4) When Christ, who is your life, is revealed, then you also will be revealed with him in glory. (5) Put to death, therefore, your earthly parts: sexual immorality, impurity, passion, evil desire, and greed (which is idolatry). (6) On account of these the wrath of God is coming [on those who are disobedient.] (7) In these you also once walked, when you were living among them. (8) But now you must put away all these things: anger, wrath, malice, slander, and filthy language from your mouth. (9) Do not lie to one another, since you have put off the old humanity with its practices (10) and have put on the new humanity, which is being renewed in knowledge according to the image of its creator. (11) Here there is no Greek and Jew, circumcised and uncircumcised, barbarian, Scythian, slave, free; but Christ is all and in all. (12) Therefore, as God's chosen ones, holy and beloved, put on compassion, kindness, humility, gentleness, and patience, (13) bearing with one another and, if anyone has a complaint against another, forgiving each other; just as the Lord has forgiven you, so you also must forgive. (14) And over all these, put on love, which is the bond of completeness. (15) And let the peace of Christ rule in your hearts, to which indeed you were called in one body. And be thankful. (16) Let the word of Christ dwell in you richly, as you teach and admonish one another in all wisdom, with gratitude singing in your hearts to God with psalms, hymns, and spiritual songs.

(17) And whatever you do, in word or deed, do all things in the name of the Lord Jesus, giving thanks to God the Father through him.

3:1. The opening of chapter 3 marks the beginning of a new subsection of the letter. The commencement of the letter body in 2:6, with a call to the readers to "walk" in a manner that is consistent with their reception of Christ Jesus as Lord, was followed almost immediately, in 2:8-23, with a warning against the "philosophy and empty deceit" that would divert them from that path. Now, in 3:1, the focus returns to a positive account of the way believers' identity and conduct are to be shaped by their participation in Christ's resurrection and their acknowledgment of him as Lord.

This is not to say that the polemics of 2:8-23 have been altogether left behind in the transition from chapter 2 to chapter 3. The final paragraph of chapter 2, in particular, lays a platform for what follows with its reminder that believers have "died with Christ to the basic principles of the world" and can therefore no longer conduct their lives "as if . . . still living in the world" (2:20). The close connection between that final paragraph of chapter 2 and the opening paragraph of chapter 3 is signaled by the conceptual and linguistic similarities between the reminder to believers in 2:20 that they "died with Christ" (*apethanete syn Christō*) and the depiction of them in 3:1 as having been "raised with Christ" (*synēgerthēte tō Christō*). It is further strengthened by the "therefore" (*oun*) in 3:1, which relies for its force on the assumption that the latter is an entailment of the former.

Reading the two paragraphs in close connection like this helps to clarify the intention of Paul's encouragement to believers in 3:1b to "seek the things above, where Christ is, seated at the right hand of God," and in 3:2 to "set your minds on the things above, not on the things that are on the earth." The teachers of the philosophy against which Paul has been warning in chapter 2 are promoting a way of life defined at a fundamental level by "the basic principles of the world" (2:20), shaped in accordance with merely human tradition (2:8). The Colossians, in contrast, are to seek as the defining goal of their lives "the things above" (that is to say, the realities associated with the place "where Christ is, seated at the right hand of God") and to shape their lives accordingly (cf. McKnight 2018, 288).

The picture of Christ as "seated at the right hand of God" echoes the language of Ps 110:1 (LXX Ps 109:1), where the invitation to sit at God's right hand comes with a promise that the enemies of the one who is honored in this way will be made "a footstool for your feet." The echo of the psalm here, therefore, carries a further reminder of the supremacy of Christ over "every ruler and authority" (2:10; cf. 1:16; Eph 1:20-23) and over the whole religio-political system that the teachers of the philosophy seek to uphold.

3:2. Verse 2 repeats the point made in v. 1, with the command to "seek the things above" (*ta anō zēteite*) giving way to the closely equivalent expression, "set your minds on the things above" (*ta anō phroneite*)—a focus that is now, in v. 2, set in explicit contrast with "the things that are on the earth." The latter expression is best understood in light of the references in 2:20-23 to "the basic principles of the world" (v. 20) and to systems of religious regulations set up "according to human precepts and teachings" (v. 22). The problem with such "earth[ly]" systems is not so much the materiality of the matters they address (though the fact that they deal, ultimately, only with things that "perish with use" has already been pointed to by Paul in 2:22 as a sign of their limitations). The larger and more basic problem with them is the fact that they are framed without reference to the rule of the risen and ascended Christ and, consequently, function to reinforce the rule of the corrupted, oppressive powers of a fallen cosmos rather than to liberate men and women from them. Paradoxically, therefore, the picture Paul paints here of a way of life determined and ruled by "the things that are on the earth" includes both the ascetic and self-humiliating disciplines of human religion and the fleshly indulgence that they claim to be a remedy for.

3:3. The reason believers should not allow their lives to be shaped and controlled by merely earthly powers and forces such as these is given in v. 3: "for you died, and your life is hidden with Christ in God." The reminder at the start of the verse that "you died" reiterates in summary form what has already been said at greater length in 2:20 ("you died with Christ to the basic principles of the world"). The statement that follows ("and your life is hidden with Christ in God") draws out the implications of 3:1a ("you have been raised with Christ") and 3:1b ("where Christ is, seated at the right hand of God") for the present existence of believers. If the ascended Christ now sits in heaven, at God's right hand, and if believers have been raised with him, then they too have a share in his exaltation and glory. The picture of the ascended Christ (and believers with him) as existing "in God" (*en tō theō*) should probably be taken in a loosely spatial sense, interpreted in light of the picture in v. 1 of Christ "seated at the right hand of God" and the parallel expression, "in glory," at the end of v. 4. Seated at the right hand of God, participating fully in the glory of the heavenly realm, Christ can be spoken of by Paul as fully, eternally, and inseparably "in God"; by virtue of their connection with him, therefore, believers too can be spoken of as being "included within the sphere of God's presence" (Beale 2019, 267).

The present situation of believers, "with Christ, in God," is not a state of affairs that is manifest to the world at large or directly, empirically verifiable by believers themselves. It is, as Paul puts it, a reality that is at present "hidden" from view; believers know it to be true not primarily on the basis of their own immediate sensory or mystical experience but on the basis of the testimony about Christ's death and resurrection (2:20; 3:1), and of the baptism and faith through which they have become participants in those events (2:11-12). In addition to this primary sense of invisibility (which Paul goes on in v. 4 to place in deliberate contrast with the manifest revelation of the age to come), the "hidden[ness]" that Paul speaks of in v. 3 is probably also intended to carry an additional sense of divine protection and security, with a possible echo of LXX Ps 26:5 (= MT Ps 27:5): "he hid me in the tabernacle in the day of my troubles" (cf. Beale 2019, 268–69 on the multiple points of correspondence between LXX Ps 26 and Col 3:1-4).

3:4. The realities that are "hidden" in the present will one day be manifest for all to see, as Paul goes on to say in v. 5: "When Christ, who is your life, is revealed, then you also will be revealed with him in glory." Because believers have been baptized into Christ, united with him in his death, burial, and resurrection, he can be spoken of by Paul not only as the one "with [whom]" their life is hidden (v. 3) but as the one who "is" their life (cf. vv. 9-11). The time to which Paul looks forward is the day of Christ's return and the general resurrection of believers (cf. Phil 3:20-21; 1 Cor 15:42, 51-53), when Christ's universal rule—at present an invisible, heavenly reality—and the vindication of his people will be manifest for all to say. On that day, believers will be revealed "with him in glory"—language that leaves room for multiple, interrelated possibilities of meaning including both a spatial sense (believers as located with Christ in the sphere of the divine presence) and a qualitative sense (believers as themselves glorified; cf. BDAG, s.v. "*en*," 2.b, and Paul's use of the same expression, *en doxē*, "in glory," in 1 Cor 15:43). The clear distinction in vv. 3-4 between the "hidden" reality of believers' present participation in the resurrection and ascension of Christ (v. 3) and the future day on which Christ (and believers with him) will be "revealed" (v. 4) is one of a number of points within Colossians at which the letter's eschatological framework leaves room for the same note of future expectation that is typically emphasized in the undisputed Pauline letters (cf. Still 2004, 128–29).

3:5. The ethical implications of the exhortations in vv. 1-2 to "seek the things above" and "set your minds on the things above, not on the things that are on the earth" are spelled out in the verses that follow, beginning with the command to the readers in v. 5 to "put to death, therefore, your earthly parts:

sexual immorality, impurity, passion, evil desire, and greed (which is idolatry)." The metaphor implied by the command to "put to death" the listed vices derives from the reminders in the preceding paragraphs that believers have "died" (2:20; 3:3) and "been raised" (3:1) with Christ. What is already true at the level of the readers' fundamental personal identity, by virtue of their incorporation into Christ, must now be expressed at the level of their conduct and in the transformation of their character (cf. Rom 6:1-14).

In describing what is to be put to death as the readers' "earthly parts," Paul uses a word (*melē*) that, when used in a literal sense, refers to the limbs and organs of the human body. Here, however, the list of vices placed in apposition to it ("sexual immorality, impurity, passion, evil desire, and greed") makes it clear that what he has in mind is not body parts *per se* or the materiality of the body as distinct from the invisible operations of the mind or soul; what he has in mind, rather, is the various faculties, functions, and dispositions of a person as they are employed in the service of "earthly" powers and influences that resist the rule of Christ (cf. the similar use of *melē* in Rom 6:19).

The particular vices that Paul selects for inclusion in the list are all sins that consist in, or arise out of, inordinate or misdirected desire. Three of the five items ("sexual immorality, impurity . . . and greed") correspond to the vices that are condemned in Eph 5:3. Here, as there, the list begins with a vice (*porneia*) that is exclusively and unambiguously sexual in nature, making use of a word that functioned in Second Temple Judaism and early Christianity as a kind of umbrella term for all forms of improper sexual activity, with marriage understood as the sole context for legitimate sexual activity (cf. the comments on Eph 5:3, above). The word *akatharsia* ("impurity") that follows next in the list is often used by Paul in close connection to *porneia* (e.g., 2 Cor 12:21; Gal 5:19) or in a context that suggests a focus on improper sexual conduct (e.g., Rom 1:24), but its range of meaning can at times be considerably broader (e.g., 1 Thess 2:3). Given the explicit generality with which the word is used in Eph 5:3 ("*all* impurity"), it seems most plausible to read it as carrying a similar breadth of meaning here. The third and fourth items, *pathos* ("passion") and *epithymia kakē* ("evil desire"), can similarly be used with a broad meaning (e.g., 4 Macc 1:1-6; Rom 7:8) or in a more narrowly sexual sense (e.g., Rom 1:26; 1 Thess 4:5). The likelihood that these terms, too, are being used by Paul in a broad rather than a narrow sense is strengthened by the fact that he concludes the list with "greed (which is idolatry)." Although it is true that the word *pleonexia* can also, at times, be used to refer to refer to sexual covetousness, it is most commonly used to refer to acquisitiveness more generally, or with particular reference to material/financial greed. The description of greed as "idolatry" strengthens the case for this interpretation, evoking the frequently stated notion in OT and Second Temple Jewish tradition that greed for money and possessions makes the objects of desire into substitutes or rivals for God himself (e.g., Job 31:24-28; Philo, *Spec. Laws* 1.23; Matt 6:24; Luke 16:13; cf. Rosner 2007, 69–100).

3:6. The urgency of Paul's call to "put to death" the vices listed in v. 5 is underlined in v, 6: "On account of these the wrath of God is coming [on the sons of disobedience]." The wording of Paul's warning is closely similar to the wording of the warning in Eph 5:6, and here, as there, the present-tense description of the wrath of God as "coming" is probably best taken not as a reference to the present manifestation of God's wrath (cf. Rom 1:18-32) but as a way of speaking about a future, eschatological judgment that is on its way but has not yet arrived (e.g., 1 Thess 1:10) (cf. Moo 2008, 259). The phrase at the end of the verse specifying the objects of God's coming wrath as "the sons of disobedience" is included in many early manuscripts of Colossians but omitted in $\mathfrak{P}^{46}$ and B. The shorter reading has in its favor the argument that it is easier to imagine a copyist inserting the extra phrase to conform to the familiar wording of Eph 5:6 than it is explain why a copyist might have deliberately or inadvertently omitted the phrase, had it been original (Beale 2019, 288). If the shorter reading were the original, however, it would be difficult to explain the "you also" (*kai hymeis*) in the following verse, and the "in them" (*en hois*) and "among them" (*en toutois*) of v. 7 would both need to be taken, somewhat redundantly, as referring back to the list of vices in (v. 5. For those reasons, therefore, the longer reading is probably to be preferred and "upon the sons of disobedience" taken as original (cf. Metzger 1994, 624–25; Wilson 2005, 246, both somewhat tentatively). Here, as in Eph 2:2 and 5:6, the phrase employs a traditional Hebraic idiom (roughly equivalent in meaning to "disobedient people") to refer to the unconverted Gentiles among whom the readers of the letter were once numbered.

3:7. If (as argued above) the longer reading of v. 6 is to be accepted as original, then v. 7 extends the thought of that verse by making explicit its connection to the pre-conversion lives of the readers. The opening phrase, *en hois*, is grammatically ambiguous. If *hois* is read as a neuter plural, its antecedent is the list of vices in v. 5 and the phrase should be translated as "in which"; alternatively, if *hois* is read as a masculine plural, then its antecedent is "the sons of disobedience" (v. 6) and the phrase should be translated as "among whom." A similar question is raised by the phrase *en toutois* at the end of the verse, which could also be read as either neutral plural ("in them [i.e., those vices]") or masculine plural ("among them [i.e., those people]").

In the closely similar set of linked statements in Eph 2:1-3, both ideas are present and stated in close succession: ". . . you were dead your trespasses and sins, in which (*en hais*) you once walked, . . . according to the spirit that is now at work among the sons of disobedience, among whom (*en hois*) we too all once conducted our lives." Here in v. 7, our decision about how best to read the *en hois* at the start of the verse is assisted by the "you also" (*kai hymeis*) that follows immediately after it, suggesting that what can be said of "the sons of disobedience" (v. 6) can also be said of "you" (v. 7) and tipping the scales in favor of translating *en hois* as "in which," referring back to the vices that were listed in v. 5. If the *en toutois* at the end of the verse adds a new thought and is not merely a repetition of the same idea, it should be read as a masculine plural and translated as "among them," referring to "the sons of disobedience" as the community to which the readers belonged before their incorporation into Christ (cf. NRSV fn: "when you were living among such people").

3:8. Although that way of life was characteristic of the readers' past, it must not continue to be so. The "once" (*pote*) of v. 7 is immediately contrasted with a "but now" (*nyni de*) in v. 8: "But now you must put away all these things: anger, wrath, malice, slander, and filthy language from your mouth." The verb that Paul uses to tell the readers to "put away" (*apothesthe*) is the same as the verb used in Eph 4:22 to introduce the change of clothing metaphor that he employs in 4:22-24. Its normal meaning is, however, quite broad and is not confined to the putting off of clothing, and even in the Eph 4:22-24 context, it is only in retrospect, once we have read the unambiguously clothing-related language of v. 24, that we can discern the presence of a clothing metaphor in v. 22. Here in Colossians 3, the "put[ting] away" that is in view in v. 8 is best understood in a broad and general sense, and it is the introduction of the verb *apekdyomai* ("put off [clothing]") in the following verse that establishes the change of clothing metaphor.

Unlike the first vice list in v. 5, which focused on sins of desire in its depiction of the pre-conversion lives of the readers, the list in v. 8 focuses on sins of anger and speech. The first four items on the list ("anger, wrath, malice, slander") all occur in Eph 4:31. Here, as there, the intended effect of the list is probably not to arrange the items into a precisely calibrated taxonomy or gradation but simply to create emphasis by accumulating a collection of near synonyms. The fourth item, "slander" (*blasphēmia*), can sometimes be used to speak of blasphemies directed against God, but its context here suggests that the primary sense in view is slanderous speech directed against fellow humans (cf. Rom 3:8; 1 Tim 6:4). The final word in the list, *aischrologia* ("filthy language"), is generally used with a meaning that focuses on the scurrilous or obscene nature of the speech that is being described, but its juxtaposition in this verse with "anger," "wrath," "malice," and "slander" probably implies that Paul's primary interest here is not in scurrility or obscenity *per se*, but in their use as verbal weapons directed against others in a malicious or defamatory attack (cf. BDAG, s.v. "*aischrologia*").

3:9-10. The focus on sins of speech with which v. 8 concludes, with its reference to "slander and filthy language from your mouth," continues in vv. 9-10, which issue the readers with a further command ("Do not lie to one another") and remind them of the basis for it in the transformation of identity that they have undergone in their conversion ("since you have put off the old humanity with its practices and have put on the new humanity, which is being renewed in knowledge according to the image of its creator"). As was the case with the command to put away filthy language in the preceding verse, the prohibition on lying is oriented primarily toward the socially corrosive dimension of the practice that is being condemned. There are, no doubt, many good arguments that could be made in favor of truth-telling in the abstract, as a general principle, but here in this verse the focus of Paul's condemnation is on the anti-social intentions and effects of lying "to one another" (cf. the focus of the ninth commandment on false witness that is borne "against your neighbor" and the similar focus implied in the language used by Paul in Eph 4:25).

The change of identity that Paul reminds his readers of in vv. 9b-10 is described using language that implies a change of clothing metaphor ("since you have put off [*apekdysamenoi*] . . . and have put on [*endysamenoi*]"). Here, as is the case in the closely similar reminder that Paul gives his readers in Eph 4:22-24, Paul uses these verbs with a personal object—"the old humanity (*ton palaion anthrōpon*)" and "the new [humanity] (*ton neon [anthrōpon]*)"— an idiom that is rare and, when it does occur, is generally used in a theatrical context (either literal or metaphorical) (cf. Starling 2019). If, as seems likely, the same theatrical background stands behind the metaphor here, the change of clothing that Paul refers to is to be understood as a change of costume and character; Paul is reminding his readers that they have laid aside the role of the old, fallen humanity and have put on in its place the role of the new humanity created by God in Christ. The choice made by the majority of English versions to translate Paul's *palaios anthrōpos* and *neos [anthrōpos]* as "old self" and "new self" is an understandable one, but it runs the risk of conveying a misleadingly individualistic impression: if the closely similar language Paul uses in Eph 2:15 is any guide, the "new self" (or, better, "new humanity") in view here as the identity that believers have been granted in Christ is an irreducibly communal reality, forged through the bringing together of Jew and Gentile in one redeemed community.

With that change of identity goes a corresponding change of character. This is described in v. 9 as something that has already taken place in principle, when (at the point of their conversion) the readers put off the old humanity "with its practices." It is also, however, to be understood as a process of transformation that is to continue in the present—a reality that is implied in v. 10 by the description of the new humanity as "being renewed in knowledge according to the image of its creator." The renewal that Paul speaks of here is renewal "in knowledge" (*eis gnōsin*); the fact that Paul chooses the preposition *eis* (which commonly carries the sense of "for" or "into") rather than *en* ("in" or "by") suggests that he is thinking of knowledge here not as the means by which the renewal takes place but as the goal toward which the process of renewal is directed (cf. 1:9-10; Eph 1:17).

The renewed humanity into which Paul tells the readers they are being formed is shaped "according the image of its creator"—language that evokes an obvious echo of Gen 1:26-27 and (within the closer context of Colossians itself) the assertion in 1:15 that Christ himself is "the image of the invisible God, the firstborn of all creation." This latter, closer echo would suggest that what God is at work to create in his people is not merely a backward-looking restoration of the lost glories of Adam but a forward-looking renewal of his people into the likeness of the risen Christ (cf. Rom 8:29; 1 Cor 15:49; 2 Cor 3:18).

3:11. The irreducibly communal nature of the "new humanity" that Paul refers to in v. 10 is further confirmed in v. 11, where the particle *hopou* ("Here") that begins the verse looks back to the new humanity of the previous verse as its antecedent and goes on to describe it as a place in which "there is no Greek and Jew, circumcised and uncircumcised, barbarian, Scythian, slave, free; but Christ is all and in all." The list of (mostly) contrastive pairs that Paul provides here to illustrate the divisions that are erased by the gospel is noticeably similar to the list in Gal 3:28 ("There is neither Jew nor Greek, slave nor free, no male and female, for you are all one in Christ Jesus"), though here in Colossians the Greek/Jew pairing is amplified by the addition of a closely similar circumcised/uncircumcised pair following immediately after it, the male/female pairing is omitted, and a new barbarian/Scythian pairing introduced.

The first two pairs in the list have an obvious relevance to the context of the readers, in which a philosophy is being propagated that places heavy emphasis on religious practices and abstentions originating in Old Testament teaching and Jewish tradition (cf. 2:8-23). The relevance of the third pair ("barbarian, Scythian") is less easy to discern. Douglas Campbell's theory (Campbell 1996) that "barbarian" connotes "free" and "Scythian" connotes "slave" (establishing a chiasm with the "slave, free" that follows) is an intriguing possibility, but the evidence he offers for a widespread association between these ideas in popular usage is thin. The simpler and more likely explanation is that Paul's thought is moving along a similar trajectory to the one that he follows in Rom 1:14, where "Greeks and barbarians" is placed in parallel with "wise and foolish." On this reading, "barbarian" and "Scythian" are an elaboration on the previous categories of "Greek" and "uncircumcised," playing on the stereotypical Greek view of the barbarian (and, still more, the Scythian) as linguistically alien and philosophically unlearned. The relevance of these categories within the context Paul is addressing in Colossae would have been heightened by the presence of a teaching that presented itself as a "philosophy" (2:8) and was propagated by teachers who, according to Paul, were "puffed up" in their own estimation by the wisdom they claimed to possess (2:18).

Closely related to the distinctions of culture and education suggested by the categories of "Greek," "barbarian," and "Scythian" is the distinction of social and economic status suggested by the final pairing, "slave" and "free." When Paul makes reference in his letters to the distinctions that are abolished by the gospel, the slave/free pairing is frequently juxtaposed with the distinction between Jew/circumcised and Greek/uncircumcised (e.g., Gal 3:28; 1 Cor 7:17-24; 12:13). If the latter distinction was fundamental for the ethno-religious construction of the world (viewed through Jewish eyes), the former was fundamental to its socioeconomic order; the presence of slave and free at the same table was as shocking a feature of early Christianity as was the table fellowship of Jew and Gentile.

The erasure of all these divisions within the "new humanity" that believers have become participants in is grounded in the fact that—as Paul reminds his readers in the final line of the verse—"Christ is all and in all." There is a sense in which this is (originally and ultimately) true for the whole of the cosmos, as Paul has already asserted in 1:16-17. Paul's primary focus in 3:11, however, is not on that larger, cosmic reality but on what is true "here," within the new humanity that has been inaugurated (and is in the process of being fully realized) in the church.

Just as significant as the variations Paul makes here in Colossians to the set of contrastive pairs that he borrows from Gal 3:28 is the change he makes to the formula's placement within the argument of the letter. In Galatians, the formula is placed within the context of an argument against the claim of the agitators that Gentiles must undergo circumcision before they can be included among the covenant people of God. Here in Colossians, however, it is placed not within the polemics of chapter 2 but in the midst of the ethical instruction that Paul gives to his readers in chapter 3. The gospel's erasure of the hostilities and divisions of the old humanity is not only the basis on which Gentiles are accepted into the covenant community; it is also fundamental to the way of life that those who enter into that community are called to live.

3:12. The ethical implications of inclusion in the covenant people are spelled out further in the following verses, with the "therefore" (*oun*) that joins v. 12 to v. 11 making that logic explicit. The readers, who have "put off the old humanity" and "put on the new," are to understand themselves, in consequence, as constituting "God's chosen ones, holy and beloved." All three of these terms echo language used in the Old Testament for the nation of Israel, whose covenant relationship with YHWH made them his "chosen ones" (e.g., Ps 105:6, 43 [LXX Ps 104:6, 43]; Isa 43:20), "holy" (e.g., Exod 19:6; Deut 7:6; 14:2), and "beloved" (Deut 4:37; Ps 78:68 [LXX Ps 77:68]). Through their incorporation into Christ, the readers have now entered into those covenant privileges and possess that identity.

As the chosen, holy, and beloved people of God, the readers are to clothe themselves with the virtues that correspond to that identity. The clothing metaphor Paul uses here is an extension of the metaphor already introduced in vv. 9-10; having "put on" the new humanity, the readers are to "put on compassion, kindness, humility, gentleness, and patience" as the dispositions in which the ethos of the new humanity is manifested.

"Compassion" (*splanchna oiktirmou*: literally, "bowels of mercy") heads the list, evoking a quality that is most commonly attributed in NT and LXX usage to God himself (e.g., Rom 12:1; 2 Cor 1:3; Ps 103:4 [LXX 102:4]) and calling on the readers to imitate it in their own affections and actions. "Kindness" (*chrēstotēs*), similarly, is a word commonly used in LXX and NT for the generous and merciful initiatives taken by God in saving and caring for his people (e.g., Ps 31:19 [LXX Ps 30:30]; Eph 2:7; Titus 3:4); this, too, is to be imitated by believers as a characteristic disposition of those who belong to the community formed by the generosity and love of God.

"Humility" (*tapeinophrosynē*), the third item on the list, carries a somewhat more complex set of connotations. In Greco-Roman usage it typically implies a negative evaluation of the person to whom it is attributed and carries a meaning of servility or lack of self-respect (cf. Epictetus, *Diatr.* 3.24.54–58; Josephus, *J.W.* 4.9.2). In Jewish and early Christian usage, it carries positive connotations and is used to speak of the proper humility that the righteous feel before God and manifest in their dealings with others, both of which are crystallized in the example given to believers by the self-humbling obedience of Christ (cf. the use of the cognate verb in LXX Ps 130:2 [MT Ps 131:2]; Phil 2:8). "Gentleness" (*prautēs*), similarly, can be used to speak of a disposition of believers that is cultivated in conscious imitation of Christ; in Jewish and early Christian usage its meaning embraces both an inward meekness of spirit (e.g., Sir 45:4) and an outward gentleness in speech and action (e.g., Sir 4:8). "Patience" (*makrothymia*), the final item in the list, is a word that is frequently used to describe the longsuffering forbearance that God shows to his people (e.g., LXX Isa 57:15; Rom 2:4); when it is used in reference to believers (e.g., 2 Cor 6:6; Gal 5:22; 2 Tim 4:2; Col 1:11; Eph 4:2) it carries a similar meaning (unlike the other commonly used word for patience, *hypomonē*, which typically refers to the steadfast endurance that bears up under adverse circumstances and waits for divine deliverance).

3:13. As is the case in the closely similar exhortations Paul gives to his readers in Eph 4:2, the attributes of "humility, gentleness, and patience" are unpacked in v. 13a in terms of the mutual forbearance that believers are to show toward one another, passing over the small offenses and irritations that are a recurring feature of life in community with others. Closely related to this habitual practice of "bearing with one another" in such small matters is a willingness, in cases where a larger grievance arises ("if anyone has a complaint [*momphē*] against another"), to approach the resolution of the grievance in a manner that leads to the possibility of forgiveness and reconciliation. The model for such an approach to the resolution of grievances is to be found in the gracious forgiveness that believers have received from Christ: "just as the Lord has forgiven you," Paul reminds the readers in v. 13b, "so you also must forgive." (The similarly worded reminder in Eph 4:32 speaks of the gracious act of "God in Christ"; here in Col 3:13, however, "the Lord" is probably referring to the Lord Jesus as the agent of forgiveness, in line with usage elsewhere in the letter [cf. 1:3; 2:6; 3:17]).

3:14. After the parenthetical elaboration on forgiveness in v. 13b, v. 14 resumes and completes the sentence that was commenced in v. 12: "And over all these [put on] love, which is the bond of completeness." Given the context of the extended clothing metaphor introduced in vv. 9-10 and continued in v. 12, the phrase "over all these" (*epi pasin . . . toutois*) is probably best taken as a further development of that metaphor, with "all these" referring back to the listed virtues of v. 12 and "over" (*epi*) encouraging us to think of love as a metaphorical mantle or belt that holds the rest of the garments in place and connects them all together. A metaphor of this sort fits well with the further description of love in the second half of the verse, where Paul tells us it is "the bond of completeness" (*syndesmos tēs teleiotētos*). The word *syndesmos* has already been used in 2:19 to refer to the ligaments that connect the limbs of a body together; it is used in a similar context but a slightly more abstract sense in Eph 4:3 speak about the "bond of peace" in which believers are to maintain the unity with one another that is granted to them by the Spirit. Here, the "completeness" (*teleiotēs*) that is fostered by or consists in love could possibly be referring to the harmonious relationships that love fosters within the body (cf. "the bond of peace" in Eph 4:3) (Pao 2012, 245). The presence of the elaborate and developed clothing metaphor in vv. 9-14, however, suggests that it is more likely referring to the complete and harmonious interrelationship of the virtues, with love summing up and integrating all the others (cf. 1 Cor 13; Rom 13:8-10, and the description in Simplicius, *In Epict. Ench.* 37.279 of friendship as the "bond of all the virtues").

3:15. Verse 15 commences with a new sentence, framed as a third person imperative: "And let the peace of Christ rule in your hearts, to which indeed you were called in one body." The idea is, however, closely related to the thoughts of the preceding verses. The new humanity with which believers are to clothe themselves is shaped and defined by the rule of the risen Christ. The ideas of "peace" and "rule" are closely connected within the thought world of Paul and his readers. The messianic promises that Christ fulfilled speak of him as "Prince of Peace" (Isa 9:5-6; cf. Mic 5:5 [LXX Mic 5:4]), and the imperial propaganda of Rome promoted the idea that peace and Roman rule were inseparable blessings. For believers in Christ, it is "the peace of Christ" (i.e., the peace established by Christ's victory over the powers) that is to rule over the hearts of believers. The verb *brabeuō* that Paul uses here to speak of the "rule" of Christ and his peace is the simple version of the compound verb *katabrabeuō*, which he used in the previous chapter to speak of the attempts made by the proponents of the philosophy he is warning against to "disqualify" those who do not comply with their regulations and prohibitions. Paul's use of the related word here, therefore, may carry an echo of the polemics in the previous chapter, reminding readers that it is Christ's peace, not the elitist and divisive teachings of the philosophy (or the "rulers and authorities" whose authority stands behind them), that is to exercise sway over their hearts.

Peace is not only the objective state of affairs established by Christ's victory and rule; it is also the way of life to which believers have been "called" (*eklēthēte*) "in one body" (*en heni sōmati*). The logic of Paul's exhortation here is a compressed version of the logic of Eph 4:1-6, where believers are reminded of the way of life to which they have been "called" (*eklēthēte*) in the gospel, encouraged in consequence to be "eager to keep the unity of the Spirit in the bond of peace" (v. 3) and reminded that "[there is] one body (*hen sōma*) and one spirit, just as you were called in one hope that belongs to your calling" (v. 4). As is the case in Ephesians, the image of the "one body" of the church can be used to speak of the universal or heavenly church (e.g., 1:18; 2:19), but its use in contexts such as this still implies that the primary context in which the peace of Christ is to be manifested is the local community of believers, as its members manifest the dispositions and behaviors called for in vv. 12-14 in their day-to-day dealings with one another. Here in col 3:15, the call to live under the rule of Christ's peace is followed immediately by a call to thankfulness—a compactly expressed reminder that the peace they have been granted in the gospel is a generous gift of God, calling for a pervasive and enduring response of gratitude on their part (cf. 1:3, 12; 2:7; 3:16, 17; 4:2).

3:16. The third person imperative of v. 15 ("Let the peace of Christ . . . rule in your hearts") is followed by another, loosely parallel third person imperative ("Let the word of Christ dwell . . .") in v. 16. "The word of Christ" is probably intended by Paul to be understood not as a subjective genitive (i.e., "the message spoken by Christ") but as an objective genitive (i.e. "the message about Christ"), in line with the earlier reference in 1:5 to "the true message of the gospel" (*tō logō tēs alētheias tou euangeliou*). Just as the word of the gospel was pictured in 1:5-6 as an active subject, "bearing fruit and growing in all the world," here in 3:16 it is pictured as making its home within the community of the church, "dwelling" in the hearts of believers (cf. v. 15) and pervasively present in their speech and song (v. 16b) (Pao 2012, 248). The description of the word as dwelling "richly" (*plousiōs*) within the community implies a sense of abundance and plurality, which Paul goes on to develop in the second half of the verse.

The participial clauses that make up the remainder of the verse ("as you teach and admonish one another in all wisdom, with gratitude singing in your hearts to God with psalms, hymns, and spiritual songs") are closely similar to the series of clauses in Eph 5:19-21 that follow Paul's command to the readers in v. 18 to "be filled with the Spirit." Here, as there, the function of the participial clauses is elaborative, painting a picture of what it looks like (in this case) for the word of Christ to "dwell richly" in the community. The first of these clauses ("as you teach and admonish one another in all wisdom") recalls the earlier description of Paul's own ministry in 1:28 ("admonishing everyone and teaching everyone in all wisdom"); here, however, the teaching and admonishing are pictured as being the work of the whole community as its members minister to one another regarding the gospel and its wisdom.

The wording of the remainder of the verse raises several questions about the meaning of its component parts and their relationship to one other. One frequently discussed issue is the meaning of the "psalms," "hymns," and "spiritual songs" that Paul goes on to refer to, with commentators typically distinguishing between the Old Testament derived "psalms" and newly composed "hymns" and "spiritual songs" (or "songs from the Spirit") (e.g., Witherington 2007, 181; McKnight 2018, 332–33). It is unlikely, however, that Paul has in mind a sharp set of distinctions between the three categories. As Beale points out, all three of the Greek words that stand behind these terms (*psalmoi, hymnoi,* and *ōdai*) can be found within the ancient Greek translations of the Psalter as roughly interchangeable descriptions of same psalms (e.g., LXX Pss 66:1; 75:1; cf. Beale 2019, 304–307), and all three are said by Paul to be forms in which "the word of Christ" resonates within the congregations, suggesting that even when the canonical songs from the Psalter are sung, they are appropriated and understood within a larger frame of Christological fulfillment.

The more difficult question to resolve is whether the "psalms, hymns, and spiritual songs" that Paul refers to should be read as a description of the means through which the congregation members teach and admonish one another (e.g., NIV; cf. McKnight 2018, 331–32; Pao 2012, 248–49) or as the content (or better, perhaps, in view of the dative cases of the three nouns, the form) of what they sing to God (e.g., NRSV, ESV; cf. Harris 2010, 167; Lohse 1971, 151). The NIV's rendering of the verse has the advantage of corresponding more closely to the way the congregation's singing is presented within the parallel passage in Eph 5:19, where the psalms, hymns, and spiritual songs are spoken "among yourselves" (*heautois*). On the other hand, the fact that Col 3:16 pictures the congregation members not merely "speaking" to one another (cf. Eph 5:19; *lalountes*) but "teach[ing] and admonish[ing] . . . in all wisdom" (cf. the language of 1:28) suggests something more is involved than merely the singing of songs, and it tips the balance in favor of a rendition of the verse along the lines of the ESV or NRSV. Nevertheless, as noted above, the singing that is described in v. 16b (no less than the teaching and admonition in v. 16a) is still presented as one of the forms in which the word of Christ "dwell[s] richly" within the congregation, suggesting that the content of the "psalms, hymns, and spiritual songs" to which Paul is referring contains a solid core of declarative praise that reiterates and celebrates the message of the gospel and functions, in its own way, as a further form of mutual catechesis.

The voiced praises and mutual encouragements that the congregation members convey to one another through their singing do not exhaust the function that the songs perform; believers, as they sing, are directing their words not only to each other but "to God," and they are singing not only with their voices but in their hearts, giving expression in song to the gratitude (*charis*) that they return to God for his grace extended in Christ (cf. the exhortation to thankfulness that concludes the previous verse).

3:17. The paragraph concludes in v. 17, with a statement that is unmistakeably comprehensive and climactic in the way it is framed: "And whatever you do, in word or deed, do all things in the name of the Lord Jesus, giving thanks to God the Father through him." The comprehensive scope of the exhortation is underlined by the repetition of "whatever" (*pan*) and "all things" (*panta*), a comprehensiveness that is further spelled out by the intervening phrase, "in word or deed" (*en logō ē en ergō*): not only is the speaking and singing of the congregation members a manifestation of the word of Christ; their deeds, too, are to be performed "in the name of the Lord Jesus." Speaking and acting "in the name of" a person can be understood in a variety of ways, the commonest of which implies a relationship of representation and/or authorization (e.g., Deut 18:20, 22; 1 Sam 25:9; Mic 4:5; 2 Thess 3:6). To speak and act "in the name of the Lord Jesus" is to serve as his representative, constrained and authorized by his rule and conveying his action and speech to others (cf. Dunn 1996, 241, who frames the meaning in terms of "a consciousness of commissioning, of acting on behalf of, in the power of"). In all things, too, believers' speech and action are to be accompanied and undergirded by the thanksgiving that Paul has already called for in both of the previous two verses. Just as the speech and action of believers toward one another and their neighbors are to be "in the name of the Lord Jesus," so the thanksgiving that they offer to the Father is to be "through him"—language that expresses the centrality of Christ's mediation in the prayer and worship of believers (cf. Rom 1:8; Eph 2:18).

Wives . . . Husbands . . . Children . . . Fathers . . . Slaves . . . Masters (3:18–4:1)

(3:18) Wives, submit to your husbands, as is fitting in the Lord. (19) Husbands, love your wives and do not be embittered against them. (20) Children, obey your parents in everything, for this is pleasing in the Lord. (21) Fathers, do not provoke your children, so that they do not lose heart. (22) Slaves, obey your fleshly masters in everything, not in eye-service, as people-pleasers, but in singleness of heart, fearing the Lord. (23) Whatever you do, do it from the heart, as for the Lord and not for people, (24) knowing that from the Lord you will receive the reward of inheritance. Serve the Lord Christ. (25) For the wrongdoer will be paid back for his wrong, and there is no partiality. (4:1) Masters, provide for your slaves justice and equality, knowing that you also have a Master in heaven.

3:18. Within 3:1-17, as Paul begins the section of the letter in which he exhorts his readers to shape their lives in accordance with the reign of the risen Jesus and their shared identity as the "new humanity" that God has created in him, his initial focus is on the unity and solidarity with which they share together in that identity. The community is to understand itself as "one body" (3:15), demonstrating and preserving that unity through its relationships of peace (3:15) and mutual love (3:14). All the things that are said and done by all the members of the community are to be said and done in one name—that of the Lord Jesus (3:17). Within this community, as Paul reminds them in v. 11, "Christ is all, and in all."

But within that unity there is a diversity of ways in which the community's various members demonstrate, in the shape of their relationships with one another, the fact that Christ is present among them by his word. In Ephesians, the diversity within the one body of the church is articulated initially in terms of the differing gifts that Christ has apportioned (Eph 4:7-16) and only subsequently in terms of their differentiated social roles (Eph 5:21–6:9). Here in Colossians 3, however, Paul's thought turns directly to the various roles that believers fill within the household, in each of which (in varied and reciprocating patterns of action) they are to relate to one another in ways that are "fitting in the Lord" (3:18).

The form in which he frames these instructions in 3:18–4:1 is a "household code"—a form that appears to have originated within early Christianity as a distinctively Christian contribution to the widely discussed *topos* of household management that was touched on by numerous political and moral philosophers and advice givers within various strands of Hellenistic Judaism and the Greco-Roman tradition. (For a discussion of the relationship between the Pauline household codes and the household management *topos* as it was dealt with in the broader cultural context, see the introductory comments on Eph 5:21–6:9 above.)

Here in Colossians, while the structure and sequence of the household code are identical to the structure and sequence of the Ephesian code, with paired sets of exhortations directed in turn to wives and husbands, children and fathers, and slaves and masters, the content is considerably less detailed (especially in the case of the words to husbands and wives and children and fathers), and a good deal less is said about the way the instructions Paul gives relate to the teachings of the Old Testament or the theological vision laid out in the preceding chapters. If, as I have argued above in the introduction to Ephesians, it is plausible to equate the letter that Paul goes on to refer to in 4:16 as "the letter from Laodicea" with the circular homily that we know as Ephesians, then readers of Colossians (both ancient and modern) are encouraged by the text to fill out the sparse and summary directions that Paul gives here in 3:18–4:1 with the more nuanced and expansive elaborations to be found in the Ephesian version of the code.

To the extent that a theological rationale is expressed at all here in Colossians, within the household code itself, it is conveyed primarily by the brief references contained with the words to wives and children about what is "fitting" (3:18) and "pleasing" (3:20) in the Lord and by the recurring references to Jesus as "the Lord" (3:22, 23, 24), "the Lord Christ" (3:24), and "a Master in heaven" (4:1) that punctuate the words Paul addresses to slaves and masters. Within the various situations in which the readers are placed in the households where they live and work day by day, the instructions of the household code exhort them to relate to one another in a way that is shaped by their allegiance to Jesus as Lord, expressing that allegiance in ways that are "fitting," in light of their differentiated social roles.

The opening exhortation of the household code is addressed to wives, who are urged to "submit to your husbands, as is fitting in the Lord." As is the case in the Ephesian code, Paul uses the word "submit" (*hypotassō*) to speak of the stance that he encourages wives to adopt toward their husbands, saving the word "obey" (*hypakouō*) for vv. 20 and 22—a verbal distinction that may reflect the difference in his mind between the child-parent and slave-master relationships on the one hand and the husband-wife relationship, in which both parties are adults and neither is enslaved to the other, on the other hand. A further hint in that direction can be found in the middle-voice form of the imperative in v. 18 (*hypotassesthe*), framing the submission he is speaking of as a posture that wives themselves adopt as a free act of their own will, acknowledging the particular responsibility that has been assigned to their husbands and choosing to relate to them accordingly. This posture of free and voluntary submission, Paul goes on to say, "is fitting (*anēken*) in the Lord"—language that borrows from the vocabulary of Greco-Roman moral philosophy (used, for example, in the Stoic literature to speak of a life lived in harmony with the natural order) but bends the idea into a new shape, urging conformity to the way of life that is "fitting" within the redeemed sphere of life "in the Lord" (cf. Dunn 1996, 247–48).

3:19. Husbands, for their part, are not instructed to "rule over" or "control" their wives (as is the case, for example, in Plutarch, *Conj. praec.* 142e) but to "love" (*agapate*) them. The content of what Paul has in mind by this is not spelled out in anything like the detail we find in Eph 5:25-33, though (as suggested above) it would seem likely that Paul expected his readers in Colossae to draw on those verses to supplement and interpret the brief word to husbands that he includes here. The only detail we are given here to expand on what he has in mind is the command in v. 19b that husbands, in loving their wives, should "not be embittered (*mē pikrainesthe*) against them." (The language of most EVV, which translate Paul's command to husbands as an exhortation against dealing "harshly" with wives, runs the risk of importing the notion that husbands' primary interaction with their wives will still be the exercise of rule, albeit gently rather than severely; this implication is rarely if at all present in the other NT and LXX uses of the verb *pikrainesthai*, which focus on anger and bitterness in interpersonal relationships rather than the heavy-handed exercise of authority.)

3:20. In vv. 20-21 Paul turns from husbands and wives to children and fathers. The word to children in v. 20 instructs them to obey their parents "in everything." Like the similar language used of wives' submission to husbands in Eph 5:24, the comprehensiveness of the expression should not be over-read, as if it left no room for exceptions. Philo, for example, interpreted the Decalogue's commandment to children to honor their parents as requiring obedience only "in everything that is just and profitable" (*Spec.* 2.236), and conventional Greco-Roman wisdom worked on a similar assumption. Musonius Rufus, for example, regarded it as being so self-evident that a son might on occasion be required to resist his parents' will in order to do what is wise and right that the question need hardly be asked (*Diss.* 16.23). Paul and his readers would presumably have shared that assumption as something that could be confidently taken for granted; his focus here, however, is on the general rule rather than on the exceptions. The reason Paul offers for why children should obey their parents in this manner is that "this is pleasing (*euareston*) in the Lord"—a rationale that has obvious similarities to v. 18b ("as is fitting in the Lord") but replaces the criterion of what is "fitting" with what is "pleasing" (cf. Eph 5:10).

3:21. Fathers, in turn, are addressed in v. 21. The command to children in v. 20 urges obedience to both parents and assumes a role for both in the discipline and teaching of children, but it is fathers who are specially addressed in v. 21, in line with the particular responsibilities carried by fathers in both Testament teaching and Greco-Roman culture (cf. Gen 18:19; Deut 6:7, 20, and Prudentius, *C. Symm.* 1.197-214; Plutarch, *Cat. Maj.* 20, quoted in Lincoln 1990, 400). Whereas the word to fathers in Eph 6:4 includes both a negative injunction ("do not provoke your children to anger") and its positive counterpart ("but bring them up in the instruction and admonition of the Lord"), the word here in Colossians focuses exclusively on the first of these ("do not provoke [*mē erethizete*] your children"), emphasizing it further by the addition of the rationale: "so that they do not lose heart." (The verb *athymeō*, which Paul uses here, typically suggests a feeling of discouragement or despair aroused by the threat of an overbearing force; e.g., Deut 28:65; Jdth 7:22; Josephus, *Ant.* 9.87.) The emphasis on fatherly gentleness is striking when compared with the sternness and severity that were typically advised by Jewish and Greco-Roman writers (e.g., Sir 30:8-13) and the unbounded rights that fathers possessed over their children under Roman law (cf. Dionysius of Halicarnassus, *Ant. rom.* 2.26.4).

3:22. In 3:22–4:1, Paul turns to address slaves and masters with a series of exhortations and reminders that is almost equal in length (and closely similar in wording) to the corresponding section of the Ephesian household code (Eph 6:5-9). It is difficult to be certain why this section of the Colossian household code is so much less terse and compressed than the preceding two sections. One possible explanation is the presence of the returned slave Onesimus (4:9) and the accompanying letter to Philemon, which would have raised issues regarding the master/slave relationship that required, in Paul's view, a somewhat more expansive treatment than the husband/wife or child/parent relationships addressed in the previous paragraphs. Alternatively (or additionally), the relatively long section of the household code that is addressed to slaves and masters may be a consequence of the way the letter body is introduced in 2:6 with a call for the readers to continue walking in line with their reception of Jesus as "Lord" (*kyrios*), establishing a theological frame that has obvious potential for elaboration in the instructions given to slaves and masters (cf. Hering 2007, 76–77; Pao 2012, 272).

Slaves, like children, are urged to obey "in everything" (presumably with the same implied possibility of exceptions in instances where what was required of them was foolish or wicked—though if a master insisted on his legal right to command, the consequences of disobedience could be severe). As in the Ephesian code, Paul's reference to their masters as "fleshly" (*kata sarka*) does not necessarily imply the same sort of negative moral and spiritual connotations that it has in passages such as Rom 8:4-5, 12-13 and 2 Cor 1:17; it does, however, prepare the way for the contrast in the following verses between the slaves' earthly masters and the heavenly *kyrios* (3:22, 23, 24; 4:1) that slave and master have in common.

The obedience that slaves are to give to their earthly masters is, as Paul goes on to say in v. 22b, to be rendered "not in eye-service, as people-pleasers, but in singleness of heart, fearing the Lord." The contrast he draws is between an attitude that is framed entirely by the desire to obtain the favor of earthly masters and avoid their punishment and an attitude that is shaped by a sincere and single-minded devotion to the Lord. (The "Lord" in question is identified explicitly in v. 24 as "the Lord Christ," retrospectively confirming the instinct of Christian readers to interpret v. 22 as an appropriation of the

Old Testament concept of the fear of YHWH, applying it to the Lord Jesus.) Masters, if Paul's exhortation is followed, retain the obedience of their Christian slaves but lose the capacity to dominate the motivations that drive their slaves' behavior through the terror of threats and the possibility of reward.

3:23. The exhortation in v. 22 that urges slaves to obey "in everything . . . in singleness of heart, fearing the Lord" is reiterated and expanded in v. 23: "Whatever you do, do it from the heart, as for the Lord and not for people."

The opening phrase, "whatever you do," reinforces the universal scope of the previous verse's "in everything," and the injunction that follows ("do it from the heart") corresponds to the call in the previous verse to obey "in singleness of heart" (replacing the *kardia* of v. 22 with the roughly synonymous *psychē*—hence the NRSV's paraphrase, "put yourselves into it"). The verse's final line ("as for the Lord and not for people"), like the identically worded expression in Eph 6:7, implies both an imaginative reframing of reality ("as if you were not working for humans, though in fact you are") and the recognition of a deeper truth that is in fact the case ("in keeping with the reality that you are, in fact, slaves of Christ, and it is ultimately Christ whom you are serving, even as you serve your earthly masters").

3:24-25. Verses 24-25 offer a rationale for the exhortations in vv. 22-23, which is framed in terms of the impartial rewards and punishments that will be dispensed (by implication, in the age to come) by Christ, the heavenly Master. The focus of v. 24 is on the promise of eschatological reward: "knowing that from the Lord you will receive the reward of inheritance; you are serving the Lord Christ." The "Lord" to whom Paul is referring in v. 24a is almost certainly "the Lord Christ," as v. 24b makes explicit. The genitive expression, "the reward of inheritance," is probably to be taken as an epexegetical genitive ("the reward that is inheritance"), pointing forward to the future day when the readers will enter into full possession and experience of the blessings and privileges to which they have become heirs in Christ (cf. 1:12).

The final line of the verse (*tō kyriō Christō douleuete*) is grammatically ambiguous and could be taken either as an indicative ("you are serving the Lord Christ") (e.g., NIV, NRSV; cf. Campbell 2013, 66; Foster 2016, 391–92; Dunn 1996, 257) or as an imperative ("Serve the Lord Christ!") (e.g., LEB; cf. Pao 2012, 275–76; Moo 2008, 313; Harris 2010, 185–86). While the imperative translation has in its favor the fact that it more easily explains the logic of the "for" (*gar*) in the following verse, the indicative translation better preserves the parallelism between vv. 24-25 (reminders, introduced by *eidotes* ["knowing"], supporting the exhortations in vv. 22-23) and 4:1b (a reminder, introduced by *eidotes*, supporting the exhortation in v. 1a) and is to be preferred for that reason.

If v. 24b is read as an indicative, not an imperative, then the main function of v. 25 is to provide support for the assertion in v. 24a that "from the Lord you will receive the reward of inheritance" (which is the primary theme of that verse and is given additional support by the reminder in v. 24b). It does so by reassuring readers of the impartiality of the judgment that will be exercised by Christ at the end of the age (cf. Rom 2:6, 16), with a focus on punishments for wrongdoing that complements and balances the focus on rewards in the previous verse. The stress of v. 25 on the impartiality of that judgment carries a clear implication that masters, no less than slaves, will be subject to this judgment: masters who have short-changed, abused, or otherwise wronged their slaves, with little or no accountability to earthly judges under the Roman legal system, will one day face a judge whose verdict is impartial and a law that is not stacked in their favor.

4:1. The word to slaves in 3:22-25 is followed in 4:1 by a word to masters, which continues the emphasis of 3:25 on the impartial judgment of Christ as the one who is the true Master (*kyrios*) of master and slave alike. Like the word to slaves in 3:22-25, this verse begins with an imperative (in v. 1a) and supports it with a reminder (in v. 1b), introduced by the word "knowing" (*eidotes*). The imperative in v. 1a is strongly worded, though its force is somewhat softened by the way it is translated in most English versions. The NIV, for example, has Paul urging masters to provide their slaves with "what is right and fair," significantly diminishing the socially leveling force of the original, which could be translated more literally as a call for masters to grant their slaves "justice" (*to dikaion*) and "equality" (*tēn isotēn*) (Vasser 2017; McKnight 2018, 365–66).

It is difficult to know precisely what pattern of conduct Paul intends that language to give rise to; the best clues we have are probably the hints and intimations he offers in the accompanying letter to Philemon (esp. Phlm 16-21) and the command to masters in Ephesians 6 that they are to desist from the practice of threatening their slaves, since "their Master and yours is in heaven, and there is no favoritism with him" (Eph 6:9). Within the context of the first century Roman slave economy, beatings and whippings (and the threat of them) were understood to be the primary way in which social order was maintained and the distinction between slave and master was exhibited and perpetuated (Bradley 1987, 113–38; Saller 1994, 133–53). In the absence of such threats, the outward form of the slave/master relationship could still persist within a Christian household, but its nature would need to be radically transformed; both parties, in differentiated ways, are to manifest

Redeeming the time (4:-6)

(2) Devote yourselves to prayer, keeping alert in it with thanksgiving, (3) at the same time praying for us as well that God may open for us a door for the word, so that we may declare the mystery of Christ, for which I am a prisoner, (4) in order that I may reveal it clearly, as I must speak. (5) Walk in wisdom in relation to outsiders, redeeming the time. (6) Let your speech always be full of grace, seasoned with salt, so that you may know in what way is necessary to answer each one.

4:2. In the paragraph that follows immediately after the household code, Paul's thoughts turn to the prayers of the community, to his own circumstances under house arrest, and to the relationships the readers have with those who are "outsiders" to the Christian community. The opening exhortation of the paragraph, in v. 2, is a call to prayer. The imperative, "devote yourselves" (*proskartereite*), implies attentiveness to an assigned task or maintenance of a habitual practice (e.g., Rom 12:12; 13:6; Acts 1:14; 6:4). The participial phrase, "keeping alert in it" (*grēgorountes en autē*), that follows immediately after the imperative reinforces this sense and adds to it a connotation of eschatological urgency that the New Testament's calls to alertness typically carry (cf. 1 Thess 5:6; Matt 24:42-43; 25:13; Rev 3:3; 16:15; cf. Eph 6:18, using the roughly synonymous verb, *agrypneuō*). Paul's call to petition God with this kind of persistence and urgency should not be taken as implying a forgetfulness of benefits already received or anxiety about what is to come; the alertness with which they pray is to coexist with the "thanksgiving" (*eucharistia*) that Paul has already spoken of as a pervasive and habitual Christian practice (1:12; 2:7; 3:16-17; cf. Phil 4:6-7).

4:3-4. The exhortation to prayerfulness in v. 2 does not include any specific indication regarding what the content of readers' prayers should be or the people for whom their petitions should be made; presumably, in Paul's mind, the scope of the prayers they are to pray is as broad as that of the prayers he calls for in the equivalent verse in Ephesians, where he urges to readers to pray "at all times in every prayer and supplication, and with this purpose keeping alert in all perseverance and prayer for all the saints" (Eph 6:18).

In vv. 3-4, however, when he goes on to ask the readers to pray "at the same time . . . for us as well," the prayers he asks them to pray for him are focused and specific, zeroing in on the primary way he envisages Christ's victory over the powers being exhibited by him within the circumstances of his imprisonment (cf. Eph 6:19-20). Three times within the space of two verses, he makes reference to the proclamation of the mystery of Christ, asking them to pray that God might open a door for the message, that Paul might proclaim it, and that his proclamation might be as manifest and clear as it ought to be. As is the case in the equivalent request Paul makes to the Ephesians (where he describes himself in 6:20 as "an ambassador in chains"), Paul relates the request explicitly to his situation as "a prisoner" (lit., "bound" [*dedemai*]). Whereas the readers might be inclined to lose heart at the news of Paul's imprisonment (cf. Eph 3:13), he urges them to pray that God might create new opportunities for the gospel's advancement even in the midst of his confined circumstances, recalling his earlier insistence in 1:24 that he is "rejoicing" in his present experience of suffering.

4:5-6. Paul's request to the readers in vv. 3-4 that they pray for him in his proclamation of the gospel is followed in vv. 5-6 by an exhortation regarding their own interactions with those outside the church: "Walk in wisdom in relation to outsiders, redeeming the time. Let your speech always be full of grace, seasoned with salt, so that you may know in what way is necessary to answer each one" (4:5-6).

Paul's focus on "wisdom" as the overarching category that ought to shape the readers' interactions with those who are not believers in Christ continues a thread that has run through the entire letter (cf. 1:9-10, 28; 2:1-3, 8, 23; 3:16). To "walk in wisdom" is to shape one's daily life in accordance with the distinctively Christian and Christ-centered vision of reality that Paul has sketched in the previous chapters, rejecting, on the one hand the old, pagan patterns of life in which they used to walk and, on the other hand, the pseudo-wisdom of the "philosophy and empty deceit" that Paul warns against in 2:8-23.

While the overall pattern of this wisdom is distinctively Christian in its shape and center, it is not a narrowly sectarian or esoteric body of knowledge; since Christ is the one in whom the whole creation hangs together (cf. 1:15-23), the wisdom that his followers are to live by ought to include the wisdom that is written into the shape and order of the created world and discernible, at least in principle, by any human observer.

The combined effect of these interrelated factors is a wisdom that is profoundly missional in character—open in its texture and universal in its scope and interests yet strikingly and distinctively Christocentric in its overall shape, generating precisely the kind of interactions with "outsiders" that Paul goes on to encourage in vv. 6b-7, beginning with the participial phrase "redeeming the time" (*ton kairon exagorazomenoi*), with which he concludes

v. 6, painting a metaphorical picture of what it means for the Colossians to relate wisely to the unbelieving society that surrounds them.

The verb *exagorazō*, which Paul uses here, can sometimes (e.g., Polybius, *Hist.* 3.42.2) function simply as an intensified form of *agorazō* (i.e., "buy up" entirely, opportunistically, or urgently). But the contexts in which Paul uses the same verb elsewhere suggest that what he has in mind may involve more than just a marketplace metaphor for opportunistic activity. The closely similar exhortation in Eph 5:16, for example, is accompanied by a reminder not that the days are short (though, no doubt, in Paul's view that is also the case) but that they are "evil," and Paul's other uses of the verb carry an explicitly redemptive sense (Gal 3:13; 4:5). Here too, in Colossians, it is not at all beyond the bounds of possibility that Paul could be picturing the speech and action of believers as an opportunity for rescuing back hours and days from the darkness of this present age (cf. Col 1:13; Eph 6:12), so as to make them occasions for goodness and truth.

The parallel with the similar exhortation in Eph 5:16 implies a broad variety of ways that Paul can envisage this occurring, including the unspoken witness conveyed by the pattern of their lives and its contrast with the prevailing social norms (cf. Eph 5:7-14). Here in Colossians, the close proximity to Paul's prayer request in 4:2-4 and the exhortations about wise answers and gracious conversation in 4:6 suggest the likelihood that, in Paul's mind, a prominent place among the various ways that the time is to be redeemed is occupied by the church's own verbal testimony to the gospel.

The primary distinctive of believers' speech, according to v. 6, is the "grace" (*charis*) that is to pervade it. The context of the similarly worded exhortation in Eph 4:29 ("Let not any bad speech come out of your mouth, but if there is something good for the building up of [the person who has] need, [let it be spoken], in order that it might give grace to those who hear") suggests that the "grace" Paul has in mind here is not a narrow reference to the gospel message about the saving grace of God but a broad reference to the generosity with which human words can function to extend goodness and blessing to others. Still, the close proximity of this exhortation here in Colossians to Paul's prayer request in 4:2-4 suggests the likelihood that in his mind the graciousness of believers' speech, like the wisdom of their actions (v. 5), plays a part within the dynamic by which the gospel is propagated and bears its fruit (cf. 1:5-6).

The readers' speech is not only to be "full of grace"; it is also, as Paul goes on to say, to be "seasoned with salt." The metaphor of "saltiness," when used by Greco-Roman writers in relation to speech, refers to conversation that is striking and engaging in its manner and content (e.g., Plutarch, *Mor.*

514E–F, 685A; Quintilian, *Inst.* 6.3.19), and it is probably that sense that the metaphor carries here (Pao 2012, 298; Dunn 1996, 266–68).

The combined effect of these two qualities in the speech of believers is spelled out in v. 6b: "so that you may know in what way is necessary to answer each one." In contexts of confrontation and inquisition, when believers are called upon to "answer" the questions and accusations that are put to them, they are to offer a response that is not surly, hostile, or frightened. Instead, they are to offer an answer that is generous, engaging, wise, and even, on occasion, witty (cf. Luke's account of Paul's own trial before Agrippa, in Acts 26:1-29).

Final commendations and greetings (4:7-18)

(7) Tychicus will make known to you all the news about me; he is a beloved brother, a faithful servant, and a fellow slave in the Lord. (8) I send him to you for this very purpose: so that he may know how you are and encourage your hearts; (9) [I am sending him] with him Onesimus, the faithful and beloved brother, who is one of you. They will tell you about everything here. (10) Aristarchus my fellow prisoner greets you, and Mark the cousin of Barnabas, concerning whom you have received instructions—if he comes to you, welcome him— (11) and Jesus who is called Justus, who are of the circumcision—these are the only ones among my coworkers for the kingdom of God; they have been a comfort to me. (12) Epaphras greets you; he is one of you, a slave of Christ Jesus always wrestling on your behalf in his prayers, so that you may stand mature and fully assured in all the will of God, (13) for I bear witness to him that he has labored much for you and for those in Laodicea and in Hierapolis. (14) Luke, the beloved physician, greets you and Demas. (15) Greet the brothers and sisters in Laodicea, and Nympha and the church in her house. (16) And when this letter has been read among you, cause it to be read also in the church of the Laodiceans; and see that you read also the letter from Laodicea. (17) And say to Archippus, "See that you complete the ministry that you have received in the Lord." (18) I, Paul, write this greeting with my own hand. Remember my chains. Grace be with you.

In keeping with the fact that it is directed to a community of believers all living within a single town, many of whom are known to Paul, the letter closes with a series of final commendations and greetings that is considerably longer than the equivalent section in Ephesians, the brevity of which is probably due to the likely function of that letter as a kind of circular homily addressed to believers in a multiplicity of different locations, many of whom would not have been known to Paul.

Tychicus ... Onesimus (4:7-9)

4:7-8. As is the case in Eph 6:21-22, Paul commences the closing section of the letter with a commendation of Tychicus, the letter carrier. The wording of vv. 7-8 is closely similar to that of the equivalent verses in Ephesians, though probably not quite as closely similar as the version of v. 8 that is followed in most EVV ("I send him to you for this very purpose: so that you may know how we are and he may encourage your hearts") would suggest. There is good manuscript support for this reading (including A, B, and D*), and it is entirely plausible that if both letters are authentically Pauline and were sent with the same letter carrier, he might have worded the commendation of Tychicus in both letters in such a closely similar manner (cf. Ignatius, *Phld.* 11.2 and *Smyrn.* 12.1). The manuscript support for the alternative reading is also strong, however (including $\mathfrak{P}^{46}$, C, and D¹), and if that was the original wording it would be easy to explain the origin of the other as an assimilation to Eph 6:22. Also worth taking into account is the further statement in v. 9, regarding Tychicus and Onesimus, that "they will tell you about everything here," which would be the third time this has been said in the space of as many verses, if the text in most EVV is followed. The variant reading attested in $\mathfrak{P}^{46}$ is probably, for those reasons, to be preferred as the more likely original (Head 2014, 312).

If that is the case, then Tychicus's commission in Colossae is a somewhat more complex and pastorally demanding one than his mission in Ephesus and the other possible destinations of Ephesians, as it is described in Eph 6:21-22. Not only is he to do what would almost always have been expected and could confidently be taken for granted as the task of a letter carrier—fill in the recipients regarding the details of the sender's circumstances, "mak[ing] known to you all the news about me" (v. 20). He is also, in the case of the Colossians, to acquaint himself in greater detail with the situation in Colossae (including the degree to which the philosophy Paul warns against in ch. 2 has made inroads within the congregation, and perhaps also, if reports of the earthquake in AD 60 have already reached Paul, the extent to which they have been affected by its impact) and tailor the encouragement that he gives to them accordingly (Head 2014, 314). On that reading, Paul's commendation of Tychicus in v. 7b, as a "a beloved brother, a faithful servant, and a fellow slave in the Lord," takes on additional importance, commensurate with the scope of the discretion and the nature of the responsibility that has been entrusted to him.

4:9. The commendation of Tychicus is followed in v. 9 by a similar, albeit briefer, commendation of Onesimus who has been sent with him. No mention is made here of the tensions between Onesimus and his master,

Philemon, or of the requests and travel plans that Paul speaks of in the letter addressed to Philemon, Apphia, Archippus, and the church that met in Philemon's house. The only hint we have of these matters here is the unqualified commendation of Onesimus as "the faithful and beloved brother, who is one of you" (cf. Phlm 16), and his inclusion, along with Tychicus, in the task of enlightening the Colossians about "everything here."

Aristarchus . . . Mark . . . Jesus . . . Luke . . . and Demas (4:10-14)

4:10-11. In vv. 10-14 the focus shifts from the letter carriers whom Paul is sending to Colossae to the people who remain with him—for now, at least—in Rome and send their greetings to the Colossians. The names listed within these verses (Aristarchus, Mark, Jesus called Justus, Epaphras, Luke, and Demas) are almost identical with the names of the people from whom Paul conveys greetings in the closing verses of his letter to Philemon (though with omission, in the case of Phlm 23-24, of a reference to "Jesus called Justus").

The first three, listed by Paul in vv. 10-11, are identified as being "of the circumcision." Given their presence with Paul and his endorsement of them as "coworkers for the kingdom of God" and "a comfort" to him, the phrase "of the circumcision" is unlikely to carry the same sense here as it does in Gal 2:12, where it is used to refer to the members of a "circumcision party" that placed pressure on Peter to withdraw from fellowship with Gentiles; here, as in Rom 4:12, it appears to refer simply to those within the community of Christ followers who are Jewish by birth, in contrast with the Gentile-background believers listed in vv. 12-14.

The first of them, Aristarchus, is presumably the same person as the Aristarchus who appears in the book of Acts as a traveling companion of Paul in his third missionary journey (Acts 19:29; 20:4) and his journey from Adramyttium to Myra (and possibly also the subsequent shipwreck-interrupted journey from Myra to Rome; cf. Acts 27:2, 6; 28:11). The description of Aristarchus as Paul's "fellow prisoner" (cf. Rom 16:7; Phlm 23) may possibly imply that he, like Paul, has been arrested and is being held in custody, but Paul's habit of using similar terms (e.g., "fellow soldier" [Phlm 2, referring to Aristarchus] and "fellow slave" [e.g., 1:7; 4:7]), somewhat loosely, interchangeably, and at times metaphorically, would suggest that Aristarchus, along with Epaphras (Phlm 23), is more likely to have been a voluntary companion of Paul in his detention.

Also mentioned in v. 10 is "Mark, the cousin of Barnabas." According to the account in Acts, Mark's mother had been a prominent member of the community of disciples in Jerusalem (Acts 12:12), and he had returned to Antioch with Barnabas and Saul after the visit to Jerusalem that they made in response to the famine prophesied by Agabus (Acts 11:30; 12:25). He subsequently accompanied them on their first missionary journey (Acts 13:5) before "desert[ing]" them in Pamphylia and returning from there to Jerusalem (Acts 13:13; 15:38). The long shadow cast by that event and the rift it created between Paul and Barnabas is probably one of the reasons Paul feels the need to give his endorsement to Mark here, reminding the readers of the "instructions" about Mark that they have received (from an unknown source) and adding his own imprimatur: "if he comes to you, welcome him."

A third, figure, "Jesus who is called Justus," is added to the list in v, 11. This is the only mention of him in the New Testament and we know nothing else about him. His Latin cognomen, Justus, means "just" or "righteous" and could be used by Jews as well as Gentiles (cf. Acts 1:23; 18:7). The fact that these three are "the only ones [of the circumcision] among my coworkers for the kingdom of God" is commented on in the second half of the verse. The inclusion of the word "only" (*monoi*) probably implies an element of sadness at how few of Paul's fellow Jews are present and partnering with him in the work of the gospel (cf. Moo 2008, 341–42, citing Phil 1:14-18); the fact that they are there at all is, nonetheless, highlighted by Paul as "a comfort" to him. The description of them as "coworkers for the kingdom of God" recalls Paul's earlier description of the salvation as a matter that involves believers being "rescued . . . from the dominion of darkness" and transferred by God "into the kingdom of the son of his love" (1:13); it is also consistent with Luke's description of Paul's time under house arrest in Rome as a season in which he "proclaimed the kingdom of God and taught about the Lord Jesus Christ" (Acts 28:31).

4:12-14. The greetings in vv. 10-11 from Paul's Jewish coworkers, Aristarchus, Mark, and Jesus called Justus, are followed in vv. 12-14 by greetings from three Gentile coworkers: Epaphras, Luke, and Demas. The greeting in vv. 12-13 from Epaphras is the longest of the three (and indeed the longest of all the greetings in vv. 10-14). This is for the obvious reason that Epaphras is "one of you" (*ex hymōn*; i.e. a native Colossian, like Onesimus) and was the one through whom the believers in Colossae first learned the gospel (1:7-8). Although he is now absent from the Colossians, he is depicted here (like Paul himself, in 1:9, 29; 2:1-5) as "always wrestling . . . in his prayers" on their behalf. The content of his prayers ("that you may stand mature and fully assured in all the will of God") is framed in categories that echo Paul's descriptions of his own prayers and the goal of his ministry (cf. 1:9-12, 28-29; 2:2), implicitly joining Epaphras's prayers to Paul's, and to Paul's warnings and exhortations in the earlier chapters of the letter. Like Paul, Epaphras wants to see the Colossians stand "mature" (*teleioi*) in Christ (cf. 1:28), "fully assured" (*peplērophorēmenoi*) (cf. 2:2) in their grasp of and commitment to the will of God (cf. 1:9)—a goal that will require both their rejection of the philosophy that Paul warns against in chapter 2 and their embrace of the positive vision for the transformation of their conduct and character that Paul lays out in 3:1–4:6.

The description of Epaphras continues in v. 13 with Paul's assurance to the Colossians that Epaphras "has labored much for you and for those in Laodicea and in Hierapolis." This, too, is reminiscent of Paul's earlier words in 2:1 about "how great a struggle I have for you, and for those in Laodicea, and for all those who have not seen my face in the flesh" (though with the broad, sweeping reference of 2:1 to "all those who have not seen my face in the flesh" replaced by a more focused reference to "those . . . in Hierapolis"). The mention of Laodicea here in v. 13 is the first of three references to that city within the final greetings section of the letter (cf. vv. 15, 16), suggesting a degree of interconnectedness between the church in that city and those in Colossae and Hierapolis that was probably, at least in part, a consequence of the regional scope of the ministry exercised by Epaphras (Pao 2012, 317).

The second and third names in the list are those of "Luke, the beloved physician . . . and Demas." The first of these we hear of again in 2 Tim 4:11 and—assuming, as seems highly probable, this is the same Luke who wrote the third Gospel and the book of Acts—in the "we" passages of the latter (cf. Acts 16:10-17; 20:5-15; 21:1-18; 27:1–28:16). The description of him as "the beloved physician" may derive its relevance from Paul's circumstances as a prisoner and the medical assistance he required as a consequence of his chronic and/or recurring health problems (cf. Gal 4:13; 2 Cor 12:7). Demas's name occurs on only here, in Phlm 24, and 2 Tim 4:10-11, where we are told that he has "deserted" Paul because he "loved the world."

The brothers and sisters in Laodicea (4:15-17)

4:15-16. Having conveyed his commendation of Tychicus and Onesimus (vv. 7-9) and the greetings those who remain with him in Rome (vv. 10-14), Paul now turns his attention to those who are at the receiving end of the letter—or more precisely, in the case of vv. 15-16, to those in their vicinity to whom the Colossians are asked to extend Paul's greetings.

First among these are "the brothers and sisters in Laodicea, and Nympha and the church in her house" (v. 15). It is difficult to say with certainty what is meant by the *kai* (here translated as "and") that links the first half of this verse to the second. It could, on the one hand, be read as implying that "Nympha and the church in her house" are a completely distinct group from "the brothers and sisters in Laodicea" and presumably resident in another town (Hierapolis?). Alternatively, if the *kai* is taken as epexegetical, it could be read as introducing some further information about the brothers and sisters in Laodicea (i.e., that they are constituted as a church that meets in Nympha's house). A third possibility (favored as the most likely in Pao 2012, 319) is that the gathering in Nympha's house was one of a number of house churches in Laodicea (just as the gathering in Philemon's house may have been one of a number in Colossae), and that Paul is singling this gathering out because Nympha, unlike the other house church hosts, was known to him. If that is the case, then the following verse's reference, in the singular, to "the church of the Laodiceans" would need to be read as an indication that the various house churches of Laodicea still regarded themselves as one *ekklēsia* and could still gather together on occasion as a large, combined group (cf. the references to "the whole church" in 1 Cor 14:23; Rom 16:23, which may imply a similar arrangement among the house churches of Corinth). The fact that Paul singles her out in this manner is an indication of her prominence, along with a number of other women such as Chloe (1 Cor 1:11), Lydia (Acts 16:40), Euodia and Syntyche (Phil 4:2-3), and the various women named in Romans 16, among the churches associated with Paul's missionary circle. It is difficult to say with any certainty what her role within the gathering would have been, aside from the patronage that she exercised by hosting it in her home, though that in itself would have been a significant social role (cf. Rom 12:8; 16:2 and the discussion in MacDonald 2005).

The believers in Colossae are not only to greet the brothers and sisters in Laodicea; they are also to see to it that the letter they have received is read out in the church at Laodicea and they, in turn are to read the letter that was sent to the Laodiceans (v. 16). If, as I have argued in the introduction to Ephesians above, it is plausible to take "the letter from Laodicea" as a reference to the circular homily known to us as Ephesians, then Paul's instruction in v. 16 can be taken as an invitation to read Colossians in close conjunction with that letter, with the latter at times reinforcing, at times complementing, and at times expanding on the former.

4:17. The instructions regarding the brothers and sisters in Colossae (vv. 15-16) are followed in v. 17 by an instruction that the readers are to pass on from Paul to Archippus, urging him to "see that you complete the ministry that you have received in the Lord." The inclusion of Archippus within the greetings conveyed in the opening verses of Philemon would suggest that he is resident in Colossae, not Laodicea. The "ministry" (*diakonia*) that he has received is not identified here in any detail, though the description of him in Phlm 2 as "our fellow soldier" perhaps suggests that his work involves labors and sufferings similar to those of Paul.

I, Paul, write this greeting . . . (4:18)

Paul's letter to the Colossians concludes in 4:18 with a final greeting written by Paul in his own hand (cf. 1 Cor 16:21; Gal 6:11; 2 Thess 3:17; Phlm 19), asking the hearers of the letter to "remember my chains" (probably, at least primarily, a request for prayer; cf. the use of "remembrance" language in connection with prayer in Rom 1:9; Eph 1:16; Phil 1:3; 1 Thess 1:2; 2 Tim 1:3; Phlm 4) before signing off with Paul's customary benediction, "Grace be with you." The letter thus ends on the same note with which it began (cf. 1:2)—an indication of the pervasive significance of the grace of God within Paul's vison for the Christian life and the prayers he prays for his fellow believers. Here in his letter to the Colossians, that customary emphasis has been further underlined by the sharp warning he has given against a spirituality driven, in his view, by an altogether different dynamic (cf. 2:8-23) and reinforced by the recurring reminders throughout the letter that the life of believers is to be one of pervasive gratitude to God (cf. 1:12; 2:7; 3:16-17; 4:2), grounded in the message about God's grace that was made known to them in the gospel (1:6).

Works Cited

Abbott, Thomas Kingsmill. 1897. *A Critical and Exegetical Commentary on the Epistles to the Ephesians and to the Colossians*. ICC. Edinburgh: T&T Clark.

Anderson, Garwood P. 2016. *Paul's New Perspective: Charting a Soteriological Journey*. Downers Grove: IVP.

Arnold, Clinton E. 1996. *The Colossian Syncretism: The Interface between Christianity and Folk Belief at Colossae*. WUNT. Tübingen: Mohr Siebeck.

Arnold, Clinton E. 1997. *Power and Magic: The Concept of Power in Ephesians*. 2nd ed. Grand Rapids: Baker.

Arnold, Clinton E. 2010. *Ephesians*. ZECNT. Grand Rapids: Zondervan.

Balch, David. 1988. "Household Codes." In *Greco-Roman Literature and the New Testament*, edited by D. E. Aune, 25–50. Atlanta: Scholars.

Barclay, John M. G. 2013. "'Because He Was Rich He Became Poor': Translation, Exegesis and Hermeneutics in the Reading of 2 Cor 8.9." In *Theologizing in the Corinthian Conflict: Studies in the Exegesis and Theology of 2 Corinthians*, edited by R. Bieringer, M. Ibita, and D. Kurek-Chomycz, 331–44. Leuven: Peeters.

Barclay, John M. G. 2015. *Paul and the Gift*. Grand Rapids: Eerdmans.

Barth, Markus. 1974. *Ephesians: Introduction, Translation and Commentary*. 2 vols. AB. Garden City: Doubleday.

Barth, Markus, and Helmut Blanke. 1994. *Colossians*. Translated by Astrid B. Beck. AB. New York: Doubleday.

Beale, G. K. 2007. "Colossians." In *Commentary on the New Testament Use of the Old Testament*, edited by G. K. Beale and D. A. Carson, 841–70. Grand Rapids: Baker.

Beale, G. K. 2019. *Colossians and Philemon*. BECNT. Grand Rapids: Baker.

Beetham, Christopher A. 2008. *Echoes of Scripture in the Letter of Paul to the Colossians*. Leiden: Brill.

Beker, J. C. 1991. "Recasting Pauline Theology: The Coherence-Contingency Scheme as Interpretive Model." In *Pauline Theology, Volume I: Thessalonians, Philippians, Galatians, Philemon*, edited by Jouette M. Bassler, 15–24. Minneapolis: Fortress.

Best, E. 1998. *A Critical and Exegetical Commentary on Ephesians*. ICC. Edinburgh: T&T Clark.

Best, Ernest. 1997a. *Essays on Ephesians*. Edinburgh: T&T Clark.

Best, Ernest. 1997b. "Who Used Whom? The Relationship of Ephesians and Colossians." *NTS* 43/1: 72–96.

Betz, Hans Dieter. 1986. *The Greek Magical Papyri in Translation: Including the Demotic Spells*. Chicago: University of Chicago Press.

Bevere, Allan R. 2003. *Sharing in the Inheritance: Identity and the Moral Life in Colossians*. JSNTSup. London: Sheffield Academic Press.

Bird, Michael F. 2016. "What Do We Do with the Household Codes Today?" In *The Gender Conversation: Evangelical Perspectives on Gender, Scripture, and the Christian Life*, edited by Edwina Murphy and David Starling, 63–72. Eugene: Wipf & Stock.

Blazosky, Bryan. 2019. *The Law's Universal Condemning and Enslaving Power: The Gentiles and the Law in Paul, the Old Testament, and Second Temple Jewish Literature*. University Park, PA: Penn State University Press.

Bormann, Lukas. 2012. *Der Brief Des Paulus an die Kolosser*. THKNT. Leipzig: Evangelische Verlagsanstalt.

Bradley, K. R. 1987. *Slaves and Masters in the Roman Empire: A Study in Social Control*. New York: Oxford University Press.

Bruce, F. F. 1984. *The Epistles to the Colossians, to Philemon, and to the Ephesians*. NICNT. Grand Rapids: Eerdmans.

Caird, G. B. 1976. *Paul's Letters from Prison: Ephesians, Philippians, Colossians, Philemon, in the Revised Standard Version*. Oxford: Oxford University Press.

Calvin, Jean. 1965. *The Epistles of Paul the Apostle to the Galatians, Ephesians, Philippians and Colossians*. Translated by T. H. L. Parker. Calvin's New Testament Commentaries. Grand Rapids: Eerdmans.

Campbell, Constantine R. 2012. *Paul and Union with Christ: An Exegetical and Theological Study*. Grand Rapids: Zondervan.

Campbell, Constantine R. 2013. *Colossians and Philemon: A Handbook on the Greek Text*. BHGNT. Waco: Baylor University Press.

Campbell, Douglas A. 1996. "Unraveling Colossians 3.11b." *NTS* 42: 120–32.

Campbell, Douglas A. 2014. *Framing Paul: An Epistolary Biography*. Grand Rapids: Eerdmans.

Caragounis, C. C. 1977. *The Ephesian Mysterion: Meaning and Content*. ConBNT. Lund: Gleerup.

Chua, Amy. 2018. *Political Tribes: Group Instinct and the Fate of Nations*. New York: Penguin.

Copenhaver, Adam. 2018. *Reconstructing the Historical Background of Paul's Rhetoric in the Letter to the Colossians*. LNTS. London: T&T Clark.

Dahl, N. A. 2000. "Kleidungsmetaphern: der Alte und der Neue Mensch." In *Studies in Ephesians*, 389–411. Tübingen: Mohr Siebeck.

DeMaris, Richard E. 1994. *The Colossian Controversy: Wisdom in Dispute at Colossae*. JSNTSup. Sheffield: JSOT Press.

Dibelius, Martin. 1913. *Die Briefe Des Apostels Paulus: die Neun Kleinen Briefe*. HNT. Tübingen: J.C.B. Mohr.

Dunn, James D. G. 1996. *The Epistles to the Colossians and to Philemon: A Commentary on the Greek Text*. NIGTC. Grand Rapids: Eerdmans.

Ehrman, Bart D. 2014. *Forgery and Counterforgery: The Use of Literary Deceit in Early Christian Polemics*. Oxford: Oxford University Press.

Elliott, John H. 1981. *A Home for the Homeless: A Sociological Exegesis of 1 Peter, Its Situation and Strategy*. Philadelphia: Fortress.

Fanning, B. M. 1990. *Verbal Aspect in New Testament Greek.* Oxford: Clarendon.

Fee, Gordon D. 1994. *God's Empowering Presence: The Holy Spirit in the Letters of Paul.* Peabody: Hendrickson.

Fitzmyer, Joseph A. 1961. "The Use of Explicit Old Testament Quotations in Qumran Literature and the New Testament." *NTS* 7: 297–333.

Foster, Paul. 2016. *Colossians.* BNTS. London: T&T Clark.

Fowl, Stephen E. 1990. *The Story of Christ in the Ethics of Paul: An Analysis of the Function of the Hymnic Material in the Pauline Corpus.* JSNTSup. Sheffield: JSOT Press.

Fowl, Stephen E. 2012. *Ephesians: A Commentary.* NTL. Louisville: WJK.

Gehring, Roger W. 2004. *House Church and Mission: The Importance of Household Structures in Early Christianity.* Peabody: Hendrickson.

Gnilka, Joachim. 1977. *Der Epheserbrief: Auslegung.* 2nd ed. HTKNT. Freiburg: Herder.

Gombis, Timothy G. 2002. "Being the Fullness of God by the Spirit: Ephesians 5:18 in Its Epistolary Setting." *TynBul* 53: 259–71.

Gombis, Timothy G. 2005. "Cosmic Lordship and Divine Gift-Giving: Psalm 68 in Ephesians 4:8." *NovT* 47/4: 367–80.

Gombis, Timothy G. 2010. *The Drama of Ephesians: Participating in the Triumph of God.* Downers Grove: IVP.

Goodhart, David. 2017. *The Road to Somewhere: The Populist Revolt and the Future of Politics.* London: Hurst.

Gordley, Matthew E. 2007. *The Colossian Hymn in Context: An Exegesis in Light of Jewish and Greco-Roman Hymnic and Epistolary Conventions.* WUNT 2. Tübingen: Mohr Siebeck.

Gupta, Nijay K. 2012. "Mirror-Reading Moral Issues in Paul's Letters." *JSNT* 34: 361–81.

Haidt, Jonathan. 2012. *The Righteous Mind: Why Good People Are Divided by Politics and Religion.* New York: Pantheon.

Harper, Kyle. 2011a. "*Porneia*: The Making of a Christian Sexual Norm." *JBL* 131: 363–83.

Harper, Kyle. 2011b. *Slavery in the Late Roman World, AD 275-425*. Cambridge: Cambridge University Press.

Harris, Murray J. 2010. *Colossians and Philemon*. EGGNT. Nashville: B&H.

Harris, W. H. 1996. *The Descent of Christ: Ephesians 4:7-11 and Traditional Hebrew Imagery*. Leiden: Brill.

Harrison, James R. 2003. *Paul's Language of Grace in Its Graeco-Roman Context*. WUNT. Tübingen: Mohr Siebeck.

Head, Peter M. 2009. "Named Letter-Carriers among the Oxyrhynchus Papyri." *JSNT* 31: 279–99.

Head, Peter M. 2014. "Tychicus and the Colossian Christians: A Reconsideration of the Text of Colossians 4:8." In *Texts and Traditions: Essays in Honour of J. Keith Elliott*, edited by Peter Doble and Jeffrey Kloha, 303–15. Leiden: Brill.

Hengel, Martin. 1983. *Between Jesus and Paul: Studies in the Earliest History of Christianity*. London: SCM.

Hering, James P. 2007. *The Colossian and Ephesian Haustafeln in Theological Context: An Analysis of Their Origins, Relationship, and Message*. New York: Peter Lang.

Hill, R. C., ed. 2001. *Theodoret of Cyrus: Commentary on the Letters of St Paul*. Brookline, MA: Holy Cross Orthodox Press.

Hirsch, Alan. 2016. *The Forgotten Ways: Reactivating Apostolic Movements*. 2nd ed. Grand Rapids: Brazos.

Hodge, Charles. 1954 [1856]. *A Commentary on the Epistle to the Ephesians*. Repr. ed. Grand Rapids: Eerdmans.

Hoehner, Harold W. 2002. *Ephesians: An Exegetical Commentary*. Grand Rapids: Baker.

Hollenbach, Bruce. 1979. "Col. II.23: Which Things Lead to the Fufillment of the Flesh " *NTS* 25: 254–61.

Hood, Jason B. 2013. *Imitating God in Christ: Recapturing a Biblical Pattern*. Downers Grove: IVP.

Hooker, Morna. 1973. "Were There False Teachers in Colossae?" In *Christ and Spirit in the New Testament: Essays in Honour of Charles Francis*

Digby Moule, edited by Barnabas Lindars and Stephen S. Smalley, 315–31. Cambridge: Cambridge University Press.

Hurtado, Larry W. 2003. *Lord Jesus Christ: Devotion to Jesus in Earliest Christianity*. Grand Rapids: Eerdmans.

Jeal, Roy R. 2000. *Integrating Theology and Ethics in Ephesians: The Ethos of Communication*. Lewiston: Mellen.

Jeremias, Joachim. 1963. "Γωνία, Κ.Τ.Λ." *TDNT* 1:791–93.

Judge, E. A. 2008. "Ethical Terms in St Paul and the Inscriptions of Ephesus." In *The First Christians in the Roman World: Augustan and New Testament Essays*, edited by James R. Harrison, 368–79. Tübingen: Mohr Siebeck.

Kaiser, Walter C. 1996. "Response to Douglas Moo." In *Five Views on Law and Gospel*, edited by Wayne G. Strickland, 393–400. Grand Rapids: Zondervan.

Kreitzer, L. J. 2004. "Living in the Lycus Valley: Earthquake Imagery in Colossians, Philemon and Ephesians " In *Testimony and Interpretation: Early Christology in Its Judeo-Hellenistic Milieu: Studies in Honour of Petr Pokorný*, edited by J. Mrázek and J. Roskovec, 81–94. London: T&T Clark.

Kroeger, Catherine Clark. 1993. "Head." In *Dictionary of Paul and His Letters*, edited by Gerald F. Hawthorne, Ralph P. Martin, and Daniel G. Reid, 375–77. Downers Grove: IVP.

Kümmel, Werner Georg. 1975. *Introduction to the New Testament*. Translated by H. C. Kee. Rev. ed. NTL. London: SCM.

Lamb, Jeffrey S. 1998. "Wisdom in Col 1,15-20: Contribution and Significance." *JETS* 41: 45–53.

Larkin, William J. 2009. *Ephesians: A Handbook on the Greek Text*. BHGNT. Waco: Baylor University Press.

Lendon, J. E. 1997. *Empire of Honour: The Art of Government in the Roman World*. Oxford: Clarendon Press.

Lieu, J. M. 1985. "'Grace to You and Peace': The Apostolic Greeting." *BJRL* 68: 161–78.

Lightfoot, J. B. 1879. *St Paul's Epistles to the Colossians and to Philemon*. 3rd ed. New York: Macmillan.

Lightfoot, Joseph Barber. 1893. *Biblical Essays*. London: Macmillan.

Lincoln, Andrew T. 1982. "The Use of the Old Testament in Ephesians." *JSNT* 14: 16–57.

Lincoln, Andrew T. 1990. *Ephesians*. WBC. Dallas: Word.

Lohse, Eduard. 1971. *Colossians and Philemon*. Hermeneia. Philadelphia: Fortress.

MacDonald, Margaret Y. 2000. *Colossians and Ephesians*. SP. Collegeville: Liturgical.

MacDonald, Margaret Y. 2005. "Can Nympha Rule This House? The Rhetoric of Domesticity in Colossians." In *Rhetoric and Reality in Early Christianities*, edited by Willi Braun, 99–120. Waterloo, ON: Wilfrid Laurier University Press.

Marshall, I. Howard. 1996. "Salvation, Grace and Works in the Later Pauline Corpus." *NTS* 42: 339–58.

Martin, Ralph P. 1989. *Reconciliation: A Study of Paul's Theology*. 2nd ed. Grand Rapids: Academie.

Martin, Troy. 1996. *By Philosophy and Empty Deceit: Colossians as Response to a Cynic Critique*. JSNTSup 118. Sheffield: JSOT Press.

Mathewson, David, and Elodie Ballantine Emig. 2016. *Intermediate Greek Grammar: Syntax for Students of the New Testament*. Grand Rapids: Baker.

McKnight, Scot. 2018. *The Letter to the Colossians*. NICNT. Grand Rapids: Eerdmans.

Metzger, Bruce Manning. 1994. *A Textual Commentary on the Greek New Testament: A Companion Volume to the United Bible Societies' Greek New Testament (Fourth Revised Edition)*. 2nd ed. Stuttgart: Deutsche Bibelgesellschaft.

Meyer, H. A. W. 1884. *Critical and Exegetical Handbook to the Epistle to the Ephesians and the Epistle to Philemon*. Translated by M. J. Evans. Edinburgh: T&T Clark.

Mickelsen, A., and B. Mickelsen. 1986. "What Does *Kephalē* Mean in the New Testament?" In *Women, Authority, and the Bible*, edited by A. Mickelsen, 97–110. Downers Grove: IVP.

Mitton, C. Leslie. 1951. *The Epistle to the Ephesians: Its Authorship, Origin, and Purpose.* Oxford: Clarendon Press.

Mitton, C. Leslie. 1976. *Ephesians.* NCB. London: Oliphants.

Moo, Douglas J. 2008. *The Letters to the Colossians and to Philemon.* PNTC. Grand Rapids: Eerdmans.

Morales, Helen, ed. 2011. *Greek Fiction: Chariton, Callirhoe; Longus, Daphnis and Chloe; Anonymous, Letters of Chion.* London: Penguin.

Morgan, Teresa. 2015. *Roman Faith and Christian Faith: Pistis and Fides in the Early Roman Empire and Early Churches.* Oxford: Oxford University Press.

Moritz, T. 1996a. *A Profound Mystery: The Use of the Old Testament in Ephesians.* NovTSup. Leiden: Brill.

Moritz, T. 1996b. "Reasons for Ephesians." *Evangel* 14: 8–14.

Moule, C. F. D. 1959. *An Idiom Book of New Testament Greek.* 2nd ed. Cambridge: Cambridge University Press.

Moule, H. C. G. 1914. *The Epistle to the Ephesians.* Cambridge: Cambridge University Press.

Moulton, J. H., and G. Milligan. 1997. *The Vocabulary of the Greek New Testament.* Repr. ed. Peabody, MA: Hendrickson.

O'Brien, Peter T. 1977. *Introductory Thanksgivings in the Letters of Paul.* Leiden: Brill.

Olliffe, M. 2017. "Is 'Faith' the 'Gift of God'? Reading Ephesians 2:8-10 with the Ancients." *The Gospel Coalition.* September 13. au.thegospelcoalition.org/article/is-faith-the-gift-of-god-reading-ephesians-28-10-with-the-ancients/.

Pao, David W. 2003. *Thanksgiving: An Investigation of a Pauline Theme.* NSBT. Downers Grove, IL: InterVarsity Press.

Pao, David W. 2012. *Colossians and Philemon.* ZECNT. Grand Rapids: Zondervan.

Porter, Stanley E. 1992. *Idioms of the Greek New Testament.* Sheffield: JSOT Press.

Reyes, L. C. 1999. "The Structure and Rhetoric of Colossians 1:15-20." *Filologia Neotestamentaria* 12: 139–54.

Robinson, Donald, W. B. 1963. "Who Were 'the Saints'?" *RTR* 22/2: 45–53.

Rogers, Cleon. 1979. "The Dionysian Background of Ephesians 5:18." *BSac* 136: 249–57.

Rosner, Brian S. 2007. *Greed as Idolatry: The Origin and Meaning of a Pauline Metaphor.* Grand Rapids: Eerdmans.

Rosner, Brian. 2013. *Paul and the Law: Keeping the Commandments of God.* NSBT. Downers Grove: IVP.

Rowe, C. Kavin. 2016. *One True Life: The Stoics and Early Christians as Rival Traditions.* New Haven: Yale University Press.

Rowe, Christopher Kavin. 2009. *World Upside Down: Reading Acts in the Graeco-Roman Age.* Oxford: Oxford University Press.

Runge, Steven E. 2010. *Discourse Grammar of the Greek New Testament: A Practical Introduction for Teaching and Exegesis.* Peabody: Hendrickson.

Saller, Richard P. 1994. *Patriarchy, Property, and Death in the Roman Family.* Cambridge: Cambridge University Press.

Sandnes, Karl Olav. 1991. *Paul, One of the Prophets?: A Contribution to the Apostle's Self-Understanding.* WUNT. Tübingen: Mohr Siebeck.

Savage, Timothy B. 1996. *Power through Weakness: Paul's Understanding of the Christian Ministry in 2 Corinthians.* SNTSMS. New York: Cambridge University Press.

Schlier, Heinrich. 1957. *Der Brief an die Epheser: Ein Kommentar.* Düsseldorf: Patmos.

Schnabel, E. 1985. *Law and Wisdom from Ben Sira to Paul.* WUNT. Tübingen: Mohr Siebeck.

Schnackenburg, R. 1991. *Ephesians: A Commentary.* Translated by H. Heron. Edinburgh: T&T Clark.

Schüssler Fiorenza, Elisabeth. 2017. *Ephesians.* Wisdom Commentary. Collegeville: Liturgical Press.

Scott, James M. 1992. *Adoption as Sons of God: An Exegetical Investigation into the Background of Υιοθεσια in the Pauline Corpus.* WUNT. Tübingen: Mohr Siebeck.

Seitz, Christopher R. 2014. *Colossians.* BTCB. Grand Rapids: Brazos.

Sellin, Gerhard. 2008. *Der Brief an die Epheser*. KEK. Göttingen: Vandenhoeck und Ruprecht.

Smith, G. V. 1975. "Paul's Use of Psalm 68:18 in Ephesians 4:8." *JETS* 18: 181–89.

Smith, Ian K. 2006. *Heavenly Perspective: A Study of the Apostle Paul's Response to a Jewish Mystical Movement at Colossae*. LNTS. London: T&T Clark.

Snodgrass, Klyne. 1996. *Ephesians*. NIVAC. Grand Rapids: Zondervan.

Starling, David. 2017. "'For Your Sake We Are Being Killed All Day Long . . .': Romans 8:36 and the Hermeneutics of Unexplained Suffering." *Themelios* 42: 112–21.

Starling, David I. 2011. *Not My People: Gentiles as Exiles in Pauline Hermeneutics*. BZNW. Berlin: de Gruyter.

Starling, David I. 2012a. "The *Apistoi* of 2 Cor. 6:14: Beyond the Impasse." *NovT* 55: 1–17.

Starling, David I. 2012b. "Meditations on a Slippery Citation: Paul's Use of Psalm 112:9 in 2 Corinthians 9:9." *JTI* 6: 241–55.

Starling, David I. 2012c. "The Yes to All God's Promises: Jesus, Israel and the Promises of God in Paul's Letters." *RTR* 71: 185–204.

Starling, David I. 2014a. "Covenants and Courtrooms, Imputation and Imitation: Righteousness and Justification in *Paul and the Faithfulness of God*." *JSPL* 4: 37–48.

Starling, David I. 2014b. "Ephesians and the Hermeneutics of the New Exodus." In *Reverberations of the Exodus in Scripture*, edited by R. Michael Fox, 139–59. Eugene: Wipf & Stock.

Starling, David I. 2014c. "'She Who Is in Babylon': 1 Peter and the Hermeneutics of Empire." In *Reactions to Empire: Sacred Texts in Their Socio-Political Contexts*, edited by John Anthony Dunne and Dan Batovici, 111–28. Tübingen: Mohr Siebeck.

Starling, David I. 2016. "Family Drama: The Ephesian Household Code in Narrative-Dramatic Perspective." In *The Gender Conversation: Evangelical Perspectives on Gender, Scripture, and the Christian Life*, edited by Edwina Murphy and David Starling, 77–88. Eugene, OR: Wipf & Stock.

Starling, David I. 2019. "Putting on the New Self: Costume and Character in Eph 4:22-24." *NovT* 61: 289–307.

Still, Todd D. 2004. "Eschatology in Colossians: How Realized Is It?" *NTS* 50: 125–38.

Stowers, Stanley K. 2016. "Paul and Self-Mastery." In *Paul in the Greco-Roman World: A Handbook: Volume II*, edited by J. Paul Sampley, 270–300. London: T&T Clark.

Suh, Robert H. 2007. "The Use of Ezekiel 37 in Ephesians 2." *JETS* 50/4: 715–33.

Talbert, Charles H. 2007. *Ephesians and Colossians*. Paideia. Grand Rapids: Baker.

Taylor, R. A. 1991. "The Use of Psalm 68:18 in Ephesians 4:8 in the Light of Ancient Versions." *BSac* 148: 319–36.

Thielman, Frank. 1994. *Paul and the Law: A Contextual Approach*. Downers Grove: IVP.

Thielman, Frank. 2007. "Ephesians." In *Commentary on the New Testament Use of the Old Testament*, edited by G. K. Beale and D. A. Carson, 813–33. Nottingham: IVP.

Thielman, Frank. 2010. *Ephesians*. BECNT. Grand Rapids: Baker.

Thompson, Marianne Meye. 2005. *Colossians and Philemon*. THNTC. Grand Rapids: Eerdmans.

Trebilco, Paul R. 1991. *Jewish Communities in Asia Minor*. SNTSMS. Cambridge: CUP.

van der Horst, Pieter W. 1978. "Is Wittiness Unchristian? A Note on *Eutrapelia* in Eph 5:4." In *Miscellanea Neotestamentica*, 2.163–71. Leiden: Brill.

van Kooten, George H. 2003. *Cosmic Christology in the Pauline School: Colossians and Ephesians in the Context of Graeco-Roman Cosmology*. Edited by WUNT. Tübingen: Mohr Siebeck.

Vanhoozer, Kevin J. 2005. *The Drama of Doctrine: A Canonical-Linguistic Approach to Christian Theology*. Louisville: Westminster.

Vasser, Murray. 2017. "Grant Slaves Equality: Re-Examining the Translation of Colossians 4:1." *TynBul* 68: 59–71.

Wallace, Daniel B. 1996. *Greek Grammar Beyond the Basics: An Exegetical Syntax of the New Testament.* Grand Rapids: Zondervan.

White, Joel. 2016. "Paul Completes the Servant's Sufferings (Colossians 1:24)." *JSPL* 6: 181–98.

Wiles, Gordon P. 1974. *Paul's Intercessory Prayers: The Significance of the Intercessory Prayer Passages in the Letters of St Paul.* SNTSMS. Cambridge: Cambridge University Press.

Williams, Jarvis J. 2015. "Violent Ethno-Racial Reconciliation: A Mystery in Ephesians and Its Jewish Martyrological Background." *CTR* 12/2: 119–34.

Wilson, R. McL. 2005. *A Critical and Exegetical Commentary on Colossians and Philemon.* ICC. London: T&T Clark.

Witherington, Ben. 2007. *The Letters to Philemon, the Colossians, and the Ephesians: A Socio-Rhetorical Commentary on the Captivity Epistles.* Grand Rapids: Eerdmans.

Wright, Christopher J. H. 2006. *The Mission of God: Unlocking the Bible's Grand Narrative.* Downers Grove: IVP.

Wright, N. T. 1986. *The Epistles of Paul to the Colossians and to Philemon: An Introduction and Commentary.* TNTC. Grand Rapids: Eerdmans.

Wright, N. T. 1990. "Poetry and Theology in Colossians 1.15–20." *NTS* 36: 444–68.

Wright, N. T. 2009. *Justification: God's Plan and Paul's Vision.* London: SPCK.

Wright, N. T. 2013. *Paul and the Faithfulness of God.* London: SPCK.